# MISCELLANIES

## CRITICAL, IMAGINATIVE, AND JURIDICAL.

# MISCELLANIES

## CRITICAL, IMAGINATIVE, AND JURIDICAL

CONTRIBUTED TO BLACKWOOD'S MAGAZINE.

BY

SAMUEL WARREN,

D. C. L. F. R. S.

OF THE INNER TEMPLE.

ONE OF HER MAJESTY'S COUNSEL.

IN TWO VOLUMES.

VOL. II.

Fred B. Rothman & Co.
Littleton, Colorado
1996

Library of Congress Cataloging-in-Publication Data

Warren, Samuel, 1807-1877.
Miscellanies critical, imaginative, and juridical : contributed to Blackwood's magazine / by Samuel Warren.
p. cm.
ISBN 0-8377-2785-5 (lib. bdg. : alk. paper)
I. Title.
PR5732.M5 1996
824'.8--dc20 96-42914
CIP

Printed in the United States of America

Text is printed on 20% post-consumer recycled paper

The paper used in this publication meets the minimum requirements of American National Standard for Information Sciences—Permanence of Paper for Printed Library Materials, ANSI Z39.48-1984.

# MISCELLANIES

## CRITICAL, IMAGINATIVE, AND JURIDICAL

CONTRIBUTED TO BLACKWOOD'S MAGAZINE.

BY

SAMUEL WARREN,

D. C. L. F. R. S.

OF THE INNER TEMPLE.

ONE OF HER MAJESTY'S COUNSEL.

IN TWO VOLUMES.

VOL. II.

WILLIAM BLACKWOOD AND SONS,

EDINBURGH AND LONDON.

MDCCCLV.

# CONTENTS OF VOL. II.

# MISCELLANIES.

---

## THE MYSTERY OF MURDER, AND ITS DEFENCE.*

THE legal profession, and the public, were equally taken by surprise, on Tuesday, the 20th November 1849, by the conspicuous appearance in the *Times* newspaper of that morning, of a correspondence, consisting of two letters, between Mr Charles Phillips,† and another member

* 1. *Correspondence relative to the Trial of Courvoisier.* With a Preface and Appendix. 1849.

2. *The Times Newspaper,* from May 7th to June 30th, 1840, and for the 20th November 1849.

3. *The Examiner Newspaper,* for 27th June 1840, 11th July 1840, 24th November 1849, and 1st and 8th December 1849.

4. *The Annual Register* for 1840. Vol. lxxxii. pp. 229–244.

5. *Minutes of Evidence, taken in Short-hand, at the Central Criminal Court.* Published by Authority. Vol. xii. pp. 216-271.

† Now Mr Commissioner Phillips. This paper appeared in the *Law Review* for March 1850; and is inserted in THE MISCELLANIES on account of the extraordinary interest of the case to which it refers; and also of the question to which it gave rise, with reference to the conduct of an advocate, placed in circumstances of sudden and almost unprecedented difficulty, by a confession volunteered privately by the prisoner during the progress of the trial to that advocate, whom he nevertheless required *"to defend him to the uttermost!"* The author expended much time and labour in thoroughly investigating the charge, perseveringly made by a weekly London journal for years, against the advocate in question, of atrocious misconduct in calling God to witness his belief that one was innocent who had just confessed himself guilty; and with attempts

of the Bar, on the subject of the former's defence of Courvoisier, the Swiss valet, who so barbarously murdered his sleeping master, Lord William Russell, in Norfolk Street, Park Lane, in May 1840. The counsel in question, in a brief note, dated the 20th November, called the attention of Mr Phillips to "an accusation recently revived against him in the *Examiner*," alluding to the following passage, which had, about a fortnight previously, appeared in that newspaper:—"How much worse was *the attempt of Mr Phillips to throw the suspicion of the murder of Lord William Russell on the innocent female servants, in order to procure the acquittal of his client, Courvoisier, of whose guilt he was cognisant!*" Mr Phillips was reminded that as this accusation had been thus renewed against him after his elevation to a responsible judicial office, he ought to lose no time in offering, as the writer of the note in question believed he could truly do, a public and peremptory contradiction to such serious allegations; and the writer added, that he had been told by Lord Denman that he had inquired into the matter, and found the charge to be utterly unfounded; that Mr Baron Parke, who was present at the trial, and had closely watched every word that Mr Phillips uttered, had given his lordship decisive testimony against the truth of the charges which had been brought against Mr Phillips on the occasion in question. To this note, Mr Phillips, a few days afterwards, replied, in an interesting letter, couched undoubtedly in indignant and contemptuous language; and the editor of the *Times*, to whom both were sent for publication by Mr Phillips, on the same day on which the correspondence appeared, called attention to it, in a leading article, temperately but emphatically pronouncing Mr Phillips' statement conclusive on the subject, forcibly observing, "that it would

to attach the crime to an innocent fellow-servant of the prisoner. After the publication of this paper, the charge was never re-asserted; and the author had the satisfaction of being assured by one of high station and authority, that the paper was characterised by judicial impartiality and temper, and that it formed an unanswerable vindication of libelled innocence.

have been well had he given to the world, nine years before, the very complete justification of his conduct in the Courvoisier trial, which appeared that morning in their columns." That "no man could afford to despise the general opinion of mankind, and least of all one who, by circumstances, whether of necessity or inclination, occupies a somewhat prominent place in the public eye." That "had Mr Phillips uttered, long before, a denial so emphatic of the charges brought against him, he would at once have silenced the slander which had so long associated his name with unscrupulous advocacy, and inhuman carelessness of the life of an innocent fellow-creature." The example of the *Times* was promptly followed by almost the whole metropolitan and provincial press; several journals, in a praiseworthy spirit of candour, adding an expression of regret that they had ever lent assistance, unconsciously, in giving currency to misrepresentation. Rarely, in short, has an old but suddenly revived accusation received so sudden and successful an answer.

On the ensuing Saturday, however, the *Examiner* reprinted its two articles of the 27th June and the 11th July 1840, containing the original charges, professing deliberately to re-affirm them; accusing Mr Phillips of having "done his best to evade every charge specifically brought against him by the *Examiner;*" and offering conclusive evidence of the truth of those charges, in the shape of extracts from the *Times* newspaper, which had reported the proceedings out of which the accusation against Mr Phillips originated. The *Examiner*, doubtless irritated by the vehement and scornful tone of Mr Phillips' letter, expressed its re-affirmed charges in very bitter terms; and also in the ensuing two numbers inserted extracts from several other newspapers; complaining also of the precipitancy of fellow-journalists in authenticating a charge of calumny against it, without having paused for its rejoinder, but presumed Mr Phillips' answer complete. Several journals, both in town and country, shortly afterwards recanted their recantation, acknowledging their rashness, and declaring their belief that their contemporary had "made good his charges to the letter." One of our professional contemporaries, on the 24th November, in handsome terms expressed regret at having ever acquiesced in the belief that a member of the profession had been guilty of cruel and unconscientious conduct, "and thereby unintentionally joined in a wrong." That they "were bound to say, that after reading the letter of the learned Commissioner, no doubt remained on their minds that his conduct was misrepresented; and that in most painful and trying circumstances he did exactly what a right-minded man and a conscientious advocate ought to have done." On the 15th December, however, the same journal announced that it had once more undergone a total change of opinion. "We have, since the 24th November, *procured the report in the* 'Times' *of June 22d* 1840; and we are bound to say that *every particular in the* 'Examiner's' *charges is strictly proved.* Mr Phillips was accused of having appealed to heaven as to his belief in his client's innocence, after receiving a confession of his guilt. We have gone into this detail, derived *from our own perusal* of the 'Times' report, in order to show that we are not *now* relying, as we did before, on an *ex parte* statement." The *Times*, however, and the great majority of the other journals, indicated by their silence, and some by replies to the *Examiner*, contentment with their originally expressed opinion. Thus the matter stands with the press. In professional circles the matters in question have afforded topics for much and grave discussion; and we have felt it our duty, as an independent organ of professional opinion, to examine into the matter temperately and candidly; regarding it as one, not of professional etiquette and usage merely, but of professional honour and morality. It is this consideration alone which has induced us to make topics appearing in the columns of the *Examiner*, a non-professional weekly journal, the subject of comment in our pages. Consideration also for Mr Phillips, as a gentleman of long and distinguished standing at the Bar, and whose reputation, save in the matters above referred to, has never, that we know of, on any occasion been sullied by even the suspicion of misconduct, conduces to urge upon us the duty of sifting this matter thoroughly, in order to see if there be any real foundation for imputing to him this solitary instance of grave misconduct. The charge is one which ought never to have been made, much less, avowedly, "from time to time" * re-asserted by any journal, or by any person, except upon the surest grounds, the clearest evidence, and after dealing with that evidence with perfect candour and impartiality. We have carefully referred to every source of information within our reach, and are now prepared to submit the result of such investigation to our readers.

In examining into the propriety or impropriety of a particular line of conduct, it is obviously desirable to be placed, as far as possible, in the position, at the time, of the individual whose conduct is the subject of examination;—to look at the doubtful and obscure aspect which it presented to him, in the order of events, and not as illuminated by those brought afterwards into existence. For this purpose we shall give, as briefly as possible, a narrative of the circumstances attending the discovery of the appalling assassination of Lord William Russell; whose murderer selected, as his leading advocate, in Mr Phillips, a gentleman of brilliant eloquence, of great experience, and characterised by a zealous devotion to the cause of his clients. In the midst of his powerful exertions on behalf of a client, whom there appears no doubt that both he and his brother advocate in the cause believed, as they still declare that they *did*, innocent—exertions but too likely to have proved successful, owing to the extraordinary mystery in which the circumstances of the case were enveloped,—his execrable client almost

* *Examiner*, 24th Nov. 1849.

paralysed him by a confession of his guilt, accompanied, nevertheless, by an injunction "to defend him to the uttermost!" * Having thus barely alluded to this signal circumstance, we request our readers to dismiss it for a while from their minds, and follow us while we narrate the leading circumstances of the murder, in the order of their occurrence, as they appear in the official short-hand writer's notes of the evidence taken at the Central Criminal Court, and published every session by authority.

On Tuesday night, the 5th of May 1840, Lord William Russell, infirm, deaf, and aged, being in his seventy-third year, retired to bed at his usual hour. He was a widower, living at No. 14 Norfolk Street, Park Lane, a small house, occupied by only himself, and three servants—Courvoisier, and two women, a cook and housemaid. The latter two had lived with him for about three years; but Courvoisier, a young Swiss valet, had been in his service for only five weeks, having come to it from that of Mr Fector, then the Member for Dover, with an excellent character. It would appear, however, that he did not like his situation as much as he had expected, and was piqued at receiving lower wages than had been given to his predecessor. He occasionally complained, moreover, of the peevishness of his new master's temper, expressing surprise how the former valet could have lived with him so long, and a doubt whether his own temper would allow him to do so. He also said, in the course of conversation with his fellow-servants, that he was not as well off in his circumstances as when he had come over to England; and on two occasions spoke to them of his master thus:—"Old Billy was a rum old chap, and if *he* had his money, he would not remain long in England!" On the housemaid (whose name was Sarah Manser) telling him that "his lordship was not a very rich man," he replied, "Ah, old Billy has money; and if I had it, I would not remain long in England." These

* Correspondence, &c., pp. 11, 27.

expressions he used twice; once, shortly before attending his master to Richmond, on the 5th of April, where they stayed till the 22d of that month; the second time, shortly before the 5th of May. He said this, however, in a jocular manner, and it attracted no attention from his fellow-servants; with whom, it may be stated, he lived on the most friendly terms. On the day last mentioned, some conversation had passed between them relative to money matters, in the course of which Courvoisier spoke of his having only £5 or £6 left, with the exception of £8 and a few shillings at the savings' bank; and that he should soon have to ask his lordship for some money. Shortly before Lord William and Courvoisier went to Richmond, the latter was observed by one of the servants to have brought his lordship's dressing-case down into the pantry,—a circumstance which had never occurred, to her knowledge, in the time of the former valet; and on the day of their going to Richmond, she also saw him there with his lordship's cash-box, which his lordship had left unlocked. Courvoisier accounted to her for it, however, by the remark, that he had brought it down *because* it was unlocked, and he knew his lordship was going to take it with him that day to Richmond. Both the dressing-case and the cash-box were always kept by Lord William in his bed-room. Another circumstance also is not unworthy of notice,—that the same fellow-servant, the housemaid, had on more than one occasion seen Courvoisier apparently peering inquisitively into the "property" in almost (she afterwards stated) "every room" in the house; and on her asking him what he was about, he answered simply that he was "looking for something."

On the 5th of May, Lord William had given Courvoisier orders for the carriage to be sent to Brookes's Club by five o'clock that afternoon, but Courvoisier forgot to communicate the orders to the coachman; and Lord William, naturally somewhat irritated, returned home in a street cab about half-past five, and rebuked Courvoisier for his forgetfulness, at first peevishly: but, as Courvoisier stated, he quickly resumed his good humour. He dined at home, alone, that day; and in the evening repaired, as was his custom, to the back drawing-room. The cook (whose name was Mary Hannell), having sate at home after dinner, working till towards nine o'clock, laid her work aside, putting her materials, including *an old silver thimble*, worth little more than a shilling, into her work-box, which she placed in the cupboard, in the kitchen, and then went out for about an hour, returning a little before ten o'clock. Courvoisier let her in by the front street door, which he then shut, closing both bolts, and barring, locking, and fastening the chain across the door. Whilst she was preparing her supper, he went out for her beer, through the area door and gate; and on his return locked both as usual. About a quarter past ten o'clock, the housemaid went up to bed, leaving Courvoisier and the cook in the kitchen, observing, as she passed the door of the back drawing-room, his lordship sitting there, with candles, as was usual with him at that period of the evening. She then went into his bed-room, where she lit his fire, and placed a rushlight—a *whole* one—in the shade, his lordship being in the habit of burning one. The bed-room had three windows, the bed being between them and the door, which was covered with green baize, had a spring on, and opened and shut noiselessly. The back bed-room adjoining was used only as a lumber-room, one door of it opening on the landing, and another communicating with the front bed-room.

On quitting the latter, the housemaid went up to her own bed-room, which was immediately over that of her master. She and the cook occupied separate beds, but in the same room, which was separated from that of Courvoisier by such a slight partition as admitted of almost the smallest noise in the latter being heard in that of the women servants'. Just before the cook retired to bed, which she did about a quarter of an hour after the housemaid, Courvoisier was summoned up stairs by his lordship's bell; and on his return went into his pantry, where he was occupied when she went to bed. Courvoisier always remained up after the other servants to attend his master. It was his business to warm the bed; and having done so, to take the warming-pan down stairs. He had once omitted to do this, and the housemaid had blamed him for leaving it on the bed-room landing.

On the women servants going to bed, they soon fell asleep, neither seeing nor hearing anything more of Courvoisier; and they slept soundly all night, not being disturbed by noise, or any occurrence whatever, nor having either of them quitted their bed-room. About half-past six o'clock the next morning, which was a little earlier than her usual time, the housemaid got up, leaving the cook, as she supposed, asleep, in bed; and neither of them having spoken, she quitted her room about a quarter to seven o'clock. She tapped at Courvoisier's door, as she was accustomed, in passing it, but he made no answer. On reaching Lord William's bed-room landing, she found the warming-pan lying there; and supposed that Courvoisier had again forgotten it. Stepping over it, she entered the back bed-room to get her broom; and then, leaving the warming-pan where she had found it, went down stairs, and opened the window in the back drawing-room. She then saw some appearance of disorder in the room—the writing-desk turned round, and "jammed up with papers," and the drawers open. She also noticed a screwdriver lying in the chair; and some papers, and a bunch of keys, lying on the hearthrug. Having before seen his lordship's papers lying about on the floor, nothing occurred to her on the subject; and she proceeded to open the windows of the front drawing-room, where everything was in the state in which she had left it on the preceding evening. On going down stairs and reaching the passage, however, she was "surprised" to see a number of articles lying in it, consisting of his lordship's blue cloak "folded up very neatly," his opera glass, a small trinket-case, and a number of articles tied up in a napkin, which she did not open, but recognised as having given it out to Courvoisier, for his lordship's dinner, on the Monday previously. This napkin, on being subsequently examined, was proved to contain a number of small gold and silver articles, the property of Lord William Russell, and generally worn about his person. On looking towards the street door, the housemaid observed that it was closed, but only by the latch,—neither chained, locked, nor bolted, so that any one could have opened it from without. Somewhat surprised, but still not alarmed, by what she saw,—attributing the state of the door to Courvoisier's forgetfulness, as had once before been the case,—she entered the dining-room to open the shutters; and then beheld that which, combined with what she had already seen, greatly alarmed her, namely, articles scattered about on the floor, and all the cupboards and drawers open. She immediately ran up stairs, much terrified, to the cook, whom she found still in bed, and hurriedly asked her, "if she knew whether anything had been the matter last night?" To which the cook answered, "No;" telling her to call Courvoisier; on which she went to his door, knocked, and exclaimed, "Courvoisier, do you know of anything being the matter last night?" To which he answered, "No;" and immediately opened the door. He was dressed as he usually was in the morning, with the exception of his coat. She said, "All your silver and things are about!" on which, "looking very pale and agitated," without making any answer he hastened down stairs, putting on his coat as he went, followed closely by the housemaid. He went down direct to the pantry; and on seeing things there in confusion,—the cupboards and drawers open,—exclaimed, "My God! some one has been robbing us!" The housemaid said, "Let us go up stairs;" and on their reaching the passage, she exclaimed, "For God's sake let us go *and see where his lordship is!*" They hurried up stairs, Courvoisier going first, she closely following him. He went by the green baize door into Lord William Russell's bedroom, the door closing on him before the housemaid could enter; she pushed it open, however, and followed him, and found him in the act of opening the middle window, having for that purpose passed the foot of the bed. As soon as she had reached it, she exclaimed, "My lord! my lord!" Courvoisier exclaimed, "There," or "here he is!" and on looking towards the bed, she did not see Lord William, but observed blood on the pillow, on which she rushed screaming from the room, running first a few steps up the attic stairs towards the cook's room, but then down stairs, and into the street, where she rang the bells of two neighbouring houses. On returning, she saw the cook near the passage, whom she told that his lordship was killed; and on hastily entering the dining-room, she saw Courvoisier sitting down, apparently writing on a slip of paper, and exclaimed with agitation, "What the devil do you sit there for? Why don't you go out, and run for some one, or a doctor?" to which he replied, "I must write to Mr Russell," meaning the son of Lord William, and who lived near Belgrave Square. The housemaid said that some one ought to be sent for him; on which Courvoisier went to the street door, and observing a labouring man passing, called him; but the housemaid said, "Don't call such a man as that;" afterwards explaining that she had not thought him a proper person to despatch on such an occasion to Mr Russell, and also not believing that Courvoisier meant to send him. Lord William Russell's coachman and groom, who had been sent for, the servants of the two neighbouring houses, the police, and the medical men, one of them the ordinary attendant of his lordship, were quickly in the house; and on entering his bedroom, beheld him lying in the bed, his face covered over with a towel; on removing which, and pulling down the clothes, a ghastly spectacle presented itself. He lay weltering in his blood, and his head was nearly severed from his body by the stroke of some weapon which must have caused instantaneous death. None was ever found in the room. No blood was on the counterpane, nor had any, with the exception of a little on the pillow, been visible till the towel and bed-clothes had been removed by the police and medical men. Courvoisier was present, standing at the foot of the bed, when they revealed the horrors, till then concealed; and on witnessing it, he elevated his hands, and sank back into a chair dreadfully agitated, exclaiming, "Oh dear! this is a shocking job; I shall lose my place, and character!" On the police casting their eyes round the room, they beheld a candle, burnt out, standing on a shelf, but too far off for any one in bed to have been reading by, and a rushlight only partly burnt, and which had not been *blown*, but apparently *burnt* out. On the floor, between the window and the bed, lay a book (the "Memoirs of Sir Samuel Romilly,") with a pair of spectacles in it; Courvoisier saying that he had left his lordship reading in bed about half-past twelve o'clock. There was a key in the door, and Courvoisier, on being asked the question, said that his lordship never locked his door at night. As soon as the medical men had looked at the wound, they desired every thing to be replaced precisely in the state first discovered; and Courvoisier assisted the police in doing so. While they were examining the state of the property, he answered their questions about it in a frank and natural manner, pointing out the absence of some valuable articles which he said he had seen in his lordship's possession only the day before, and others which he showed the police; one of whom, on observing that they were more valuable than those described as missing, observed, probably in a pointed manner to Courvoisier, "It is a very curious thief to leave all this valuable property behind!" to which he replied, "It is certainly very strange!" Taking up a note-case, he opened it; and on finding it empty, remarked, "There was a £10 and a £5 note here, yesterday," and also explained that his lordship's watch, and rings and pins, were missing. He was much agitated; continually exclaiming, "What shall we do? what shall we do?" While putting aside some of the articles of property in the dressing-case, in the presence of one of the police, he said, "I have lived with his lordship only five weeks, and what shall I do for my character?"—All the three servants were immediately placed under the eye of the police, to prevent communication with one another. The inspector (Tedman) went up stairs with Courvoisier, to his bed-room, where he opened his box, and showed him everything in it; but there was nothing to occasion the slightest suspicion, "nor anything at all tending to explain the case;" and on his hands and person being also examined, there was no mark or spot of any kind to be seen. In short, all the three servants voluntarily offered their boxes to be searched by the police, who found nothing whatever calling for observation. On one of them going down with Courvoisier to the basement, the latter went suddenly up to the door leading into the back area, and partly open, on which he pushed it wide open and exclaimed, "Oh, here is where they came in!" pointing at the same time to sundry marks and bruises on the edge of the door and door-posts. "Some of you in the house have done this deed," said the inspector; and Courvoisier answered, "If they have, I hope they will be found out." "There is not much fear," he replied, "but what they will." Suffice it to say, that on examining the state of things at the back of the house, it appeared, on consideration, to show conclusively that no one could have entered the house that way, without having left distinct traces of his passage; and also that the marks pointed out to them on the door appeared spurious—not those of burglars. Though some of the police at first thought that the marks had been made from without, they expressed themselves as afterwards satisfied that they had been made from within, and in such a manner as to lead to the suspicion that the object had been to counterfeit a breaking into the house. On a policeman showing Courvoisier the screwdriver lying in the back drawing-room, and asking him if it belonged to the house, he said, "I believe it does." "Did his lordship use it yesterday?" inquired the policeman; to which Courvoisier replied, "I am sure I can't tell you." On going to the sideboard in the dining-room, and finding the drawers pulled out, and plate and plated articles lying on the floor, the policeman said, "Is there anything missing here?" Courvoisier answered, "Some spoons and forks, but I cannot tell you how many at present." On seeing the cloak and other articles lying in the passage, the policeman asked Courvoisier if they were his lordship's property; and on being answered "Yes," the policeman said, "No thief would ever leave this property behind;" to which Courvoisier replied, "It is certainly very odd." Being asked how he had left the street-door over night, he immediately put up the chain, bolted, and locked it, and said that he had so left it; and then unchaining, unlocking, and unbolting it, and putting the spring of the lock back on the hook, said, that such was the state in which he had found the door that morning.

The consternation with which this dreadful occurrence filled all London, and, indeed, the country at large, we well recollect, as doubtless do most of our readers. A coroner's inquest was held the next day, the foreman of the jury being the Right Hon. G. Dawson: at which Courvoisier and the women servants were examined, but gave their evidence in such a way as to allay all suspicion of their having been concerned in, or cognisant of, the murder. Mr Dawson said that Courvoisier's former master, Mr Fector, had given him, that morning, an excellent character of Courvoisier,—a fact immediately corroborated by another member of the jury. The principal of the police, Inspector Tedman, deposed as follows:—"I did not see the slightest marks of blood about any of these people, or in any part of the house. I examined all the places I possibly could, and there was not the slightest tinge of blood about them, on the linen, bed-curtains, or anywhere else in any part of the house." At the close of the inquiry, the coroner and the foreman, with the rest of the jury, concurred in the propriety (with a view to allaying public excitement, and checking unjustifiable rumours and suspicions) of at once returning a verdict of "Wilful Murder against some person or persons unknown;" leaving the inquiry to be vigorously prosecuted by the police. The three servants returned to the house of Lord William Russell, not in custody, but simply in the company and presence of the police, who never quitted the place, and took care to prevent any communication between them, otherwise than in the presence of the police. None of them tried to escape, nor did their conduct indicate anything beyond the distress which was natural to persons so circumstanced. A leading article in the *Times* of the ensuing day (8th May) thus commences:—"At the close of the second day after the commission of a barbarous murder at the house in London, of a nobleman, it appears that the police are without any clue that can lead to the discovery and apprehension of the murderer." In another part of the paper it was said, "The general opinion in the neighbourhood is, that the murderer, whoever he may be, must have been secreted in the house from an early hour in the evening, or possibly might have got down the area steps soon after ten o'clock, when the valet went to get the beer for the cook's supper." Public censure began to visit the police, for their alleged inefficiency; and, on the same day, their diligence, and that of others, was stimulated by the appearance of a reward of £450; of which £200 was contributed by the Government, and £200 by the family of the deceased nobleman, with £50 for the discovery of a considerable quantity of missing plate.

Here we deem it of great importance to present, from the evidence subsequently given at the trial, an account of the progressive discoveries alleged to have been made by the police, in the box of Courvoisier, beginning with the search by Inspector Tedman, to which allusion has been already made. He appears to have been an excellent officer, at once shrewd and candid; and who, though he afterwards gave destructive evidence against Courvoisier, was justly complimented by Mr Phillips on the fairness with which he had done it. The following is his evidence as to what occurred on his first examination of Courvoisier's room and box, on the morning of the discovery of the murder:—

"Courvoisier showed me into his bed-room: I found a purse containing a £5 note and six sovereigns: I gave them up: I asked him how he had got the note: he said he had given his lordship change for it a day or two before, and the rest of the money was his own: he had had it some time: he showed me his box containing his linen: I examined everything in it as I went along, but saw nothing tending to explain the case at all: I pulled the things out, and laid them on the bed, but I certainly did not examine so accurately as I did subsequently: I unfolded but did not shake them: I and Beresford merely unfolded the shirts on the bed: I examined Courvoisier's hands when I examined his room: I did not see the slightest scratch or mark: all the servants wished me to examine their trunks, and I did: I examined Courvoisier's trunk to see if there was any weapon, or any article with marks of blood on it: I satisfied myself on that subject: I searched as carefully as I possibly could: I found two shirts, looked at them, and found them free from spots: I took out every article in the trunk: and I and Courvoisier replaced them: there was no speck of blood on anything I saw in the trunk: I saw no gloves in the shirts: I cannot say whether in unfolding the shirts a pair of gloves might have been there, and I did not see them—there might be: I did not find any weapon in the trunk." Beresford, another policeman, said, "that he was present on that occasion: in a black trunk or box, between two waistcoats, about the centre of the box, he found a chisel; Courvoisier seeing it, but making no observation: we took the clothes off the bed *very carefully one by one:* I went to the trunk for the purpose of examining its contents: I took them out: I think I recollect two shirts: I opened them merely to look at the wristbands: I did not shake nor turn them out: I do not think I took all the articles quite out; for when I got just to the bottom, I believe I turned them from one end of the box to the other: *I examined sufficiently to convince myself that there was nothing suspicious to be found.*"

On the 8th of May, the day on which the reward was offered, the prisoner's box was again searched by two of the police, Shaw and Pearce; but, as far as concerned any discovery prejudicial to Courvoisier, in vain. The former said in his evidence at the trial, "our search was a minute one: we do not make a careless search when our object is to find anything suspicious: I paid every attention my duty required me to pay: we took all the things out of the box, one by one: we took each article up in our hands, and placed it on the bed: we left nothing behind that we considered suspicious: we took everything out and put it on the bed, so as to see that the box was empty and contained nothing more: I recollect seeing a shirt-front like this produced: I recollect seeing this: I had it in my hand: I recollect no [pocket] handkerchief." These facts were all elicited by Mr Phillips on cross-examination, the witness not having been examined to them in chief! Pearce said, "I turned the things out: I did not find anything that attracted my attention: I made the search with every degree of minuteness: I generally do so: I went to make a minute search: I saw some clean linen; looked at and examined it: I might have opened some, but do not recollect opening every one: there might have been some that I did not open." *Q.* "Did you not turn out every individual article?" *A.* "I took them out with my hand: I think there were two clean shirts: I took them out: to the best of my belief I did not unfold them: I took out everything, and put them, and left them, on the bed: if there had been any blood-stained articles, I think I should have seen them: I believe I should have seen them if they had been there." Late in the evening of the same day, and, according to the evidence of one of the police, before he had heard of the reward, a strict search was made in Courvoisier's pantry; and several articles, afterwards proved to have belonged to Lord William Russell, were found secreted behind the skirting of the sink, and under the floor: viz., a purse, with five gold rings, and five gold coins; then a Waterloo medal, and a £10 note folded up. These were immediately taken up-stairs, and shown to Courvoisier, by the policeman Pearce, who said, "I have found these things concealed in your pantry, behind the skirting board;" to which he represented Courvoisier to have answered, "I know nothing about them: I am innocent: my conscience is clear: I never saw the medal before." He was then taken down-stairs, and shown where the articles had been found: on which he said again, "I am innocent; I know nothing about them." Another policeman (Collier) said to him, on the same occasion, "It is a most shocking thing;" to which Courvoisier answered, "It is! I am innocent of it; but it would not have looked so bad against me, had not the property been found in my pantry." The policeman said, "that it looked very suspicious:" to which Courvoisier replied, "I shall say nothing, at least until I hear that the whole truth is told." He was then taken up-stairs, and searched, but nothing suspicious was found on him: and that evening he was taken into strict custody, but not removed from the house. On the ensuing morning, a gold seal, a signet-ring, and a gold locket were found concealed in the scullery. On Sunday night Courvoisier was taken to gaol. On the ensuing Tuesday another discovery was made: a watch-key, and a watch, all of which had been the property of Lord William Russell, were found similarly concealed in the scullery; and, on the next day (Wednesday, the 13th), a sovereign was found under the floor of the pantry. On the evening of the 13th May, the prisoner's uncle, a respectable man, the butler of the late Sir George Beaumont, called at the house of Lord William Russell, at the request of his nephew, then, of course, in charge of the police, for some linen, a clean shirt and stockings. His request was not, however, complied with till the following morning, when Inspector Tedman, to whom the application had been made, went up with a brother policeman to the prisoner's box, the one which had been searched before; took out a shirt, and unfolded it, holding it up by the collar; and on shaking it, *there dropped out a pair of gloves slightly stained with blood!* They were white cotton gloves, such as servants wear when in attendance on their masters. He had unfolded this very shirt on the 6th, and had not discovered the gloves; and on the day of thus discovering them, he afterwards examined the prisoner's hands, but did not see the slightest mark or scratch. Shortly afterwards, on the same morning, two other policemen went up to the room where the gloves had been found; and, lying very near the top of the portmanteau, found two handkerchiefs, one cotton and one silk, marked "B. C." with spots or marks of blood on both, and a shirt-front. "We found them directly: no one could search the portmanteau without seeing them, if they had any eyes: I should not think any person could fail to see the handkerchiefs when they looked into the portmanteau. * * * I was present a few days before when it was searched, and attended to the examination: I cannot swear that I noticed either of these things then: I did not find any shirt anywhere that the shirt-front would match: I found the shirt-front a little below the handkerchiefs: a torn shirt-front would attract attention, and attracted mine: I do not know how any one could miss seeing it,—I could not, I know: if a person took each article, one by one, out of the trunk, I do not think he could have missed seeing it, or the handkerchiefs either, if they had been there: I believe it was Shaw and Humphries who searched it with me [on the former occasion]: they searched more particularly than I did: I did not search the box minutely myself: they appeared to me to be minutely searching the box: I observed none of these things on that day." It was abundantly proved, that many of the police and others had access to the boxes and portmanteau where these gloves, handkerchiefs, and shirt-front were so strangely first omitted to be seen, and afterwards more strangely seen.—We may here inform the reader that shortly before Courvoisier was executed, he made a full confession (a portion of which we shall give hereafter) of all the circumstances attending the murder; and in that confession, he made the following distinct statement relating to these discoveries:—"The gloves were never placed in the shirt by me, or to my knowledge. When I left Mr Fector's, I gave all my white gloves to the coachman. The handkerchiefs that were found in my portmanteau were never put there by me. I know nothing whatever of the shirt-front."

Five or six public examinations at Bow Street preceded the final committal of Courvoisier to Newgate, on the 29th of May; and, notwithstanding the strength of the suspicions existing against him, the public mind was in a state of extreme disquietude and excitement, lest, on the one hand, an innocent man should be sacrificed, or, on the other, an atrociously guilty one should escape. On turning to the *Times*, we find almost daily comments on the alleged remissness of the police, and the doubtful nature of the case, even as it was progressively developed by each day's discoveries. It is also stated that Courvoisier, on being told that his pantry was about to be searched, exhibited much uneasiness; and on hearing of the discoveries which had been made both there and in the scullery, " turned as white as his shirt," and was even " taken suddenly ill." It was first intimated to him that he was in actual custody, as soon as the £10 bank-note had been found. " His agitation was extreme; but he persisted in declaring his innocence." When suddenly taken to Bow Street, at twelve o'clock at night on Sunday the 10th, he rose, dressed, and prepared himself, with alacrity, " making no other remark than a fervent declaration of his innocence." A day or two afterwards, we find that he " frequently expressed his opinion that he should be honourably acquitted, and told Serjeant Driscol that when at liberty he should not forget him for all the civility he had shown him." On the ensuing day, we find him " not in the slightest degree depressed in spirits, and stoutly persisting in his entire innocence." After Sarah Manser and Mary Hannell had been examined before the magistrate at great length, Mr Flower, who conducted Courvoisier's defence, with a confident air assured the magistrate " that the prisoner was extremely anxious for the fullest possible inquiry to take place." A day or two afterwards, " the prisoner still persisted in protesting his entire innocence." On the 25th May, we learn that the public " felt the utmost possible anxiety to know if anything of a *decisively criminating* character had been discovered:" this being after the examination on the preceding day, on which we notice, as being present, Sir George Beaumont, at whose expense, from a strong persuasion of the prisoner's innocence, his defence was afterwards conducted. On the 29th May, his last examination took place, and all the depositions were read over in his presence. " He entered the dock with a light step and cheerful countenance; and it may be added that his appearance indicated increased confidence as the protracted evidence drew to a close." On that day he was committed to Newgate, to take his trial for the murder. As an exponent of the state of public feeling at that time on the subject of Courvoisier's guilt, we may again allude to the fact that the late Sir George Beaumont, as we now learn from his private solicitor,* generously pitying a foreigner exposed to mortal, and, as Sir George conceived it, unjust peril, supplied the funds for defending the prisoner on his trial at the Old Bailey.

That trial commenced on Thursday, the 18th of June 1840, before the late Chief Justice Tindal, Mr Baron Parke sitting beside him. The counsel for the prosecution were the late Mr Adolphus, Mr Bodkin, and Mr Chambers; those for the prisoner, Mr Phillips and Mr Clarkson. The trial lasted three days, and no fewer than thirty-five witnesses were examined. The evidence for the prosecution had been prepared with care and skill: and it may be important to apprise non-professional critics, that the prisoner's counsel was, as is always the case, thoroughly informed of the evidence which had been given by all those witnesses who had been examined in the previous stages of the inquiry; whereby any discrepancies between their former testimony and that given at the trial, would be amply available on behalf of the prisoner. This will explain many questions put by the prisoner's counsel in cross-examination, which might otherwise appear unaccountable, and even unjustifiable. The prisoner, being an alien, was of course entitled to be tried by a jury composed equally of foreigners and Englishmen. On being asked, he said that he preferred being tried by a jury of Englishmen. Mr Adolphus opened the case to the jury, in a lengthened and elaborate address, characterised by his usual ability, and presenting several remarkable features, naturally challenging severe observations on the part of the prisoner's counsel. We shall content ourselves, for several reasons, with the following account of the general character of his address, given in the *Annual Register*:—†

* Correspondence, &c., pp. 27, 28. Letter of Christopher Hodgson, Esq.

† Vol. lxxxii. p. 230, A.D. 1840.

"The report of his speech occupies four or five columns of the *Chronicle's* broad sheet" [and three and a half of the columns in the *Times*]. "He went into a minute, elaborate, and very able statement of all the circumstances connected with the murder, presenting a mass of circumstantial evidence against the prisoner—*pausing frequently to remove any impression favourable to him, and suggesting a guilty motive for all that he said and did.*" This severe observation, we are compelled to own, appears to us justified by the report of the speech as given in the *Times.* Mr Adolphus admitted the case to be one entirely of circumstantial evidence, and repeatedly pressed on the jury the weight which was due to such evidence—doubtless apprehensive of the effect which might be produced by his eloquent and ingenious opponent. One or two passages of this speech throw so much light on that of Mr Phillips, that it is necessary to present them to the reader, as given in the *Times*—begging the non-professional one to bear in mind that the counsel for the prosecution was also aware of all the evidence which had been given in the previous stages of the case, and the use which might be made of it by his opponent.

"Having discovered these things," said Mr Adolphus in the course of his narrative, "the police went with the prisoner up to his own bed-room, and searched his box, but found nothing in it material to this inquiry. *He saw that this made some impression on the jury;* and he would only observe, that if the prisoner were guilty, and possessed of even moderate cunning, he would hardly put any of the stolen articles into his box, which he must be sure would be subjected to investigation. His box was searched; and he, Mr Adolphus, *did not rely on anything found in that box on any occasion.* He felt that he was speaking to men who heard and read what was published to the world. Something might have transpired *with respect to linen found in the prisoner's box,* marked in a particular way; but he, Mr A., *attributed no weight to it;* and he repeated that *nothing arose, in the present case, from anything discovered in the prisoner's box.*"

When Mr Adolphus made these observations, he was aware of the facts already laid before the reader; and what the witnesses were about to depose to before the jury respecting the gloves, handkerchiefs, and shirt-front. He proceeded—

"*Englishmen* were not in the habit of committing murder as a prelude to plunder; *with foreigners it was different!* for they imagined that if they extinguished the life of the person they robbed, there would exist no direct testimony against them!"

He then proceeded to answer, by anticipation, certain topics which he supposed would be urged on behalf of the prisoner.

"Another mode of [impeaching?] the evidence he foresaw, *from the newspapers*, was this—that one of the witnesses, Sarah Manser, was unworthy of credit. It was not in his power to call witnesses to set up her credit; but in answer to the general declamation which might be heard against them, he would say this, that her character was unblemished in every particular. * * * If it *should* be said that she was unworthy of credit, he hoped the jury would not consider her testimony prejudiced by any mere declamation, or the use of hard terms and bad names."

"*A similar attack might be made on the police.* It might be said that their exertions had been stimulated by a very large reward," &c.

"The illustrious family for whom he appeared had no desire to hunt a helpless foreigner into the jaws of death, as if actuated by feelings of personal revenge. The Bedford family prosecuted here as the mere petitioners for public justice, not to gratify any feeling of private revenge."

The effect which such a speech as that made by Mr Adolphus, on such an occasion, was likely to produce on the prisoner's counsel, it is not difficult to imagine.

The first witness called was Sarah Manser, the housemaid, whose examination occupies seven pages and a quarter of the closely-printed *Sessions Minutes.* Her cross-examination by Mr Phillips occupies five pages, and appears to have been close and severe, but in no degree, in our opinion, unjustifiably so. He endeavoured to establish discrepancies between the evidence she had given on that occasion, and on her previous examinations at the police-office. She admitted that she had several times before spoken of having seen Courvoisier "looking not only into *one* room, but every room," without mentioning, as she had that day done, that "she saw him *looking after his lordship's property.*" She was also pressed with having said before the coroner that she "saw his lordship *murdered on the bed,*" instead of merely seeing "*some blood on the pillow.*" She was asked why she had said "Let us go and see *where his lordship is?*" instead of "Let us go and *tell his lordship the house is robbed?*" "*Q.* Did you think anything was the matter with my lord, then?" "*A.* I did not know what to think: he was unprotected, and nobody went to see; I found my fellow-servants safe. * * * I expected to find him in his bed-room: I did not know whether he was there or not: I had been in every room but the kitchen. I had not been into his bed-room: I did not know where he was: I did not expect any mischief was done to him at that time: I was anxious to see where he was: I had no doubt where he was." Her testimony was not really shaken; but Mr Phillips elicited the fact, that on the glass door leading into the back area, "through which she had gone scores of hundreds of times," *she had observed no marks before the police came into the house;* that she had *never* noticed any, nor heard of any experiment made on it *since* the police entered. She also stated that a ladder, found standing in the back yard, by which any one could have got over into the adjoining area, had been taken there by Courvoisier on the day of the murder, by her desire, as it was in her way while cleaning the passage. The last of the eight witnesses examined on that day, was a policeman named Baldwin, whose testimony was utterly destroyed by the cross-examination of Mr Phillips; and Chief Justice Tindal told the jury to place no reliance on it whatever! Grosser equivocation on the subject, in particular of his knowledge of the reward which had been offered, we have seldom seen.

Up to this time there was but too much probability of the difficulties of the case proving too serious to be successfully encountered by justice. The prosecutors were, however, that afternoon placed unexpectedly in possession of an item of evidence, serious, indeed, for the prisoner and his defenders, viz., the discovery of the missing plate, and of evidence that it had been left by the prisoner at the place where it was found, about a week, perhaps only a very few days, *before* the committing of the murder. The parcel contained silver spoons, forks, a pair of gold auricles—all unquestionably the property of the unfortunate nobleman; and the only question remaining was, whether Courvoisier was the person who had so left it. If he were, it would of course fearfully increase the *probabilities* that it must have been he who subsequently committed the murder, and with the object of plunder. On the ensuing morning, the person who had made this discovery (Mrs Piolaine, the wife of a Frenchman who kept a place of entertainment called L'Hôtel de Dieppe, in Leicester Place, Leicester Square), was shown a number of prisoners in the prison-yard, one of whom was Courvoisier, whom she instantly recognised as the person who had left the plate with her, and also had formerly lived in her employ. Courvoisier also suddenly recognised her, and with dismay. The immediate effect of his panic was the astounding confession of his guilt to his counsel, at the bar of the court, a few minutes afterwards, coupled with his desire, nevertheless, to be defended to the utmost. From this last circumstance, we infer that the object of the guilty wretch, in making the confession, was simply to prepare his counsel against the forthcoming evidence. Mr Phillips, who declares* that "up to that morning he and Mr Clarkson believed most firmly in the prisoner's innocence," (and his statement is confirmed by Mr Clarkson,)† has given a brief but graphic account of the effect of this communication. He stood, as well he might, awhile aghast; and on recovering from the shock, said, "Of course, then, you are going to plead guilty?" "No, sir; I expect you to defend me to the utmost;" on which Mr Phillips and Mr Clarkson returned to their seats. "My position," says Mr Phillips,‡ with perfect truth, "at this moment was, I believe, without a parallel in the annals of the profession. I at once came to the resolution of abandoning the case, and so I told my colleague." Had Mr Phillips yielded to this impulse, in the horror of the moment, he would have abandoned his duty; and we have his own authority for saying that such is now his own opinion. "I am satisfied that my original impression was erroneous. I had no right to throw up my brief, and turn traitor to the wretch—wretch though he was—who had confided to me."§ It was the influence of his zealous and able colleague, Mr Clarkson, which saved him from committing this grievous error, and overcame his determination by suggesting that they should take the opinion of the eminent judge, Mr Baron Parke, who sat during the trial beside the Chief Justice, but did not share in trying the cause. Mr Baron Parke acted with that kindness and discretion, in the terrible dilemma so unexpectedly brought under his notice, which the judges almost always exhibit in dealing with the Bar. He "requested to know distinctly whether the prisoner insisted on my defending him; and on hearing that he did, said, I was bound to do so, and to *use all* FAIR ARGUMENTS ARISING ON THE EVIDENCE."‖ How

* Correspondence, p. 11. † *Ibid.* p. 27. Appendix.
‡ *Ibid.* p. 11. § *Ibid.* p. 15. ‖ *Ibid.* p. 12.

promptly, justly, and felicitously was here laid down the true rule of advocacy applicable to the awful situation, for awful it was, in which Mr Phillips was placed, through no fault of his own! "It was not till after eight hours of my *public* exertions before the jury that the prisoner confessed; and to have abandoned him then would have been virtually surrendering him to death."* That in this he was right, no one, whose opinion is worth having, will deny; and even the *Examiner* does not presume to question that right. "I therefore retained the brief," continues Mr Phillips; "and I contend for it that every argument I used *was* 'a fair commentary on the evidence,' though, undoubtedly, *as strong as I could make it.*"† This is bold and decisive; and the question is, whether the facts, as far as now ascertainable, sustain Mr Phillips' affirmation, or the counter-affirmation of his accusers; and on them, of course, lies the burden of proof.

The first witness called into Court on the morning of this blighting confession, almost immediately after it had been communicated to the bewildered advocate, and while he was fresh from his interview with Mr Baron Parke, was a policeman, the first of *seven*, examined during the day. It was Inspector Tedman, who gave very strong and apparently conclusive evidence against the prisoner. How every answer must have told on his advocates, it is easy to imagine. His evidence occupies nearly six pages. The cross-examination by his then crest-fallen questioner, scarcely exceeds half a page! and is confined to a few calm questions, and limited to two topics—the blood-stained linen, its non-discovery on the 6th, its discovery on the 14th of May; and the marks on the back area door. His answers on the former point are incorporated in the foregoing narrative; and he added that "he found no weapons in the prisoner's trunk on the 6th of May." As to the latter point, he made the following frank statement:—"*There was no mark on the area door, with the glass to*

* Correspondence, p. 16. † *Ibid.*

*it, on the* 6*th of May:* I examined it for the purpose of seeing whether there were any marks: *there are now a number of marks on that very door*, and also on the posts of that door, *which had none on the* 6*th:* they appear to have been made with some kind of instrument: the prisoner was under the inspection of the police from the very time of our entering the house: Serjeant Pullen was appointed over the prisoner." On re-examination, he said, "I was not present when the marks were made on the door: I did not see who made them, knew nothing of any being made, and ordered none to be made." "*Mr Adolphus:* There were none on the 6th, but there were afterwards? *A.* Yes; they are there now." This was the last answer given by the witness; and when Mr Phillips came to comment on the evidence of this critical witness, he concluded, according to the report in the *Times*, by saying of him that he was "an officer who had given his evidence most fairly." The next policeman was William Rose, to whom Mr Clarkson put one question only. The next policeman was Henry Beresford, who gave important evidence, and at considerable length; but Mr Phillips cross-examined very briefly as to the examination of the prisoner's trunk, and the marks on the area door. The next policeman was Nicholas Pearce. He also gave important evidence, in considerable detail, and was cross-examined severely and ably, but by Mr Clarkson, as to the marks on the door, the discoveries in the prisoner's trunk, and as to the expressions he had used to Courvoisier, on suddenly exhibiting to him the articles which had been discovered in the pantry and scullery. The witness had stated, on his examination-in-chief, that he said to the prisoner, "I have found these things concealed in your pantry." Mr Clarkson extorted from him an admission, however, that he had added the words, "Can you now look me in the face?" and severely questioned him as to his object in making this suppression; and in having put the question to the prisoner as to whether he had not done it to extort a confession, and under the expectation of obtaining part of the reward payable on conviction—an expectation which the witness avowed, when pressed by Mr Clarkson. The next policeman was George Collier, who also gave cogent evidence, especially as to finding the blood-spotted handkerchiefs and the shirt-front in the trunk, which he had not found on a previous search, though he admitted that "no one, if they had any eyes, could have searched the portmanteau without seeing them!" Mr Phillips cross-examined him as to one point only—the searches in the prisoner's trunk; and his answers were somewhat confused and unsatisfactory. He admitted that "anybody might have had access to the room in which the prisoner's box was, for what he (the witness) knew." The next policeman was Frederick Shaw, who spoke, in his examination-in-chief, solely to his discovering the gold seal, seal-ring, and gold locket in the pantry and scullery. Mr Phillips cross-examined him only as to the searches into the prisoner's trunk, eliciting highly important evidence as to the non-discovery of any linen or other articles spotted with blood, on the 8th of May, in company with Pearce. The last policeman was Paul Cronin, who deposed to the discovery of the property secreted in the pantry and scullery, and neither Mr Phillips nor Mr Clarkson examined him. The next ten witnesses were not cross-examined at all by either Mr Phillips or Mr Clarkson, with the exception of a single question by the latter, immaterial for the present purpose, though both the Court and jury, ignorant, be it borne in mind, of the confession, put questions to several of the witnesses. The next witness was Charlotte Piolaine, who spoke to the prisoner as the person who had left with her the parcel containing the plate and other articles, and explained how she came to make the discovery, and only so lately as after the trial had commenced. Mr Phillips cross-examined this important witness, but not at great length, eliciting that their hotel "was not kept exclusively for guests"—that there was a billiard-table there, at which "any body could go in and play that liked; any stranger might go in and play;" but she denied that it was a gambling-house, or that the police or any one had ever taken out any gang of suspected persons. "She *thought* she could swear that, as she had never heard any noise, and was never down in the billiard-room. She was not aware that there were a great many gambling-houses in Leicester Place—not that she was aware of: she had never inquired much whether there were any there: she had lived there two years next September." On being asked, she said she had heard of the murder the day after it was committed, and was much shocked, but had not heard continual conversations during the ensuing five weeks—never among the people who came to her house: had never heard her husband speak of it, to her knowledge: had never seen posted up in large letters "The murder of Lord William Russell:" and she had never spoken about the murder to any body, being generally occupied with her own affairs." The remaining eight witnesses were scarcely cross-examined at all. Mr Phillips did so only twice, and in a question or two. So much for his cross-examination of the witnesses for the prosecution, after he had become unexpectedly and unwillingly the depositary of the prisoner's confession. From that moment his fire slackened, and was directed thenceforth to only two or three points, and these, unless we are grievously mistaken, really vulnerable portions of the case, and justifying, in our opinion, after much consideration of the facts elicited on cross-examination, the gravest suspicions.

On the ensuing morning, after a sculptor had been called to speak to the accuracy of the model of Lord William Russell's house, which had lain before the jury during the trial, and Sarah Manser and Inspector Tedman had been recalled by the prosecutor, who put only one apparently immaterial question to each, Mr Phillips rose to address the jury; and if he did not do so under circumstances entitling him to the sympathy of all who knew and could appreciate the misery of his position,—with the ominously watchful eye and ear of Mr Baron Parke being upon him during every syllable of his speech, and a consciousness that the fatal secret of the confession would in a few hours' time be universally known,—no advocate ever was, or can be, entitled to such sympathy. We think it proper to give the opening paragraphs of his address, *verbatim*, from the *Times*, which is also given almost *totidem verbis* in the *Annual Register*.*

"Mr Phillips addressed the jury for the prisoner:—

"He supposed, he need hardly say, that after twenty years' experience in courts of criminal justice, he had seldom risen to address a jury under more painful and more anxious sensations. There were certain circumstances in this case, revealed before the magistrates, which had caused him much anxiety; and he left them to conjecture how much that anxiety must be increased by the production, without any notice whatever, of evidence by which the life of the unhappy man at the bar might be placed in the greatest peril. He said, 'might,' because he did not consider even that additional proof, for reasons which he should state to them, by any means *conclusive*. He felt that, in the situation in which he stood, he should have their kindest sympathies; he should also have the sympathy of his associates. They were embarked together in a common cause; they had incurred together a common responsibility; the life of a fellow-creature was intrusted to their keeping; and so surely as they dealt with that life *unjustly*, so surely would they have to answer for it to the God who made them.

"He had not merely the facts of the case to deal with, but the odious prejudices which the preliminary investigations must have engendered, filled him with apprehension.

"The horrid nature of the crime itself, the rank of the deceased, the numerous connexions mourning their bereavement, the opinions promulgated before the prisoner could be heard, the fact that his case had not been left to the ordinary instruments of justice, but that speculation had been stimulated by the offer of a Government reward,—as if the grave knew any aristocracy,—these things did fill him with apprehension. And when he looked around him on that crowded court, and saw the intensity of the public gaze, and

* Vol. lxxxii. pp. 233–236.

almost heard the throb of popular indignation; and when he turned him to the dock, where the wretched object of this outburst stood, —alone amid this multitude, far from his native land, far from the friends that loved, and the associates that in his hour of danger would have crowded around him,—a poor, solitary, isolated, helpless foreigner,—he did own that he should feel his spirits fainting fast within him, were it not for the anchor by which he held, an anchor that was centred in the breasts of the jury. He relied upon their integrity, upon their sense of justice; he participated in that generous reliance which the prisoner showed, when he refused all foreign interference, and trusted his life to a jury of Englishmen.

"He thought that the prisoner was right; he had no fear in appealing to such a tribunal. He knew that the case, whatever it was, would by such a tribunal be fairly, fully, impartially heard, and justly decided. He should proceed, then, to consider the most extraordinary and unheard-of circumstances of this case; and, having done so, he should submit that in such a case, wrapped up in clouds, in mystery, and darkness, there was not only nothing upon which they could safely convict the prisoner, but that here and there probabilities started up which might make them suspect that he had been made the victim of an unjust and depraved conspiracy!"

What was the object of that probable conspiracy, thus guardedly suggested, and what were the means by which it had been sought to obtain the object, must long ago have occurred to any attentive reader of the foregoing pages.

We had marked many passages in the powerful address of Mr Phillips, for quotation, as specimens of what may be admirably accomplished by a skilful advocate, in even the most disheartening and desperate cases. Want of space, however, and a desire to adhere to the real points of the present controversy, compel us to be content with merely indicating the course of his topics. He proceeded to say that "he had much to complain of in the opening address of Mr Adolphus," particularly in his attempting to answer a prisoner's defence, by anticipation of what it might possibly turn out to be. Then Mr Adolphus had said, "the man is a foreigner; and foreigners always murder when they rob:" a proposition which he scouted in terms of vigorous and indignant eloquence. Then as to the possible motive for the crime: "it was not," said Mr Adolphus, "necessary for a man to have a motive to commit crime." The prosecutor had been obliged to say this, because he acknowledged he could assign no motive for Courvoisier's murder of his noble, kind, and confiding master. Had it been avarice, he had many ways of obtaining his wishes easily, without resorting to murder. "This was not a case in which they had clear proofs before them; it was one of circumstances only, as the prosecutor had himself told them: and, therefore, every minute observation with which it might be his painful duty to trouble them, would, he was sure, be taken into consideration. It was not his case, it was their own case. His duty performed, not upon his feeble breath, thank God, would the irrevocable doom depend. Upon them it would; and, therefore, when the arduous task committed to himself and his friends was performed, their consciences would be clear." He proceeded to remark on the proved and admitted absence of assignable motive on the part of the prisoner, for the murder; and then urged an obviously important topic of his defence, of any defence, especially in cases of mere circumstantial evidence, namely, that it lay on the prosecutor, to make out clearly a case of guilt against the prisoner, whose innocence is of course presumed by the law. "The counsel for the prosecution had undertaken to prove that the crime had been committed by the prisoner. He believed it would be laid down by the learned Judge, that it was the duty of the prosecutor to bring home to the prisoner, without any reasonable doubt whatever, the commission of this offence. It was not his (Mr Phillip's) business to prove who did it; that was the task *they* had undertaken. Unless that were proved, he would beseech the jury to be cautious how they imbrued their hands in this man's blood. The omniscient God alone knew who did this crime.* He was not called on to rend asunder the dark mantle of the night, and throw light on this deed of darkness. They were bound to shew the prisoner's guilt, —not by inference, by reasonings, by that subtle and refined ingenuity which he was shocked to hear exercised in the opening address of his friend, but to prove it by downright, clear, open, palpable demonstration. How did they do this? What said Mr Adolphus, AND HIS WITNESS SARAH MANSER? AND HERE HE WOULD BEG THE JURY NOT TO SUPPOSE, FOR A MOMENT, IN THE COURSE OF THE NARRATIVE *with which he must trouble them, that he meant to cast the crime upon* EITHER OF THE FEMALE SERVANTS. It was not at all necessary to his case to do so. He wished not to asperse them. [God forbid that any breath of his should send tainted into the world persons perhaps depending for their subsistence upon their character. It was not his duty, nor his interest, nor his policy to do so." †] The *Examiner*, in originally stating this part of its charge against Mr Phillips, on the 27th June 1840, quoted, and very conspicuously, *only the last two sentences*, above included in brackets, *taking no notice whatever of the far more important sentences immediately preceding them!*

Mr Phillips, however, having thus guarded the jury at the outset, against entertaining erroneous notions as to his intentions with reference to the women servants, thus proceeded;—and to the whole of this paragraph, particularly the portions in small capitals, we would direct the special attention of our readers—" The first imputation on the

* The reader will continue to bear in mind that we are quoting from the report in the *Times;* and as to this sentence some observations will be found hereafter (*post*, p. 63).

† The *Morning Chronicle* report thus commences this important paragraph: —" In the first place, says my friend, Mr Adolphus, and says his witness, Sarah Manser,—and here I beg to do *an* ACT OF JUSTICE, and to assure you that I do not for a moment," &c., "that this crime may have been committed by the female servants." The *Herald:*—" But let me do *myself* justice, and OTHERS JUSTICE, by now stating," &c. The *Post:*—" Let me do *myself* justice, and OTHERS JUSTICE, by begging you not to suppose that I am *in the least degree* seeking to cast the crime upon ANY OF THE WITNESSES."

prisoner by Mr Adolphus, was his AGITATION. Let them try that by the test of their own hearts and consciences. The prisoner had seen his master retire to his peaceful bed, and was alarmed in the morning by the housemaid, who was up before him, with a cry of robbery, and some dark mysterious suggestion of murder. 'Let us go,' said she, 'and see where my lord is.' He did confess that that expression struck him as extraordinary. If she had said, 'let us go and tell my lord *that the house is plundered*,' that would have been natural; but why should she suspect that aught had happened to his lordship? She saw her fellow-servants safe, no taint of blood about the house, and where did she expect to find her master? why, in his bed-room to be sure. What was there to lead to a suspicion that he was hurt? Courvoisier was safe, the cook was safe, and why should she suspect that her master was not safe too? If he had heard the character of that nobleman right, there was never a man who breathed who had less reason to suspect or dread a foe. But Courvoisier did as he was desired. He and Sarah Manser went to the bed-room. The prisoner walked up to the window, as he was in the habit of doing; he opened a shutter; and then the female servant saw a speck of blood upon the pillow, and ran screaming out of the room. He had put a question to the witness respecting the account she had given before the Coroner. The depositions taken before the Coroner were then before the learned Judges; and, perhaps, they would consider it their bounden duty to tell the jury, whether that woman swore before the Coroner as as she did before the Court.* His conscience was clear. He had discharged his duty by throwing out that sugges-

* It may be necessary to apprise the non-professional reader of the reason why Mr Phillips did not at once settle the point, that there was a variance between an answer given by the witness at the trial, and one given when she was examined before the Coroner. If he had done so, he would have made these depositions evidence, and so have entitled the counsel for the prosecution to a reply. Whether or not, in the present instance, Mr Phillips was likely to allow a speech in reply from Mr Adolphus, after such an opening as his, it is for the experienced reader to say.

tion. The question he had put to the witness was this; 'Upon the oath you have taken, did you not tell the Coroner that you saw, instead of "some blood on the pillow," "his lordship murdered on the bed?"' That was matter for the jury to consider. He should now pass on. The window was opened, the daylight let in on the dreadful spectacle, and could they expect Courvoisier, or any human being who did not disguise within a human shape the heart of a wild beast, to remain unmoved at the exhibition? To see rank and age, a nobleman, seventy-three years old, weltering in his blood; how did the jury think that *they* could have borne the spectacle? Mr Adolphus said, they must show no agitation at it! that if they did, it must be taken as a proof of guilt! What would have been said if Courvoisier had remained calm, and looked on unmoved? Would they not have thought, and thought justly, that the man who was unmoved, who did not shudder with agitation at such a sight—was himself capable of committing the deed? But when Mr Adolphus called on them to mark the agitation of the prisoner, as a proof of guilt, what became of the women, who showed the very same feelings? HE THOUGHT THE BETTER OF THESE WOMEN FOR DOING SO: GOD FORBID HE SHOULD INSINUATE IT WAS A PROOF OF THEIR GUILT: IT WOULD APPEAR TO HIM, ON THE CONTRARY, TO BE A PROOF OF THEIR INNOCENCE! He wished his learned friend had been where he, Mr Phillips, had accidentally happened to be,—in Hyde Park, some days since, when the murderous attack on the Queen was made! He wished his friend could have seen the emotion of the bystanders when it became known; how the stoutest man stood appalled; and every face betrayed the most painful *agitation*. If THAT were a proof of guilt, there was not a man in the Park who should not have been considered the murderer. Agitation, indeed!" The *Morning Herald* thus reports the passage above quoted in small capitals from the *Times*;—"But Mr Adolphus talks of the prisoner's agitation being a proof of guilt. Let me remind him that the female servants, his own witnesses, were in the same state of agitation, and I THINK THE BETTER OF THEM FOR IT: for I hold, that in such a case, agitation, so far from being a proof of guilt, IS A PROOF OF INNOCENCE." The *Morning Chronicle* gives it thus:—"But when Mr Adolphus calls on you to say that the prisoner's agitation was a proof of his guilt, what is to become of the women? They showed similar agitation. Mr Adolphus says, agitation on the part of the man, was a proof of his guilt. I SAY, THAT AGITATION, IN THEM, WAS A PROOF OF THEIR INNOCENCE; AND THAT IS THE DIFFERENCE BETWEEN US!" The passages above-quoted from the *Times*, in small capitals, have never been cited by the *Examiner* in any of its articles during the last ten years! as far as we have been able to discover (certainly not in those placed at the head of this article), though the attention of the writer of them was of course directed to the report in the *Times*, which, doubtless, he has carefully and repeatedly studied, to discover whether it really bore out the assertion, that Mr Phillips deliberately imputed to the women servants, or insinuated against them the imputation, that they had been guilty of the crime of murder! And the only proof which the *Examiner* has to offer of so horrible an imputation, is contained in the foregoing brief extract, beginning, "the prisoner had seen his master retire to his peaceful bed," and ending, "why should she suspect that her master was not safe too?"*

Pursuing the course of Mr Phillips' defence, there follows a series of acute and striking comments on various points of the evidence which had been pressed by Mr Adolphus strongly against the prisoner. One of them related to the ineffectual search by Inspector Tedman of the prisoner's box on the 6th of May; and Mr Phillips remarked, with equal force and justice, on the probability that the gloves, handkerchiefs, and shirt-front had found

* *Ante*, p. 407.

their way fraudulently into the prisoner's trunk,—which, instead of having been immediately sealed up and secured, out of justice to the prisoner and the public, after Inspector Tedman's search on the 6th of May had satisfied him that there was nothing in it to criminate the prisoner, had "remained open and accessible to the women servants and the whole gang of policemen," down to the day when the articles in question were so strangely discovered. "*Who put them there*, between the 6th and 14th of May? his learned friend had demanded, Who murdered Lord W. Russell? *He* (Mr Phillips) was not bound to show that; but he had a right to know who put those bloody gloves in the prisoner's trunk, between the 6th and 14th of May, after the first minute examination by Inspector Tedman, and when the prisoner had been three days in gaol! * Had there not been *practice* here? 'Thus bad begins; but worse remains behind.' This man, it was evidently determined, should be made the victim of some foul contrivance. Then, as to the handkerchiefs, shirt-fronts, and frill: who put these into the trunk, and for what purpose? They were not there on the 6th of May. It was clear Courvoisier had not put them there; it was physically impossible: he was in his dungeon at the time, three miles off. Some villains must have been at work here, to provide proofs of guilt against the prisoner, and endeavour to make the jury instrumental in rendering him the victim, not of his own guilt, but their own machinations. He was not wrong in saying that there existed a strong suspicion, if not actual proof, that the trunk had been practised on." Mr Phillips then proceeded to comment severely on the conduct of the policeman Pearce, who had suppressed a portion of his remark to the prisoner ("Dare you look me in the face?"), yet said he had not intended

* In the report of the *Morning Herald*, as cited by the *Examiner* on the 8th Dec. 1849, there appears, in this part of the speech, the following bold avowal by Mr Phillips, in the presence of the judge and jury:—"I say, freely and fearlessly, that the articles were placed there by some of the police, for reasons best known to themselves!"

to "intimidate." Mr Phillips charged him with an attempt to extort a confession, and added, "yet the fellow who did all this, told the jury he expected to share in the plunder,—the £450 reward,—which was to be divided over the coffin of Courvoisier. He had hoped the days of blood-money were past. These rewards might be offered by Government from the purest of motives. They might induce men to hunt out evidence, but their effect was, also, to make them invent, fabricate, colour, distort, and exaggerate it, to attain the end they had in view." Then came Baldwin, whom Mr Phillips accused of "shuffling, equivocation, and lying on his oath;" and, as we have already intimated, the Judge agreed with Mr Phillips, and directed the jury to dismiss from their minds the evidence of this man, as worthless and dangerous! Mr Phillips proceeded to explain several other portions of the evidence, as being of an inconclusive character, and even consistent with the prisoner's innocence. He observed on the absence of the slightest wound or scratch on the prisoner's person, or stain of blood on any portion of his clothes; that it was absurd to suppose he would, if guilty of the murder, have placed gloves, handkerchiefs, &c., marked with blood, where they were certain of being instantly discovered; and the same observation he applied to the articles which had been found in the pantry and scullery. He also asked how the cook's silver thimble, an utterly worthless article, came to be in the hall, among the other articles found there; and called attention to the undoubtedly remarkable circumstance, that so much could have been done, door-breaking and all, during the night, by Courvoisier, who slept in a room immediately adjoining that of the women servants, without having once disturbed them. He pointed out the strange position, and the contradictory character of the evidence, as to the marks said to have been found on the area door. On coming to the startling addition to the case for the prosecution, afforded by the evidence of Mrs Piolaine, he complained loudly that he had not been apprised of it, and of the name of the witness, (as he certainly might have been) over night. "A night, at least, should have been given, to allow inquiries to be made into the character of the witnesses. This new evidence had been sprung on him like a mine. He knew nothing about Mrs Piolaine; how should he? The prosecution had taken care that he should know nothing about her. * * * He hoped the jury knew something of Leicester Place. If they did, they knew the character of this hotel, with a billiard-room attached to it, where, unlike at a respectable hotel, any stranger, not being a guest, might enter and gamble. This was the evidence of Mrs Piolaine, who though," &c.; and he went on to remark justifiably on the air of improbability worn by a portion of her evidence, and the possibility of her being mistaken as to the identity of the prisoner. "But supposing all this was admitted (and he was sure that the jury, could they find their way out of this case, consistently with the ends of justice, without shedding the prisoner's blood, would be glad to do so), was this evidence conclusive as to the murder? On this question they would have the valuable opinion of his lordship; yet he might say of this evidence, that though, if true, it might be conclusive of the robbery, yet it was by no means conclusive of the murder. And with respect to the commission of the murder, the jury might have a strong suspicion, or even a moral conviction; but it was not on a strong suspicion, or a moral conviction, that a man was to be declared guilty of murder. If, notwithstanding that suspicion, they felt bound to acquit the prisoner, he was still answerable for the robbery, if guilty; and even supposing him guilty of the murder, which, indeed, was known to Almighty God alone, and of which, for the sake of his eternal soul, he (Mr Phillips) hoped the prisoner was innocent, it was better far that in the dreadful solitude of exile he should, though not in the sight of man, but before the presence of God, atone, by a lingering repentance, for the deed, than that he should now be sent, in the dawning of his manhood, to an ignominious death, in a case where the truth was not clear. And having now travelled through this case of mystery and darkness, his anxious task was done; that of the jury was about to begin: might God direct their judgment! * * * His had been a painful and an awful task; but still more awful was their responsibility. To violate the living temple which the Lord had made, to quench the fire that His breath had given, was an awful and tremendous responsibility. The word once gone forth, was irrevocable. Speak not that word lightly. Speak it not on suspicion, however strong; on moral conviction, however cogent; on inference, or anything but a clear, irresistible, bright, noonday certainty. * * * IF THEY PRONOUNCED THE WORD LIGHTLY, its memory would never die within them."—And would it? These words were addressed, by one who was, as will be admitted, bound to act as though he were not the depositary of the fatal secret confided to him, to twelve men who were, as the Chief Justice almost immediately afterwards in impressive terms reminded them, sworn to decide ACCORDING TO THE EVIDENCE. "They sate in that box under the solemn sanction of an oath, and were bound by that oath to deliver their verdict according to the evidence laid before them; they were bound to decide upon that evidence and upon that evidence alone, so that, in coming to their verdict, their understandings and consciences should agree." If the jury should pronounce their dread verdict irrespectively of the evidence, that is, "lightly," they would have unquestionably violated their oaths, and that, too, in the case where the life of a fellow-creature was at stake. We have omitted, equally from want of space in this protracted article, and as needless to our present purpose, several passages of powerful rhetoric, ably enforcing the appeal which appears above.

Such was the defence of Mr Phillips, on certain isolated

portions of which, alone, it has been sought to support the gross charge alleged against him.

The summing up of the Chief Justice, which lasted for three hours and a-half, was characterised by that rigorous impartiality and clearness for which he was so pre-eminently distinguished. So long and elaborate a summing up alone amply evidenced the real doubt which he deemed to surround the proved facts of the case, and the necessity which existed for a careful and unbiassed consideration of them. He put it prominently to the jury, whether the murder and robbery were perpetrated by different persons, on the same night, or by the same person; and whether the marks of burglary and robbery exhibited within the house, and on the back door, were genuine or spurious? Were the articles of property so disposed within the house, and the marks so made on the door, to divert the attention of the officers of justice, in order that the guilty parties might escape? If thieves had entered to plunder, would they have left behind property so easily disposable about their persons? He advised the jury "by no means to rely on the prisoner's expressions when first met with in the morning, or his agitation, as a mark of guilt," but to act upon their oaths as to proved facts. He regarded the discrepancies between the evidence of the two women servants, and the suggested variance of expression attributed to the housemaid on the occasion of her first entering Lord William Russell's bed-room, as immaterial. "It was stated in the course of the trial, that the words of Sarah Manser, 'Let us go and see where his lordship is,' were 'rather extraordinary.' But in looking at expressions made use of by parties in a state of anxiety and alarm, the jury would not have to confine the words to their strict interpretation." "Nor was much weight to be attached to the language attributed to the prisoner, about 'Old Billy being a rum old chap,' &c.; it was little more than the kitchen gossip of servants about their masters. The discrepancy imputed to the statement of Sarah Manser, between 'seeing' blood on the pillow, and 'my lord murdered in the bed,' was not to be strained too far;" for, after all, "it really appeared a trivial one, and not to amount to a contradiction;" and he thought that Sarah Manser's testimony ought to be believed. "With respect to the question which had been put to the prisoner by the inspector, there could be no objection to his doing so; but if it had been for the purpose of entrapping him into a confession which might be used in evidence against him, it was most unfair. If the words, 'Dare you look me in the face?' were used with an honest intention, the officer was not to blame." As to the gloves and handkerchiefs, "some observations had been made about finding the gloves and handkerchiefs secreted in the prisoner's portmanteau; and it was stated that they must have been placed there to bring the prisoner within the consequence of a verdict of guilty. The jury would consider whether, in the previous search, when all the shirts were taken out and placed on the bed unfolded, the gloves and handkerchiefs could have escaped notice; and whether any one could be capable of making up the chain of circumstances, in order to convict the prisoner at the bar. They would also consider whether, if this had been intended, more decisive steps would not have been taken, for scarcely any blood appeared on the gloves and handkerchiefs; and it might be supposed, that if the party who committed the murder wore those articles at the time, they would not exhibit more marks than those produced. * * * As to the handkerchiefs, it might be said, that if the prisoner were the guilty party, he would never have placed them in his portmanteau, where they could not by possibility escape detection." "As for the operation of rewards, many crimes would go undiscovered without them; but it was for the jury to consider how far the credibility of witnesses was affected by the expectation of reward." In speaking of Baldwin's evidence, his lordship said, "The witness John Baldwin, the police constable, gave evidence as to the state of the leads and the walls; but he gave this testimony in such a way, that it would be dangerous, in such a serious inquiry as this, to give any credit to it." His lordship then remarked on the favourable evidence as to the prisoner's character, explaining its true value and tendency, as operating only in cases of doubtful facts, not where the facts were so strong ("though he did not mean to say they were so in this case") as to leave no reasonable doubt in the minds of the jury as to the guilt of the accused. After remarking on the difficulty of assigning the true motives of human action, and saying that a court of justice had to deal with facts only, and to reconcile them with the act charged against an accused, his lordship thus concluded his righteous and luminous summing up:—"After carefully considering the whole matter, it was for the jury to say whether the prisoner was guilty, or not guilty, of the crime with which he was charged."

The jury retired to consider their verdict; and, after an absence of an hour and twenty-five minutes, returned with a verdict of Guilty; on which the prisoner was sentenced to death,—the Chief Justice telling him "that his guilt had been brought to light in a manner clear and convincing to all. The murder in itself, with the single exception of one direct circumstance against you, which subsequently appeared in the course of the trial, was involved in mystery. It was committed and planned by you with so much secrecy and cunning, aided by peculiar facilities of which you took advantage, that you considered yourself safe from the consequences of the crime."*

* The following is the conclusion of Courvoisier's confession, duly signed by him, and attested, and sent to the Home Office. It goes into details which, with the following exceptions, accord with the evidence adduced at the trial:—"The gloves were never placed in the shirt by me, nor to my knowledge. When I left Mr Fector's, I gave all my white gloves to the coachman. The handkerchiefs that were found in my portmanteau were never put there by me. They were in my drawer where I used to keep my dirty linen, or in my bag, with my dirty linen, in the pantry. If there is blood upon then, it must have been from my nose, as it sometimes bled. I know nothing whatever of

We have now laid before our readers, with all possible accuracy and fidelity, the whole proceedings of this memorable affair; and the question now to be considered is,—Did Mr Phillips discharge his duty as an advocate, consistently with the dictates of honour and morality; or did he irretrievably compromise his character, and, in so doing, cast a stigma on the great profession of which he is a member? The *Jurist*, in the article in which it admitted the sufficiency of Mr Phillips' explanations, thus speaks of the duty of the advocate, and Mr Phillips' due discharge of those duties:—"If the law has laid down, for the general protection, some certain rules of evidence, or otherwise, according to which, only, the legal conclusion of a man's guilt is to be arrived at, it is the duty of counsel to do as Mr Phillips did—to retain his brief, and to use every endeavour that his intellect can suggest, to take care that his client shall not be condemned except by a conclusion strictly deducible, by applying the fixed rules of the law to the evidence produced."* Mr Baron Parke tersely defined to Mr Phillips that duty to be, "using all fair arguments arising on the evidence;" and the *Examiner* admits his duty to have been, "to confine himself to weighing the sufficiency of evidence, and examining flaws in its links;" that had he done this, "he

the shirt-front. I turned up my coat and shirt sleeve of my right hand when I committed the murder. I did not use the pillow at all. After I had committed the murder, I undressed and went to bed as usual. I made the marks on the door on the outside, none of them from the inside, for the purpose of having it believed that thieves had broken in. I never made use of the chisel or the fire-irons. I placed the things about the house, to give the appearance of robbery. It is not true that the bottom bolt was never used to secure the door; it was bolted that night. I took the jewellery after I had committed the deed. All the marks on the door were made from the outside on the Monday night, for I got out of the pantry window and broke in at the door, and while getting out of the pantry window, made a little mark on the wall outside, near the water-pipe, which the witness Young saw, and mentioned in his evidence. I went to bed about two o'clock. I burned nothing. I did not wash my hands or the knife in the bedit in his lordship's bed-room. Sarah Manser knew nothing about it; neither did the cook, nor any of the other servants. I am the only person who is at all guilty.—FRANCOIS BENJAMIN COURVOISIER; June 22, 1840."—*Annual Register*, vol. lxxxii. p. 238.

* Jurist, 24th Nov. 1849.

would at least have avoided wrong and danger to others, in the defence of an assassin:" and "its objections to Mr Phillips' defence applied to the points in which he became the assailant or accuser of witnesses, whose truth he had no reason to suspect after Courvoisier's confession; and also to his solemn pretences of the prisoner's innocence." This was the wording of the charge nearly ten years ago. On the 24th of November 1849, the *Examiner* thus declared its deliberate adherence to the charge:—"Our plain and distinct averment against Mr Phillips is, that with a perfect knowledge where the guilt lay, *he endeavoured to cast the suspicion of the guilt upon the innocent.* To that averment we in all respects adhere." In the same number, also, it is stated, in allusion to their original accusation, "We did not accuse Mr Phillips of solemnly *protesting* his belief in Courvoisier's innocence, but of solemnly *acting* it! in short, our charge was restricted to his solemnly *acted* belief in the innocence of a murderer!" They were pleased to "admit Mr Phillips' right, in the peculiar circumstances of the case, to retain his brief 'even after the confession;'" and expressed their opinion that "his defence should turn, in such case, on the sufficiency of proof, and on technical points."

We have already placed our readers in a position to form their own judgment on this subject, and shall presently offer a few observations which have occurred to ourselves. But, in the first instance, we would ask how can the *Examiner* get rid of the distinct and emphatic testimony of the illustrious Judge who tried the case, and his very eminent brother Judge who sate beside him, and who states "that he had a reason, which the Chief Justice did not know, for watching Mr Phillips;" both of whom concur in stating that "Mr Phillips had *carefully abstained from giving any personal opinion* in the case," and that he had never "appealed to Heaven as to his belief in Courvoisier's innocence?" while it is further expressly stated by two gentlemen of unquestionable veracity, honour, and standing at the Bar, who publicly give their names,* that they heard the late lamented Chief Justice, shortly after the trial, and after the charge had been made against Mr Phillips, state that "Mr Phillips' observations had been much misunderstood;" that "he had, under circumstances of extraordinary difficulty, properly discharged a most painful duty;" that the Chief Justice not only "exculpated him from the precise imputations," but made such a representation of the case as tended "to remove *every impression* to Mr Phillips' prejudice;" that "the Chief Justice declared distinctly that he deeply regretted the attacks which were made on Mr Phillips, and strongly declared that there was no foundation for them." Can anything possibly be more decisive? To say nothing of similar strong concurrent testimonies from various gentlemen, independent and disinterested, who were present at the trial, heard, and closely attended to, all that Mr Phillips said, and have come forward honourably to bear such testimony—it must occur to any one, that the emphatic, undisputed testimony of two of the most gifted, distinguished, and high-minded Judges who ever adorned the seat of justice, is conclusive on the question. Consummately qualified for the task, they are equivalent to any conceivable number of the most thoroughly competent witnesses speaking to any facts which have come under their personal observation. Their integrity was, as the *Examiner* may possibly admit, beyond all question; their intellectual capacity far beyond a high standard of mankind; they had incomparable opportunities and facilities for observation; and one of them, a man remarkable for his acuteness and strength of intellect, declares that he "narrowly watched" this harassed advocate, and testifies to the unexceptionable manner in which he discharged his duty. How could, then, these two Judges have been mistaken? How could they ever have brought themselves

* Mr Mellor of the Midland, and Mr Flowers of the Oxford Circuit.—*Correspondence*, pp. 25, 28.

deliberately to vouch the propriety of conduct of which they even entertained the slightest doubt?

Let us, however, see what are the specific charges of the *Examiner*, and how they are borne out by the evidence on which they are professedly founded. They were originally thus expressed, and have been ever since adhered to:—That, after the confession of Courvoisier to Mr Phillips, he "threw out the cruellest insinuations against the witness Sarah Manser, and advanced the foulest charges against the police."* As to the former branch of this charge, there are just grounds for serious complaint against the *Examiner*. Nearly ten years ago, it originated the charge of "throwing out the cruellest insinuations against the witness Sarah Manser." We have ever since been under the impression, as doubtless have been the other readers of the *Examiner*, till the publication of Mr Phillips' letter in answer to his friend's challenge, that the *Examiner* had quoted frankly and fairly, without any suppression, from the *Times*' report of that part of Mr Phillips' speech on which the *Examiner* founded its imputations. We unfeignedly regret to say, however, that we find ourselves to have been altogether mistaken; that a single sentence has been picked out of a strong *bonâ fide* disclaimer, and placed conspicuously alone, as if it were the only sentence of the kind or tendency; and no allusion whatever is made to those immediately preceding it, containing an anxious, positive, emphatic exoneration of the female servants, *such as the public never would have heard of*, as far as the *Examiner* was concerned, even unto this day, but for Mr Phillips' letter, and our own careful reference to the *Times*' report! With the following pregnant words under its eye—uttered the instant after Mr Phillips had first mentioned the name of Sarah Manser,—"*and here he would beg the jury not to suppose for a moment that he meant to cast the crime upon either of the female servants*," — the *Examiner* contents

* *Examiner*, 27th June 1849.

itself with quoting the ensuing:—"God forbid that any breath of his should send tainted into the world persons perhaps depending for their subsistence upon their character! It was not his duty, nor his interest, nor his policy to do so."

The following is the entire passage, as given in the *Times*:—

"What said Mr Adolphus, and his witness, Sarah Manser? *Here he would beg the jury not to suppose for a moment, in the course of the narrative with which he must trouble them, that he meant to cast the crime upon either of the female servants.* It was not at all necessary to his case to do so; he wished not to asperse them. God forbid that any breath of his should send tainted into the world persons perhaps depending for their subsistence upon their character. It was not his duty, nor his interest, nor his policy to do so."

The following is the mode in which the *Examiner* originally (27th of June 1840) cited *one portion only* of the above:—

"The intended line of defence (query, *lie* of defence?) was not changed by the communication [of the confession]. The cruellest insinuations were thrown out against the witness Sarah Manser, and the foulest charges advanced against the police.

"Mr Phillips disclaimed the intention to criminate the female servants. No, forsooth!

"'God forbid that any breath of his should send tainted into the world persons dependent for their subsistence upon their character! It was not his duty, nor his interest, nor his policy to do so.'

"But did he, or did he not, make the attempt in this passage?

"The prisoner had seen his master," &c.

[Quoting the passage beginning with these words, and given *ante*, p. 32.] Thus the *Examiner*, on the 27th of June 1840, totally suppressed the all-important passage in question, which had given a tone to the entire speech: and on the 24th of November 1849, deliberately reprinted the article of 1840, without supplying or alluding to the deficiency! and in its own article of the former date, thus summarily and obscurely deals with this same apparently unwelcome passage, in professing to quote from the *Times*:—

"*And here he would beg*, &c. *He wished not to asperse the female servants*, *God forbid!* &c. &c. It was not at all necessary to his case to do so."*

How is all this to be explained, and on what principle can it be justified? and in a writer avowing, in the same article, that he "writes *with the file of the* "Times" *before him?*" Did it never occur to the writer or writers of all these articles, as very material that such passages as we have now called to their attention should be publicly noticed by them; and credit given for them to the gentleman whom they were so cruelly assailing?

Is this dealing fairly?—The *Examiner*, having thus prefaced this garbled extract (for such we must call it) with the words, "Mr Phillips disclaimed the intention to criminate the female servants. No, forsooth!" subjoins, "But did he, or did he not, make the attempt in this passage?" and then quotes the brief passing comment of Mr Phillips, legitimately made on an answer given by the witness in open court; and this is positively its only proof of the grave charge, that he attempted to fasten the guilt of the murder upon the female servants! Again totally suppressing, not only a still more impressive and conspicuous disclaimer, in the very same portion of the speech from which the *Examiner* is quoting, of all imputation on the women servants,—but a distinct assertion that he regarded their agitation, on the occasion in question, as a "PROOF OF THEIR INNOCENCE;" adding, even,

* This last passage is printed in a column parallel to the quotation from Mr Phillips' letter; which circumstance may possibly be assigned by the *Examiner* as a reason for referring to it only by the leading words of the sentence, and an "&c."

"GOD FORBID HE SHOULD INSINUATE IT WAS A PROOF OF THEIR GUILT!" We ask, how is it possible to suppose that these signal passages could have escaped the sharp eyes scrutinising the paragraph in which they occur—scrutinising it, too, not from a zealous desire to exculpate and to defend, but to inculpate and accuse? And if they were seen, why were they deliberately and perseveringly suppressed, while an attempt was made, by citing an isolated passage, as if it were the only one of that character or tendency, to sustain the charge *which those former passages so clearly contradicted?* The *Examiner* itself has unwittingly supplied evidence of the extent to which it has misled the journals relying upon its accuracy and fairness; for it has quoted extracts from their columns, conclusively showing the ignorance of the writers that such passages were to be found in Mr Phillips' speech, as are given in this article, but were *not* supplied by the *Examiner!* Again, it is of the last importance to remark, that the solitary and strictly legitimate comment of Mr Phillips, on the remark which fell from Sarah Manser, which he said simply had "struck him as extraordinary" occurs in the midst of that passage of the speech in which he is refuting Mr Adolphus' first proposition, that the prisoner's *agitation* was a proof of his guilt: Mr Phillips immediately, and with evident eagerness, seizing an opportunity to make that second declaration of his belief of the women servants' innocence, on which the *Examiner* has ever been so suspiciously silent! What becomes of the alleged cruel and infamous "insinuation" in the solitary comment in question, *preceded* as it is, and *followed* as it is, by full, emphatic disclaimers and protests? Regarded fairly as a link in the chain of argument, the real drift of that comment is, that the jury might regard what fell from Sarah Manser, on this and other occasions, as *inaccurate*—as an exclamation *not justified by the appearances around her at the time;* for proved circumstances are recited showing that she could *then* have had no *reason* for suspecting personal injury to her master. It is really sickening to have to deal with such perversion and over-straining as that here exhibited by the *Examiner*, which sees in this comment only "imputations of a knowledge of the murder" by the housemaid, "previous to Courvoisier's knowledge of it!" This one comment of Mr Phillips is the only *scintilla* of evidence offered by his accuser in support of the dreadful charge of deliberately attempting to destroy the innocent, in order to shield the guilty! There is not the faintest allusion to the women servants, except such as we have quoted: nor is there throughout the entire three hours' speech, wherever reported, as far as we have seen, the slightest attempt to suggest or insinuate that "*any of the witnesses*" * had committed the murder, or were in any way cognisant of it; but, on the contrary, an explicit and straightforward disclaimer of any such imputation. What motives, indeed, could Mr Phillips have had for resorting to such an unjustifiable topic of defence (and in the presence of Mr Baron Parke), when he had already one amply sufficient for his purpose,—one strictly legitimate, and established by the sworn evidence in the cause, as we shall presently demonstrate, and must, indeed, be already apparent to our readers, and to which he pointedly referred at the very outset of his speech? This attempt, then, to dislocate the solitary brief passage in question, and wrest it into a wrong significancy, appears to us to resemble the style of procedure of those who would, as Lord Erskine said, prove the Psalmist guilty of blasphemously asserting that "there is no God," by suppressing the preceding words — "the fool hath said in his heart." There is really not a shadow of pretence for this grievous accusation. Nothing could have sustained it but proof that the *general tendency* of Mr Phillips' speech was to save his client, by incriminating the women servants: whereas, it was precisely the reverse! How, indeed, could Chief Justice Tindal have failed to notice such an attempt

* *Morning Herald*, June 22, 1840.

in his summing up, and exonerate an outraged female's character from so foul and unfounded an imputation? Yet that acute and watchful Judge uttered not a breath of censure—not a suggestion as to a harsh or unjustifiable comment or insinuation on the part of Mr Phillips! How, again, could Mr Baron Parke, sitting beside him, have tolerated the slightest tendency or approach towards such an imputation, without an instant and indignant interference to stop that which he would have known to be so revolting a display of depravity? and to which, by his silence, he would almost have made himself a party: for *quì non prohibet, cùm prohibere possit, consentire videtur!* How, finally, could the Chief Justice, after hearing subsequently of the confession, have testified to the "proper" discharge by Mr Phillips of "a most painful duty," and the "groundlessness of the imputations" upon him? To the cross-examination of Sarah Manser, before the confession, no one can possibly object, nor, that we know of, ever has. It does not appear to us in any way objectionable; and yet the *Examiner* recently * professed to recite an advertisement issued on behalf of Sarah Manser, in 1840, in order to sustain its charge against Mr Phillips (of course, in respect of his *speech*), which expressly attributes her mental and physical prostration to the "harassing *interrogations* to which she was subjected, *preceding* the providential discovery of the guilt of Courvoisier!" † To all the foregoing disproofs of this shocking imputation, we must add the silence of the leading organs of public opinion at the time. The *Times* would, assuredly, never have passed by such a flagrant instance of forensic turpitude; nor are we aware of any other journal, except the *Examiner*, and the few who too hastily adopted its

* *Examiner*, 24th Nov. 1849.

† The *Examiner* states, in a note, that "to the above 'advertisement' unhappily no effectual response was made"—a circumstance suggesting a significant inference. Had Sarah Manser been the victim into which it has since been sought to convert her, the British public would not have been appealed to in vain on her behalf.

accusation, that countenanced such imputations. In the *Annual Register* no notice whatever is taken of such a disfiguring feature of the defence, which is thus epitomised:—"Mr Phillips then elaborately dissected the evidence; pointing out some discrepancies, taking advantage of every piece of testimony which could raise a presumption of the prisoner's innocence, and artfully insinuating that he was the victim of a conspiracy among the policemen to divide the large reward of £450 over Courvoisier's coffin."* Could this impartial chronicler have overlooked, after the public disclosure of the confession, the more hideous feature of the advocate's falsely imputing the known guilt of an assassin to an innocent woman, if such feature had really existed? And as to the "artful insinuation" respecting the policemen, let us now see how far the expression was justifiable.

The next head of charge against Mr Phillips is, "his advancing the foulest charges against the police, the groundlessness of which he knew, as well as his client's guilt." This appears to be not only equally unsustained, but equally disproved, by the evidence, with the former charge; and also to have been advanced in defiance, or at least in total oblivion of the proved facts. Mr Phillips *bonâ fide* believed that there had been unfair "practices" among the police, to fabricate evidence in support of a case otherwise too doubtful, in his opinion, to warrant that conviction on which depended their participation in the large reward. That this belief was perfectly consistent with his own private knowledge of Courvoisier's guilt,—a fact which was unknown to the police,—is obvious to any one of common candour or sense; and we have taken care to lay before our readers the premises from which they may draw their own inferences, as to the reasonableness and *bona fides* of Mr Phillips' belief. We are, ourselves, utterly unable, on considering the evidence, to account satisfactorily for the blood-spotted gloves and handker-

* Vol. lxxxii. pp. 234, 235.

chiefs found in the prisoner's box on the 14th of May, having been there on the 6th and 8th of May, and yet, on the latter two occasions, escaping the observation of the acute and practised police, who searched expressly for the purpose of making such discoveries! What would the Judge, what would the Bar, what would the jury, what would the public, have thought and said, of the advocate who, his lips hermetically sealed as to the confession, and addressing himself anxiously and exclusively to the evidence, according to which alone the jury were to decide, should have passed over these glaring topics of defence—topics which Mr Adolphus had, in his opening, not only shrunk from adopting as a part of his case, but expressly and significantly discarded? Why, but because he suspected the evidence in question to be spurious, and calculated to damage the case for the prosecution. Nevertheless, the advocate of the prisoner was ignominiously to disregard these advantages, and yet have credit for doing his duty by that prisoner! Would not an undying clamour have arisen against a British advocate, as having shamefully sacrificed his client to British prejudices, and given him over, bound hand and foot, to the great ducal family so pointedly alluded to by Mr Adolphus? We ask again,—why did Mr Adolphus discard this evidence, and *also anticipate an attack on the police?* Why "place no reliance on anything at any time found in the trunk," but because he, who had seen all the depositions, had heavy misgivings as to the *bonâ fide* character of that part of the evidence, and sought to obviate, by anticipation, the powerful comments which he knew would be made upon it on behalf of the prisoner? Where, then, is the evidence of Mr Phillips' knowledge of "the groundlessness of these charges?" Will any competent reader of the foregoing pages concur in opinion that these charges *were* groundless, that Mr Phillips knew them to be so, and should have altogether passed by such topics? In speaking, however, of his "unjustifiable attacks on the police," what is to be said of the policeman Baldwin, whose evidence the Chief Justice, in his summing up, actually declared that Mr Phillips had annihilated? Yet the *Examiner*, without alluding to this most decisive fact in the case, actually ventures to speak of the attack on Baldwin as "still more unjustifiable"* than that on a former witness! The latter being a policeman named Pearce, to whose evidence we refer the reader,† and which the Chief Justice left altogether to the jury to decide upon, with reference to the imputation of Mr Phillips, founded solely on the answers given by the witness, whether he had dealt fairly or unfairly with the prisoner, and attempted to extort from him a confession; adding, "that if they thought that such had been his intention, nothing could have been more unfair." But when a policeman gives what Mr Phillips deemed honest evidence, as in the case of Inspector Tedman, he deals very differently; and, in the last-mentioned instance, positively compliments Tedman before the jury, "as" (according to the report in the *Times*) "an officer who had given his evidence most fairly:" while Mr Phillips is thus reported in the *Morning Chronicle:*—"I have great pleasure, first of all, in bearing my testimony to the conduct of the witness, Inspector Tedman, and in reference to the whole course of proceedings which he has adopted in this case; * * * an honest man, who examined the trunk on the 6th, and went again to it on the 13th, with a fair and proper reason." Yet this witness had given evidence telling with deadly effect on Mr Phillips' client; but it was immediately after Mr Phillips had received his client's astounding confession. What then became of Mr Phillips' "advancing the foulest charges, the groundlessness of which he knew," against the police? And why was not the striking fact of this discriminating treatment of the police, noticed by a candid inquirer into truth? With reference to the other policemen, Mr Phillips' attack upon

* *Examiner*, June 27, 1840. † *Ante*, p. 29.

them, both in question and comment, was, as we have seen, confined strictly to those parts of their evidence which appeared to him inconsistent with each other and with truth, but consistent with the belief that they were using unfair means to earn a large reward, by completing the links in a chain of evidence which *they* reasonably enough deemed imperfect. He asked not a question as to any of the other facts to which they deposed; nor, in his address to the jury, sought in the least degree to discredit their evidence as to such facts. A more unfounded charge, then, than this can scarcely be imagined. We are surprised, indeed, that Mr Phillips should, himself, have altogether overlooked so strong a part of his own case, in his letter to his friend. He could not have had before him the original *Examiner*, which contained the easily disprovable charge in respect of the police; yet the recent *Examiner* * positively reproaches him with this omission! We, too, must, in our turn, ask Mr Phillips how he came to do so? and not only that question, but how *he* came to overlook the pregnant paragraph to which we have already called attention, with reference to his explicit exculpation of the women servants, and which, in *his* case, is utterly inexplicable, except on the supposition of a too hasty reference to the "files of the *Times*." The policy of offering rewards for the discovery of crime, may well be a moot point; and Mr Phillips' objections to this topic in addressing the jury, are put tersely and forcibly. He had elicited from the witnesses, especially the trustworthy Inspector Tedman, that the box of Courvoisier, in which were made such mysterious discoveries, had remained accessible from morning to night to the police and others interested in entitling themselves to the very large reward. If there were, *on the evidence*, a fair ground for imputing to the police that they were trading in "blood-money,"—that is, that they were manufacturing proofs of guilt, and in a capital case, in order to entitle themselves

* 24th Nov. 1849.

to that money,—is there any language too forcible or severe to be applied to such execrable criminality? And is it not beneath contempt, in such a case, to dwell hypercritically on mere expressions?

The next item of accusation against Mr Phillips is his "defaming the character of Mrs Piolaine," and uttering "gross imputations," and "wicked and unfounded aspersions" on her "and on her husband." In support of this charge, the *Examiner* simply quotes the following passage from Mr Phillips' speech, as if it had been purely a gratuitous and unfounded slander of his own:—"He hoped the Jury knew something of Leicester Place. If they did, they knew the character of this hotel, with a billiard-room attached to it, where, unlike at a respectable hotel, any stranger, not being a guest, might enter and gamble." On referring to the evidence of this witness, it will be seen * whether Mr Phillips went beyond it, or did more than comment on an admission made by the witness herself! He also made other just comments on other portions of her evidence, already before the reader, whom we invite to consider whether they were such as he would have been himself inclined to credit. That she gave true evidence, in the main, as to the identity of the person who had left the plate with her, cannot now be doubted; but had not Mr Phillips a perfect right to "use all fair arguments arising on the evidence," according to the canon of Mr Baron Parke, to "weigh the sufficiency of proof, and examine flaws in its links;" according to the concession of the *Examiner* itself? Mr Phillips desired undoubtedly to convey to the jury the idea that the "hotel" of the Piolaines was not of a superior kind; that any one, out of the street, might go in and play at the billiard-table there: he undoubtedly suggested that there was gambling there, though the witness denied the fact of its being a gambling-house, both to him, and, on re-examination, to Mr Adolphus. Of the manner of such

* *Ante*, p. 31.

denial, however, the reader will judge for himself, and couple with it the not unreasonable complaint to the jury of Mr Phillips, that he had not had the slightest opportunity afforded him by the prosecution of inquiring beforehand into the character and circumstances of so critical a witness.

The remaining accusation of the *Examiner*, against Mr Phillips, was one of a fearful description, but which it has seen since fit essentially to modify. In the first paper in which Mr Phillips' defence of Courvoisier was mentioned, viz., on the 27th June 1840 the *Examiner* quoted a paragraph from the *Times*, beginning thus:—"A correspondent of the *Times* states—" and then followed the paragraph in question, professing to repeat a complaint of Mr Phillips, in court, of a gross and false statement concerning him. "The effect of the statement was, *that he had made a solemn appeal to God of Courvoisier's innocence;*" and the paragraph went on to state that Mr Phillips had spoken to both the learned Judges upon the subject, and they assured him they had purposely watched his speech, and felt quite convinced that he never attempted to use the language attributed to him. Many others in court gave similar testimony. The *Examiner* then thus proceeds: —"In the *Times* report we find this emphatic assertion: '*The Omniscient God alone knew who did this crime.*' This was said by the man who himself knew who did the crime, and who profaned the name of the Deity by thrusting it into a solemn assertion, of the untruth of which he was cognisant." And in the conclusion of the article, it distinctly specified, as one of its two heads of objection to Mr Phillips' defence, "*his solemn pretences of the murderer's innocence.*" In this shape the charge has ever since had currency, conveying probably to thousands of persons the idea that Mr Phillips had distinctly avowed and professed his belief in Courvoisier's innocence, in a speech made after the miscreant's confession to him. We are not without suspicion that the word "pretences," in the above extract, may have been originally written "professions," or "protestations;" as founded by the writer on the charge above quoted by the *Examiner* from the correspondent of the *Times*, viz., that Mr Phillips had "made a solemn appeal to God of Courvoisier's innocence." Probably also the writer in the *Examiner* had seen the absurd statement which had been put forth in a since defunct newspaper, that Mr Phillips had said, in his speech to the jury, "On my soul, I believe Courvoisier innocent of the crime!" Finding it expedient, therefore, neither to abandon nor assert the charge in terms, the writer possibly contented himself with substituting the word "pretences" for "profession," or "protestation," "of the murderer's innocence." "Solemn 'pretences' of innocence," is evidently a forced and unnatural expression: while "solemn 'professions,' or 'protestations' of innocence," is simple and natural. The testimony adduced by Mr Phillips, on this point, in his letter, appear to us irresistible. Taking the newspaper in which the charge was contained, to the two Judges who had been present at the trial, he asked them whether he had ever used any such expression? "*You certainly did not*, Phillips," replied Chief Justice Tindal, "and I will be your voucher whenever you choose to call me." "And I," said Mr Baron Parke, "had a reason, which the Lord Chief Justice did not know, for watching you narrowly; and he will remember my saying to him, when you sate down, 'Brother Tindal, did you observe how carefully Phillips abstained from giving *any personal opinion* in the case?' To this the learned Chief Justice instantly assented."* We have personal reason to know, independently of Mr Phillips' putting forward this statement, that it is strictly correct. Mr Baron Parke is aware of it, and could have instantly contradicted, or can now † contradict it, if it be

* Correspondence, pp. 14, 15.

† This paper has been carefully read by this distinguished Judge, and the author has conversed with him on the subject more than once.

in any respect inaccurate. If then, this testimony be true, in our minds it settles the question. It is mere drivelling to quibble about forms of expression, as against the evidence of two such men as the late Chief Justice Tindal and Mr Baron Parke. The *thing*—the very substance of the matter so pointedly called to their attention was, whether Mr Phillips had expressed any opinion of his own, "any personal opinion" in the case, as to Courvoisier's guilt or innocence, in whatever form he might have expressed it: whether as solemnly declaring the fact of guilt to be known to the Deity alone, or as declaring the speaker's belief that Courvoisier was not the guilty person? Mr Baron Parke distinctly vouches, that, knowing as much as Mr Phillips so unfortunately knew, he had for that reason "narrowly watched" him, doubtless weighing, as Mr Baron Parke can and does weigh whatever is said before him, especially in his judicial capacity, every word and turn of expression of Mr Phillips. And on his sitting down gave expression to the result of his "narrow watching," viz., "how carefully Phillips had abstained from giving any personal opinion on the case." The Chief Justice "instantly assented;" and this assent was given, after he, also, had been made aware of the cruel position in which Courvoisier had placed his counsel. What but a perfect confidence in his innocence could have emboldened Mr Phillips to make this pointed appeal to two judicial personages, whose answer in the affirmative, or silence, would have withered the appellant? Both were high-minded men, and would not have given the decisive and peremptory answer in the negative, if they had not been perfectly clear on the matter. After this, we will presume everything in favour of Mr Phillips, and against his accusers.

Staggered, doubtless, by this unexpected evidence, the *Examiner* of November 24th last altogether changed its ground: gave a new colouring to its original assertion of Mr Phillips' "solemn pretences of the murderer's innocence;" and declared that "they did not accuse him of solemnly *protesting* his belief in Courvoisier's innocence, but of solemnly ACTING it." Such are the dismal shifts of determined disingenuousness! What is the meaning of an advocate's acting a belief of his client's innocence? Would the *Examiner* have him do the reverse, and ACT a belief of his client's guilt? Would they have an advocate go through a "solemn" and cruel mockery, only, of defence? Would they have his looks, his gestures, his topics, "solemnly" belie the purpose for which he had professedly risen? It is a matter which does not bear an instant's arguing. The *Examiner* proceeded further to endeavour to explain its new position:—"We asserted that Mr Phillips invented a falsehood, to profess, not faith in his client's innocence, but ignorance of his guilt;" and "profaned the name of the Deity by using it to give solemnity to this falsehood." If we *must* follow the *Examiner* into this new position, we say, first, assuming that Mr Phillips actually used the precise expressions attributed to him by the *Times*, viz., "The omniscient God alone knew who did this crime," is it not cruel and monstrous to suppose that Mr Phillips deliberately *intended* to appeal to the Almighty to attest the truth of an assertion that he was ignorant of his client's guilt? While objecting strongly to the strain of allusion to the Deity in parts of the speech, common candour suggests that in the passage in question no more was really meant than a conventional, though most irreverent mode of telling the jury, that as far as concerned them, who could know nothing but what the evidence told them, no one but God knew who had committed the guilty act; that they would forget their oaths, if they travelled for a moment out of the evidence to decide the question submitted to them. In this very case, the Chief Justice, as will have been seen, impressively cautioned the jury on the subject, at the commencement of his charge. But in the present instance, could Mr Phillips have really and deliberately *intended* to declare that the Deity alone knew that which the speaker, Mr Baron Parke, Mr Clarkson, Mr Flower, and the wretched prisoner himself knew? Common sense and common candour revolt from the suggestion. It should, on every legitimate and fair principle of interpretation, be regarded as a mere figure of speech, most improper undoubtedly, but involving no more of deliberate moral turpitude than the too frequent conversational expression, "God knows!"—or "God *only* knows!"—a fact which one instant's reflection would show the irreverent speaker must be known to one, two, or many persons. Nothing but a reckless determination to draw harsh inferences, would induce a man to persevere in torturing the expression attributed to this eloquent advocate, into an impiously deliberate appeal to the Deity to attest a known falsehood! But did Mr Phillips, in fact, use the expression? We verily believe that he did not, but one which might be very easily misunderstood for it. The report in the *Times* is given in the third person, and not professedly *verbatim;* and the slightest turn of expression, unconsciously, would make all the difference. We have made inquiries on this subject, and find that a member of the Bar who was present at the trial,—a gentleman of long standing in the profession, of ability, of high character, and unquestionable honour—Mr Fortescue,—paid close attention to Mr Phillips, and will state on oath, without the slightest hesitation, as he has ever since stated on innumerable occasions when the subject was mentioned, that Mr Phillips' exact words were—"But you will say to me, if the prisoner did it not, who did it? I answer, *ask the Omniscient Being above us, who did it:* ask not me, a poor finite creature like yourselves: ask the prosecutor who did it;—it is for *him* to tell you who did it; it is not for *me* to tell you who did it; and until he shall have proved, by the clearest evidence, that it was the prisoner at the bar, beware how you imbrue your hands in the blood of that young man."* How easy for even the ablest reporter (and the report of these proceedings in the *Times* evinces the utmost ability and fidelity), in throwing the above sentence into the third person, to adopt the phraseology, on the literal accuracy of which it is now sought to impale the reputation of a distinguished advocate!

But even admitting that Mr Phillips, in the course of a three hours' speech, was betrayed into the momentary adoption of this expression—which we are satisfied, for reasons above stated, was not the fact—is it not the height of injustice and uncharitableness to put upon it the very worst construction of which the words are susceptible —to weigh with malignant nicety verbal expressions, uttered, too, on such a fearful occasion, in golden scales? We believe that the profession and the public are too just to tolerate such a thing for a moment; and we almost fear that we have expended too much pains in demonstrating to be erroneous the representations and misconstructions of this self-constituted censor. For aught we can tell, those who have made these accusations against a distinguished member of our profession, are not themselves members of it, know nothing practically of the duties of advocacy, and are unacquainted with the principles of legal investigation. One leading principle on which it is conducted, we wish them to understand, is to examine thoroughly into facts before coming to conclusions, and especially before hazarding destructive imputations on character; to state evidence with rigid impartiality, avoiding equally the *allegatio falsi*, and the *suppressio veri;* to put a liberal construction on doubtful acts; always presuming against, and not in favour of, dishonourable and wicked motives and intentions.

We should not pass over a last shred of objection, pre-

* This gentleman has informed us, that the moment he heard of the statement attributed to Mr Phillips, he said to his informant, "I know the passage which must have been misunderstood:" repeated the words as above given, and immediately went to Mr Phillips, repeated them to him, and offered to communicate it to the newspapers.

sented with all the emphasis which can be derived from italics and small capitals; we allude to the natural solemnity and fervour with which Mr Phillips cautioned the jury against violating their oaths by "pronouncing," and that while dealing with the life of a fellow-creature, "the word 'guilty' lightly." And can any words be too stringent and impressive in giving such a caution? Is it not one uniformly pressed in such cases by counsel, the ablest and best that ever did honour to the Bar? And is it not fair to impute even an excess of earnestness on this point to Mr Phillips' natural anxiety to conceal from the jury the blighting secret which was "weighing upon his heart," —to resist its benumbing influence? Those who would deliberately convert this into a serious accusation, must indeed be driven to straits. And can it be tolerated that an able and zealous advocate is to be dragged forth week after week,* and sought to be made ridiculous, odious, or criminal, because, in a case of life and death, he clothes in fervid words his appeal to those in whose hands lies his client's life,—that life which he has solemnly promised to do his utmost to defend? It would be an insufferable usurpation, and tend to palsy the genius of advocacy, and in doing so, inflict deadly and irreparable injury, not on the Bar, but on those who are compelled to avail themselves of the exertions of the Bar, in desperate and mortal exigencies! We protest against the assumption by the one, or the recognition by the other, of any such right.

The cruel charges with which we have been dealing, and of which we trust we have satisfactorily and finally disposed, are of almost as serious a character as can be conceived. Mr Phillips has been charged by the *Examiner*, on its own recent admission, from "time to time,"* during the last ten years, with the horrible impiety of deliberately calling on the Deity to attest a falsehood; and

* *Examiner*, Nov. 24, 1840. On the very day on which we are writing (Saturday, the 26th of January 1850), the *Examiner* goes out of its way to make an insulting allusion, on the subject of these charges, to Mr Phillips, and even calls him by a nick-name!

with the execrable attempt to procure the acquittal of an assassin who had confessed to him his guilt, by throwing that guilt upon an innocent woman, whom Mr Phillips' misconduct drove into a lunatic asylum! These are charges of terrible gravity, requiring to be established by the clearest and most cogent evidence, given with rigorous fairness to the accused. That those of the *Examiner* have not been so sustained, we conscientiously believe, and are unwilling to impute the errors which we have detected, to personal malignity, or a deliberate intention to do wrong. It can never be too late to repair an act of injustice; and it is almost an atonement for even long-continued misrepresentation, to come forward with a magnanimous avowal of error. Who can be interested in thus casting dark shadows over the evening of an unoffending and honourable man's life? What act during Mr Phillips' whole career justifies the belief that he could have committed the atrocities imputed to him? Was he suddenly bereft of both integrity and understanding?

After a long, a dispassionate, and a thorough investigation into all the facts on which the *Examiner's* pertinacious accusation against him is professedly based, we have come to the conclusion that Mr .Phillips' conduct has been from first to last most cruelly misrepresented with reference to his defence of Courvoisier. We have watched every turn of the case, and seen in this gentleman's conduct of it nothing inconsistent with honour, or calculated to do anything but reflect credit on that great profession of which he has been so long one of the most brilliant ornaments. We doubt whether his position, at and after the paralsying confession to him of his client's guilt, has a parallel in the annals of advocacy. Every presumption should surely be made in favour of one suddenly placed at such a desperate disadvantage. But Mr Phillips needs not the aid of presumptions. Most fortunately for him, his defence against these cruel and persevering accusations rests on evidence irrefragable—that of two witnesses, in the late distinguished Chief Justice Tindal, and the present equally distinguished Baron Parke, each in himself a host of consummately qualified witnesses. It is impossible to rate human testimony higher than that which exonerates Mr Phillips from those sedulously circulated charges of cruelty and impiety, which we believe to be now finally disposed of. And to those who have originated and perpetuated that charge, we recommend a more strict obedience to both the letter and the spirit of the divine commandment, *Thou shalt not bear false witness against thy neighbour.*

# MODERN STATE TRIALS.*

## No. I.

## THE WELSH RIOTERS.—HIGH TREASON.

THE idea of this work is happily conceived, and carried into effect, in the two volumes before us, with no little judgment and ability. The subject is at once interesting, useful, and important; and the author was in many respects well qualified to deal with it, by his talents, his accomplishments, his professional acquirements, and his experienced observation. It will be seen that we use different tenses, in speaking of the author, and of his work; and there is a melancholy significance in the distinction. Within a few days of his sending to us, personally, these two volumes, he died, unexpectedly, in the flower of his age, and just as he had attained an honour

* *Blackwood's Magazine*, October 1850.

*Modern State Trials:* Revised and Illustrated, with Essays and Notes. By WILLIAM C. TOWNSEND, Esq., M.A., Q.C., Recorder of Macclesfield. In 2 vols. 8vo. Longman & Co. 1850.

It was and is one of the objects of this short series of papers, which attracted much attention in America, and also at home, to aid in bringing into notice the work on which they were founded, written by an accomplished and experienced friend of the author. The latter has, however, treated every topic entirely in his own way, and introduced many not to be found in the two eloquent and valuable volumes in question. The author has bestowed great pains upon these papers, in the hope of interesting both professional and general readers. For detailed and correct accounts of the cases themselves, reference must be made to Mr Townsend's volumes; for they contain what the author of these papers does not know to be collected elsewhere.

which he had long coveted—that of being raised to the rank of Queen's Counsel. On the first day of last Easter term, he presented himself in each of the courts at Westminster, in his "silk" gown, exchanging the customary obeisances with the Judges, the Queen's Counsel, and the great body of his brethren behind the bar, on being formally called by the Lord Chief Justice "to take his seat within the bar, Her Majesty having been pleased to appoint him one of Her Majesty's Counsel." He looked pleasurably excited: alas, how little anticipating that the last day of that same term would see him stripped of his long-coveted insignia, and clothed in the dismal vesture of the grave! For on that day he died, after a brief but severe illness, in his forty-sixth year. A serious attack of rheumatic fever, several years before, had permanently impaired his physical energies, though not to such an extent as to prevent the exercise of his profession. His practice, till latterly, had been chiefly at the Cheshire and Manchester sessions, from which he gradually rose into considerable business, both civil and criminal, on the North Wales circuit. On being raised to his briefly-held rank, the prospect of a successful career opened before him; for he knew his profession well, as those were aware who were able and disposed to push him forward. During Easter term he was engaged before a committee of the House of Commons, to conduct a case of some importance. This was a lucrative branch of practice, which he was naturally eager to cultivate. Fatigue, anxiety, and excitement induced the return of an old complaint, accompanied by new and somewhat startling symptoms; but though utterly unfit for business, he could not be restrained from attending the committee room, though it was necessary to carry him in a chair up the long flight of steps leading to the corridor in the new House. He was soon, however, obliged to return as he had gone. The palsying hand of Death had touched the eager lawyer! After much suffering, he expired on the 8th of May, the last day of Easter term, and on the 13th was buried in the vaults of Lincoln's Inn, of which he had only a few days previously been elected a Bencher! He was a member of Queen's College, Oxford, where he graduated, we believe with honours, in 1824; was called to the Bar in 1828; and elected Recorder of Macclesfield in 1833.—As a speaker he was correct and fluent, though not forcible; as an advocate, judicious and successful. He was a man of classical tastes, extensively read in literature, and exceedingly familiar with political history, and constitutional law. What he knew, he could use readily and effectively, both as a writer and a speaker. He was extremely industrious with his pen, during every interval between his professional engagements; and has left behind him, independently of his contributions to periodical literature, three works—the *History of the House of Commons, from* 1688 *to* 1832; the *Lives of Twelve Eminent Judges*, and the work now before us. The first of these was published in 1843-4, in two volumes octavo. The author's professed object was to present "a popular history of the House of Commons, with biographical notices of those members who have been most distinguished in its annals; and describing the changes in its internal economy, powers, and privileges," during the space of a hundred and forty-four years elapsing between two memorable periods—the "noble introduction" to Parliamentary Records, "afforded by the Convention Parliament of 1688," and the "eventful close" witnessed in the second Parliament of William IV., which passed "the Reform Bill." This space he subdivided into three distinguishing eras:—

"The *first* includes a space of thirty-nine years, from the abdication of James to the death of George I. in 1727, characterised by master spirits, critical events, and stirring debate. The *second* era, a sort of mezzo-termino, comprehends the reign of George II., when men in office were corrupt, and public morals low, and the general topics of discourse resembled parish vestry discussions, but still a prosperous reign, the sound common-sense of Walpole promoting, even by inglorious acts, the national welfare, and Chatham's genius rescuing the age from mediocrity.

"The regular publication of the debates, and troubles in America, usher in the *last*, and most glorious epoch, the days of North and Burke, of Pitt and Fox, of Windham and Canning, of Tierney, Brougham, and Peel, illustrated by oratory enduring as the language, and with memories of statesmen that can never die."

Mr Townsend's second work was published, about four years afterwards, viz., in 1848, also in two volumes, and entitled *Lives of Twelve Eminent Judges of the Last and Present Century*. These were—Lord Alvanley, Mr Justice Buller, Lord Eldon, Lord Ellenborough, Lord Erskine, Sir Vicary Gibbs, Sir William Grant, Lord Kenyon, Lord Loughborough, Lord Redesdale, Lord Stowell, and Lord Tenterden. This work consisted of memoirs, which the author had previously published in the *Law Magazine*, where they had attracted considerable attention from the profession; as they contained many interesting and entertaining anecdotes, and information not easily attainable elsewhere. Both of these works are of an entertaining character. They are written in an easy, flowing style, occasionally, however, somewhat loose and gossiping. It must be owned that the author's *forte* does not lie in the delineation of character, either moral or intellectual. If he really possessed a quick and searching insight into it, he would seem to have felt a greater pleasure in grouping about each individual who was the subject of his pencil, the general incidents of his position, than in penetrating his idiosyncrasy, and detecting the operation of those incidents upon it. He does not conceive distinctly of *his man*, keeping his eye steadily upon him, with a view to the development and exhibition of character; but is apt, if we may be allowed so to speak, to lose him, in his very life. Still the work is a creditable acquisition to popular and professional literature, and, equally with its predecessor, evidences the mild and candid temper and character of the author.

Thus much we thought it only fair to premise, in justice to the memory of an amiable and accomplished member of the English Bar, and a man of letters; one, too, who in his political opinions, was a staunch and consistent upholder of those to which *Blackwood's Magazine* has from the first been consistently devoted. In no instance, however—in neither of the two works at which we have been thus glancing in passing, nor in that now lying before us—did Mr Townsend suffer his political opinions to bias his judgment, or betray him into the faintest semblance of partiality or injustice.

It is time now to direct attention to his last work, which he barely lived to see published—his *Modern State Trials,* spread over two goodly octavo volumes, containing nearly eleven hundred pages, and these, too, pretty closely printed. Upon this work much thought and labour have evidently been bestowed in the collection of his materials, and dealing with them, as in the volumes before us, in such a manner as to render the product at once interesting and instructive to both general and professional readers.

---

It is no slight matter to make one's-self thoroughly master of a Great Case, in all its bearings; to seize its true governing characteristics; to select, condense, and arrange facts and incidents; to assign to every actor, whether judge, jury, witness, counsel, or party, his proper proportion and position; and all this with a view to interesting and instructing widely different classes of readers —and those, again, general and professional. To do all this effectually, requires powerful talents, much knowledge of life and character, practical acquaintance with the law of the country, sound judgment, and a vivid imagination. There is scarcely any point of view in which a great trial will not appear deeply interesting to a competent observer, watching how each individual plays his part in the agitating drama. Whether the judge hold the sacred scales even; whether he see clearly and act promptly, calmly, resolutely, in detecting fallacy, in order to shield an unsophisticated jury from its subtle and deleterious agency; whether, for this purpose, his intellect and his knowledge be superior, equal, or inferior to those of the advocates pleading before him. How those advocates conduct themselves, intellectually and morally; whether they be clear-headed, acute, ready, learned—or cloudy, obtuse, superficial, and ignorant; whether evenly or over-matched; whether they play the gentleman or the scoundrel; whether they will, however difficult the task, nobly recognise the obligations of truth and honour, or villanously disregard them, to secure a paltry triumph in defeating justice! How the witnesses discharge their momentous duties; whether constantly mindful of their oath, or forgetful of it, or wilfully disregarding it, from hostility or partiality to the prisoner, or any other wicked motive. Whether the judge, or the advocates, be equal to the discomfiture of a wicked witness. How the jury are conducting themselves—whether with watchful intelligence, or stolid listlessness. How the prisoner, standing in the midst of all these, with life, honour, character, liberty, everything at stake, and depending on the word which one of that jury will utter,—how *he* is demeaning himself, knowing, as he does, the truth or falsehood of the charge on which he is being tried; what he may be thinking of the exertions of his counsel, of the temper and spirit of the witnesses, of the jury, of the judge; whether he advert at all to the spectators around him, and the feelings by which they are animated towards him; whether he be aware of, or appreciates, the true strain and pressure of the case—the sudden chances and perils occurring in its progress.

How striking and instructive to observe the abstract rules of justice brought to bear with readiness and precision, equally upon ordinary and extraordinary combinations of circumstances!—to witness the dead letter of the law become animated with potent vitality, for the regulation of human affairs!

Again, it has often occurred to us that there is another point of view from which important trials, nay, almost any trial, may be contemplated with lively interest, by a logical observer, with reference to *the use made of facts* by judicial and forensic intellect. How little even the acutest layman could have anticipated such dealing with facts as that which he here beholds; how he must appreciate the practised, watchful art with which the slightest circumstance is seized hold of, and in due time so combined with others with which it seemed, at first, to have no conceivable connexion, as to justify conclusions exactly the reverse of those which had till then seemed inevitable! What totally different aspects the same facts may be made to wear, by different dealers with them, having different objects in view! By their different arrangement and combination, what unexpected inferences may be drawn from the self-same facts, and even when similarly arranged and combined! How exciting to see a defence constructed by experienced astuteness and eloquence, out of the slightest materials, out of a hopeless case, in the teeth of one really overpowering for the prosecution! The desperate determination, the exquisite subtlety, the consummate judgment, often exhibited on such occasions by eminent advocates—struggling, too, at once with their own sense of right and wrong, and the desire to do their utmost for one who has entrusted his all to them—conscious, too, that though a jury of twelve plain common-sense people may be unable to see through the fallacies which are presented to them, it will doubtless be far otherwise with one who has to follow, who has the last word! and with that last word may at once lay bare the sophistries of forensic effrontery, and perhaps rebuke him who attempted to trifle with and mislead the understandings of those so solemnly sworn to give a just and true verdict, according to the evidence. "But what is one to do?" exclaims the anxious advocate. "How am I to defend yonder trembling being who has selected me to stand between him and—the scaffold, it may be—if I am to play the judge, and not the advocate; to yield pusillanimously to an array of fearfully plain facts, and make no attempt to square them with the hypothesis of my client's innocence, or persuade a jury that they are, whatever my own secret opinion, pregnant with too much doubt to warrant a verdict of guilty?" Only one who has been placed in the situation can conceive the faintest idea of what is endured on such occasions by the sensitive and conscientious advocate; who is called upon in desperate emergencies, in moments of intense eagerness and anxiety, the spasms, as it were, of which are publicly exhibited, and before gifted and critical rivals and merciless public censors, to see and observe the delicate but decisive line of right—of duty; to maintain at once the character of the zealous, effective advocate, and the Christian gentleman.

If sufficient allowances were made for persons placed in such circumstances of serious embarrassment and responsibility, less uncharitable judgments would be passed on the manner in which advocates exercise their functions than are sometimes seen; judgments formed and pronounced, too, in the closet—by those speaking after the event—calm and undisturbed by anxieties and agitation, which have probably never been personally experienced. This topic, however, we may hereafter treat more at large, in giving to the volumes before us that extended examination which is at present contemplated. They contain a series of trials of undoubted public interest and importance; and have been selected, upon the whole, judiciously, with a view to the end which the author had proposed to himself; though the propriety of the title which he has chosen—*i. e.* "Modern *State* Trials"—is not at first sight apparent. The idea conveyed by these words is, trials directly affecting *the State*, political prosecutions in respect of political offences. It is difficult to bring trials for murder, duelling, forgery, abduction, libel, blasphemy, and conspiracy, under this category; and this Mr Townsend felt. Such, nevertheless, constitute a large proportion of the trials contained in these volumes, and are, in our opinion, also those of most popular interest, and worthiest of being dealt with, as it was Mr Townsend's expressed intention to deal with them.

The "trials" contained in the volumes before us are fifteen in number, of which only four, or at most five, (Mr Townsend seems to have thought six,) have any pretensions to be designated "*State* trials." These five are—John Frost, Edward Oxford, and Smith O'Brien for high treason; Daniel O'Connell, and eight others, for a treasonable conspiracy; and Charles Pinney, for alleged neglect of his duty as mayor of Bristol, during the fiery and bloody "Reform Riots," as they were called, in that place, in October 1831. The remaining ten trials consist of two for duelling—the late James Stuart for killing Sir Alexander Boswell, and the Earl of Cardigan for shooting Captain Tucket; three for murder, (in addition to James Stuart, who was tried for the *murder* of Sir Alexander Boswell)—viz. Courvoisier, for the murder of Lord William Russell; M'Naughton, for the murder of Mr Drummond; Hunter and others, for conspiracy and the murder of John Smith, the Glasgow cotton-spinner, in 1837; Alexander Alexander (the titular Earl of Stirling), for forgery; Lord Cochrane, and seven others, for a conspiracy to raise the funds; the Wakefields, for conspiracy, and abduction of an heiress; John Ambrose Williams, for a libel on the Durham Clergy; and Mr John Moxon, for blasphemy, in publishing the poems of Percy Bysshe Shelley. It will be observed that all these are *criminal* trials, and occurred in England, Scotland, and Ireland; affording thus a favourable opportunity for comparing the different methods of proceeding in their respective courts, and the characteristics of their respective judges and advocates. The English trials are ten, the Scottish three, and the Irish two in number: and whether they are precisely those which could have been most advantageously selected, it were needless for present purposes to inquire. Mr Townsend made his choice, and thus generally states his objects and intentions:—

> "The present edition of *Modern State Trials* is meant to include those of the most general interest and importance which have occurred during the last thirty years. None are inserted in these volumes which have been previously comprised in any collection; but the editor regrets want of space, which compels him to omit several not uninstructive. In making a selection, he has endeavoured to present a faithful, but abridged, report of such legal proceedings as would be most likely to command the attention of all members of the community, and to be read by them with pleasure and profit. This appears to be the popular description of the term 'State Trials,' in which Mr Evelyn and Mr Hargreave acquiesced, or they would not have included convictions for witchcraft, and the prosecution of Elizabeth Canning for perjury, in their collection. Were the definition restricted to political offences merely, the work, however logically correct, would be wanting in spirit and variety."—(Introd. vol. i. p. 5.)

After stating that no technical objection can be raised to those of the above trials which immediately affect the State, he observes, that, "for the propriety of inserting the rest under the same title, a just apology may be made." The trial of the Earl of Cardigan, before the House of Lords, is represented as interesting, from the rank of the accused and from the rarity of the trial, as being the first time that duelling was attempted to be brought within a recent statute, (1 Vict. c. 85,) enacting that the shooting at a person, not with premeditated malice, but deliberately, and causing a bodily injury dangerous to life, should be a capital offence; and that whoever should shoot any person with intent to commit murder, or to do some grievous bodily harm, should, though no bodily harm were inflicted, be guilty of *felony*, and liable to transportation or imprisonment. The social position of the titular Earl of Stirling, and the extraordinary nature of the evidence, are said to justify the insertion of *his* trial; while, "in the records of criminal jurisprudence, there occur few proceedings of more deep and painful interest than the prosecution of Lord Cochrane, for conspiracy to commit a fraud on the Stock Exchange." The two cases of Courvoisier and M'Naughton respectively "involve topics of absorbing interest at the period of the occurrence, and of enduring interest to all time: in the one being involved the rights and duties, the privileges and immunities of counsel for prisoners; in the other, the fearful question of responsibility for crime—whether moral insanity, alone, may exonerate the alleged subject of it from the temporal consequences of his guilt." This latter topic is also involved in Oxford's case. The trials of Mr Stuart for killing Sir Alexander Boswell, and of Mr Moxon for blasphemy, are inserted for one and the same reason—namely, "a desire to embalm the very beautiful speeches of Lord Cockburn, Lord Jeffrey, and Mr Justice Talfourd." As to the trial of Ambrose Williams, it is inserted on account of the celebrated speech in defence by Lord Brougham—"one of the most vivid specimens extant, in either ancient or modern literature, of keen irony, bitter sarcasm, and vehement vituperation." The prosecution of the Wakefields for conspiracy, and the abduction of Miss Turner, "forms a singular chapter in legal history; interesting not less to the student of human nature, on account of its characters and incidents, than to the lawyer, for the elaborate discussions on the Scottish law of marriages, and the right of the wife, even should there have been a legal marriage, to appear as a witness against the offending husband—matters argued with profuse learning and ability."

"In setting forth, under a condensed form," says Mr Townsend,* "this and the other most interesting trials of our time, it has been the object of the editor to free the work from dry severity by introducing the '*loci lætiores*' of the advocates, the salient parts of cross-examination—those little passages of arms between the rival combatants which diversified the arena, the painting of the forensic

* Introduction, vol i. pp. 7, 8.

scene, the poetry of action of these legal dramas. He has sought to give the expressed spirit of eloquence and law, upon occasions which peculiarly called them forth; pruning what was redundant, rejecting superfluities, weeding out irrelevant matter, but omitting no incident or episode that an intelligent witness would have been disappointed at not hearing."

We present the ensuing paragraph, which immediately follows the preceding, because it will afford us an opportunity of making a remark applicable to the entire structure of the work before us.

"In the extracts here given from some of the most celebrated speeches of modern days, the editor has also had the great advantage of the last corrections of the speakers themselves, and has thus been enabled to preserve the *ipsissima verba*, by which minds were captivated and verdicts won; those treasures of oratory which would have gladdened the old age of Erskine, could he have seen how his talisman had been passed from hand to hand, and the mantle of his inspiration caught. The vivid appeals of Whiteside, the magnificent defence of Cockburn, the persuasive imagery of Talfourd, will exist as κτήματα εἰς αεὶ—trophies of forensic eloquence, beacon lights, it may be, in the midst of that prosaic mistiness which has begun to creep around our courts."

The remark to which we have alluded is this: that the work before us is pervaded by a tone of uniform, excessive, and undistinguishing *eulogy;* which, however creditable to the amiable and generous dispenser of it, is calculated to lower our estimate of his critical judgment, and even, unless one should be on one's guard, to provoke a harsh and disparaging spirit towards the subjects of such undue eulogy, and a suspicion that here "praise undeserved," and the remark is applicable equally to praise excessive, "is censure in disguise!" No judge, no counsel, can say or do anything, in the course of any of the trials here brought under our notice, without speaking and acting in such a way as to merit applause for exhibiting the highest qualities of mind and character! Let it not be supposed, that, in making these observations, we wish to apply them to the particular instances cited by Mr Townsend of

Messrs Whiteside, Cockburn, and Talfourd—all of whom are distinguished, accomplished, able, and eloquent advocates; but we believe that each would, in spite of the fondest self-love, in his own mind, somewhat mistrust his title to the amount of applause here bestowed upon him. What more than he has said of them, could he have said of the greatest orators and advocates whom the world has produced? In a corresponding strain, Mr Townsend speaks of every one, senior and junior counsel, and every writer, great and small, whom he has occasion to mention. Those who knew him, and appreciated his simple and manly character, will refer the defect which we have felt compelled thus to point out, to its true cause, the kindliness of his heart; and we believe that, had he lived to see these observations, his candour would have caused him promptly to recognise their justice.

Each of the trials is preceded and followed by "Introductory Essays" and "Notes."

"The Essays, chiefly historical, have been introduced in order to familiarise the reader with the subject, and prevent the monotony which, but for these occasional dissertations, might pervade so many recurring trials. The notes are added with a similar object." * We may say generally, that these "Essays" and "Notes" always display judgment, and the writer's complete knowledge of his subject. No reader should enter on the trial, without carefully perusing the "Essay" which ushers it in, shedding light upon all its details, and the circumstances attending the committing of these offences, indicating, with distinctness, the leading features of interest and importance. In the report of the trial itself, great pains have evidently been taken, and successfully, to observe rigid impartiality, and secure accuracy of statement; and the conflicts of counsel with each other and with witnesses —the temperate, and timely interpositions of the judges, and their satisfactory summings-up to the jury, are pre-

* Introduction, p. ix.

sented to the reader with no little vividness. The fault of Mr Townsend's style is, diffuseness, a tendency to colloquiality, and a deficiency of vigour. With these little exceptions, added to that above noticed, we have no hesitation in commending these volumes as an acquisition to popular and professional literature, reflecting credit on the author's memory, and the Bar to which he belonged.

Having thus briefly indicated the general character of this work, and given the author's own account of it, we propose in the present, and few following articles, to take our own view of some of the leading "Trials" thus collected by Mr Townsend, incidentally observing on his treatment of the subject. With him, we regard several of these trials as exhibiting features of remarkable interest; and are much indebted to him for having so disposed his materials as to rouse and rivet the attention of all classes of intelligent readers, but in an especial degree that of the youthful student of jurisprudence. Without further preface, we shall commence with that which stands first in Mr Townsend's collection—the trial of Frost, for high treason.

This affords a very favourable specimen of Mr Townsend's capabilities. He appears to have worked it out perhaps more exactly to his own idea, than any of the ensuing ones; and, by his able and judicious treatment of the subject, has given us an opportunity of exhibiting in glowing colours a forensic battle-field: the stake, life or death; the combatants, evenly matched, the very flower of the Bar; their tactics clear and decisive, with the odds tremendously against one party—that is to say, facts too strong for almost any degree of daring or astuteness to contend against hopefully. Let us see, under such circumstances, how the combatants acquitted themselves; or, if one may change the figure, let us see how was played a great game of chess on the board of life, by skilful and celebrated players. Who were they?

Four in number—Sir John Campbell and Sir Thomas Wilde, then respectively Attorney and Solicitor-General, representing the Crown; Sir Frederick Pollock and Mr Fitzroy Kelly, Queen's Counsel for the prisoner. Ten years have since elapsed, and behold the changes in the relative positions of these gentlemen! Sir John Campbell is a peer of the realm, and Chief Justice of the Queen's Bench: having also, during the interval, become a laborious and successful biographer of the Lord Chancellors and Chief Justices of England. Sir Thomas Wilde is also a peer of the realm, and became Lord High Chancellor, having been previously Attorney-General and Chief Justice of the Common Pleas. Sir Frederick Pollock, having been subsequently appointed Attorney-General, is now Chief Baron of the Exchequer; while Mr Kelly, having since become Solicitor-General, lost office on the break-up of Sir Robert Peel's ministry, and remains—such are the chances and changes of political life —plain Sir Fitzroy Kelly, but occupying a splendid position at the Bar. These four were the leading counsel; but besides the Attorney and Solicitor-General, the Crown was represented by two gentlemen of great legal learning and eloquence, since raised to the Bench—Mr Justice Wightman and Mr Justice Talfourd;* and by Mr Serjeant Ludlow, since become a Commissioner of Bankruptcy; and the Hon. John C. Talbot, now so highly distinguished in Parliamentary practice.† The judges sent as the special commission consisted of the late Chief Justice Tindal, the present Mr Baron Parke, and the late Mr Justice Williams, forming, it is superfluous to say, an admirably constituted court—the chief being consummately qualified for his post by temper, sagacity, and learning.

* The sudden, affecting, and awful death of this amiable, gifted, and accomplished judge, while in the act of charging a Grand Jury at Stafford, occurred in the Spring Sessions of 1854.

† Mr Talbot died almost suddenly, about two years after this article was written, worn out by his labours as the leading member of the Parliamentary Bar.

It was the business of the Attorney and Solicitor-General to establish a case of high treason against the prisoner, and of Sir Frederick Pollock and Mr Kelly to defend him, *à l'outrance;* but God forbid that we should say, *per fas aut nefas.* It were idle to characterise the intellectual and professional qualifications of these four combatants; the eminence of all is undisputed, though their idiosyncrasies are widely different from each other. Suffice it to say, that everything which great experience, sagacity, learning, power, and eloquence could bring to bear on that contest might have been confidently looked for. One circumstance is proper to be borne in mind—that the prisoner's counsel (of course, abhorring the acts imputed to their client) were stimulated to the uttermost exertion, by the fact that their own political opinions were notoriously adverse to those entertained by the prisoner, and those, viz., Chartists, who so confidently summoned two Tories, to the rescue of their imperilled brother Chartists.

All the main facts of the case were universally known before the trial took place, together, of course, with the legal category to which they must be referred, to satisfy the conditions of high treason. The nature of that offence was thus tersely and beautifully explained by the Chief Justice,—*

"Gentlemen, the crime of high treason in its own direct consequences, is calculated to produce the most malignant effects upon the community at large; its direct and immediate tendency is the putting down the authority of the law, the shaking and subverting the foundation of all government, the loosening and dissolving the bands and cement by which society is held together, the general confusion of property, the involving a whole people in bloodshed and mutual destruction; and, accordingly, the crime of high treason has always been regarded by the law of this country as the offence of all others of the deepest dye, and as calling for the severest measure of punishment. But in the very same proportion as it is dangerous to the community, and fearful to the offender from the weight of punishment which is attached to it, has it been

* Townsend, vol. i. pp. 1, 2.

thought necessary by the wisdom of our ancestors to define and limit this law within certain express boundaries, in order that, on the one hand, no guilty person might escape the punishment due to his transgression by an affected ignorance of the law; and, on the other, that no innocent man might be entangled or brought unawares within the reach of its severity by reason of the law's uncertainty."

The following were fearful words to be heard, or afterwards read, by those who were charged with the defence of Frost. They occur, like the preceding passage, in the luminous charge of the Chief Justice to the Grand Jury, on the 10th December 1839:—

"An assembly of men, armed and arrayed in a warlike manner, with any treasonable purpose, is a levying of war, although no blow be struck; and the enlisting and drilling and marching bodies of men are sufficient overt acts of that treason, without coming to a battle or action. And, if this be the case, the actual conflict between such a body and the Queen's forces must, beyond all doubt, amount to a levying of war against the Queen, under the statute of Edward. It was quite unnecessary to constitute the guilt of treason that the tumultuous multitude should be accompanied with the pomp and pageantry of war, or with military array. Insurrection and rebellion are more humble in their first infancy; but all such external marks of pomp will not fail to be added with the first gleam of success. The treasonable design once established by the proper evidence, the man who instigated, incited, procured, or persuaded others to commit the act, though not present in person at the commission of it, is equally a traitor, to all intents and purposes, as the man by whose hand the act of treason is committed. He who leads the armed multitude towards the point of attack, and then retires before the blow is struck—he who remains at home planning and directing the proceedings, but leaving the actual execution of such plans to more daring hands—he who, after treason has been committed, knowingly harbours or conceals the traitor from the punishment due to him, all these are equally guilty in the eye of the law of the crime of high treason."

The head of treason applicable to the facts of the case under consideration is the third, in statute 25 Edward III. c. 2, which concisely declares it to exist "if a man do *levy war* against our lord the King in his realm." This has been the law of the land for just five centuries, *i. e.*, since the year 1351. But in the application of these words, of fearful significance, the object with which arms are taken up must be a GENERAL one—"the *universality of the design* making it a rebellion against the state, a usurpation of the power of Government, and an insolent invasion of the King's authority"—"under pretence to reform religion and the laws, or to remove evil counsellors, or other grievances, whether real or pretended."* Or, to adopt the definition of Mr Kelly, in addressing the jury in this very case, it is necessary to prove "that the prisoner levied war against her Majesty, with intent by force to alter the law, and subvert the constitution of the realm."† To appreciate the position of the prisoner, and the difficulties with which his counsel had to struggle, it may here be mentioned, that he admitted the prisoner to be a Chartist, as it was called—that is, a supporter of the following five points of sweeping change in the political institutions of the country—"Universal suffrage, vote by ballot, annual parliaments, no property qualification, and payment of members of parliament." This was also, during the trial, avowed by the prisoner.‡

Having thus got a clear view of the law, let us briefly indicate the *facts*—the palpable, notorious, leading facts, known to be such by the prisoner's counsel, as soon as they had perused their briefs.

A body of ten thousand men, principally miners from the surrounding country, headed, in three divisions, by Frost, and two other men, Jones and Williams, Frost having five thousand under his command, and armed indiscriminately with muskets, pikes, axes, staves, and other weapons, was to make a descent upon the peaceful town of Newport, during the night of Sunday, the 3d November 1839! Tempestuous weather prevented the preconcerted junction of these three bands; but, between eight and nine o'clock on the Monday morning, Frost's division, five thousand strong, marched into the town—

* 4 Black. Com. 81-2. † Townsend, vol. i. p. 54. ‡ Ibid. vol. i. p. 45.

and headed, after a fashion, by him, commenced an attack upon a small inn, where they knew that a handful of troops was stationed, about thirty in number, under command of a lieutenant. As soon as the mob, who formed steadily, saw the soldiers drawn up in the room, the windows of which were thrown open, they cruelly fired into it, and also rushed through the doors into the passage. On this, the lieutenant gave the word of command to fire. He was obeyed—and with deadly effect, as far as regarded some thirty or forty, known to have received the fire, many of whom were shot dead on the spot. But this cool promptitude and determination of the troops put an end *instanter* to the insane insurrection. This vast body of supposed desperadoes fled panic-struck in every direction; and Frost himself, who was unquestionably on the very spot, at the very time, when and where the attack commenced, fled in ridiculous terror,* and was arrested that evening at a friend's house adjoining his own, armed with three loaded pistols, and having on him a powder-flask and a quantity of balls. His brother heroes, Williams and Jones, were also arrested, together with many others; and there ended the formidable outbreak, which had more astounded than alarmed the public; leaving, however, the instigators and conductors to a speedy and dismal reckoning with that same public. The active management of matters by Frost was beyond all doubt, and it seemed never to have been wished to conceal it. He was the Jack Cade of the affair. He planned the order of march; the time, place, and mode of attack; and explained the immediate and ulterior objects of the movement. Shortly before the outbreak, he was asked by one of his adherents, "*what he intended to do?*" He answered—

"First, they should go to the new poor-house, and take soldiers and arms; then, he said, there was a storehouse, where there was plenty of powder; then, they would blow up the bridge, that would stop the Welsh mail which did run to the north, and that would be

* "I thought *he was crying*," said one of the witnesses!—P. 23.

tidings; and they would commence there in the north on Monday night, and he should be able to see two or three of his friends or enemies in Newport."—Vol. i. p. 36.

Similar observations he made to another of his followers, who asked him, on hearing him give orders for the guns to take the front, the pikes next, the bludgeons next—"in the name of God, what was he going to do? was he going to attack any place or people?" he said—

"He was going to attack Newport, and take it—and blow up the bridge, and prevent the Welsh mail from proceeding to Birmingham: that there would be three delegates there, to wait for the coach an hour and a half after the time; and if the mail did not arrive there, the attack was to commence at Birmingham, and be carried thence to the North of England, and Scotland, *and that was to be the signal for the whole nation.*"—i. p. 33.

The coal and iron trade in these parts, from which the population derived their subsistence, had seldom been more prosperous than at the time when this preposterous movement was concerted and made: employment was easily obtained; wages were high; and those concerned in the affair had no private grievances to redress. At the same time, it was notorious that political agitation, on the subject of the Charter aforesaid, had for some time prevailed there; that the population had been organised for combined and effective action by affiliated societies; and Frost, the prime mover—a pestilent agitator, who, occupying the position of a decent tradesman, a linendraper, in Newtown, had been rashly raised to the local magistracy, from which he was soon degraded for sedition—declared his object to be, to make the Charter the law of the land. All these, and many other facts, which had been elicited during the preliminary examinations, were known to the prisoner's counsel, who had copies of all the depositions which had been made by the witnesses; and also knew the precise terms in which the indictment was framed, and the name, calling, and residence of every witness to be produced in proof of that indictment.

How was this towering array of facts to be encountered, with these enlightened judges to conduct the inquiry, and guide the jury, and very able and determined counsel to elicit and arrange those facts, and enforce them on the jury—and *have the last word* with the jury in so doing? We may well imagine how anxious and disheartening were the consultations of the prisoner's counsel, before going into court. Neither they, nor their attorneys, could disguise from themselves the desperate nature of the case in which they were concerned. They would probably determine to cross-examine the witnesses cautiously and rigorously, with a view to breaking down important links in the case; and it is likely that their paramount object in conducting the defence, would be to aim at supplying Frost with some other than *a general object*—something else than establishing the Charter as the law of the land. A hopeful prospect! But besides all this, it must have been determined, of course, to throw no single chance away, whereon—however, whenever it presented itself—to fight the fearful case for the Crown inch by inch, and foot by foot—contesting every technical point, with a view to detecting any possible slip in either the preliminary or any other part of the proceedings of the experienced and watchful Crown officers. Here, again, was a hopeful prospect! Their proceedings had been doubtless advised beforehand by the Attorney and Solicitor-General, and conducted by Mr Maule, the Solicitor of the Treasury, in person—himself a barrister, and perfectly qualified for his post. He was also a humane man; always anxious to discharge his duties firmly, but at the same time to afford a prisoner every degree of consideration and indulgence consistent with the public interest.

By this time the reader may be aware how very serious a thing is the conduct, on the part of the Crown, of a prosecution for high treason, in every one of its stages—in the slightest particulars—especially where the great *facts* of the case are so clear against the prisoner, as to compel his advocate to watch and test every link in the chain fixed around his client. Here, in fact, correlative duties are cast on the opposing parties—to *take* every possible objection; and to be beforehand *prepared for* every possible objection, by vigilant exactitude in complying with every legal requisite.

It is important, now, to bear in mind the *dates* immediately following.

On the *eleventh* day of December 1839, the Grand Jury returned a true bill for high treason against John Frost and thirteen of his followers; and on the very next day, viz., Thursday the *twelfth*—in order to oblige the prisoner, by giving him the longest possible time for availing himself of the important information contained in the *indictment*, and the *jury list*—copies of these instruments were delivered to him by the Solicitor of the Treasury. On the ensuing Tuesday, the 17th, he delivered to the prisoner a *list of the witnesses;* and, the trial having been appointed to take place on the 31st December, five days previously to the latter day—viz., on the 26th December—Sir Frederick Pollock and Mr Kelly were assigned to John Frost, as his counsel, on his application, pursuant to the statute, to Mr Bellamy, the clerk of the Crown. It is here essential, in order to appreciate the immense importance of the earliest moves in this life-and-death game, to weigh every word in the following brief enactment, under which the above documents were delivered to the prisoner: the humane object of the legislature being to afford him ample time to prepare his defence:—"When any person is indicted for high treason, a list of the *witnesses*, and of the *jury*, mentioning the names, profession, and place of abode of the said witnesses and jurors, shall be also given at the same time that the copy of the indictment is delivered to the party indicted—which copy of the indictment shall be delivered ten days before the trial."* Thus it will be

* Stat. 7 Anne, c. 21, § 11.

seen that, as the trial was to take place on Tuesday the 31st December, Mr Maule might have delayed delivering these documents to the prisoner till the 20th, and perhaps till the 21st December; but, solely to favour the prisoner, he delivered two of them—viz., the indictment and jury list—so early as the 12th, and the list of witnesses so early as the 17th December. Let us see, by and by, whether anything comes of this, and of the lengthened study, by the prisoner's astute and experienced counsel, of these three documents.

On Tuesday the 31st December 1839, all the fourteen prisoners were arraigned on an indictment consisting of four counts: two for levying war against her Majesty in her realm; a third for compassing to depose the Queen from her royal throne; and the last, for compassing to levy war against the Queen, with intent to compel her to change her measures. To this indictment each of the fourteen prisoners pleaded not guilty; and it is to be particularly observed that they all did so without making any objection, on any score. Thus was taken the first move by the Crown counsel, who may possibly, for aught we can at present see, have thereby gained some great advantage. Let us now conceive the solemnly-exciting scene of the court-house at Monmouth, on this memorable trial. Three judges sitting, in their imposing scarlet and ermine vestments, calm and grave; a phalanx of counsel sitting beneath them; the prisoners standing at the bar, on their deliverance, silent as the grave, while the fate-fraught procedure of the court is methodically going on; the spectators crowding every part of the court that they can occupy, and all silent, nothing heard but official voices; while without that court all is excitement—repressed, however, by the stern presence of the civil and military power; detachments of troops at that moment scouring the adjacent hills in quest of malcontents, and preventing any fresh rising of the population.

The first step taken by the prisoner's counsel was to

state that they appeared for John Frost alone, and should challenge the jury separately: on which all the other prisoners were removed from the bar, John Frost remaining to take his trial alone. Then came the swearing of the jury—the name of every one, with his calling in life, and place of abiding, being known to the prisoner and his counsel, who objected to the very first step taken by the clerk of the Crown. He had begun to call over the names in their alphabetical order on the panel—the usual course for a great series of years; but Sir Frederick Pollock objected to his doing so, insisting on each juror's name being taken from the ballot-box. The Chief Justice was about to have overruled the objection; but the Attorney-General intimated that he consented to the course proposed by the prisoner's counsel. Each witness was sworn first on the *voir dire* (i. e., *dicere verum*), as to his qualification, before he was sworn to try. First came a juryman, who was challenged peremptorily on the part of the Crown; but the prisoner's counsel, doubtless for very good reasons, wishing him to remain on the jury, insisted, first, that the Crown had no such right—an objection at once overruled; secondly, that the Crown was too late, as the juror had actually got the New Testament into his hand to be sworn to try, before the Crown challenged. But, on the court's inquiry, it turned out that the witness had himself taken the book, without having been directed to do so by the clerk of the Crown. Under these circumstances, the court decided that the Crown were in time with their challenge—and the juryman was excluded. In this kind of out-skirmishing the whole of the first day was consumed!—a full jury not having been sworn till the evening, when they were "charged" with the prisoner and then dismissed for the night—but with the unpleasant information from the court, that they themselves were thenceforth prisoners, though with every kind of proper indulgence, till the trial was over.

On the next morning, just as the Attorney-General was

rising to state the case for the Crown, he was interrupted by Sir Frederick Pollock, and doubtless sufficiently astonished by what fell from him: "I feel myself bound, at the earliest moment, and this is the first opportunity that I have had, to take an objection which must occur the moment that the first witness is put into the box,—namely, that the prisoner has never had a list of the witnesses, pursuant to the statute, and that therefore *no witness can be called!*" What could be the meaning of this? inquired the Attorney-General's companions among themselves, with no little anxiety; but he himself somewhat sternly censured the interruption, as premature, as it certainly was, and proceeded with his address to the jury. He made a lucid and temperate statement of the case, drawing attention prominently to the necessity imposed on him of proving that what had been done by Frost and his companions was with a *general*, and not a particular object,—a *public*, and not a private purpose. His proposed proof was crushing: but immediately on the Solicitor-General's calling the name of the first witness, Sir Frederick Pollock rose, and required him to prove the delivery of a list of the witnesses, containing the particular one in question, pursuant to the statute. The Attorney-General then called Mr Maule, who proved having done what has already been explained: whereupon Sir Frederick Pollock disclosed the exact objection, which he himself had been the first to detect, that whereas the statute required all these documents, *i. e.*, the indictment, the jury list, and witness list, to be delivered "*at the same time*," in the present instance that had not been done, the first two having been delivered on the 12th, and the list of witnesses on the 17th December! This was a formidable move on the part of the prisoner: who stood at the bar on his deliverance, the jury being bound to convict or acquit according to evidence, and if this objection should prevail, none could be offered them! If that *were* so, he must of necessity be pronounced not guilty, and be for ever safe. The objection was urged with extreme tenacity and ingenuity by both the prisoner's counsel, who insisted on the statute of Anne receiving a strict literal construction of the words "at the same time," admitting the benevolent intentions by which Mr Maule had been actuated. The Attorney-General argued very earnestly against this startling objection, denying that it had any validity; asserting that the statute had been substantially complied with; that the objection, if valid, had been waived; and that it was made too late—viz., not till after the prisoner had pleaded to the indictment, and the jury been charged with the prisoner. The Attorney-General's astute argument, however, was interrupted by the Chief Justice stating that the court had a sufficient degree of doubt on the point to reserve it for further consideration by the Judges at Westminster, should it become necessary: for, if their objection were valid, it affected every one of the fourteen prisoners awaiting their trial!

Then came another desperate attempt of Sir Frederick Pollock to secure his client the benefit of *an acquittal*, in the event of the Judges ultimately deciding that the objection ought to have been decided in the prisoner's favour at the trial. This, however, the Attorney-General again strongly opposed; and the court cautiously ruled, that, in the event contemplated, the prisoner would be entitled then to the same benefit to which he would have been entitled at the trial, without saying what that would have been. The witness thus provisionally objected to was then admitted; but only to be, at first, sworn on the *voir dire*, on which a lengthened examination and some argument ensued; each of the Judges delivering judgment on the excessively refined and astute objection to the manner in which the witness's place of abode had been described in the list—which was such as that it was just imaginable, and nothing more, that an inquirer might have been misled! The objection was overruled in the case of the first witness; but on the ensuing two witnesses, and most important ones, being called, a similar objection was taken, but too successfully, and their evidence, consequently, altogether excluded!—excluded solely on account of the anxious "*over*-particularity" of the Crown! Nor were these the only witnesses whose testimony was, on such grounds, rendered unavailable to the Crown.

Then came the usual contests, from time to time, as to acts and declarations of third parties, which were offered as evidence against the prisoner, though done and said in his absence, and before and after the actual outbreak—viz., to what extent he had rendered himself liable for the consequences of such acts and declarations, by embarking in a common enterprise, having a common intent with these third parties. The result of such contests was practically this,—The court acted on the rule of law, as well established, that, in treason and conspiracy, the Crown may prove either the conspiracy, which renders admissible as evidence the acts and declarations of the co-conspirators; or the acts and declarations of the different persons, and *so* prove the conspiracy. A witness, for instance, said that he was at a party at a Chartists' lodge on the 2d November, when a man named *Reed* gave them directions to go to Newport on the following night, and explained for what purpose they were to go: but the witness did not see Frost till two days *afterwards*, when on his march to Newport. The Chief Justice overruled the objections of Sir F. Pollock and Mr Kelly, and received the evidence which they had attempted to exclude.

A great mass of proof was given during the trial, establishing satisfactorily the acts and doings of Frost, throughout the progress of the conspiracy, and down to the very moment of the actual attack on the inn, and the Queen's troops stationed in it—a mass of proof on which the attempt to make an impression seemed absurd.

There was only one faint ray of hope for the prisoner's counsel, throughout the palpable obscure—that they might be able to escape from the generality and publicity of object attributed to the prisoner, by persuading the jury that the object was a private, temporary, and specific one—viz., to effect the release of one Vincent, a Chartist, then in confinement at Monmouth! To pave the way for this hopeful line of defence, first, an artful turn was sought, in cross-examination, to be given to the evidence of one of the early witnesses. He swore that he had heard one of those who attacked the inn, exclaim at the time, presenting his gun at one of the special constables at the door, "Surrender *yourselves* our prisoners;" to which the gallant answer was, "No, never!" On this Mr Kelly warily cross-examined the witness, with a view of showing that, in the confusion, he could not hear distinctly, so as to report distinctly, as to precise expressions; that the mob intended merely to rescue Vincent; and that the expressions used must have been, not "Surrender *yourselves* our prisoners," but "Surrender up our prisoners!" or simply, "Surrender our prisoners,"—thus rejecting, from the witness's answer, the single significant word "yourselves." The attempt, however, was wholly ineffectual; but out of two other witnesses were extorted, on cross-examination, the following, so to speak, crumbs of comfort: from one—"I have heard Vincent's name mentioned many times; I have heard Williams, one of the leaders of the three bands forming the ten thousand, say that Vincent was a prisoner at Monmouth: the people there liked him very much; the people knew he was in jail. I have heard them speak about him." Another witness said, "I knew of Vincent's being sent to prison: I believe the Chartists took a great interest in his fate: I do recollect something of dissatisfaction about Vincent's treatment, and about a petition to be drawn up: I recollect people's minds being dissatisfied about it." Another witness, however, deposed, "that at midnight on the Sunday, the 3d November, Williams came to his house with a number of armed men:" the witness inquired, "Where are you going?" "Why do you ask?" said Williams. "Because," answered the witness, "some of the men who were with me, have told me, this morning, that they were going to Monmouth, to draw Vincent out of prison." "*No*," replied Williams, "*we do not attempt it:* we are going to give a turn as far as Newport."

The Attorney-General closed his case with the arrest of Frost, heavily armed, and in concealment, on the evening of the day on which he had attacked the inn with his five thousand men; and thus stood the matter, when, after a considerable interval for repose and reflection, courteously conceded by the Chief Justice, at the implied request of Sir Frederick Pollock, that able and upright advocate rose to address the jury for the defence. Judging from the specimens afforded us by Mr Townsend, Sir Frederick Pollock's address appears to have been pervaded by a strain of dignified and earnest eloquence, and also characterised by a candour in dealing with facts which was in the highest degree honourable to him, and also equally advantageous to the prisoner, on whose behalf such conduct was calculated to conciliate both the judges and the jury. His line of defence was, that, admitting enormous indiscretion on the part of Frost in assembling so vast a body of men, and marching and appearing with them as he did at Newport, there was no satisfactory evidence of his having done so with a *treasonable* purpose. He had been guilty of a heinous misdemeanor; but the treasonable declarations and exclamations, put into his and their mouths, in order to give the affair a treasonable complexion, had been either misunderstood or perverted by the witnesses. The sole object of Frost and his friends was the release of Vincent; that they had never dreamed of taking, or attacking the town of Newport—least of all, as an act of general rebellion; that all they had meant was to take a "turn" as far as Newport, to get Vincent out of prison; and that "that was the true character of the whole proceedings;" that Frost did not know that the military were in the inn; and that, the instant they had become visible, and had fired, the crowd succumbed, threw down their arms, and ran away—*i. e.*, they did this "the very moment there was any prospect of what they were doing being construed into treason." That Frost could not have contemplated treason, and throwing the whole country into confusion, would be evidenced by proof, and his having made provision for the payment of a bill of exchange, and actually paying it on the very Monday on which the outbreak occurred. Sir Frederick Pollock properly insisted on the burthen of proving treason lying on the Crown, and not of disproof on the prisoner. Then were called one or two witnesses, with a view to showing expressions of the crowd that they had come to Newport in quest of their prisoners who were there; but the evidence proved ridiculously insufficient and contradictory. Then was read, with the Attorney-General's consent, a letter of Frost's in the previous September, to one of the visiting magistrates of the gaol of Monmouth, requesting some relaxation of the prison discipline to which Vincent and other prisoners were subject; and it appeared, also, that a similar application had been made to the Lord-Lieutenant of the county. Then was proved Frost's having taken up his acceptance on the 4th November; and his character for humanity as specially instanced in his having protected Lord Granville Somerset from personal violence, during the Reform riots of 1832. Finally was called a witness, with the view of negativing the design imputed to Frost of preventing the Welsh mail from going to Birmingham, by showing the absurdity of that course, since a new and different mail started from Bristol to Birmingham, and not the same coach which had come from Newport. But to this witness were quietly put the following significant, and probably unsuspected, questions:—

"*Attorney-General.* You took an interest, I suppose, in Vincent? *A.* I did so.

"*Attorney-General.* You had not been told that there was to be any meeting for Vincent on the 4th of November, had you? *A.* No.

"*Attorney-General.* You, living at Newport, can tell us that there was no notice by placard, or in any other way, of a meeting to be held on the 4th November? *A. I never saw any.*

"*Attorney-General. Nor heard of any? A. No.*"

Such was the meagre case in behalf of the prisoner in point of evidence. And at its close, his second counsel, Mr Kelly, rose to address the jury on his behalf—a privilege accorded to no prisoner, except one tried on a charge of high treason. We shall present the reader with an extract from the opening passage in Mr Kelly's address, inasmuch as it is highly characteristic of that eminent counsel's style of advocacy, his imposing display of fervent confidence in his case, his terse and nervous expression, and the clearness and precision of his reasoning. We have some ground for believing that the following is exactly what fell from his lips:—

"The Attorney-General, in his opening, seemed to anticipate that we might deviate from the straight and honourable course before us, in defending the prisoner, into something like an attempt to induce you to depart from the strict letter of the law. So far from this, it is in the law, in the strict undeviating performance of the law, that I place my hope, my only trust. It is my prayer, therefore, that you should follow it; that you should be guided and governed by it; that you should attend and adhere to the law, and to the law alone; because I feel that, by that law, I shall prove to you clearly and satisfactorily, that the prisoner, whatever may have been his misconduct in other respects, however high the crimes and misdemeanors for which in another form he might have been indicted or punished—I feel that, by the law of high treason, he is as guiltless as any one of you, whose duty, I hope, it will soon be so to pronounce him. Gentlemen, if the prisoner at the bar be at this moment in any jeopardy or danger, it is from the law not prevailing, or not being clearly and perfectly understood. It is because the facts, which are in evidence before you, undoubtedly disclose a case of guilt against him; because they do prove that he has committed a great and serious violation of the law; because he has subjected himself to indictment and to punishment, that the danger exists—a danger from which it is for me, by all the humble efforts I can command, to protect him—that you, finding that he has offended against the justice of the country, should condemn him, not for the misdemeanor which he has really committed, but for the great and deadly crime with which he is charged by this indictment. I therefore, gentlemen, beseech your calm and patient attention, while I endeavour, as shortly, as concisely, and, I will venture to add, as fairly and candidly as I can, to lay before you, subject to the correction of their lordships, the law, as it affects this high and serious charge. And if I should be fortunate enough to do so, I undertake then to satisfy you—to convince the most doubting among you, if there be any more doubting than the rest, when I shall refer you to the testimony of the witnesses,—that this charge is not only not proved, but that it is absolutely and totally disproved, even by the evidence for the prosecution. The question here is,—not whether a great and alarming riot has been committed; the question is, not whether blood has been shed, whether crimes, which are, as they ought to be, punishable by law, have been perpetrated by many who may be the subjects of this indictment; but the question is, whether the prisoner at the bar has, by competent legal proof, been proved, beyond all reasonable doubt in the mind of any one of you, to have levied war against Her Majesty, with the treasonable intent which is stated in this indictment? The Crown must satisfy you that the prisoner at the bar has levied war; that he has levied war against Her Majesty—that is, that he has conducted these armed multitudes, and committed, if he has committed, outrages with them, and concerted with them, or engaged them, to commit them; and not merely that he has done all these acts, but that he has done them against the Queen, that he has levied war against the Queen and her Government. And then, further, it must be proved to you that that was done with the intent, with the design, which is stated in this indictment."—(I. pp. 52, 53.)

Mr Kelly's speech was long, elaborate, eloquent, and most ingenious, adhering closely to the line of defence taken by Sir Frederick Pollock; pressing on the jury, in every possible way, with many varied illustrations, the improbability of Frost having contemplated the rebellious objects imputed to him, and the alleged certainty that his only view had been the rescue of Vincent. He vehemently assailed the credibility of those witnesses who had given the strongest evidence against Frost; and concluded with a most impassioned appeal to the feelings of the jury. When he had concluded, the Chief Justice accorded still another privilege to Frost—viz., that of himself then addressing the jury, after both his counsel had done so; to which Frost prudently replied—"My lord, I am so well satisfied with what my counsel have said, that I decline saying anything upon this occasion."*

The Solicitor-General then rose to reply on the part of the Crown; and if any one inexperienced in forensic contests were incredulous as to the potency of *the last word*, from competent lips, in any case, civil or criminal, let him read the outline of this reply, with the copious specimens of it, given with much judgment, by Mr Townsend. It is true that Sir Thomas Wilde's case was in itself crushing, but his dealing with it made that crushing character fearfully clear to the plainest capacity. Its opening passages seemed tinctured by some sternness of allusion to the concluding topics of Mr Kelly's address; but the remainder of the reply is characterised by mingled moderation and power; by irresistible closeness and cogency of argument, and by extraordinary skill in dealing with facts, in combining and contrasting them, and pointing out a significancy lurking in them, which the prisoner's counsel had possibly not chosen to see, or skilfully striven to conceal. Our limits restrict us to one or two samples of the present [1850] Lord Chancellor's mode of advocacy when at the Bar. After explaining that it was the real object contemplated by the prisoner, viz., to raise rebellion, with which the jury had to deal, the Solicitor-General thus pithily disposed of all arguments which had been drawn from the prisoner's want of power to do all that he intended:—

"It is also immaterial to this case whether or not he had the power to do all he intended. We need not talk of punishing successful rebellion—it is unsuccessful rebellion that comes under the cognisance of the law. I cannot restrain the expression of some surprise at the course of argument that was taken by the learned

* Townsend, vol. i. p. 71.

counsel who last addressed you. His course of argument was this: when the prisoner was interrupted in what he was doing, 'Look and see what he has done;' where he has accomplished his purpose, 'Do not believe the witnesses.' The party having been dispersed by the soldiers, the learned gentleman says, 'See if they went to the post-office; see if they went to the bridge; see if they went to other places'—he knowing that they were stopped before they reached those places; 'but as to marching there with arms to take the town, that I dispose of by asking you not to believe the witnesses; so that, as regards what was prevented, I ask you to see what was done; and as regards what was done, I ask you to disbelieve the witnesses, and there is an end of the charge.'"—(I. p. 75.)

This single paragraph annihilated a third of the case set up on behalf of Frost; as did the following a second third:—

"They could not have raised these men with a view to relieve the prisoners at the Westgate, because at the time they collected on the mountain they had not been taken. But had it any relation to Vincent? What is their intention? We have been told again and again that Mr Frost must not be supposed likely to do absurd things; that he is a man of the world, and a man of intelligence. What then, gentlemen, do you think of an attempt to induce the Monmouthshire magistrates to relax the prison discipline in favour of a person who has been convicted of sedition, or seditious libel, or something of that sort, by marching into Newport with ten thousand men armed? What do you think of a man of the world resorting to that mode of inducing the magistrates to relax in favour of a prisoner? Is Mr Frost a man of intelligence? Is he a man of the world? Suppose he had been the worst foe that Vincent ever had; suppose that he had desired to procure additional restrictions to be put upon him, and had wished that he should sustain the last hour of the sentence which had been pronounced upon him, could he have resorted to a more maliciously effective mode than by showing that those who were connected with Vincent were persons so little acquainted with their duty, so little obedient to the law, so little to be depended upon for their peaceable conduct, as that they would march at that hour of the night into a town, alarming and frightening everybody?"—(I. p. 79.)

Again:—

"Gentlemen, will you judge of the criminal intentions of persons engaged in an insurrection by the probability of their success? If you do, you will judge of a mob by a rule that never was found correct yet. They always imagine—and they would not begin if they did not imagine, though they always imagine wrong, but they never will learn wisdom—they always imagine that they can accomplish more than they can; of course they begin, not with the idea of fastening a halter round their necks, but with the idea that they shall succeed, and by their success escape. With those thousands of men (you will see as I pass on what the number of the soldiers were), was it an unnatural thing that, coming at between one and two o'clock in the morning, they should surprise the poorhouse; that the soldiers, not being aware that they were coming, might not be prepared—might be taken by surprise—might be either overcome or murdered before they could put themselves in a condition to defend themselves?

"Are their sayings inconsistent? What conspiracy ever was consistent? You would indeed give the most perfect freedom to conspiracy, rebellion, and treason, if you disbelieved witnesses coming to prove declarations inconsistent if made at the same time, though not inconsistent when made at different times. They may at first think the soldiers to be Chartists and their friends, and, in the next moment, talk of attacking them in their barracks. But will you give a *carte blanche* to conspirators and traitors by saying, that if witnesses prove inconsistent declarations, they are not to be believed? It is not, gentlemen, the inconsistency of the witnesses, but of those engaged in transactions, the conduct and management of which must vary from hour to hour, according as circumstances arise; and that which a man may contemplate one minute, may the following minute, or the next hour, be inconsistent with the views that had prevailed, arising out of the then existing circumstances."—(I. p. 89.)

The circumstance of Frost's having been found with the loaded pistols, and not having attempted to use them, is thus significantly disposed of:—

"Give him the benefit of the circumstance that *he did not use* the three loaded pistols which he had about him. But I think, unfortunately, that they speak much more strongly as indicating violent intentions *when those pistols were provided*, than they speak peaceable intentions when he was apprehended."—(I. p. 24.)

There has been no counsel at the English Bar, in modern times, whose reply was more dreaded by an opponent than Sir Thomas Wilde; and that reply, in Frost's case, abundantly shows how well founded was that apprehension.

Thus, then, the counsel on both sides having played out their parts in the case, it stood awaiting the intervention of the Chief Justice—the very model of judicial excellence. Tranquil, grave, patient; exact, ready, profound in legal knowledge, and of perfect impartiality—all these high qualities and qualifications were exhibited by him in his luminous and masterly summing up on this occasion. In order to give all due weight to the sole substantial suggestion offered on behalf of the prisoner—*i. e.*, that his object had been the liberation of Vincent—the Chief Justice read to the jury the following important passage from that great authority, Sir Matthew Hale—"If men levy war to break prisons, to deliver *one or more particular persons* out of prison, this was ruled, on advice of the Judges, to be not high treason, but only a great riot; but if it was to break prisons, or deliver *persons generally* out of prison, this is treason." * Having taken at once a minute and comprehensive view of the evidence, he left the following as the exact question for their determination,—"Whether it was Frost's object, by the terror which bodies of armed men would inspire, to seize and keep possession of the town of Newport, making this a beginning of an extensive rebellion, *which would be high treason;* or whether he had no more in view than to effect, by the display of physical force, the amelioration of the condition of Vincent and his companions in Monmouth jail, if not their liberation, *which would be a dangerous misdemeanor only;* and the jury were to look at the evidence with all possible candour and fairness, and see if the Crown had conclusively disproved this limited object and design." † We conceive that neither Frost nor any one of his ten thousand dupes, on that "day of dupes," which had led to this inquiry, could have taken objection to this mode of submitting the all-critical question to his

* Hale's *Pleas of the Crown*, part i., c. 14.

† Townsend, p. 95.

jury—a jury of his peers, with the selection of whom he himself had had as much concern as the Crown.

That jury retired from court for half-an-hour, and then returned, amidst the solemn excited silence of the court—crowded to suffocation—with the fatal verdict, "Guilty;" adding, "My lords, we wish to recommend the prisoner to the merciful consideration of the court." Sentence was not immediately passed upon him. He was removed from court; and on its re-assembling on the ensuing morning, Zephaniah Williams was placed at the bar, tried, and in due course found guilty; on which William Jones was in like manner arraigned, tried, and found guilty; each being recommended by the jury to mercy. Scared by this result, five of the ringleaders resolved to throw themselves on the mercy of the Crown, withdrawing their pleas of not guilty, and pleading guilty—it having been intimated that the sentence of death should be commuted into transportation for life. The Attorney-General thought it expedient, in the case of the remaining four prisoners, who were less deeply implicated, to allow a verdict of not guilty to be recorded.

On the 16th January, Frost, Williams, and Jones were brought up to the bar to receive sentence of death, which the Chief Justice prefaced by a solemn address, listened to in breathless silence. An imposing scene of judicial solemnity and terror, indeed, the court at that agitating moment exhibited. Without were strong detachments of soldiery, foot and horse, guarding the public peace: within were an anxious auditory, commanded to keep silence under pain of fine and imprisonment, while sentence of death was being passed upon the prisoners. There were, in the midst of the throng, two groups awfully contrasted in character and position—the three prisoners, standing pale and subdued; and, sitting opposite, the three judges, each wearing his black cap; while the following heart-sickening words fell from the lips of the Chief Justice:—

"And now nothing more remains than the duty imposed upon

the court, to all of us a most painful duty, to declare the last SENTENCE OF THE LAW; which is that you, John Frost, and you, Zephaniah Williams, and you, William Jones, be taken hence to the place whence you came, and be thence drawn on a hurdle to the place of execution, and that each of you be there hanged by the neck until you be dead; *and that afterwards the head of each of you shall be severed from his body, and the body of each, divided into four quarters, shall be disposed of, as her Majesty shall think fit. And may Almighty God have mercy on your souls!*"

Whether the words placed in italics should ever again be pronounced on such an occasion, barbarously prescribing a revolting outrage on the dead, which it is known, at the time, cannot be perpetrated in these days of enlightened humanity, is a point which cannot admit of debate. The practice ought forthwith to be abolished, and by statute, if such be necessary.

Under the mortal pressure of this capital sentence remained these three unhappy and misguided men, from the 16th till the 28th of January. On the 25th, an elaborate argument was had at Westminster before the fifteen Judges, which lasted till the 28th, on a case framed by Chief Justice Tindal for their opinion, on the point which had been raised at the trial by Sir Frederick Pollock. The Chief Justice submitted these two questions for consideration,—"First, whether the service of the list of witnesses was a good service, under the statute 7 Anne, c. 21, sec. 11; secondly, whether, at all events, the objection was taken in due time." There was a great array of counsel on both sides; but the argument was conducted by the Attorney-General alone on behalf of the Crown; and by Sir Frederick Pollock, Sir William Follett, and Mr Kelly, on behalf of the prisoners. The utmost possible ingenuity was displayed on both sides; and with such effect, that at the close of the argument, the Chief Justice of the Common Pleas wrote a letter to the Secretary of State for the Home Department, the Marquis of Normanby, announcing the following somewhat perplexing result,—that "first, a majority of the Judges, in the proportion of NINE to SIX, were of opinion that the delivery of the list of witnesses was NOT a good delivery in point of law:

"But, secondly, a majority of the Judges, in the proportion of nine to six, were of opinion that the OBJECTION to the delivery of the list of witnesses was *not taken in due time.*

"All the Judges agreed, that if the objection had been made in time, the effect of it would have been a *postponement of the trial*, in order to give time for a proper delivery of the list."

The AYES on this occasion were—*Justices* Littledale, Patteson, Williams, Coleridge, Coltman, Erskine; *Barons* Parke, Alderson, Rolfe.

The NOES—Chief Justice Denman, Chief Justice Tindal, Chief Baron Abinger; *Justices* Bosanquet, Maule, and Baron Gurney.

These last (the NOES) decided also that the objection had not been taken in time; and three of the former class (the AYES), viz., Baron Alderson, Baron Rolfe, and Justice Coleridge concurred in that decision.*

Here was a question for the Executive to decide! A capital conviction for high treason, with a decision of the majority of the Judges of the land, that a statutory requisition as to the period for delivery of a list of the witnesses had not been exactly complied with, but that the prisoner did not make the objection till the time had gone by for making it; and that, had he made it in time, the utmost effect would have been to cause a postponement of the trial for a few days. The prisoner's objection was

* 1 Townsend, pp. 99, 100; and see the argument reported at length in Regina *v.* Frost, 9 Carr and Payne, 165–187. Of these fifteen Judges, only six are still [1850] on the Bench — Barons Parke, Alderson, Rolfe; and Justices Patteson, Coleridge, and Maule—nine having disappeared during the last ten years. It will be observed that the three chiefs of the courts were of one way of thinking, viz., that there *had* been a good delivery of the list of witnesses, in point of law. Only four of these six are now [1854] on the Bench — Justices Coleridge and Maule, and Barons Parke and Alderson. Baron Rolfe, since created Lord Cranworth, is now Lord Chancellor.

avowedly *strictissimi juris;* and he did not affect to show that he had suffered the slightest detriment from the over-anxious kindness of the Crown solicitor. That, under these circumstances, the lives of the three traitors were absolutely at the mercy of the Crown, is indisputable; and no one, we conceive, could have censured the Government, if they had advised the Crown to carry the capital sentence into effect. They inclined, however, to the merciful exercise of their anxious discretion; and the capital sentence was remitted, on condition of the three prisoners being transported for the term of their natural lives. They have now been ten years at the Antipodes; and how many times, during that lengthened period of bitter, dishonoured existence, they have cursed their own folly and crime, who can tell?

Have they ever appreciated the skill and vigilance with which they were defended? It is true that this one chance objection, which it is wonderful should have occurred to any one at all, was ultimately pronounced, only, however, by a majority of the Judges, after lengthened debate, to have been taken too late; but if it had not occurred to the vigilant advocate when it did—if no one had taken it at any time—would not the three traitors have been executed? Unquestionably; public justice, the public safety required it. Whether Sir Frederick Pollock purposely delayed making the objection till the moment when he did—and the Attorney-General insinuated, before the fifteen Judges, that such was the case*—thinking that course more advantageous to the prisoners, or whether the objection had not, in fact, occurred to him till it was too late, we do not here profess to say. This much, however, we can say, in conclusion, that we are much indebted to the late Mr Townsend for having enabled us to present this entertainment—for such we hope it has proved—to our readers; who may hereafter look with enhanced interest on a great trial, especially if they have the opportunity of witnessing it.

* 9 Carr and Payne, pp. 175, 176.

They may then appreciate the exquisite anxieties and responsibilities imposed on those concerned in conducting it; the difficulties with which they have to contend on the spot, without time for consideration, though life itself be the stake played for. They will also, probably, be of the opinion, that in the great game at Monmouth all the players played their parts well,—may we not say admirably?—that the uttermost justice was done on both sides.

Two practical deductions from the whole may yet be made: first, have a look-out, gentlemen prosecutors, in taking every step of your course, however apparently unimportant at the time it may seem to you; bearing in mind that, in proportion to the desperate exigencies of the defence, will be the piercing scrutiny to which every formality will be subjected; so that a blow may be hit which might easily have been avoided, but, when hit, is fatal. Secondly, in your turn, gentlemen counsel, be encouraged by the result of this interesting and instructive trial, to watch every step of your opponents—even those in which error, omission, or miscarriage is least likely—with sleepless vigilance, and be prompt in action. Thus much for the trial of John Frost.

# MODERN STATE TRIALS.

## No. II.

## HIGH TREASON AND MURDER—MORAL INSANITY.

IMPELLED by motives which we own it hard entirely to justify, and which we must resolve into an overmastering anxiety to behold how doomed human nature can confront terror-inspiring circumstances, felt sufficient to palsy one's own soul, we found ourselves, on Sunday morning, the 5th of July 1840, in the front seat of the stranger's gallery in the Chapel of Newgate, in order to hear the condemned sermon preached to Benjamin Courvoisier,* and witness the demeanour of one who was to be publicly strangled on the ensuing morning, and in the ensuing evening buried within the precincts of the prison. Callous must he have been who could witness the scene of that morning without being profoundly affected. It was the house of God; and yet—with reverence be the allusion made—in one sense, alas! a *den of thieves*—of outcasts from society; whose laws they had, or were charged with having, disregarded and openly violated. Some were there under the pressure of violent suspicion, amounting to a moral, soon to pass into a legal, certainty; of various kinds and degrees of guilt: others bore the blighting brand of established crime, and were suffering, or about to suffer, its penalty. With what feelings would they enter the house of Him

* *Vide ante,* The Mystery of Murder, p. 1.

who is of purer eyes than to behold iniquity; to Whom all hearts are open, all desires known, and from Whom no secrets are hid! Would any of that guilty throng take their places there, brutally ignorant, indifferent, reckless, or desperate? Would their polluted souls be swelling with ill-suppressed feelings of impiety and blasphemy? Would any approach with broken and contrite spirits, having been shaken, by the stern hand of offended human law alone, out of a life's lethargy and insensibility? How would the holy accents of warning, of expostulation, of mercy, of dread denunciation, sound in the ears of those who were presently to fill that dismal chapel—dismal only from its locality, and the character of its occupants? With what feelings would *one* enter,—the death-doomed,—for whom, and for whom alone, was reserved that solitary central, ominous black bench? Who was so terribly far advanced in his passage from a human tribunal to that of the dread Eternal! On whose brow already faintly glistened the dread twilight between here and hereafter,—the black night of time, breaking before the dawning of an eternal day!

They come! Yonder gallery, curtained off, is filling with the female prisoners; no sounds audible but their rustling dresses, and perhaps a half-choked sigh, or sob. It is well, poor souls! that you are hidden from the public gaze—from the rude eye of your male comrades in crime! They are now entering below, silent and orderly, the eye of the governor upon them, as they are led by burly turnkeys and inspectors to their appropriate places, classed as untried and convicted, the latter according to their respective kinds and degree of punishment. All, at length, are seated. What an assemblage! Almost all clad in prison costume; many with sullen, determined countenances, others with harassed features and downcast look; one or two exhibiting equivocally an air of insolent and reckless defiance, but all conscious of the stern surveillance under which they sate. Alas, *those boys!*

some already, others about to be, condemned—all gazing, terror-struck, at the black seat in the centre.

The chaplain enters the desk immediately under the pulpit, which, attached to the blank wall, faces the communion-table. He, also, casts an ominous glance at the black bench before him, in the centre of the floor, to which all faces are directed, amidst moody and troubled silence. At length a door on the left is heard being unbolted; a turnkey enters, followed by the great criminal—one whose name was at that moment ringing in the ears of the public—one on whom every eye is instantly fixed with sickening intensity. It is Courvoisier—the monster who, a few weeks before, had barbarously murdered his sleeping lord!

He was led to his seat, a glass of water being placed near him, in case of his faintness, and on one side of him sate a turnkey. Courvoisier knelt down; and then, a prayer-book having been given him, which he held with a firm hand, took his seat, not far from the reading-desk, covering his eyes for a few moments with his left hand. His demeanour was signally calm and self-possessed, and his motions were deliberate. He was a man about twenty-four years of age. His countenance wore such an expression of pensive good-nature and docility, as rendered it a consolatory reflection that he had unequivocally and spontaneously confessed the fiendish act of which the law had pronounced him guilty, and for which, under holy sanctions, it was on the morrow to take away his life.* Yes, there he sate, where we had seen sitting, also, his blood-stained predecessor Greenacre; and, moreover, Fauntleroy

* How must the following verses in the Psalms of the day have affected him, if the wretched being were not too bewildered to appreciate them! "Turn Thee unto me, and have mercy upon me, for I am desolate and in misery. The sorrows of my heart are enlarged; O bring Thou me out of my troubles. Look upon my adversity and misery, and forgive me all my sins" (Ps. xxv. 15, 16, 17). "O shut not up my soul with the sinners, *nor my life with the blood-thirsty*" (Ps. xxvi. 9). If the murderer's heart did not thrill when these last words were read out by the chaplain, with fearful distinctness, it must have been the only one that did not.

the forger; also a young banker's clerk, a widowed mother's sole support, her only child, for forging a trifling check. Alas, alas! how he wept during the whole service! but how calmly he behaved the next morning, on the gallows!

After gazing long and earnestly on the central figure in the gloomy picture, our eyes were casually attracted by a very different one,—that of a youth, sitting on the steps of the altar, as though he had been a privileged spectator. We regarded him as a friend of some subordinate functionary of the gaol. He seemed a silly, vulgar, little dandy, who had put on his best clothes for the occasion. He looked about eighteen or nineteen years old, and was of slender figure, and a little under the average height. His hair was full and curly, displayed in a most affected style. He wore a sort of second-hand blue surtout with velvet collar, a black satin stock, a light figured waistcoat, and light slate-coloured trousers,—the latter a trifle too short, and strained down by a pair of elongated straps, so as to reach as nearly as possible to the brightly-polished boots. Beside him was a hat, of which he seemed very careful, and smoothed it round delicately, once or twice, with his hand. His eyes were quick, and inquisitive; and he seemed to share the interest with which others contemplated Courvoisier. Several times, during the service, his fingers passed jauntily through his hair, as if to dispose it effectively round his temples. A prayer-book was handed to him, to which he seemed tolerably attentive; but during the sermon he was evidently more occupied with his dress than the exciting and instructive topics of the chaplain; frequently pulling off and putting on his gloves, and arranging different portions of his dress, as though he feared they did not sit upon him sufficiently becomingly. When, however, the chaplain addressed himself personally, and with fearful solemnity, to the murderer before him, the young occupant of the altar-steps was roused into attention, and he listened a few minutes, his eyes fixed now on the preacher, then on the condemned. When the service was over, Courvoisier, whose demeanour had been throughout most satisfactory, solemn, composed, and reverent, was beckoned out to the door through which he had entered, and he obeyed, walking with complete self-possession. We had looked our last on him!

"Do you see that young fellow on the altar-steps?—do you know who he is?" said a gentleman who approached us for the purpose. "No; he seems a vulgar little puppy," we exclaimed, "whoever he may be." "It is Oxford, who shot at the Queen, and is to be tried this week!" was the reply; and while we turned round to gaze at him, he was in the act of quitting the chapel, holding his hat very carefully, and gazing towards the gallery with an expression of cheerful inquisitiveness. Had it occurred to him that, in all human probability, a week or two would behold *him* an occupant of the black bench just quitted by the murderer?

Yes! that was Edward Oxford, the little caitiff, first of a small and ignominious series of similar ones, who had, on the preceding 9th of June, twice deliberately fired at his young Queen, as she was driving, in fancied security, with her consort, up Constitution Hill, and on each occasion apparently with ball! The following was his own free-and-easy account of the matter, on being examined before the Privy Council:—

> "A great many witnesses against me. Some say I shot with my left, others with my right. They vary as to the distance. After I had fired the first pistol, Prince Albert got up, as if he would jump out of the coach, and sate down again, as if he thought better of it. Then I fired the second pistol. This is all I shall say at present. (Signed) "EDWARD OXFORD."

In the case of this young miscreant (for it is difficult to speak of him temperately), however, was, within four days' time, to be resolved a problem of unspeakable difficulty and moment, by such means as the law of the country could command,—viz., responsibility or irresponsibility for criminal acts, according to the state of mind supposed to be existing at the time of committing them. It is needless to affirm that this is a question of public, permanent, universal interest; one in which every individual, young or old, *may* become personally concerned; one which no human jurist, practical or speculative, can approach without lively anxiety; one worthy of frequent and deep consideration by every one concerned in the administration of criminal justice. To punish an individual utterly unconscious of the difference between right and wrong at the time of committing the alleged crime, shocks one's sense of natural justice, and confounds all the principles on which it can be administered by man. How can we hang a maniac who, in a paroxysm of madness, kills the keeper who was endeavouring to soothe or to restrain him? Or one who shoots another whom, under the veritable and sole influence of delusion, he believed to be in the act of killing *him*, and that he was therefore acting solely in self-defence? These are plain cases, as stated; but still they require, of course, very clear proof of the facts from which the law is to deduce a perfect irresponsibility for his acts. The subject is one environed with immense practical difficulties, which are often unexpectedly visible in applying apparently clear and correct principles to simple combinations of fact. The most sagacious judges, the most conscientious juries, have grievously miscarried in such cases; some sending persons to the scaffold under circumstances far weaker than those held by others demonstrative of irresponsibility, and, consequently, demanding an acquittal. Many painful and dreadful cases might be cited; but two shall suffice.

In the year 1837, an industrious, affectionate, poverty-stricken father strangled his four children, avowedly to prevent their being turned into the streets. They all slept in one room. Having strangled two, he left the room; but, after meditating for some time, came to the conclusion that he might as well be hanged for killing all four; on which he returned, and strangled the other two —having shaken hands with them before he did it! He then quitted the house, and went to a neighbour's, to whom he did not mention what he had done; but on being apprehended the next day, and taken before the coroner, he confessed the above facts. No witness had ever observed a trace of insanity about him. The physician to a lunatic asylum offered to prove that the prisoner's grandmother and sister had been under his care, the latter for entertaining a desire to destroy herself and her children —evidence which the judge rejected; and under his direction the jury convicted, and he passed sentence of death on the prisoner.* In the year 1845, a young servant girl, quiet and docile, having taken a knife from the kitchen, on some trivial pretence, went up to the room where her master's child lay, and killed it. She then went down stairs, and told the horrifying fact to her master. She was quite conscious of the crime she had committed, and showed much anxiety to know whether she would be hanged or transported. There was not the slightest tittle of evidence that she had been labouring under any delusion; yet she was acquitted on the ground of insanity! † Can anything be more grievously unsatisfactory than such a state of things as this, in the administration of the criminal justice of the country? One of the causes which conduced to such results was the too ready deference paid to speculative medical men, professing to have made disordered intellects their peculiar study, and who came forward, from time to time, confidently and authoritatively pronouncing that such and such circumstances indicated unequivocally the existence of "insanity," of "moral insanity," at the time of the act committed. Nay, they would sit in court, listening to a detail of facts, from which they would then enter the witness-box, and authoritatively

* He was subsequently respited, owing to the zealous interference of some medical men, who succeeded in satisfying the Secretary of State of the prisoner's insanity. See Taylor's *Medical Jurisprudence*, p. 792.

† *Ibid.* pp. 803, 804.

declare their opinion that, if such were the facts, the prisoner was *insane*, and therefore irresponsible, when the act in question was committed! Many held that the mere absence of assignable motive indicated such insanity! and many, that the mere committal of the particular act should be so regarded! Notions more dangerous and monstrous cannot be conceived. Well might the late Mr Baron Gurney declare, "that the defence of insanity had lately grown to a fearful height, and the security of the public required that it should be watched."*

There are two trials contained in Mr Townsend's first volume, which afford memorable illustrations of the difficulty with which these questions are encountered in our courts of justice. They are those of Oxford, for shooting at the Queen, and of M'Naughten for the murder of Mr Drummond, the private secretary of the late Sir Robert Peel. In both cases there were acquittals, on the alleged ground of insanity; and we take leave to intimate that, in our opinion, there should have been convictions in both. The escape of the cold-blooded murderer, M'Naughten, who deliberately shot his unsuspecting victim in the back, horrified and disgusted the public. "It had not been anticipated," says Mr Townsend, "and created a deep feeling in the public mind, that there was some unaccountable defect in our criminal law. People of good sense appeared panic-stricken, by this new danger, from venturing into the London streets; and called upon the legislature to discover some preservative against the attacks of insane passengers in public thoroughfares."† Indignation was loudly expressed in Parliament. In the House of Commons, an honourable Irish baronet moved for leave to bring in a bill to abolish the plea of insanity in cases of murder, except where it could be proved that the person accused was publicly known and reputed to be a maniac; and he asked the House to suspend the standing orders to accelerate the progress of his bill. His motion, however,

* Rex *v.* Reynolds. Taylor's *Med. Jurisp.* p. 801.

† Vol. i. p. 320.

found no seconder. A similar casualty had befallen Mr Windham, in 1800, who, in the course of a debate which ensued in bringing in a bill to meet such cases as that of Hadfield, who had just been acquitted, on the ground of insanity, from the charge of firing at George III., suggested that an offender, *even if insane*, should be subjected to some sort of punishment, for the sake of example! On the same evening in which the attempt of Sir Valentine Blake was made in the House of Commons, the matter was discussed anxiously in the House of Lords, by Lords Lyndhurst, Brougham, Cottenham, Campbell, and Denman. Lord Campbell expressed the general feeling of the House, when he said, "There may be great difficulty in convicting persons who were not in a state of mind to be responsible for their actions; but it is monstrous to think that society should be exposed to the dreadful dangers to which it is at present liable, from persons in that state of mind going at large."* At length, on the suggestion of the Lord Chancellor, Lord Lyndhurst, it was agreed that the Judges should be called upon to declare the true state of the criminal law on this momentous subject; and five questions were carefully framed for that purpose, and submitted to them for grave consideration. The following are these questions and answers—both of which, as containing a solemn and authoritative enunciation of the law of the land, we shall present to our readers, whom we request to bestow on them a careful perusal, before proceeding to read what we have to offer on the two trials above alluded to. We are the more anxious that they should do so, because of the recent remarkable case of Pate, who struck her Majesty with a cane, last summer; and whose case was dealt with in strict conformity with the rules which follow:—

QUESTION I.—"*What is the law* respecting alleged crimes committed by persons afflicted with insane delusion, in respect of one or more particular subjects, or persons:—as, for instance, where, at

* Townsend, vol. i. p. 46.

the time of the commission of the alleged crime, the accused knew he was acting contrary to law, but did the act complained of, with a view, under the influence of insane delusion, of redressing or revenging some supposed grievance or injury, or of producing some public benefit?"

Answer.—"Assuming that your lordships' inquiries are confined to those persons who labour under such partial delusions only, and are not in other respects insane, we are of opinion that, notwithstanding the party did the act complained of with a view, under the influence of insane delusion, of redressing or revenging some supposed grievance or injury, or of producing some public benefit, he is nevertheless punishable according to the nature of the crime committed, if he knew, at the time of committing such crime, that he was acting contrary to law; by which expression we understand your lordships to mean the law of the land."

Questions II. and III.—(1.) "What are the proper questions to be submitted to the jury, when a person alleged to be afflicted with insane delusion, respecting one or more particular subjects or persons, is charged with the commission of a crime (murder, for example), and insanity is set up as a defence?"

(2.) "In what terms ought the question to be left to the jury, as to the prisoner's state of mind at the time when the act was committed?"

Answers.—"The jury ought to be told, in all cases, that *every man is presumed* to be sane, and to possess a sufficient degree of reason to be responsible for his crimes, until the contrary be proved to their satisfaction; and that, to establish a defence on the ground of insanity, it must be clearly proved that, at the time of the committing of the act, the party accused was labouring under such a defect of reason, from disease of the mind, as not to know the nature and quality of the act he was doing; or, if he did know it, that he did not know he was doing what was wrong. The mode of putting the latter part of the question to the jury, on these occasions, has generally been whether the accused, at the time of doing the act, knew the difference between right and wrong—which mode, though rarely if ever leading to any mistake with the jury, is not, as we conceive, so accurate when put generally and in the abstract, as when put to the party's knowledge of right and wrong with respect to the very act with which he is charged. If the question were to be put as to the knowledge of the accused, solely and exclusively with reference to the law of the land, it might tend to confound the jury, by inducing them to believe that an actual knowledge of the law of the land was essential in order to lead to a conviction, whereas the law is administered upon the principle that every one must be taken conclusively to know it, without proof that he does know it. If the accused was conscious that the act was one which he ought not to do, and if that act was at the same time contrary to the law of the land, he is punishable; and the usual course, therefore, has been to leave the question to the jury —whether the party accused had a sufficient degree of reason to know that he was doing an act that was wrong; and this course, we think, is correct, accompanied with such observations and explanations as the circumstances of each particular case may require."

QUESTION IV.—"If a person, under an insane delusion as to the existing facts, commits an offence in consequence thereof, is he thereby excused?"

ANSWER.—"The answer must of course depend on the nature of the delusion; but making the same assumption as we did before—that he labours under such partial delusion only, and is not in other respects insane—we think he must be considered in the same situation, as to responsibility, as if the facts with respect to which the delusion exists were real. For example—if, under the influence of his delusion, he supposes another man to be in the act of attempting to take away his life, and he kills that man, as he supposes, in self-defence, he would be exempt from punishment. If his delusion were that the deceased had inflicted a serious injury to his character and fortune, and he killed him in revenge for such supposed injury, he would be liable to punishment."

QUESTION V.—"Can a medical man, conversant with the disease of insanity, who never saw the prisoner previously to the trial, but who was present during the whole trial and the examination of all the witnesses, be asked his opinion as to the state of the prisoner's mind at the time of the commission of the alleged crime, or his opinion whether the prisoner was conscious, at the time of doing the act, that he was acting contrary to law, or whether he was labouring under any, and what, delusion at the time?"

ANSWER.—"We think the medical man, under the circumstances supposed, cannot in strictness be asked his opinion in the terms above stated; because each of those questions involves the determination of the truth of the facts deposed to, which it is for the jury to decide; and the questions are not mere questions upon a matter of science, in which case such evidence is admissible. But where the facts are admitted, or not disputed, and the question becomes substantially one of science only, it may be convenient to allow the question to be put in that general form, though the same cannot be insisted on as a matter of right."

Such being the authoritative enunciation of the law by

its legitimate exponents, which superseded the necessity of legislative interference, it is right to observe that it has by no means satisfied the professors of medical jurisprudence, and the members of the medical profession. One of them, Mr Taylor, has observed,* that the law here appears to "look for a consciousness of right and wrong, and a knowledge of the consequences of the act." This legal test "is insufficient for the purpose intended: it cannot, in a large majority of cases, enable us to distinguish the insane homicide from the sane criminal. * * * A full consciousness of the illegality or wrongfulness of the act may exist in a man's mind, and yet he may be fairly acquitted on the ground of insanity. * * * There *are* no certain legal or medical rules whereby homicidal mania may be detected. Each case must be determined by the circumstances attending it; but the true test for irresponsibility in these ambiguous cases appears to be, whether the individual, at the time of committing the act, had, or had not, *a sufficient power of control* to govern his actions. If, from circumstances, it can be inferred that he had this power, he should be made responsible, and rendered liable to punishment. If, however, he was led to the perpetration of the act by an *uncontrollable* impulse, whether accompanied by deliberation or not, then he is entitled to an acquittal as an irresponsible agent."† This doctrine is utterly repudiated, however, by our Judges, as will appear from two decisive instances. In directing the jury, in Pate's case, in July last, Mr Baron Alderson thus somewhat sarcastically disposed of the dangerous plea of "uncontrollable impulse:"—"The law does not recognise such an impulse. If a person was aware that it was a wrong act he was about to commit, he was answerable for the consequences. *A man might say that he picked a pocket from some uncon-*

* *Medical Jurisprudence*, p. 794, 3d edition. This is, in our opinion, the best book extant on medical jurisprudence.

† *Ibid.* p. 798.

*trollable impulse; and in that case the law would have an uncontrollable impulse to punish him for it!*" Another acute and eminent Judge, Baron Rolfe,* on a recent occasion, in trying a boy aged twelve years, for deliberately and cunningly poisoning his aged grandfather, thus gravely dispelled this favourite delusion of the medical jurists:—" The witnesses called for the defence had described the prisoner as acting from 'uncontrollable impulse.' In my opinion, such evidence ought to be scanned by juries with very great jealousy and suspicion, *because it may tend to the perfect justification of every crime that may be committed.* What is the meaning of not being able to resist moral influence? Every crime is committed under an influence of such a description, and the object of the law is to compel persons to control these influences. If it be made an excuse for a person who has committed a crime, that he has been goaded to it by some impulse, which medical men may choose to say he could *not* control, I must observe, that such a doctrine is fraught with very great danger to society." This stern and sound good sense prevailed; and the youthful murderer was convicted. We have been thus full and distinct in explaining the wholesome doctrine of our English law, because of its immense importance; and we desire it to be understood, far and wide, especially by the medical profession, that these fashionable but dangerous modern paradoxes, borrowed from Continental physicians, concerning *the co-existence of moral insanity* with intellectual sanity, will not be tolerated in English courts of justice.

Let us now proceed to deal with the two remarkable cases of Oxford and M'Naughten: the former of whom was placed at the bar of the Old Bailey four days after the execution of Courvoisier.

It is unspeakably painful, humiliating, and disgusting, to reflect that our Queen, who has always shown a disposition to trust herself unreservedly among her subjects,

* Now Lord Cranworth, Chancellor.

should have been subjected to no fewer than five public outrages, the last of which inflicted actual injury on the royal person; that of a lady, a young queen, ascending the throne of this mighty empire, at the age of eighteen! —Outrages in every instance perpetrated by despicable beings of the male sex, properly characterised by Mr Townsend as "crazed knaves, or imbecile monomaniacs." First came, on the 10th June 1840, Edward Oxford, aged nineteen; then, on the 30th May 1842, John Francis, aged twenty; then, on the 3d July 1842, John William Bean, a deformed stripling aged seventeen; then, on the 19th May 1849, William Hamilton; finally—God grant that the degraded series may never be increased!—on the 27th June 1850, Robert Pate—alas! a gentleman of birth and fortune, and who had recently borne her Majesty's commission!

We shall place our readers, briefly and distinctly, in possession of the state of the law applicable to wilfully injuring, or attempting to injure, The Royal Person.

Its progress is painfully interesting. The attempt to inflict, and the actual infliction of such injury, are of course high treason; both the trial and punishment being attended, till recently, with all the solemn formalities of high treason, as explained in our last paper. This heinous offence comes under the first head of the statute of treason, (25 Edward III. c. 2,) viz., "When a man doth *compass* or *imagine* * the death of our Lord and King." By "compass and imagine" is signified the purpose or design of the mind or will, evidenced by an open or *overt* act. On the 15th May 1800, James Hadfield fired a horse-pistol, loaded with two slugs, at King George

* "Is it not extraordinary," asked the learned Mr Barrington, *Observations on the Ancient Statutes*, p. 270, "that the life of an Englishman prosecuted by the Crown should continue to depend upon the critical construction of two obsolete French words?" (fait *compasser* out *imaginer* la mort nôtre seigneur le roi.) There is practically no force in these remarks, made nearly a century ago; as the words have a perfectly defined and recognised legal signification, and which is that mentioned above.

III., as he was entering his box at Drury Lane Theatre.* He was tried for high treason in the Court of Queen's Bench, and defended by Mr Erskine with splendid eloquence.† He was acquitted on the ground of insanity, committed at once to Bedlam, and died there in January 1841, after forty years' incarceration. In the course of his defence, Mr Erskine made an observation which led to an immediate interposition of the legislature. In speaking of the state of the law which interposed protective delay in cases of high treason, Mr Erskine observed:—"Where the intent charged affected *the political character* of the sovereign, the delay, and all the other safeguards provided, were just and necessary; but a mere murderous attack on the king's person, not at all connected with his political character, seemed a case to be ranged and dealt with like a similar attack upon any private man."‡ On the 28th July, in the same year, were passed statutes 39 and 40 Geo. III. c. 93, carrying out Mr Erskine's judicious suggestion, by enacting that, where the overt act of this head of treason should be the assassination of the King, or any direct attempt against his life or person, whereby his life might be endangered or his person suffer bodily harm, the *trial* should be conducted in every respect like a simple trial for murder; but, on conviction, the sentence should be pronounced and

* His Majesty's noble demeanour, calm, courageous, and dignified, on that agitating occasion, has always been justly applauded. The audience was of course highly excited; and Mr Sheridan composed, on the spur of the moment, the following spirited addition to the National Anthem. It was sung by Mrs Jordan thrice that evening:—

"From every latent foe,
From the assassin's blow,
God shield the King!
O'er him thine arm extend;
For Britain's sake defend
Our father, prince, and friend—
God save the King!"

† Sir William Follett, then Solicitor-General, in addressing the jury in prosecuting M'Naughten, alluded to the speech of Mr Erskine as "one of the most eloquent and able speeches, probably, that was ever delivered at the Bar."

‡ Adolphus's *Hist. of England*, vol. vii. p. 277.

carried into effect as in other cases of high treason. On the same day was passed another statute, also occasioned by the trial of Hadfield, that in all cases of trial for treason, murder, or felony, if evidence be given of the prisoner's insanity, at the time of the commission of the offence, and he be acquitted, the jury shall be required to find specially whether he was insane at the time of committing the offence, and to declare whether they acquit on account of such insanity; and if they do, the court shall order the prisoner to be confined in strict and safe custody during his Majesty's pleasure. Under the former of these two wholesome statutes were tried Oxford and Francis, the latter being convicted of having fired a pistol against the Queen, loaded with powder and "certain other destructive materials and substances unknown;" on which sentence of death was pronounced by Chief Justice Tindal, as in other cases of high treason. He sobbed piteously* on being convicted; and after two consultations of the Cabinet had been held on his case, his life was spared, in contemptuous clemency to the worthless offender, and in deference to the humane feelings of her Majesty, and he was transported for life.

Within almost one month after this questionable act of mercy, her Majesty was subjected to a similar outrage—a pistol being presented towards her, by Bean, on Sunday, as she was going to the Chapel Royal. The pistol was cocked, and the click of the hammer against the pan was heard, but there was no explosion; and the pistol was loaded with only powder, wadding, and one or two minute fragments (about the size of ordinary shot) of pipe. He was tried for misdemeanor, and sentenced to eighteen months' imprisonment in the penitentiary; Lord Abinger remarking, at the conclusion of the trial, that "whipping at the cart's tail would be the fitting sentence, in future." The public disgust and indignation demanded some more effectual remedy to be provided for such disgraceful cases,

* Townsend, vol. i. p. 104.

should any unhappily occur in future; and within a fortnight of Bean's conviction, viz., on the 16th July 1842, was passed statute 5 and 6 Vict. c. 51, entitled, "An act for providing for the further security and protection of her Majesty's person." It recites the expediency of extending the provisions of statute 39 and 40 Geo. III. c. 93, to "any attempt to injure, in any manner whatsoever, the person of the Queen," and of "making further provision by law for the protection and security of the person of the sovereign of these realms." It then proceeds to enact, that—

> "If any one shall wilfully discharge or attempt to discharge, or point, aim, or present, at or near to the person of the Queen, any gun, pistol, or other description of firearms, or of other arms whatever—whether the same shall or shall not contain any explosive or destructive material; or discharge, or attempt to discharge, any explosive substance or material near to the Queen's person; or wilfully strike, or attempt to strike, or strike at the Queen's person with any offensive weapon, or in any other manner whatsoever; or wilfully throw or attempt to throw any substance, matter, or thing whatsoever at or upon the Queen's person, with intent to break the public peace, or whereby the public peace may be endangered, or to alarm her Majesty; or if any person shall, near to the Queen's person, wilfully produce or have any gun, pistol, or other description of firearms, or other arms whatsoever, or any explosive, destructive, or dangerous matter or thing whatsoever, with intent to use the same to injure the Queen's person or alarm her Majesty, the offender shall be guilty of a high misdemeanor, and liable at the discretion of the court to be transported for seven years, or imprisoned with or without hard labour for any period not exceeding three years; and during such imprisonment to be publicly or privately whipped as often and in such manner and form as the court shall direct, not exceeding thrice."

This salutary statute, proposed by the late Sir Robert Peel, was passed unanimously; Lord John Russell justly remarking, that, "as the offence to be punished was that of bad and degraded beings, a base and degrading punishment was most fitly applied to it." Her Majesty enjoyed a seven years' respite from the insufferable annoyance to which she had been subjected—viz., till the 19th May

1849—when, about four o'clock in the afternoon, as she was driving in an open carriage with three of her children, a pistol was fired in the direction of the carriage by "one William Hamilton, an Irish bricklayer." The pistol was fired point-blank at the person of General Wemyss, one of her equerries, who happened to be in the line of her Majesty's person. This stolid wretch was tried on the 14th June ensuing, under the above statute, when he pleaded guilty, and was sentenced to be transported for seven years. Again, on the 12th of July last, it was rendered lamentably necessary to call this statute into operation, and with the like effect as in the preceding case: but we shall reserve our observations upon the case of Pate till after the completion of what we have to offer on those of Oxford and M'Naughten. We have just returned from a personal examination of those two notorious persons, in Bethlehem Hospital; and shall by and by convey to the reader the result of our own careful observations, made since the earlier portions of this article were committed to the press.

---

## OXFORD'S CASE.

The Judges who presided at the trial, which took place at the Old Bailey, and lasted three days (the 9th, 10th, and 11th July 1840), were Lord Denman, Baron Alderson, and Justice Maule. The counsel for the Crown were—the Attorney and Solicitor-Generals (Sir John Campbell and Sir Thomas Wilde), Sir Frederick Pollock, the present Mr Justice Wightman, Mr Adolphus, and Mr Gurney; those for the prisoner were the late Mr Sydney Taylor, and Mr Bodkin. The indictment contained two counts, respectively applicable, in precisely the same terms, to the two acts of firing, charging that Oxford, "as a false traitor, maliciously and traitorously did compass, imagine, and intend to put our lady the Queen to death; and, to fulfil and bring into effect his treason and treasonable compassing, did shoot off and discharge a certain pistol loaded with gunpowder and a bullet, and thereby *made a direct attempt against the life of our said lady the Queen,*" —in the words of statute 39 and 40 Geo. III., c. 93, sec. 1. The trial, as already observed, differed in no respect from an ordinary trial for felony; and neither the Crown nor the prisoner challenged a single juryman. "Oxford," says Mr Townsend, "stepped into the dock with a jaunty air, and a flickering smile on his countenance; glanced at the galleries, as if to ascertain whether he had a large concourse of spectators; and, leaning with his elbow on the ledge of the dock, commenced playing with the herbs* which were placed there before him. He kept his gaze earnestly fixed on the Attorney-General during the whole of his address, twirling the rue about in his fingers; but became more subdued in manner towards the close of the speech."† The facts constituting the outrage lie in a nutshell:—The prisoner was seized instantly after having discharged two pistols, as the Queen and the Prince-consort were driving up Constitution Hill, in a low open carriage. He had been observed, for some time before the approach of the royal carriage, walking backwards and forwards with his arms folded under his breast. As the carriage approached, he turned round, nodded, drew a pistol from his breast, and discharged it at the carriage, when it was nearly opposite to him. As it advanced, after looking round to see if he were observed, he took out a second pistol, directed it across the other to her Majesty, who, seeing it, stooped down; and he fired a second time— —very deliberately—at only about six or seven yards'

* At the Old Bailey, *rue* is placed plentifully on the ledge of the dock; whether in capital cases only, we do not know. The monster Maria Manning furiously gathered the rue that lay before her, and flung it amongst the counsel sitting at the table beneath her! Prisoners have been known, and that not unfrequently, to devour, unconsciously, much of the nauseous herb before them, during the agony and suspense of their trials.

† Townsend, vol. i. p. 113.

distance. The witnesses spoke to hearing distinctly a sharp whizzing sound "close past their own ears." The prisoner, on seeing the person who had snatched from him the pistols mistaken for the person who had fired, said, "It was me—I did it. I give myself up—I will go quietly." At the police-office he said, "Is the Queen hurt?" Some one observed, "I wonder whether there was any ball in the pistol?" on which the prisoner said, "If the ball had come in contact with your head, if it were between the carriage, you would have known it." The witness who spoke to these words appears, however, to have somewhat hesitated when pressed in cross-examination; but he finally adhered to his statement that the prisoner declared there were balls in the pistols. A few days previously the prisoner had purchased the pistols for two sovereigns, about fifty percussion-caps, a powder-flask, which, with a bullet-mould and five bullets fitting the pistols, were found at his lodgings. He had also been practising firing at a target, and, on purchasing the pistols, asked particularly how far they would carry. The Earl of Uxbridge deposed that, when he saw Oxford in his cell, he asked, "Is the Queen hurt?" on which Lord Uxbridge said, "How dare you ask such a question?" Oxford then stated that "he had been shooting a great deal lately—he was a very good shot with a pistol, but a better shot with a rifle." "You have now fulfilled your engagement," said the Earl. "No," replied Oxford, "I have not." "You have, sir," rejoined Lord Uxbridge, "as far as the attempt goes." To that he was silent. The most rigid search was made to discover any bullets, but in vain. Two witnesses, gentlemen of rank, and well acquainted with the use of firearms, spoke confidently to having seen bullet-marks on the wall, in the direction in which Oxford had fired; but the Attorney-General expressed his opinion that the evidence was entitled to no weight, as probably mistaken; declaring himself, however, positive that there must have been balls in the pistols, but that the pistols had been elevated so high that the balls went over the garden-wall. One of the witnesses said to the other, immediately after seizing Oxford, "Look out—I dare say he has some friends;" to which he replied, "You are right —I have." At his lodgings were found some curious papers, in Oxford's handwriting, purporting to be the rules of a secret club or society called Young England; the first of which was, "that every member shall be provided with a brace of pistols, a sword, a rifle, and a dagger, the two latter to be kept at the committee-room." A list of members-*factitives*' [sic] names were given. "Marks of distinction: Council, a large white cockade; President, a black bow; General, three red bows; Captain, *two red bows;* Lieutenant, one red bow." There were also found in Oxford's trunk a sword and scabbard, and a black crape cap with *two red* bows—one of the "rules" requiring every member to be armed with a brace of loaded pistols, and to be provided with a black crape cap to cover his face, with his marks of distinction outside. Three letters were also found in his pocket-book, addressed to himself at three different residences, purporting to be signed by "A. W. Smith, *secretary*," and to contain statements of what had taken place, or was to take place, at the secret meetings of the society. They were all headed "Young England," and dated respectively, "16th May 1839," "14th Nov. 1839," and "3d April 1840." Oxford said he had intended to destroy these papers in the morning, before he went out, but had forgotten it. All these papers—the "rules" and letters—were sworn by Oxford's mother to be *in his own handwriting;* and it should have been mentioned that there was not a tittle of evidence adduced to show that there were, in fact, any such society in existence, or any such persons as these papers would have indicated; nor, up to the present moment, has there been the least reason for believing that such was the case.

Thus closed the case for the Crown,—undoubtedly a formidable one. No attempt was made by the prisoner's counsel, who appear to have conducted the defence temperately and judiciously, to alter, by evidence, the position of the proved facts; which, therefore, were allowed to stand before the jury as almost conclusively establishing the case of high treason. Mr Taylor, however, strongly impaired the Attorney-General's notion that there had been in the pistols balls, which had gone over the wall; because his own witnesses had spoken decisively to the bullet-marks on the wall; yet no flattened balls had been produced, after all the search that had been made. Mr Taylor, therefore, inferred that the pistols had contained powder only: "a great outrage, unquestionably, but still not the *treason* charged." There was, again, he contended, there could have been, no *motive* for killing the Queen; and the idea of the Treasonable Society was mere moonshine, a pure invention concocted by a lunatic, one who had inherited insanity, and himself exhibited the proofs of its existence: for Mr Taylor undertook to prove the insanity of Oxford's grandfather, his father, and himself. The proof broke down as far as concerned the grandfather, a sailor in the navy; for it was clear that his alleged violent eccentricities had been exhibited when he was under the influence of liquor. The insanity of Oxford's father was sought to be established by his widow, the mother of the prisoner. If her story, "told with unfaltering voice and unshaken nerve," were correct, her husband had undoubtedly been a violent and brutal fellow, with a dash of madness in his composition. It is possible that the mother, in her anxiety to save her son from a traitor's death on the scaffold, had, by a *quasi pia fraus*, too highly coloured her deceased husband's conduct. If this were not so, she had indeed been an object of the utmost sympathy. He forced her to marry him, she said, by furious threats of self-destruction if she did not: he burnt a great roll of bank-notes to ashes in her presence, because she had refused, or hesitated, to become his wife. He used to terrify her, during her pregnancies, by hideous grimaces, and apish tricks and gesticulations: the results being that her second child was born, and within three years' time died, an idiot. Her husband pursued the same course during her pregnancy with the prisoner, and presented a gun at her head. The prisoner had always been a headstrong, wayward, mischievous, eccentric youth—subject to fits of involuntary laughing and crying. He was absurdly vain, boastful, and ambitious; and wished his mother to send him to sea, where he would have nothing to do but walk about the deck, give orders, and by and by become Admiral Sir Edward Oxford! This was the utmost extent of the facts alleged in support of the defence of insanity. The prisoner's whole life had been traced, by evidence, while he was at school, and in three distinct services; and he had never been confined, or in any way treated as mad. His sister spoke to his going out on the day of the outrage, and detailed a conversation evincing no symptoms of wandering. He used to have books from the library—*The Black Pirate*, *Oliver Twist*, and *Jack Sheppard*. On leaving home that day, about three o'clock in the afternoon, he told his sister that he was going to the Shooting Gallery, to buy some linen for her to make him some shirts, and to bring home some tea from a particular shop in the Strand. A nursery-maid, to whom he had written a ludicrously-addressed letter a few weeks before, said, "I considered him in a sound state of mind, but sometimes very eccentric:" than which, no words were fitter to characterise the true scope and tendency of all the evidence which had been offered to prove him insane. Of that evidence, according to the genius and spirit, and also the letter of English law, twelve intelligent jurymen were the proper judges, under judicial guidance; and greatly to be deprecated is any attempt to deprive them of their right, and their fellow-subjects, the public at large, of the protection afforded by its unfettered exercise.

We therefore earnestly beg the reader to assume that he

is given credit for an average degree of intelligence, and only a moderate amount of moral firmness—to imagine himself a juryman, charged with the solution of this critical problem. We ask—On the facts now laid before you, do you believe Oxford to have been no more conscious of, or accountable for, his actions, in twice deliberately firing at the Queen, than would have been a baby accidentally pulling the trigger of a loaded pistol, and shooting its fond incautious mother or affectionate attendant?

If Oxford, instead of shooting at the Queen, had shot himself that afternoon: would you, being sworn "to give a just and true verdict *according to the evidence*," have pronounced him insane—totally unconscious and irresponsible? Would you have declared him such, if required to say *aye* or *no* to that question on a commission of lunacy? Would you have declared his marriage, on that afternoon, null and void, on the ground of his insanity? Would you have declared his will void? or any contract, great or small, into which he had entered? Would you have declared his vote, in a municipal or parliamentary election, invalid? If he had committed some act of petty pilfering or cheating, would you have deliberately absolved him from guilt on the ground of insanity? Would you, in each and every one of these cases, have declared, upon your oath, that you believed Oxford was "*labouring under such a defect of reason, from disease of the mind, as not to know the nature and quality of the act he was doing,—or, if he did know it, that he did not know he was doing wrong?*"* We entreat you to forget altogether the enormity of the offence imputed to Oxford—an attempt to take the life of his Queen: dismiss it, and all consideration of consequences, as a disturbing force, and address your reason exclusively to the question last proposed. What would be your sworn answer? We beg you also to bear in mind from whom has proceeded the chief evidence in support of the defence of insanity—a mother, seeking to rescue her son from the

* Opinions of the Judges, *ante*, p. 118.

fearful death of a traitor; and that the attempt to impugn his mental sanity is not made till after such a terrible occasion has arisen for doing so. Had it been their interest to establish *his sanity*, in order to uphold a will of his bequeathing them a large sum of money, who sees not how all their evidences of insanity would have melted into thin air, and the attempt to magnify and distort petty eccentricities into such, have been branded as cruel, unjust, and disgraceful?

But there came five doctors on the scene, and at their approach the light of reason was darkened. These astute personages, mysterious in their means of knowledge, and confident in their powers of extinguishing the common sense of both judges and jury, came to demonstrate that the unfortunate young gentleman at the bar was no more the object of punishment than the unconscious baby aforesaid; no more aware of the nature and consequences of the act which he had done than is the torch with which a haystack is fired, or the bullet, cannon-ball, or dagger with which life is taken away! But let them speak for themselves—these wise men of Gotham—these confident disciples of the "*couldn't help it*" school!

FIRST DOCTOR.—*Question* by the prisoner's counsel and the Court—"Supposing a person, in the middle of the day, without any suggested motive, to fire a loaded pistol at her Majesty, passing along the road in a carriage; to remain on the spot; to declare he was the person who did it; to take pains to have that known; and afterwards to enter freely into discussion, and answer any questions put to him on the subject: would you, from those facts alone, judge a person to be insane?"

*Answer.*—"I should."

*The Court.*—"You mean to say, upon your oath, that if you heard these facts stated, you should conclude that the person would be mad?"

*The Doctor.*—"I do."

*The Court.*—"Without making any other inquiry?"

*The Doctor.*—"Yes! * * * If, as a physician, I was employed to ascertain whether a person in whom I found these facts was sane or insane, I should undoubtedly give my opinion that he was insane."

*The Court.*—"As a physician, you think every crime, plainly committed, to be committed by a madman?"

*The Doctor.*—"Nothing of the kind; but a crime committed under all the circumstances of the hypothesis!"

As to the hypothesis proposed, the reader will not have failed to observe how inapplicable it was to the proved facts. Oxford certainly "remained on the spot," because he could not possibly have got away; there being a high wall on one side, high park railings on the other, and an infuriate crowd, as well as the Queen's attendants, on all sides. He also certainly "declared he was the person who did it;" but how absurd to deny what so many had witnessed?

SECOND DOCTOR.—He is asked the same question which had been proposed to the first Doctor, with the addition of "hereditary insanity being in the family" of the person concerned.

*Answer.*—"I should consider these circumstances of strong suspicion; but other facts should be sought before one could be warranted in giving a positive opinion."

*Question* by the Prisoner's Counsel.—"Are there instances on record of persons becoming suddenly insane, whose conduct has been previously only eccentric?"

*Answer.*—"Certainly. Supposing, in addition, that there was previous delusion, my opinion would be that he is unsound. Such a form of insanity exists, and is recognised."

*Question* by the Counsel for the Crown.—"What form of insanity do you call it?"

*Answer.*—"Lesion of the will—insanity connected with the development of the will. It means more than a loss of control over the conduct—morbid propensity. Moral irregularity is the result of that disease. Committing a crime without any *apparent* motive is an indication of insanity." * * *

*Question* by the Court.—"Do you conceive that this is really a *medical* question at all, which has been put to you?"

*Answer.*—"I do: I think medical men have more means of forming an opinion on that subject than other persons."

*Question.*—"Why could not *any* person form an opinion, from the circumstances which have been referred to, whether a person was sane or insane?"

*Answer.*—"Because it seems to require a careful comparison of particular cases, more likely to be looked to by medical men, who are especially experienced in cases of unsoundness of mind."

THIRD DOCTOR.—"I have 850 patients under my care in a lunatic asylum. I have seen and conversed with the prisoner. In my opinion he is of unsound mind. I never saw him in private more than once, and that for perhaps half an hour, the day before yesterday; and I have been in court the whole of yesterday and this morning. These are the notes of my interview with him:—'A deficient understanding; shape of the anterior part of the head, that which is generally seen when there has been some disease of the brain in early life. An occasional appearance of acuteness, but a total inability to reason. Singular insensibility as regards the affections. Apparent incapacity to comprehend moral obligations—to distinguish right from wrong. Absolute insensibility to the heinousness of his offence, and the peril of his situation. Total indifference to the issue of the trial; acquittal will give him no particular pleasure, and he seems unable to comprehend the alternative of his condemnation and execution: his offence, like that of other imbeciles who set fire to buildings, &c., without motive, except a vague pleasure in mischief. Appears unable to conceive anything of future responsibility.'"

*Question* by the Court.—"Did you try to ascertain *whether he was acting a part* with you, or not?"

*Answer.*—"I tried to ascertain it as well as I possibly could. My judgment is formed on all the circumstances together."

FOURTH DOCTOR.—To the same general question put to first and second Doctors.

*Answer.*—"An exceedingly strong indication of unsoundness of mind. A propensity to commit acts without an apparent or adequate motive, under such circumstances, is recognised as a particular species of insanity, called *lesion* of the will: it has been called moral insanity."

*Question.*—"From the conversation you have had with the prisoner, and your opportunity of observing him, what do you think of his state of mind?"

*Answer.*—"Essentially unsound: there seems a mixture of insanity with imbecility. Laughing and crying are proofs of imbecility—assisting me to form my opinion. * * * When I saw him, I could not persuade him that there had been balls in the pistols—he insisted that there were none. He was indifferent about his mother when her name was mentioned. His manner was very peculiar: entirely without acute feeling or acute consciousness—lively, brisk, smart—perfectly natural—not as if he were acting, or making the least pretence. The interview lasted about three quarters of an hour."

LAST DOCTOR.—"A practising surgeon for between three and four years. Had attended the prisoner's family."

*Question.*—"What is your opinion as to his state of mind?"

*Answer.*—"Decidedly that of imbecility—more imbecility than anything: he is decidedly, in my judgment, of unsound mind. His mother has often told me there was something exceedingly peculiar about him, and asked me what I thought. The chief thing that struck me was his involuntary laughing: he did not seem to have that sufficient control over the emotions which we find in sane individuals. In Newgate, he had great insensibility to all impressions sought to be made on him. His mother once rebuked him for some want of civility to me; on which he jumped up in a fury, at the moment alarming me, and saying 'he would stick her.' I think that was his expression."

Questioned by the Counsel for the Crown.—"I never prescribed for the prisoner, nor recommended any course of treatment, conduct, or diet whatever. I never gave, nor was asked for any advice. I concluded the disease was mental—one of those weak minds which, under little excitement, might become overthrown."

With every due consideration for these five gentlemen, as expressing themselves with undoubted sincerity and conscientiousness; with the highest respect for the medical profession, and a profound sense of the perplexities which its honourable and able members have to encounter in steering their course, when called upon to act in cases of alleged insanity—encountering often equally undeserved censure and peril, for interfering, and for not interfering!—we beg to enter our stern and solemn protest on behalf of the public, and the administration of justice, against such "*evidence* of insanity" as we have just presented to the reader. It may really be stigmatised as "The safe committal of crime, made easy to the plainest capacity." It proceeds upon paradoxes subversive of society. Moral insanity? Absurd misnomer! Call it rather "*im*moral insanity," and punish it accordingly. Is it not fearful to see well-educated men of intellect take so perverted a view of the conditions of human society—of the duties and responsibilities of its members? Absence of assignable motive an evidence of such insanity as should exempt from responsibility! Inability to resist or control a motive to commit murder a safe ground for immunity from criminal responsibility!—that "criminal responsibility which," as the present Lord Chancellor,* in replying for the Crown in Oxford's case, justly remarked, "secures the very existence of society."

Let us look at another aspect of the medical evidence given on this memorable occasion. Doctor the *first* pronounced his authoritative decision solely on the evidence given in court: influenced, it may be, by his having, many years before, been called in to attend the prisoner's father when labouring under symptoms of poisoning by laudanum. Doctor the *second* gave merely speculative evidence, without, as it would seem, having even previously seen the prisoner, and founded solely on what had passed at the trial. Doctor the *third* never saw the prisoner before the trial but once, and then for "*perhaps half an hour*," on the first day of the trial, or the day before it! How potent that half-hour's observation! Doctor the *fourth* saw the prisoner with doctor the third, for "*perhaps three-quarters of an hour!*" Doctor the *fifth* was a practising surgeon of not four years' standing—owning how "short a time he had been in practice." Let us only surrender our understandings to this queer quinary, and we arrive at a short and easy solution: very comfortable, indeed, for the young gentleman at the bar, who is doubtless filled with wonder at finding how sagaciously they saw into the thoughts which had been passing through his mind—the precise state of his feelings, views, objects, and intentions, when he fired at the Queen. But in the mean time we ask, can it be tolerated that medical gentlemen should thus usurp the province of both judge and jury? We answer, no! and shall place here on record the just and indignant rebuke of Mr Baron Alderson to a well-known medical gentleman, who had thus autho-

* Afterwards Lord Truro.

ritatively announced his conclusion on the recent trial of Robert Pate.

Dr ———.—"From all I have heard to-day, and from my personal observation, I am satisfied the prisoner is of unsound mind."

*Baron Alderson.*—" Be so good, Dr ———, as not to take upon yourself the functions of both the judge and the jury. If you can give us the results of your scientific knowledge in this point, we shall be glad to hear you; but while I am sitting on this bench, *I will not permit any medical witness to usurp the functions of both the judge and the jury.*"

It has already been stated that it fell to the lot of Sir Thomas Wilde to reply for the Crown, in Oxford's case, as in that of Frost; and he discharged the responsible duty with his usual clearness and cogency. As to the facts, irrespective of the question of insanity, a single sentence disposed of them.

"What would be the condition of society—exposed as we all are to such attacks, and the infliction of death by such means—if, with the evidence of previous preparation of the means; the use of balls and pistols; inquiries as to the effect of their discharge, and whether the party was hurt, coupled with admission, incidental and direct, of the fact that balls were in the pistols: what would be the state of society, if evidence like this left an assassin the chance of escape merely because the balls could not be found?"

And, with this terse summary of the proved facts before our eyes, we ask a question of our own: What overwhelming evidence of insanity would not an intelligent and honest juryman require, to refer such a case to the category of criminal irresponsibility?

Sir Thomas Wilde vigorously and contemptuously crushed under foot the mischievous sophistries of the medical evidence.

"If eccentric acts were proof of insanity, many persons who were wrenching knockers off doors, knocking down watchmen, and committing similar freaks, *were laying up a large stock of excuses for the commission of crimes!*"

"The trick of laughing suddenly, without cause, was so common, that if this were token of imbecility, the lunatic asylum would overflow with gigglers"

"The prisoner had all along displayed a morbid desire to be talked about; and the letters and documents produced had been written with that feeling and object. A criminal should not be permitted to write out for himself a certificate of lunacy!"

"Was his making no attempt to escape, a proof of an unsound mind? If he *had* made such an attempt, it would have been a great proof of madness! He was surrounded on all sides by the multitude. He took such a reasonable view of his situation, as to see that he had no chance of escape, and gave himself up quietly!"

"The prisoner had been allowed the unrestrained use of firearms and powder, and was well acquainted with their fatal effects on human life. Would his mother have *trusted a madman with them?* and left her mad son in the same house with her daughter?"

"The medical men went to Newgate *pre-disposed and pre-determined to see a madman.*"

"Suppose the prisoner unfeeling, violent, indifferent to his own fate, and preferring notoriety to any other consideration: what evidence did that supply of his being in a state of moral irresponsibility—that moral irresponsibility which secured the very existence of society?"

All this surely sounds like an irresistible appeal to good sense.

Lord Denman directed the jury with corresponding clearness and decision, and also in full conformity with the views of the Solicitor-General, and with the subsequent annunciation of the law by the Judges.*

"If you think the prisoner was, *at the time*, labouring under any delusion which prevented him from judging of the effects of the act he had committed, you cannot find him guilty. He might, perhaps, have been labouring under a delusion affecting *every* part of his conduct, and not directed to one object alone: if that were so at the time of his firing, he could not be held accountable for it. But if, though labouring under a delusion, he fired the loaded pistols at the Queen, knowing the possible result—though forced to the act by his morbid love of notoriety—he is responsible, and liable to punishment."

"There may be cases of insanity, in which medical evidence as to *physical* symptoms is of the utmost consequence. But as to *moral insanity*, I, for my own part, cannot admit that medical men have at all more means of forming an opinion, in such a case, than

* *Ante*, p. 118.

are possessed by gentlemen accustomed to the affairs of life, and bringing to the subject a wide experience."

"The mere fact of the prisoner's going into the park, and raising his hand against the Queen, is not to be taken as a proof of insanity—particularly if we suppose that he is naturally reckless of consequences. It is a mark, doubtless, of a mind devoid of right judgment and of right feeling; but it would be a most dangerous maxim, that the mere enormity of a crime should secure the prisoner's acquittal, by being taken to establish his *insanity.* Acts of wanton and dangerous mischief are often committed by persons who *suppose* that they have an adequate motive; but they are sometimes done by those who have *no* adequate motive, and on whom they can confer no advantage. A man may be charged with slaying his father, his child, or his innocent wife, to whom he is bound to afford protection and kindness; and it is most extravagant to say that this man cannot be found guilty, because of the enormity of his crime!"

The jury, thus charged with the principles of a humane and sound jurisprudence, retired, and after three-quarters of an hour's absence returned with this special verdict:—"We find the prisoner, Edward Oxford, guilty of discharging the contents of two pistols; but whether or not they were loaded with ball, has not been satisfactorily proved to us—*he being of unsound mind at the time.*" In other words, "We find that he did not fire a pistol loaded with ball, because he was not of sound mind!" They were sent back, with a mild intimation that this was nonsense; that they had not sufficiently applied their minds to the true question—viz., Did the prisoner, aye or no, fire a pistol *loaded with ball* at the Queen? The foreman, "We cannot decide the point, because there is no satisfactory evidence produced before us, to show that the pistols were loaded with bullets." They retired, to return with a verdict of "'Guilty,' or 'Not Guilty,' on the evidence." After an hour's absence, they finally brought back their verdict, "Guilty, he being at the time insane!"

*Lord Denman.*—"Do you acquit the prisoner, on the ground of insanity?"

*Foreman of the Jury.*—"Yes, my lord; that is our intention."

*Lord Denman.*—"Then the verdict will stand thus: 'Not guilty, on the ground of insanity.' The prisoner will be confined in strict custody, as a matter of course."

"The prisoner," says Mr Townsend,* "walked briskly from the bar, apparently glad that the tedious trial was over."

Upon the whole matter we are of opinion,—*First*, That there was satisfactory evidence that the pistols were loaded with ball, and that the jury ought to have found their verdict accordingly. *Secondly*, If they remained of opinion, to the last, that there was no satisfactory evidence on this point, they ought unquestionably to have pronounced the prisoner Not Guilty, independently of any question as to the prisoner's state of mind. In Scotland, the jury would, in such a case, have returned a verdict of *Not Proven;* but in England, deficient evidence—*i. e.*, such as leaves the jury finally in doubt—is regarded as leaving the charge unproved, and requiring the verdict of Not Guilty. *Thirdly*, The defence of insanity utterly failed, and the evidence offered in support of it was scarcely worthy of serious consideration. *Lastly*, It is possible that the verdict was given, though by men anxiously desirous of acting with mingled mercy and justice, under a condition of mental irresolution and confusion, and with a deficiency of moral courage. The jury either shrank from the fearful consequences of a verdict of Guilty, on a charge of high treason, and yet feared to let the prisoner loose again upon society; or there was a compromise between those who believed that there *was*, and there was *not*, sufficient evidence of the pistols having contained bullets; and also between those who were similarly divided on the subject of the prisoner's sanity. Thus stood, thus stands, the case; and Oxford has ever since been an inmate of Bedlam: though Mr Taylor, to whose work on *Medical Jurisprudence* we have already referred, and who is a decided and able supporter of that theory of "moral insanity" to which we, in common with all the Judges, are so strongly op-

* Townsend, vol. i. p. 150.

posed, admits expressly that, with the exception of M'Naughten's case, "there is perhaps none on record, in English jurisprudence, where the facts in support of the plea of insanity were so slight as in that of Oxford."*

---

### M'NAUGHTEN'S CASE.

The case of Daniel M'Naughten, which was tried at the Old Bailey about two years and a half after that of Oxford, viz., on the 3d and 4th March 1843, cannot be approached without a shudder, as one recalls the direful deed for which he was brought to trial—the assassination of Mr Drummond, whom the murderer had mistaken for the late Sir Robert Peel! To a candid philosophical jurist, this case is one of profound interest, and of considerable difficulty. The abrupt interposition of the presiding Judge, the late Chief Justice Tindal,—a step unusual on such an occasion, and especially so in the case of that signally patient and cautious Judge,—occasioned much remark at the time; and a general, if not almost universal expression of regret, that he had not allowed a case of such magnitude to run on to the end, and so have afforded the jury the vast advantage of hearing that consummate reasoner and lawyer Sir William Follett's commentary upon the case, set up in behalf of the prisoner. The unexpected issue of this dreadful case led, as has been already explained, to Parliamentary discussion, and a solemn declaration by the assembled Judges of England of the true principles applicable to such cases. We shall not examine the proceedings as minutely as in the case of Oxford; but endeavour to enable the thoughtful reader to apply to the leading facts the rules of law laid down by the Judges for the conduct of these critical investigations. He can then form an opinion as to what might have been the result, if those

* *Medical Jurisprudence*, p. 801.

principles had been strictly adhered to, and the case had gone on to its legitimate conclusion. It will be borne in mind that, as stated at the close of our account of Oxford's case, even Mr Taylor treats the case of M'Naughten as an acquittal proceeding on facts, alleged in support of the defence of insanity, "as slight as those in Oxford's case!"

Mr Drummond, the private secretary of the late Sir Robert Peel, then prime-minister, was returning alone to his residence in Downing Street, having just quitted Drummond's banking-house at Charing Cross, in the afternoon of Friday the 20th January 1843, when a man, Daniel M'Naughten, came close behind him, and deliberately shot him in the back with a pistol which he had been seen to take from his left breast. While Mr Drummond staggered away, and the man who had shot him was seen quickly, but deliberately, taking another pistol from his right breast with his left hand, cocking it, and then transferring it to his right hand, he was tripped up by a police officer; and a desperate struggle occurred on the ground, during which the pistol went off, providentially without injuring any one. M'Naughten strove to use his right arm against the officer, but was overpowered, the pistols taken from him, and he was led to the station-house. As he went, he said "*He*" [or "she" —the witness was uncertain which word was used] *shall not break my peace of mind any longer.*" On being searched, a banker's receipt for £745, two five-pound notes, four soverigns, and ten copper percussion caps fitting the nipples of the pistols which he had discharged, were found on his person; while bullets exactly fitting the barrels were discovered at his lodgings. The unfortunate gentleman who had been thus assassinated, died, after great suffering, on the 25th January. He had borne a strong personal resemblance to the late Sir Robert Peel; and it was beyond all doubt that it had been Sir Robert Peel whom M'Naughten thought he had shot, and had intended to shoot. On the ensuing morning, when asked if he knew whom he had shot, he replied, "It is Sir Robert Peel, is it not?" and on being reminded that what he said might be given in evidence, he replied quickly, "*But you won't use this against me?*" He had shortly before said that, when brought before the magistrate, he would "give a reason, a short one," for what he had done; and also observed, that he was an object of persecution by the Tories—that they followed him from place to place with their persecution. He appeared calm; and gave a correct and connected account of his recent travelling movements. He was the natural son of a turner at Glasgow, from which, some months previously, he had come to London, and had then paid a short visit to France. Down to the moment of his committing this appalling act, he had been a man of rigorously temperate habits; and no one with whom he lodged or associated, entertained the slightest suspicion that his reason was in any way affected: though he appeared peculiarly reserved, and even sullen, which his landlady had attributed to his being out of a situation and poor; for, though punctual in his small payments, he was frugal even to parsimony. She had no idea that he possessed so large a sum as £750. During the previous fortnight, he had been observed loitering so suspiciously in the neighbourhood of Sir Robert Peel's private and official residences, as to challenge inquiry, which he parried by casual observations. In the month of November previously, he had remarked to a companion, on being shown Sir Robert Peel's house in Whitehall, "D——n him! Sink him!" or words to that effect. His other remarks were perfectly rational, and his companion entertained no notion "that his mind was disordered." The following two documents in his handwriting, dated in the May and July preceding the murder, are very remarkable, as indicating great caution, shrewdness, and thrift on the part of the writer.

The first was addressed to the Manager of the Glasgow Bank, and is as follows :—

"GLASGOW, 23*d May* 1842.

"SIR,—I hereby intimate to you, that I will require the money, ten days from this date, which I deposited in the London Joint-Stock Bank through you. The account is for £745. The account is dated August 28th 1841, but is not numbered! As it would put me to some inconvenience to give personal intimation, and then remain in London till the eleven days' notice agreed upon has expired, I trust this will be considered sufficient.—Yours, &c.

"DANIEL M'NAUGHTEN."

Two months afterwards, viz., in July, he purchased the fatal pistols of a gunsmith near Glasgow, giving him very precise directions as to their make, and on the 19th of July replied to the following advertisement, which appeared in the *Spectator* newspaper of the 16th of July :—

"OPTIONAL PARTNERSHIP.—Any gentleman, having £1000, may invest them, on the most advantageous terms, in a very genteel business in London, attended with no risk, with the option, within a given period, of becoming a partner, and of ultimately succeeding to the whole business. In the meantime, security and liberal interest will be given for the money. Apply by letter to B. B., Mr Hilton's, bookseller, Penton Street, Pentonville."*

M'Naughten's answer, which here follows, cannot be too closely scrutinised, and its general tone and tendency too anxiously weighed, by a dispassionate judicial mind, regard being had to the evidence hereafter to be adverted to, with reference to the alleged condition of the writer's mind, long previously to, at, and after the date of the letter.

"GLASGOW, 19*th July* 1842.

"SIR,—My attention has been attracted to your advertisement in the *Spectator* newspaper, and as I am unemployed at present, and very anxious to obtain some, I have been induced to write, requesting you to state some particulars regarding the nature of the business in which you are engaged. If immediate employment can be given or otherwise, what sort of security will be given for the money, and how much interest? I may mention that I have

* Townsend, p. 337.

been engaged in business on my own account for a few years, am under thirty years of age, and of very active and sober habits.

"The capital which I possess has been acquired by the most vigilant industry, but, unfortunately, does not amount to the exact sum specified in your advertisement. If nothing less will do, I will be sorry for it, but cannot help it; if otherwise, have the goodness to write to me at your earliest convenience, and address D. M. N., 90 Clyde Street, Anderton's front land, top flat." *

He went to London during the same month; appears to have gone for about a fortnight to France, returning to Glasgow; went a second time to London in September, and resided there, in the lodgings which he had formerly occupied, down to the day on which he shot Mr Drummond. His landlady accurately described his habits, and stated that "she never thought him unsettled in his mind;" and, on the very morning of the fatal day, "did not observe anything about his manner." Such was the tenor of all the evidence offered for the prosecution—some of it stretching back to the years 1840, 1841, when he attended anatomical lectures in Glasgow. A Writer to the Signet, who also attended them, and the physician who lectured, expressly declared that they had never seen anything in him to indicate "disordered mind," or that "he was not in his right senses."

The following was the statement which he made and signed, when examined on the charge at Bow Street. This document, like the preceding, is worthy of great consideration:—

"The Tories in my native city have compelled me to do this. They follow and persecute me wherever I go, and have entirely destroyed my peace of mind. They followed me into France, into Scotland, and all over England: in fact, they follow me wherever I go. I cannot get no rest for them night or day. I cannot sleep at night, in consequence of the course they pursue towards me. I believe they have driven me into a consumption. I am sure I shall never be the man I formerly was. I used to have good health and strength, but I have not now. They have accused me of crimes of which I am not guilty; they do everything in their power to harass

* Townsend, vol. i. p. 338.

and persecute me; in fact, they wish to murder me. It can be proved by evidence. That 's all I have to say."*

On Thursday the 2d February, that is to say, exactly a fortnight after the murder, M'Naughten was arraigned at the Old Bailey. When called upon, in the usual manner, to say whether he was Guilty or Not Guilty, he remained silent, with his eyes directed steadily towards the bench. At length, on being authoritatively required to answer, he said, after some hesitation, "I was driven to desperation by persecution." On being told that he must answer, "Guilty," or "Not Guilty," he replied that he was guilty *of firing*. On this Lord Abinger interposed, "By that, do you mean to say you are not guilty of the remainder of the charge—that is, of *intending to murder Mr Drummond?*" The prisoner *at once* said, "Yes;" on which Lord Abinger ordered a plea of Not Guilty to be recorded. It appears to us that there is great significance in what passed on this occasion.

An application was then made to postpone the trial, on affidavits stating that, by the next session, material evidence could be adduced to show the insanity of the prisoner when he shot Mr Drummond. The Attorney-General, Sir Frederick Pollock, at once humanely assented to the application, and it was granted; as also ample funds, out of the £764 found on the prisoner, to prepare effectively for the defence. Let us here pause for a moment, to contrast the treatment which M'Naughten—whose undisputed act had filled the whole country with horror and indignation—received on this occasion, with that experienced by his predecessor Bellingham, thirty years before, whose case closely resembled that of M'Naughten in some fearful points. We can with difficulty record calmly that Bellingham's counsel, fortified by strong affidavits of the prisoner's insanity, and that witnesses knowing the fact could be brought from Liverpool and elsewhere, applied in vain for a postponement of the trial; the Attorney-

* Townsend, vol. i. p. 345.

General of that day barbarously, and even offensively, opposing the application, which was consequently at once overruled. Within seven days' time, Bellingham shot Mr Percival, was committed, *tried*—if it be not a mockery to use the word—convicted, and executed. On Monday, the 11th May 1811, Bellingham shot his unfortunate victim, and on that day week, Monday, the 18th May 1811, the assassin's dead body lay on the dissecting table! This vindictive precipitancy affords an awful contrast to the humane temper in which M'Naughten's application was entertained by the Attorney-General, the Judge, and the justly-excited country at large. It supplied the eloquent advocate, the present Solicitor-General,* Sir Alexander Cockburn, who was subsequently retained by the prisoner, with a potent weapon of defence, of which he failed not to make effective use. It is not too much to say, that all who can concur in the acquittal of M'Naughten, must regard Bellingham as judicially murdered. We concur heartily with M'Naughten's advocate in the remark, that "few will read the report of Bellingham's trial without being forced to the conclusion that he was either really mad, or, at the very least, the little evidence which alone he was permitted to adduce, relative to the state of his mind, was strong enough to have entitled him to a *deliberate and thorough investigation of his case.*"†

On Friday, March 3d, M'Naughten took his trial before the late Chief Justice Tindal, the late Mr Justice Williams, and Mr Justice Coleridge. The prosecution was conducted by the late Sir William Follett, then Solicitor-

* Now [1854] Attorney-General.

† We have heard high authorities strongly disapprove of the conviction and execution of Bellingham; and it certainly appears impossible to reconcile with true principles of jurisprudence, the different fates awarded to Bellingham and M'Naughten, supposing the facts to be, as alleged, in each case. A military officer, present at the execution of Bellingham, and very near the scaffold, told us that he distinctly recollects Bellingham, while standing on the scaffold, elevating one of his hands, as if to ascertain whether it were raining; and he observed to the chaplain, in a calm and natural tone and manner, *"I think we shall have rain to-day!"*

General, and the prisoner defended by the present Solicitor-General, then Mr Cockburn, Q.C. Nothing could exceed the temperate and luminous opening statement of Sir William Follett, who, in our judgment, laid down the rules of English law, applicable to the difficult and delicate subject with which he had to deal, with rigorous propriety.

"If you believe," said he, "that the prisoner at the bar, at the time he committed this act, was not a responsible agent—that, when he fired the pistol, he was incapable of distinguishing between right and wrong—that he was under the influence and control of some disease of the mind which prevented him from being conscious that he was committing a crime—that he did not know he was violating the law both of God and man—then undoubtedly he is entitled to your acquittal. But it is my duty to tell you that nothing short of *that* will excuse him, upon the principles of the English law. To excuse him, it will not be sufficient that he laboured under partial insanity upon some subjects—that he had a morbid delusion of mind upon some subjects, which could not exist in a wholly sane person; that is not enough, *if* he had that degree of intellect which enabled him to know and distinguish between right and wrong—if he knew what would be the effects of his crime, and consciously committed it; and if, with that consciousness, he *wilfully* committed it."

The witnesses for the prosecution established a case, if unanswered, of perfect guilt; the facts of the assassination were indisputable, and the evidence of the prisoner's sanity cogent in the extreme. Mr Cockburn addressed the jury at very great length, and in a strain of sustained eloquence and power, his object being to persuade the jury "that the prisoner was labouring, at the time of committing the act, under a morbid [?] insanity, which took away from him all power of self-control, so that he was not responsible for his acts. I do not put this case forward as one of total insanity; it is a case of delusion, and I say so from sources upon which the light of science has thrown her holy beam." Those who have read what has gone before, concerning Oxford's case, will appreciate this observation of Mr Cockburn, and gather from it his adoption, for the purpose of that defence, of the theory of moral insanity, which he enforced and illustrated by many striking and brilliant observations, calculated to produce a strong impression on the minds of the jury; such as required the utmost exertions of Sir William Follett in reply, and finally of judicial exposition to efface, if fallacious—or modify to any extent rendered necessary by inaccuracy or exaggeration. Ten witnesses, all of them from Glasgow, were called, for the purpose of establishing the fact that the prisoner had, for some eighteen months previously to January 1843, appeared to labour, and had continually represented himself as labouring, under a persuasion that he was the victim of some such indefinite, mysterious, and incessant persecution as he spoke of in his statement before the magistrate at Bow Street.

We are bound to say that the force of this testimony, coming chiefly from persons above all suspicion, and in a superior rank of life, is irresistible as to the existence of such an insane delusion, down to the time of his quitting Glasgow. Not a witness, however, gave evidence of his exhibiting that tendency after his last return to London, before his shooting Mr Drummond. The only mention of Sir Robert Peel's name, was by one of these ten witnesses, a former fellow-lodger of the prisoner's; who told him, in July 1842, that he had heard Sir Robert Peel speak in the House of Commons; preferred his speaking to that of Lord John Russell and Mr O'Connell; and said "he thought Sir R. Peel had arrived at what Lord Byron said of him—that 'he would be something great in the state.'" Mr Cockburn asked the witness, "Did you ever, on that or any other occasion, hear him speak at all disrespectfully of Sir Robert Peel?" *Answer.*—"Certainly not." One or two witnesses spoke to singularities of demeanour as early as the years 1835 and 1836. One of his landlords, in the former year, got rid of him as a lodger, "for one reason, in consequence of the infidel doctrines he maintained, and the books of such a character which he was in the habit of reading." A witness, who had succeeded him in his business, remonstrated with him, towards the end of 1842, about his notions as to being persecuted, telling him it was all imagination — that there were no such people as he supposed. He said that, "if he could once set his eyes on them, they should not be long in the land of the living," and became shortly afterwards very much excited. Sometimes he said he was "haunted by a parcel of devils following him." His landlady seeing the brace of pistols which he had in September, just before his return to London, said — "What, in the name of God, are you doing with pistols there? He said 'he was going to shoot birds with them.' I never saw the pistols after that." He told the Commission of Police that the "persecution proceeded from the priests of the Catholic chapel in Clyde Street, who were assisted by a parcel of Jesuits." In August 1842, he told the same witness that "the police, the Jesuits, the Catholic priests, and Tories, were all leagued against him."

Mr Cockburn having thus "laid a broad foundation," says Mr Townsend, "for medical theories, *upon them* was built by the nine physicians and surgeons, who confirmed each other's theories, a goodly superstructure of undoubted insanity. Had the workings," continues Mr Townsend, sarcastically, "of the troubled brain been as distinctly visible to the eye, as the labours of bees seen through a glass hive, they could not have held the fact to be more demonstratively proved. Positive beyond the possibility of mistake, and infallible as theologians, they explained all that might appear without the aid of science inexplicable; and proved, as if they were stating undoubted facts, an irresponsible delusion."

One of the physicians attested his conviction, from an interview with the prisoner shortly before his trial, "as a matter of certainty, that M'Naughten was not responsible for his acts?" Well may Mr Townsend add, "By an excess of lenity, the counsel for the prosecution allowed these scientific witnesses to depart from the ordinary rules of evidence, *to give their own* conclusions from the facts proved, and usurp the province of the jury." * After going through the evidence (if the word can be used with propriety under such circumstances) of the other medical gentlemen, Mr Townsend observes, "Each physician and surgeon, as he stepped into the witness-box, seemed anxious to surpass his predecessor in the tone of decision and certainty; each tried to draw the bow of —— (mentioning the first physician who had been called, and who had also been called in Oxford's and Pate's case, in which latter he was rebuked by Baron Alderson, †) and shoot, if possible, still further into empty space." And this gentleman, Dr ——, had asserted, under cross-examination by Sir William Follett, "his positive conviction that he could ascertain the nicest shade of insanity! that the shadowy trace of eccentricity, dissolving into madness, could be palpably distinguished!" ‡ The last of these confident personages was permitted to make this extraordinary statement: "I have not the slightest hesitation in saying that the prisoner is insane, and that he committed the offence in question whilst afflicted with a delusion under which he appears to have been labouring for a considerable length of time!!!"

We feel constrained to say that this appears to us, in every way, monstrous.

"Nine medical witnesses," significantly observes Mr Townsend, "had now spoken, with a wonderful unanimity of opinion, *and the court surrendered at discretion.*" §

If such a course is to be allowed again in a court of justice, what security have any of us for life, liberty, or property?

Chief Justice Tindal here interposed, to ask Sir William

* Townsend, vol, i. p. 398. † *Ante*, p. 139.
‡ Townsend, vol. i. p. 396. § Ibid. p. 400.

Follett whether he was prepared with evidence on the part of the Crown to combat that of the medical witnesses,—

"Because, if you have not," said the Chief Justice, "we think we are under the necessity of stopping the case. Is there any medical evidence on the other side?"

*Sir William Follett.*—"No, my lord."*

*Chief Justice Tindal.*—"We feel the evidence, especially that of the last two medical gentlemen who have been examined, and who are strangers to both sides, and only observers of the case, to be very strong, and sufficient to induce my learned brothers and myself to stop the case."†

After this authoritative intimation from the court, in a capital case, in favour of the prisoner, it would have been obviously to the last degree inexpedient for the Solicitor-General, in his position of peculiar and great public responsibility, to "press for a verdict against the prisoner." ‡ Saying distinctly, and therefore telling the jury, that, "after the intimation he had received from the Bench, he felt that he should not be properly discharging his duty to the Crown and the public, if he asked them for a verdict against the prisoner," he withdrew, in deference to "the very strong opinion entertained by the Lord Chief Justice, and the other learned Judges present," that the evidence, especially the medical evidence, sufficed to show that the prisoner, when he shot Mr Drummond, was labouring under insanity. "*If* he were so," added Sir William Follett, with a pointed reservation of his own opinion, "he would be entitled to his acquittal." He intimated, however, distinctly, that he adhered to "the doctrines and authorities" on which he had relied in opening the case, "as being correct law; our object being

* It is said that the two physicians selected by Government to examine the prisoner, in company with those who did so on behalf of the defence, did not differ from them in opinion; and Mr Cockburn taunted Sir William Follett with not having called them, though they sat beside him in court. By that time Sir William Follett might have seen, during the progress of the trial, sufficient to make him distrust medical evidence altogether, come from whom it might.—Townsend, vol. i. p. 378.

† Ibid. p. 400. ‡ Ibid.

to ascertain whether the prisoner, at the time when he committed the crime, was—*at that time*—to be regarded as a responsible agent, or whether all control over himself was taken away. The learned Judge, I understand, means to submit that question to you. I cannot press for a verdict against the prisoner, and it will be for you to come to your decision."

The Chief Justice then briefly addressed the jury, offering to go through the whole evidence, if the jury deemed it necessary, which *he* "thought to be almost unnecessary;" adding—

"I am in your hands; but if, in balancing the evidence in your minds, you think that the prisoner was, at the time of committing the act, capable of distinguishing between right and wrong, then he was a responsible agent, and liable to all the penalties which the law enforces. If not so—and if, in your judgment, the subject should appear involved in very great difficulty—then you will probably not take upon yourselves to find the prisoner guilty. If that is your opinion, then you will acquit the prisoner. If you think you ought to hear the evidence more fully, in that case I will state it to you, and leave the case in your hands. Probably, however, sufficient has now been laid before you, and you will say whether you want any further information."

*Foreman of the Jury.*—"We require no more, my lord."

*Chief Justice Tindal.*—"If you find the prisoner not guilty, say on the ground of insanity; in which case proper care will be taken of him."

*Foreman.*—"We find the prisoner not guilty on the ground of insanity."

We repeat emphatically our deep respect for the late Chief Justice Tindal, and for his brethren who sate beside him on this momentous occasion; and we also acknowledge the weight due to the observation of Mr Townsend, that "none can form so correct an estimate of the facts proved, and their illustration by science, as those who actually saw what was going on; and the three able Judges who presided seem to have been fully impressed with the conviction that the prisoner ought not to be considered amenable to punishment for his act, being insensible, at the time he committed it, that he was violating the law of God and man."

And, again, "It is far more just and merciful to take care alike of the accused and of society, by confining in secure custody the doubtfully conscious shedder of blood, than to incur the fearful hazard of putting to death an irresponsible agent."* Nevertheless, we concur in the unanimous opinion of the five law lords, expressed in their places in Parliament—the Lord Chancellor, Lord Brougham, Lord Cottenham, Lord Denman, Lord Campbell—that it would have been better to let the trial proceed regularly to its conclusion. The whole facts of the case demanded, not less than the theories of the medical witnesses, that thorough sifting, and the application of that masterly and luminous practical logic, which both the Solicitor-General and the Chief Justice were so pre-eminently capable of bestowing. If, after such a dealing with the case, an acquittal on the ground of insanity had ensued, who could have gainsaid it? At present, see what a candid and scientific writer on medical jurisprudence, as we have several times observed, a strong favourer of the notion of moral insanity, has felt himself compelled to place permanently on record,† with reference to the acquittal of M'Naughten.

"When we find a man lurking for many days together in a particular locality, having about him loaded weapons—watching a particular individual who frequents that locality—a man who does not face the individual and shoot him, but who coolly waits until he has an opportunity of discharging the weapon unobserved by his victim or others—the circumstances appear to show such a perfect adaptation of means to ends, and such a power of controlling his actions, that one is quite at a loss to understand why a plea of irresponsibility should be admitted, except upon the fallacious ground that no motive could be discovered for the act—a ground, however, which was not allowed to prevail in the case of Courvoisier, Francis, and the perpetrators of other atrocious crimes. Observe the lively sense of his danger, and of his rights and interests, as an accused person, exhibited by M'Naughten almost im-

* Townsend, vol. i. p. 325. † Taylor's *Medical Jurisprudence*, p. 799.

mediately after committing the act—when, fearful lest an inadvertent admission should be given in evidence against him, he said to the officer* — '*But you won't use this against me?*' Note the matter-of-fact astuteness with which he attended to his pecuniary interests in May and July; the total absence of any evidence of the existence of his delusions during his last sojourn in London; the presence of such proof of careful, deliberate, and too successful perpetration, as to time, opportunity, and means; his expression in November towards Sir Robert Peel—'D——n him!' But, above all, is to be noted the time when he first gives utterance to anything directly and cogently favouring the notion on which his life depended—his insane delusion with regard to Sir Robert Peel—viz., after he had been for some time incarcerated in Newgate, and when he knew that he was being examined by a physician, in order to ascertain what had been his state of mind at the time in question! Dr Munro has there recorded it † He said—'Mr Salmond, the Procurator-Fiscal, Mr Sheriff Bell, Mr Sheriff Alison, and *Sir Robert Peel*, might have put a stop to this system of persecution if they would!' * * * 'We were afraid of going out after dark for fear of assassination: that individuals were made to appear before him like them he had seen in Glasgow.' * * * 'That he imagined the person at whom he fired at Charing Cross to be one of the crew—a part of the system that was destroying his health. He observed, that, when he saw the person at Charing Cross at whom he fired, every feeling of suffering which he had endured for months and years rose up at once in his mind, and that he conceived that he should obtain peace by killing him.'"

Surely it would have conduced, especially in the painful excitement of the public mind on the subject at the time, to the satisfactory administration of justice, if it had been allowed Sir William Follett, without his being placed in the invidious position of appearing to press unduly against a prisoner being tried for his life, to combine and contrast these various circumstances, as he, of almost all men, could have best combined and contrasted them. The jury should have had their minds solemnly and authoritatively directed to the question, for instance, whether this last observation of M'Naughten made to Dr Munro was a spontaneous, genuine indication of utterly subverted mental faculties, continuing from the moment of his shooting Mr Drummond;

* *Ante*, p. 145. † Townsend, vol. i. p. 395.

or an effort of anxious astuteness to give effect to the suggestion which he may have believed would save his life. And, moreover, this and other circumstances should have been accompanied by a direction to the jury, in accordance with that of Lord Denman in Oxford's case,* and with the following canon, subsequently laid down by the Judges in their answer to the first question proposed by the Lord Chancellor†—viz., "That notwithstanding the party did the act with a view, under insane delusion, of *redressing* or *revenging some supposed grievance or injury*, he is nevertheless punishable, if he knew at the time that he was acting contrary to the law of the land." Could M'Naughten be again tried on this charge, this is the precise question which would be left to the jury. Mr Alison, in his *Principles of the Criminal Law of Scotland*,‡ thus lays down the rule applicable to such cases, in commenting on that of Bellingham:—

> "Unquestionably, the mere fancying a series of injuries to have been received will not serve as an excuse for murder—for this plain reason, that, supposing it true that such injuries had been received, they would have furnished no excuse for the shedding of blood. On the other hand, however, such an illusion as depriving the pannel of the sense that *what he did was wrong*, amounts to legal insanity, though he was perfectly aware that murder in general was a crime."

Responsibility more awful than is devolved upon all parties to the judicial investigation of this question, can scarcely be imagined. A deliberate and thorough investigation of every, even the minutest circumstance adduced, guided steadily by correct legal principles, is demanded imperiously by justice. Difficult, almost hopeless, as may be the attempt to grope into the turbid mind of a madman, to ascertain its true condition at a given moment of time the attempt *must* be made, a decision *must* be pronounced—distinguishing between real and simulated imbecility or madness—between irresponsible insanity and responsible eccentricity. These are questions, we repeat, of infinite

* *Ante*, p. 140. † *Ante*, p. 118. ‡ P. 658.

importance, of great difficulty; and the interests of the entire community, and of individual members of it, demand a steady adherence to the principles of a humane and enlightened jurisprudence. Recent dreadful instances have served to remove several sources of dangerous error, in dealing with these cases of criminal jurisprudence. No one dare now infer madness from the mere *absence of motive*, and from the *very enormity of the act committed;* nor accord immunity to the fancied victim of "*uncontrollable impulse.*" That is, at all events, a point gained in favour of society. In England, at all events, we sternly repudiate this last sickly and spurious theory, which would place the innocent and virtuous entirely at the mercy of the most base and ruffianly impulses of our fallen nature. It would relax all the bonds of self-restraint, and afford a premium on the indulgence of ungovernable passions.

The recent lamentable case of Robert Pate affords a valuable illustration of the truth of these remarks; and Mr Baron Alderson's charge to the jury not only conduced to the firm administration of justice in the particular case, but was calculated to be of great and permanent public service, by dispelling the morbid and mischievous notions which have latterly prevailed, and exhibiting expressively the stern simplicity and common sense of English law. On the 27th June last, a gentleman, who had only recently sold his commission in the 10th Hussars, and was residing as a gentleman of fortune in London, suddenly struck her Majesty on the forehead a violent blow with a cane, which actually caused blood to flow! He could give no account of his reason for committing this execrable outrage; but the defence set up for him was, simply, uncontrollable impulse; and evidence was adduced certainly showing him to be of a very eccentric character, and actuated by strange whims and delusions. He was tried on the 12th July last at the Old Bailey, before Baron Alderson, under statute 5 and 6 Vict. c. 51, § 2.* The indictment con-

* *Ante*, p. 126.

tained three counts, charging him with striking the Queen "with an offensive weapon—that is, a stick," with intent (1st) to injure her person; (2d) to alarm her; (3d) to break the public peace. Again came the doctors—one speaking of "some strange sudden impulse, which he was quite unable to control;" and the other confidently pronouncing the prisoner to have been insane. The jury convicted the prisoner on the first and third counts, which the judge told them had been clearly made out by evidence, discarding the defence of insanity; and the following was the summing-up of Mr Baron Alderson, in strict accordance with the principles laid down in 1843 by the judges:—*

"The law throws on the prisoner the *onus* of proving that, at the time the offence was committed, he was in an unsound state of mind: and you will have to say, after hearing my explanation of the law, whether this has been made out to your satisfaction. In the first place, you must clearly understand that it is not because a man is insane that he is unpunishable: and I must say, that *upon this point there exists a very grievous delusion in the minds of medical men.* The only insanity which excuses a man for his acts is that species of delusion which conduced to, and drove him to commit, *the act alleged against him.* If, for instance, a man, being under the delusion that another man would kill him, killed that other, for, as he supposed, his own protection, he would be unpunishable for such an act; because it would appear that the act was done under the delusion that he could not protect himself in any other manner: and there the particular description of insanity conduced to the offence. But, on the other hand, if a man has a delusion that his head is made of glass, that will be no excuse for his killing a man. He would know very well that, although his head were made of glass, that was no reason why he should kill another man, and that it was a wrong act; and he would be properly subjected to punishment for that act. These are the principles which ought to govern the decision of juries in such cases. They ought to have clear proof of a formed disease of the mind—a disease existing before the act was committed, and which made the person accused incapable of knowing, at the time he did the act, that it was a wrong act for him to do. This is the rule which I shall direct you to be governed by. Try the case by this test.

* *Ante,* p. 118.

Did this unfortunate gentleman know, at the time, that it was wrong to strike the Queen on the forehead? Now, there is no doubt that he was very eccentric in his conduct; but did that eccentricity disable him from judging whether it was right or wrong to strike the Queen? Is *eccentricity* to excuse a man for any crime he may afterwards commit? The prisoner is proved to have been perfectly well aware of what he had done immediately afterwards, and in the interview which he had had since with one of the medical gentlemen, he admitted that he knew perfectly well what he had done, and ascribed his conduct to some momentary uncontrollable impulse. The law does not acknowledge such an impulse, if the person was aware that it was a wrong act he was about to commit; and he is answerable for the consequences. A man might say that he picked a pocket from some uncontrollable impulse; and, in that case, the law would have an uncontrollable impulse to punish him for it. What evidence is there, then, in this case, to justify you in coming to the conclusion, that when the prisoner struck the Queen, he did not know it was a wrong act—in fact, that what he was doing was wrong?—[Mr Baron Alderson then read over the whole of the evidence for the defence, commenting upon it as he proceeded.]—That the prisoner is an object of commiseration, is quite clear; and that he should also have been taken better care of, is equally true: but the question you have here to decide is, Are you satisfied that, at the time, he was suffering from a disease of the mind which rendered him incapable of judging whether the act he committed towards the Queen was a right or a wrong act for him to do? If you are not satisfied of this fact, you must say that he is guilty; but if you think he was not aware what he was about, or not capable of distinguishing between right and wrong, you will then say that he is not guilty, on the ground of *insanity*."

If the case of M'Naughten had been thoroughly tried out; if the medical witnesses, above all, had been checked, and restrained within their proper province, as they were by Baron Alderson; and if the summing up by the Chief Justice had been in accordance with that of Baron Alderson in Pate's case—we do not venture to say what would have been the result: but whatever it might have been, it would have satisfied the country. Whether, at the moment when M'Naughten took out his long-prepared pistol, and, after a fortnight's watching, fancied he had found Sir Robert Peel, and deliberately shot his victim in the back; whether M'Naughten was, at that awful moment, insanely ignorant of what he was doing—utterly unaware that he was doing wrong—is a question which there exist no longer any human means of determining; but it is open to us to examine the principles applicable to such an investigation in a court of criminal justice.

Upwards of seven years have elapsed since the trial of M'Naughten, more than ten years since that of Oxford; and both of them are, at the present moment, inmates of Bethlehem Hospital. Since commencing this article, we have been permitted, through the courtesy of the acute and able physician to whom the superintendence of that important institution has been for some years intrusted, to see and converse with the two persons with whose fate we have herein so anxiously concerned ourselves. Neither knew of our going; and we were accompanied by the gentleman in question.

M'NAUGHTEN was standing in the court-yard, dressed in the costume of the place, a pepper-and-salt jacket and corduroy trousers, with his hat on, knitting. He looks about forty years old, and in perfect health. His features are regular, and their expression is mild and prepossessing. His manner is tranquil. Usually he wears his hat somewhat slouched over his eyes, and sidles slowly away from any one approaching him, as if anxious to escape observation. On this occasion, however, he at once entered into conversation with our companion, calmly and cheerfully, and afforded us a full opportunity of watching him. Had we seen him casually elsewhere, and as a stranger, we should have thought his countenance indicative of a certain sort of cheerful quiet humour, especially while he was speaking; but to us it seemed certainly to exhibit a feeble intellect, shown chiefly by a faint flickering smile, even when he was speaking on the gravest subjects. When asked what had brought him where he was, he replied, drily, "*Fate.*" "And what is fate?" "The will of God

—or perhaps," he added quickly, "of the devil,—or it may be of both!" and he half-closed his eyes, and smiled. [The reader will bear in mind what was deposed at the trial, as to his infidel tendencies.*] When told by us suddenly, that Sir Robert Peel was dead, he betrayed no emotion, nor exhibited the slightest interest. "One should have thought that, considering what has happened, you would feel some interest in that gentleman." He looked rather quickly at the speaker, and said calmly, with a faint smile, "It is quite useless to talk to me on *that* subject: you know quite well I have long and long ago made up my mind never to say one word about it. I never have, and I never will; and so it would be quite childish to put any questions."† * * *

"How are you, M'Naughten?" He slightly sighed, and said, "I am very uncomfortable. I am very ill used here; there is somebody [or something] always using me ill here. It is really too bad! I have spoken about it many, many times; but it is quite useless. I wish I could get away from this place! If I could just get out of this place, and go back to Glasgow, my native place, it is all I would ask for: I should be quite well there! I shall never be well or happy *here*, for there is always some one ill-using me here."

"Well, but what do they do to you?" "Oh," shaking his head and smiling, "they are always doing it; really it is too bad." "Who are they?" "Oh, I am always being ill-used here! My only wish now is, to get away from this place! If I could only once get to Glasgow, my native place!" This is the continual burthen of his song. It is needless to say that his complaints are altogether unfounded: he is treated with the utmost kindness consistent with his situation; and, as he has never exhibited violence nor ill-behaviour, it has never been necessary to resort to personal coercion, with one exception.

* *Ante*, p. 151.

† This he has always said, and has adhered to his resolution.

Two or three years ago, he took it into his head that, as he could not get away, he would starve himself; and he persevered for such a length of time in refusing all kind of food, that he began to lose flesh fast. At length he was told by the physician that, since he would not eat voluntarily, he must be made to eat; and it was actually necessary to feed him for a considerable time mechanically, by means of the stomach pump. Under this treatment he presently regained his flesh, in spite, ludicrous as it may seem, of himself; and at length suffered himself to be laughed out of his obstinacy, and has ever since taken his food voluntarily. He seemed himself even to be tickled by a sense of the absurdity of which he was guilty. Not a doubt of his complete insanity was entertained by my acute companion, who has devoted much observation to the case. Shortly after we had quitted him, and were out of his sight, he put away his knitting, placed his hands in his jacket pockets, and walked very rapidly to and fro, his face bent on the ground; and he was apparently somewhat excited. Whatever may have been the state of M'Naughten at the time to which our inquiries have been directed in this article, we entertain little, if any doubt, that he is now in an imbecile condition.

OXFORD was in another part of the building, standing alone, at the extremity of a long corridor, gazing through a heavily-grated window, towards the new Houses of Parliament. His hat was on; he was dressed like M'Naughten, and his jacket was buttoned. We scarcely recognised him, owing to the change of his dress. He is fond of attracting the notice of anybody; and conversed about himself, and his offence, in the most calm and rational manner conceivable. He has lost much of his hair,—a circumstance which he appeared somewhat to regret, for the front of his head is bald; but he looks no older than his real age, thirty. He is mortally weary of his confinement, and says he has been terribly punished for "his foolish act."

"*Foolish!*" we exclaimed—"is *that* all you can say of your attempt to shoot her Majesty?" He smiled, and said, "Oh, sir, *I* never attempted to shoot her; I never thought of such a thing. I aimed at the carriage-panels only." "Then why did you put balls in your pistols?"

"I never did," he replied, quickly. "I never dreamed of such a thing. There were no balls."

"Oh, then you have not heard of the discovery that has just been made—eh?"

"Discovery!—what?"

"The bullets."

"Oh, there have been more found than ever *I* used, at least; for I assure you I never used any!"

"What made you do what you did?"

"Oh, I was a fool; it was just to get myself talked about, and kick up a dust. *A good horse-whipping was what I wanted*," he added, with a faint sigh. These were his very words.

"Should you have done it, if you had thought of coming *here?*"

"No, indeed I should not; it has been a dreadful punishment! * * * I dare say public opinion [his very words!] says nothing about me now; I dare say it thinks I have got what I very well deserve—and perhaps I have; but possibly if I were put quietly out of the way, and sent abroad somewhere, public opinion might take no notice of it." He has taught himself French, Italian, and German, of which he has a fair knowledge. He also used to draw a little, and began to write a novel; but it proved a sorry affair, and, being discouraged, he threw it up.

"Do you recollect," we inquired, "hearing the condemned sermon preached to Courvoisier?"

"Oh, yes, very well. It was a most excellent sermon."

"Did Courvoisier seem to attend to it?"

"Oh, yes, very much; and he seemed much affected. It was certainly an appropriate sermon; I liked it much."

"Did not you think that it might soon be your fate to sit where he was?"

"What! in the condemned seat?"

"Yes."

"Oh, no; that never occurred to me. I never expected to be condemned for high treason. Some gentleman, I forget who he was, said I should be transported for fourteen years. I thought that was the worst they could do to me; for I knew I had never meant to do any real harm, nor tried to do it."

"Yes; but the Judge and Jury thought very differently."

"Oh, I was fairly tried; but I never expected to be brought in *mad*. I was quite surprised at *that*, for I knew I was not mad, and I wondered how they were going to prove it." We asked him if he had ever seen *us;* to which he replied, gazing steadily, "Yes, I think I have—either at the Privy Council, or in Newgate Chapel."

"Where did you sit on the Sunday when the condemned sermon was preached to Courvoisier?"

"I sate on the steps near the altar."

"How were you dressed?"

"Oh, a blue surtout, with velvet collar;" and he proceeded to describe his dress almost exactly as we have described it at the commencement of the article.

He exhibits considerable cleverness: whatever he does, whether in playing at fives, or working, (*e. g.*, making gloves, &c.) he does far better than any one else, and shows considerable tact and energy in setting his companions to work, and superintending them. He admits that he committed a very great offence in having done anything to alarm the Queen, and attributes it entirely to a mischievous and foolish love of notoriety. He said, "I thought it would set everybody talking and wondering;" but "never dreamed of what would come of it—least of all that I was to be shut up all my life in *this* place." * * *

"That list of conspirators, and letters from them, that were found in your lodgings—were they not real?"

"Oh, no," he replied, with rather an anxious smile, "all mere sham—only nonsense! There was never anything of the sort!"

"Then, why did you do it?"

"It was only the folly of a boy; I wasn't nineteen then—it was very silly, no doubt."

"And their swords and dresses, and so forth—eh?"

"Entirely nonsense! It was a very absurd joke. I did not think it would come out so serious. I did not *appreciate* the consequences, or I never would have done it." The word "appreciate" he used with a very marked emphasis.

We entertain no doubt whatever of his perfect sanity; *and, if so*, as his crime was great, so his punishment is fearful.

---

NOTE APPENDED TO THE ABOVE PAPER, IN THE NUMBER OF "BLACKWOOD'S MAGAZINE" ENSUING THAT IN WHICH IT APPEARED.

A physician, in a responsible official situation, affording him great opportunities for observation, has addressed to us a note, from which we extract the following passages. Our only object is to aid in eliciting truth; and our anxiety to do so is proportionate to the difficulty and importance of the subject to which the ensuing letter has reference.

"The article on Oxford and M'Naughten has interested me very much; and though I cannot at all admit the principle of punishing a man for his misfortune, I am yet satisfied that the doctors have assumed too much, and have helped to let loose upon society some who deserved hanging as much as any who have ever suffered the extreme penalty. The test of insanity, as laid down by the Judges on the solemn occasion to which you refer, is manifestly of no value; for it is, I might almost say, *the exception* for an insane person *not* to know the difference between right and wrong. Many of them deliberately commit acts which they know to be wrong. Dadd killed his father, and immediately fled to France to avoid the consequences of his crime; and nobody ever doubted that he was one of the maddest, if not the maddest, of the mad. Touchet shot the gunmaker, not only with a full knowledge of the nature of the crime, but for the express purpose of bringing about his own death. He has entertained various delusions: amongst others, the notion that certain passages of Scripture have special reference to himself personally. And, as regards those in actual confinement on account of their mental malady, the majority know perfectly well that it is wrong to tear, break, and destroy, to injure others, and indulge their various mischievous propensities. So well satisfied are many of them that they are doing wrong, that they will try to conceal acts which they know are not permitted; and, in this way, a propensity to bite, or kick, is indulged in only when it is believed that it can be done unobserved. It seems to me that, in these most painfully embarrassing cases, every one must stand on its own particular merits; and, as neither judges nor doctors can say where sanity ends, and insanity begins, so no possible rule that can be devised will be alike applicable to all; but the previous habits and course of life of the person accused, together with the absence or presence of any motive, will go far to remove the difficulties which necessarily beset the question. I am not at all prepared to say that, because any degree of mental disturbance has been shown to exist, a person should be held *irresponsible*. It is a doctrine fraught with such dreadful danger to society, that it is very properly viewed with jealousy; but, when clearly proved that the mind was so far disturbed as to entertain delusions before and at the time of committing the offence, I would never resort to capital punishment. The Omniscient alone can tell how far the disease has gone, and to what extent the unfortunate being was really responsible for his actions to his fellow-men."

*** The author, in reprinting this Note, begs to subjoin that he adheres strongly to the opinions advocated in the preceding paper. [1854.]

# MODERN STATE TRIALS.*

## No. III.

## THE ROMANCE OF FORGERY.

A BOLD stroke for a peerage, certainly, was that of "Alexander Humpreys, *otherwise* Alexander, claiming the title of Earl of Stirling," whether the reader be disposed to accept or repudiate the verdict pronounced by an Edinburgh jury, after a week's trial before the High Court of Justiciary, in the year 1839. This gentleman stood at the bar charged with having concocted a wonderful scheme of fraud and forgery, the alleged object of which was neither more nor less than to win the title of Earl of Stirling, with great estates and territories in Scotland and British North America, and the right of creating Nova Scotia Baronets! The indictment charged him with "using and uttering as genuine, forged documents, knowing the same to be forged;" with "wickedly and feloniously fabricating false and simulate writings, to be used as evidence in courts of law, and so using the same as genuine, and knowingly uttering and using them as such, by producing the same as evidence in courts of law, having formed the fraudulent design of procuring himself to be recognised as Earl of Stirling in Scotland, and of obtaining certain great estates or territories in North America

* *Blackwood's Magazine,* April 1851.

*Modern State Trials: Revised and Illustrated, with Essays and Notes.* By WILLIAM C. TOWNSEND, Esq., M.A., Q.C., Recorder of Macclesfield. In 2 vols. 8vo. Longman & Co. 1850.

and Scotland, with the pretended right of conferring the honours and bestowing the titles of Baronets of Nova Scotia, as being the representative, and entitled to the honours, privileges, and estates of William, first Earl of Stirling; and of procuring loans or advances of money from ignorant and credulous persons on the faith of his being entitled to those estates and privileges, as he falsely represented." He sate, sustaining the burthen of this fearful charge, beside an officer and a gentleman of spotless honour, and of distinction in the military service, who thereby signified his complete conviction of his friend's innocence, with chivalrous devotion—a circumstance very singular in the eyes of an English lawyer. This gentleman was Colonel George Charles D'Aguilar, Deputy Adjutant-General of the Forces in Ireland. "I was treated with such affectionate kindness and hospitality," said he, with moving simplicity, in giving his evidence, "when we were class-fellows at school, near Birmingham, and where he invariably took me with him to his father's house, as I shall never forget; it was, indeed, unbounded: and I am here this day to repay it." For thirty years, however, while the Colonel was on service in India, he and the prisoner were separated; but on the former's return in 1829, he renewed the intimacy, *i. e.*, ten years before the trial, and kept up that intimacy personally and by correspondence. "He wrote to me," said the Colonel, "about his claims; and there was no event of his life, more especially if connected with the proceedings regarding his title, which he did not communicate with the most perfect confidence." "From your long and intimate intercourse with Lord Stirling," he was asked by the prisoner's counsel, "what is your opinion of him, as a man of honour and a gentleman?" "I think my presence here to-day is the best answer to that question," answered the high-minded soldier. "Nothing on earth would induce me to stand where I do, before this court, if I did not believe Lord Stirling to be incapable of doing a dishonourable action." Evidence of this kind, when there exists a real and a serious doubt as to the prisoner's guilt, is of great value to both the accused, and the public, interested in the success of justice alone; but where the facts, and the intention which they evidence, are clear, such evidence is utterly worthless; nay, a good character may positively form an element of aggravation, since the possession of that character may facilitate the commission of crime, by disarming suspicion. It is for this reason that evidence of good character is, in trials, reserved for the close of the inquiry, during which *the facts* may have been elicited, which it will be for the jury to pronounce clear or doubtful.

Now, in the remarkable case before us, we have reversed this order of procedure, that the reader may enter upon a lengthened and deeply interesting inquiry, in a spirit of perfect fairness to the accused; who stands upon the presumption of his innocence as upon a rock, till dislodged by overpowering proof, which, in the reader's unbiassed judgment, the counsel for the crown may have failed to adduce. Was the individual charged with this enormous offence INNOCENT, or GUILTY? is the question now before the reader. He declared then that he was innocent; it is rumoured that he says so still, and protests that he is Earl of Stirling, and has means which he intends to use, in due course of law, of proving himself such. We, however, are concerned only with that which occurred in a public court of justice in this kingdom. If there was a miscarriage, we are not responsible for it; if he prove to have been erroneously convicted, nothing can be more lamentable—no one entitled to deeper sympathy: if he were acquitted, though really guilty, then the reader might be disposed to concur in Mr Townsend's observation, that "the prisoner, in the height of his pretensions, and the ability with which they were supported, soared above all competitors, and has left a name unrivalled in imposture since the days of Perkin Warbeck."*

* Vol. i. p. 407.

Put the case, prospectively and retrospectively, of a total stranger claiming a peerage, by means of what he knows to be a fictitious pedigree. First, *prospectively*—every link in the chain will have to be forged with mingled boldness and adroitness, for it will inevitably be tested rigorously. Truth must be so skilfully intermingled with falsehood, as to baffle practised acuteness: facts and declarations, written and oral, must be arranged, with reference especially to dates, with such a comprehensive caution as not to admit of conflict with any item of hostile and undoubted proof, though disclosed accidentally! A single frail link, and chain and anchor are gone! What consummate sagacity, what extensive knowledge, what unfaltering patience and resolution, are indispensable as conditions of success in this guilty enterprise! The astute schemer must calculate on having, after he has once started, a bloodhound on his track.—Having matured his plans, what a moment is that of going into action—of openly starting his case! With what tremulous anxiety does he contemplate each successive stage of development! How start, in dismay, at the possibility of some suddenly discovered deficiency, inconsistency, contradiction, impossibility, or unlooked-for consequences of steps deemed to have been profoundly well considered!

And *retrospectively*—when the fictitious pedigree has been annihilated—with what feelings of mortification must the defeated schemer review his course of procedure, wondering at the shortsightedness which had failed to provide against this, that, or the other contingency—which, *as it has turned out*, could have been done so easily and safely!

> "A curse upon my pate,
> That this foul blot my stupid hoodwink'd eye
> Perceived not." *

For it is frequently found, by those versed in such inquiries, that the most consummate impostors prove to

* *The Pilgrim.*

have been guilty of some one act, or omission, fatal to the best-concerted scheme—to have gone much too far beyond, or fallen far short of, what was necessary. It may be called being wise after the event; but so it *is*, and is perhaps ordained to be: a truth consolatory to be borne in mind by those charged with the responsibility of conducting legal investigation, and vindicating public justice; stimulating them to the exhibition of patient vigilance.

How far the foregoing remarks may prove applicable, if at all, to the facts of the case now under consideration, we shall leave the reader to determine when he shall have been put in possession of them; for till then we intend to withhold the result of the trial—the verdict of the jury—which may, in some respects, not a little surprise him. The whole case appears to us pervaded by the very spirit of romance—exciting and sustaining curiosity and interest to the very last. We propose, first, to collect the facts which afforded the materials for investigation before the High Court of Justiciary; which, we take the opportunity of saying, appears to us to have performed its duties admirably. At present, we cheerfully bear our testimony to the discretion, urbanity, dignity, and vigilant sagacity, exhibited by the court, as well as the acuteness, learning, and eloquence of the counsel on both sides. The present is probably one of the most remarkable trials occurring in the whole annals of Scottish jurisprudence. It will be our endeavour to extricate the facts of the case from the technicalities and complexities in which they were necessarily involved at the trial;—as we go on indicating several points of interesting contrast between Scottish and English criminal procedure.

We regret being unable conscientiously to express our obligations to Mr Townsend, with respect to his account of "The trial of Alexander Alexander, claiming to be Earl of Stirling, for the crime of forgery." He is indebted for his materials, without acknowledging it, to Mr Swinton, an advocate at the Scotch Bar, and now Professor of Civil

Law in the University of Edinburgh, who, in 1839, published an elaborate and authentic account of the trial, in an octavo volume;* having the advantage of careful revision by the presiding judge, and the counsel, of those parts of the case more immediately concerning the part which they respectively bore in the proceedings. The evidence is also given at length, as well as several interesting documents tendered in proof, but rejected, yet throwing light on some of the most obscure parts of the case. The alleged forgeries were divided into three classes, and one of them, incomparably the most interesting (a map, with a great number of indorsements upon it), forms the subject of a large sheet of *fac-simile.* Mr Townsend, we are compelled to say, does not seem to have thoroughly mastered the case; the facts of which, as presented in the full report of the trial, undoubtedly demand some effort in order to present them at once accurately and popularly, so as to reward the attention bestowed on them by general readers, and students in jurisprudence. His introductory observations, however, are interesting and pertinent. He points attention † to "the marked increase in all the crimes which *require superior intelligence*, rather than brute force, for their successful accomplishment, and which can be effected only by the misapplied union of talent and education;" and also "to the temptation afforded to persons of comparative refinement—of cool head and callous heart—by the abolition of the punishment of death for crimes against property, to adventure in forbidden ways of enriching themselves at the expense of their neighbours, where failure and detection would not involve their personal safety" [by which he means their lives.] He proceeds to give, briefly, three or four "modern instances," amongst which are the monstrous fabrication of a mural tablet, "with all the signs of antiquity and convenient

* *Report of the Trial of Alexander Humphreys or Alexander, claiming the title of Earl of Stirling,* &c. By ARCHIBALD SWINTON, Esq., Advocate. Edinburgh: Thomas Clark, Law Bookseller, 1839.

† Vol. i. p. 404.

dates," in the late celebrated "Tracy Peerage" case, and which created such a vivid display of indignation in the House of Lords; and another recent case, that of a minister of religion, "the Rev. William Bailey, Clerk, LL.D.," which is of such an astounding character, that we shall present its leading features to the reader previous to entering on that which is the subject of the present paper.

The Reverend Dr Bailey, minister of St Peter's, Queen Square, Westminster, was, till within the last few years preceding his trial, an attractive preacher, and highly respected by his congregation. Happening to see a paragraph in a newspaper announcing the recent death of an obscure miser named Smith, of enormous wealth, with no near relations, and so uneducated as to be scarcely able to write his name, the deadly idea occurred to him, suggested by that Evil One against whose temptations his life had been spent in warning others, of setting up a fictitious claim to a large sum of money, as due to his sister, from the deceased miser! He pitched, doubtless for greater probability's sake, upon the fractional sum of £2875; and in due time forwarded to the executors copies of two instruments, an "I O U," and a promissory note for that amount, purporting to have been signed by the miser, and given to "Miss Anne Bailey, of 45 Upper Arthur Street, Belfast, for value received from her, in cash advanced by her on loan to me. *Witness*—William Bailey, Clerk, LL.D., minister of St Peter's, Queen Square, Westminster." Not a little astonished by this sudden application, their testator having died worth several hundred thousand pounds, and no trace existing among his papers of any transaction in which the name of Bailey occurred—none of his acquaintances having ever heard of the name of Bailey, as known to the testator—the executors resolved to resist the action, and put the plaintiff to sworn proof in a public court of justice. The reverend gentleman stepped boldly into the box; first produced an account-book, containing various entries of loans by his sister to Smith, the deceased miser; and then swore point blank to his having witnessed the miser's signature to the "I O U," in the vestry-room of St Peter's! *just before divine service!* at seven o'clock on the evening of Thursday the 12th August! His evidence was totally disbelieved; his pretended vouchers were impounded; and he was committed on the charge of forgery. How shall we proceed with the frightful facts elicited at his trial for that offence? First of all, it was proved beyond all doubt that, at the precise period pitched upon by the miserable forger as that on which he had witnessed the signature of the miser, the latter had been in company for two hours with a friend, a builder in the Hampstead Road, whose reason for remembering the circumstance was, that it was his wedding-day! But scarcely half of this tale of horror has yet been told. Not contented with having committed perjury himself, he procured, and endeavoured to procure, others to perjure themselves, in order to support this dismal fable concerning Smith's signature! He had met in the Brompton Road a poor Irishman who sold fruit by the roadside, and asked him if he would become a witness at the trial of an action! "I looked at him," said the man, "and *admired* what he meant, but I said 'Yes,' to see what his motive was." The reverend delinquent then gave him a shilling, and told him to call at his house the next day; and on his doing so, gave him a written paper, which he was to commit to memory—the purport being, that he had seen Smith go into the vestry of St Peter's, and come out again in five minutes, followed by Dr Bailey in his surplice, on the evening of the 12th August! The man preserved, and exhibited in court, at the trial of Dr Bailey, this blighting evidence of guilt! The witness had been taken to the Exchequer Office, and there had signed his false depositions; but when sent down to swear publicly in court to the falsehood, "his flesh," he said, "crawled on his bones, and he ran away!" Yet again—the prisoner had given £30 to a reduced tradesman to swear to the same falsehood, and he did so swear, as he confessed!—the Doctor having told him that, "unless he did, the Doctor's sister was in danger of being robbed of £3000!" Dr Bailey's written instructions to both witnesses were produced in court, and proved, on his trial! Nor have we even yet reached the depth to which this abandoned of God descended in the abyss of guilt. He called several unfortunate women—discharged servants, milliners, and others—whom he had tutored to swear to different portions of the imaginary transaction between himself and Smith! But the prosecution, aided by secret memoranda which they had discovered in Dr Bailey's desk, easily rent asunder this black tissue of perjury. Finally, as though to add an infernal glare to these atrocities, Dr Bailey succeeded in producing several witnesses, of unquestionable respectability, who conscientiously deposed to his eminence as a preacher, and the estimation in which he was held as a man of moral worth! All, however, was in vain: he was found guilty, and transported for life. "How venial," justly observes Mr Townsend, "in comparison with his double guilt, yet how sad in contrast, the sin and punishment of Dr Dodd!" We conceive that few cases blacker than this are on record in the annals of crime. It were vain to speculate on the state of mind and of feeling of an accepted and successful minister of religion, who could conceive, and proceed deliberately to carry into execution, as he did, the idea of such enormous atrocity!

It is time, however, to come to the remarkable case of the claimant of the Stirling peerage. The trial occurred twelve years ago,* at Edinburgh, before a Scottish jury consisting of *fifteen*, instead of twelve, as in England and Ireland—the decision of a majority being sufficient to determine the result. There were four judges, consti-

* In 1839.

tuting the High Court of Justiciary—Lord Meadowbank, Lord Mackenzie, Lord Moncrieff, and Lord Cockburn. The case of the crown was conducted partially by Mr Rutherfurd, then the Lord-Advocate, but principally by the then Solicitor-General, Mr Cosmo Innes, and Mr Handyside; that of the prisoner, called in Scotland "the *panel*," by Mr Robertson, Mr Anderson, and Mr Inglis.* The court was crowded to excess throughout the whole trial, which lasted an entire week, attracting great attention, not only in this country, but at Paris, which supplied witnesses eminent as antiquaries and otherwise. The appearance of the prisoner at the bar was attended, as we have seen, by a singular and touching manifestation of chivalrous devotion to his interests, and enthusiastic confidence in his integrity and honour, on the part of Colonel Charles D'Aguilar. This gentleman not only took his seat, in the first instance, beside the prisoner, but remained there till the last moment of the trial, when the prisoner was carried out of court in a swoon, on hearing the verdict announced.

Evidence of the prisoner's character, similar to that borne by the Colonel, was given by another gentleman of unquestionable honour and position in society, Mr Hardinge, of Bole Hall, near Tamworth, a relative of the late Sir Robert Peel.

"*Q.*—You know the prisoner intimately?

"*A.*—I have constantly corresponded with him, and know him—so far as one man can know another.

"*Q.*—What is your opinion of him as a man of moral principle and honour?

"*A.*—If I were to point out a man as remarkable for the strictest honour, I would name Lord Stirling. When

* During the fifteen years which have [A.D. 1854] elapsed, the following changes have occurred among the judges and counsel engaged in this trial. Three of the four judges are dead, and one (Lord Meadowbank) has retired into private life. Of the counsel, the then Solicitor-General (Ivory), Mr Rutherfurd, Mr Robertson, Mr Handyside, and Mr Anderson have become judges, and the latter is dead. Mr Innes is still at the Bar, and Mr Inglis is Dean of Faculty.

at school, he was universally beloved by every individual. * * * I introduced him to Sir Robert Peel. In his letters to me I never saw an expression that was not honourable to his head and heart. There is no man in existence more honourable, in my opinion, than he: as to that, from the knowledge I have of him, I think myself entitled to speak with confidence." *

Of such evidence as this, the prisoner's counsel, as it may be imagined, did not fail to make the most; but the Solicitor-General assailed it thus:—

"It cannot avail the prisoner *here*. Evidence to character may avail the accused where the case hangs *in dubio*, but not where the evidence is clear against the party. The circumstances in which the prisoner was placed, and the very end at which he was aiming, must have made it part of his game to preserve and keep up the good character which he seems originally to have possessed. He was aiming to obtain high honours and extensive lands and estates, and it was necessary for his success that he should conduct himself as a gentleman. I have no doubt that, being a very clever man, he could so conduct himself as to preserve the good impression which had from the first been laid in the early attachment of unsuspecting and affectionate boyhood. But all this must yield, if there be real evidence of crime." †

To this, which, however just and forcible, would be considered, at the English Bar, as *perhaps* pressing somewhat severely upon a prisoner so situated, his counsel answered by urging on the jury the unreasonableness of imputing such foul crime to "a man of unsullied character—or rather, as my learned friend seems to say, having got up a false good character for villanous purposes, like the man who was said to have fraudulently concealed his own insanity." ‡

The presiding Judge thus dealt with the topic:—

"Gentlemen, I believe every tittle of this evidence,

* Swinton's Rep., pp. 189, 190. † Ibid. p. 268. ‡ Ibid. p. 273.

given with an earnestness which, if it told on your minds as it did on mine, must have been by you felt as most deeply affecting. It is, however, at best, but evidence as to the *character* of the prisoner; and if the case be not *clear* against him, he will be entitled to the benefit of that character. But even if he had not obtained it, if the case had so stood, he would equally have been entitled to the benefit of the doubt. Still, you have got that evidence to character, and, still more, on account of it will you be disposed to listen to the suggestions of your own minds, and if the grounds for convicting the prisoner be not entirely satisfactory, in that case acquit him of these charges by a verdict, providing either that he is not guilty, or that, however suspicions may attach to him, the guilt has not been legally proven." *

It will be not a little interesting, in the event, to see to what extent the jury acted upon this temperate and sound judicial advice. We now entreat the reader to peruse the ensuing narrative with a suspended judgment, keeping his eye steadily fixed on the true points of inquiry. It was *not* one of them, whether the prisoner's claims to the Earldom of Stirling were valid or not, but simply and exclusively whether certain documents were, in fact, forgeries; and if so, whether the prisoner had either forged them, or uttered them with a guilty knowledge that they were forgeries. It is of the utmost moment to distinguish between these two questions, for every one of the documents may have been forged, and even designed by the forger, and intrinsically calculated, to advance the interests of the claims and pretensions imputed to the prisoner; and, further, the latter may have even availed himself of those forged documents for that purpose, and yet been as ignorant of the fact of forgery, and in all respects as innocent of a guilty uttering, as any of the judges before whom he was being tried. Thus there are three questions before us: I. Were the documents in question, or any of them, forged? II. If so,

* Swinton, p. 334.

were they forged by the prisoner, or by others with his knowledge? III. Or, lastly, did he utter any of them, knowing them to be forged?

ALEXANDER HUMPHREYS, the prisoner, was the son of respectable parents, and born in Warwickshire. His mother's name was Hannah, and she was the youngest child of the Rev. JOHN ALEXANDER, a Presbyterian minister at Dublin. His father was a merchant of considerable affluence, and living in suitable style, and very hospitably, at a place near Birmingham called "Digleth," from which, in 1798–1799, he removed to a place in the same neighbourhood called Fairhill, but subsequently "The Larches." "Nobody in Birmingham," said Mr Hardinge, "lived better. They kept their carriage and a pair of fine gray horses, and had half-a-dozen servants at least."* Their son Alexander was born about the year 1784, and he went to a school near Birmingham kept by the Rev. Mr Corrie, the brother of an important witness in the case. Young Humphreys was a great favourite among his companions, two of whom were, as has been seen, Colonel D'Aguilar and Mr Hardinge. In his eighteenth year, he accompanied his father on some errand of business, as it is supposed, to France, during the short peace of 1802, both of them being, unfortunately, among the English detained prisoners by Napoleon. The father died, in 1807, at Verdun, where his son remained till the peace of 1814. Two years previously to that event he married Fortunata Bartoletti, a Neapolitan lady, by whom he was introduced to a personage, one Mademoiselle le Normand, who was destined to figure prominently in his after history. She was an authoress of some little repute, but better known as the Parisian *Sybil*—in plain English, she was a fortune-teller by means of cards, *Tireur des cartes;*† and she told Mr Humphreys his fortune, he paying her five napoleons—viz., "that he would encounter many toils and distresses,

* Swinton, p. 189. † Ibid. p. 155.

but at length arrive at great honours." How he supported himself in France is unknown; but, in 1814, he and Mrs Humphreys came over to England, and settled at Worcester with very limited means. He became an usher at a respectable school, then called Netherton House, but shortly afterwards was the master of the establishment. It would seem, also, that he carried on, to a little extent, about the same time, the somewhat incongruous business of a wine merchant, and, in fact, appeared to be in straitened circumstances.

How it came to pass seems a mystery; but about a year after his inauspicious settlement at Worcester, viz., in 1815 and 1816, he conceived the bold idea of claiming the old Scottish Earldom of Stirling, together with estates in Scotland, and vast possessions in British North America, alleged to be annexed to the title. The dazzling link of assumed connexion with these aristocratic pretensions, was his mother. She and her husband seem to have gone down to their graves, however,—he in France in 1807, and she in England in 1814,—without ever having even hinted the existence of any such claims as their son was now starting within a little more than a year after his mother's death; unless, indeed, reliance is to be placed upon the extraordinary statements made some eleven or twelve years afterwards by Mr Humphreys' sister, a lady at Manchester, named Eliza, but commonly called Lady Eliza Pountney, who deponed that she had often heard her mother say to her children that "they had noble blood in their veins," and had heard her deceased father "frequently call her mother his countess;" but that her mother, "being a person of great humility, and perfectly unostentatious, did not take upon herself the title;" that her mother had repeatedly said that she had heard *her* mother say that she had an emblazoned pedigree of the Earls of Stirling, setting forth their marriages, issue, and descent, but which had been surreptitiously taken away or stolen from her; together with divers other family papers and valuable documents respecting the title and descent of the Earl of Stirling to her family; and she had also heard her mother say that she had two brothers, *John* and *Benjamin*, who had fully intended assuming their peerage honours, had not early death cut them off in the prime of life; also that they died unmarried, as did her eldest sister, Mary; whereby she (the mother of the deponent) said she believed herself to be the last of her family of the Alexanders, who were entitled to be Earls of Stirling: all which particulars the deponent considered "were matters of notoriety in the then circle of her mother's friends; but she did not know of any of their friends who were then alive."* The value, however, which was set upon these reminiscences, by those most affected by them, may be inferred from the fact, that this lady was not, though she might have been, called as a witness on behalf of her brother at the trial, and though the prisoner's counsel were challenged by the Crown to produce her,† and the deposition containing these critical statements was printed with the "Additional Defences" given in by the prisoner. It is for the reader to judge of the probability that such a state of facts really existed: that Mr and Mrs Alexander could have entertained the idea, and freely spoken of such critical family matters, without any disinterested respectable person being producible to attest the fact of their having done so, and of their having taken a single step to investigate their supposed rights, or prosecute their imposing claims. The reader's attention, however, is called to the fact of this lady having made these statements *so early as January* 1826, and of her brother, the prisoner, then availing himself of them. The nature of some of these representations may hereafter throw light upon dark and intricate passages in this remarkable history; but it must be remembered that this lady's statements were not brought before the jury.

The first evidence of the prisoner's stirring in the matter of his claims to the peerage, consisted of a statement

* Swinton, Appendix, p. 88.

† Ibid. p. 179.

made at the trial by a Mr Corrie, a solicitor at Birmingham, who had acted in that capacity to the prisoner's father, and been a trustee under his will. He said that he first heard from the prisoner himself, of his claims, in 1815 or 1816; but that on his saying "he had *no documents*, or no *effectual* documents, to support them," Mr Corrie had "declined to act for him then."* Sometime afterwards, however, he met with persons exhibiting greater zeal and enterprise on his behalf; but they do not come on the stage till after an interval of nearly seven or eight years—by which time he would seem to have entered into confidential relations with more than one professional adviser—among whom was a Mr Thomas Christopher Banks, the author of a work on dormant and extinct peerages,† and who will presently appear on the scene frequently and to act pretty decisively. Acting under this gentleman's advice, early in the year 1824, Mr Humphreys applied for and obtained a royal licence to assume his mother's maiden name of Alexander—also that of the Stirling family—but without any intimation, to the authorities, of any particular reason which he had for doing so. Thenceforward, he wrote himself "Alexander Humphreys Alexander."‡ Acting on the advice of counsel, and his legal agents, he ventured next to take up the peerage title of the noble family of which he aspired to be the representative; and on the 2d June 1825, actually attended at the election of a Scottish representative peer in the room of the recently deceased Lord Balcarres; answered to the name of *The Earl of Stirling;* and having tendered his vote, it was necessarily recorded by the official clerks! This feat he long afterwards justly characterised as "a serious blunder;" adding,

* Swinton, p. 183.

† 1 Townsend, 409.

‡ It is a commonly received notion that a person cannot change his *surname* without a royal licence; but this is altogether erroneous. Any person may change, or add to, or sink his surname, at his will, "and work his way in the world with his new name as he best can," said the late Chief Justice Tindal, in the case of Davies *v.* Lowndes (1 *Bingham's New Cases,* 618), "provided it be not for the purpose of fraud." The royal licence serves only to authenticate and facilitate the *evidence* of such change.

that "it was beginning where he should have ended."* He founded his claim, be it observed, on this occasion—as, indeed, ever after—upon "a royal charter, or letters patent of Novodamus, under the Great Seal of Scotland, dated the 7th December 1639, granted by King Charles I. in favour of William, Earl of Stirling." This alleged charter is the chief corner-stone of the entire structure, whether of fact or of fiction, with which we have to deal. It is necessary now, however, briefly but clearly to set before the reader the time and manner of the original ennobling of the Stirling family.

Sir William Alexander, a courtier, and at the time Secretary of State of James I., obtained from him in A.D. 1621 a charter granting to him the territory of Nova Scotia; and seven years afterwards, viz., on the 2d February 1628, he received from Charles I. a grant of the province since called Canada. Two years subsequently, viz., on the 4th September 1630, he was raised to the peerage by the title of Viscount of Stirling, by patent to him and "his *heirs male;*" and finally, three years afterwards, viz., on the 14th June 1633, on occasion of the latter king's coronation, he was advanced to the dignity of Earl of Stirling and Viscount Canada, by patent to him and, again be it noted, "his *heirs male.*" He took possession of all the vast territory which had been granted to him; and his son spent some time in America, regulating the affairs of the colony. The first earl died in London in February 1640; and with his death, suffice it shortly to state, terminated the connexion of the Stirling family with Nova Scotia and Canada. It is not altogether needless to advert to the various changes of ownership between England and France which those provinces underwent, down to the Treaty of Utrecht in 1713.

* This statement is taken from a book published by the prisoner in 1836, entitled, "Narrative of the Oppressive Law Proceedings, and other Measures resorted to by the British Government, and numerous private individuals, to overpower the Earl of Stirling, and subvert his lawful rights. Written by himself."

The first Earl of Stirling had nine children—*i. e.*, seven sons and two daughters. He had four successors in his earldom, the last of whom, Henry, the fifth earl, died without issue on the 4th December 1739. The link in the chain of descent with which we are specially concerned is that of JOHN, the fourth son of the first earl: since the prisoner's case was, that he was descended from *this son John*. The prisoner appears to have been the second claimant of the peerage. The first was a *William Alexander*, surveyor-general of the State of New Jersey, and afterwards a general in the American army. In 1759-60 this gentleman, whose name, position, and claim must be borne in mind, assumed the title, and presented to the sovereign, for the recognition of his honours, a petition, which was remitted to the House of Lords. Two years afterwards, however, on the 10th March 1762, a Committee of Privileges resolved that he had not established his claim, and that in the mean time he, or any person claiming under him, should not be admitted to vote at the elections of peers of Scotland, and that he "be ordered not to presume to take upon himself the said title, honour, and dignity, until his claim shall have been allowed in due course of law."* There the matter ended; and the dormant title of Stirling had rest for fifty-three years, viz., till the year 1815, when the prisoner so suddenly revived it in order to claim it as his own.

When we parted with him, viz., on the 2d June 1825, he was claiming to vote in the election of a representative peer of Scotland. We next find him instituting legal proceedings in Scotland, on the 7th February 1826, for procuring himself to be declared heir to *his mother*: on which occasion he styled himself "Alexander Humphreys Alexander, Earl of Stirling." On this occasion two documents were produced,† of great importance, and of which more will be presently said: viz., an affidavit alleged to have been made by a Henry Alexander, 16th

* *Journal of the House of Lords*, vol. xxx. p. 186. † Swinton, p. 105.

July 1723, and "a statement" by a William Gordon, dated the 14th January 1723; both attested by a Thomas Conyers, on the 10th and 20th July in the same year;—the whole tending to establish the fact of the then existing charter of *Novodamus*, on which the prisoner's claim was founded, and also some links in his pedigree. This preliminary step having been taken, he appears to have returned to Worcester, and there carried on an extensive correspondence, having for its objects the discovery of evidence in support of his claims, and raising loans on the security of his alleged rightful possessions in America and Scotland. Mr Banks was despatched to North America to publish and assert the prisoner's rights as Earl of Stirling, and also to search for evidence; and he soon sent home flourishing accounts of the success of his mission. "By all," says the prisoner in a letter to a friend at Glasgow,* "he was received in a most flattering manner. The British consul had tendered him his services in a very handsome manner by letter. It is now confidently anticipated the Congress will grant me a location of *five millions of acres* (which is found to be *not one-twentieth part* of the lands originally granted—all convertible at once, at common market price, into cash!) and will be more than one million sterling." Eight months afterwards (25th July 1827) he exultingly announced fresh feats on the part of his successful agent and pioneer, Mr Banks:—"I make haste to inform you that the charter of Nova Scotia is upon the record of the Great Seal at Edinburgh. Mr Banks has in his possession, and is using at this time, with complete effect, in America, all the office copies of that and the other charters which the first Earl of Stirling obtained." "By degrees all the valuable papers *of which my grandmother was robbed* about the time that the general" (the William Alexander already

* Swinton, p. ix., note.—Letter dated 24th November 1826. (The letters appearing here are among those seized at the prisoner's house, and deposited at the Justiciary Office.)

referred to) "preferred his claims to the earldom, are finding their way back to me. I have had the great satisfaction of learning, by these letters, that Mr Banks has positively ascertained the existence of another copy of that document." On returning from America, in the spring of 1828, Mr Banks was despatched on a similar errand to Ireland; and in one of his earliest letters to the prisoner, dated the 2d May 1828, he alludes to a communication made to him by the latter concerning some "late *Parisian* information," adding, "and I believe that all the latent windings are about to be brought to light. Your extracts are most encouraging; and indeed it is more than extraordinary that so much truth has been mentioned, where the circumstances of past events were never told. Thus, what is to come may be most fairly looked up to as a surety of the wonderful works of Providence in the way of retribution, which, though slow in occurring, is nevertheless true in taking place at the due time, but which human endurance, in the interim, can barely be brought to have the patience to await, or sustaining severe trials with fortitude."*

Mr Banks was despatched a second time to Ireland in the spring of the ensuing year, and in a letter to the prisoner, dated Carlow, 17th March 1829, not put in evidence, announced a great and gratifying event—neither more nor less than his discovery of an old document purporting to be a duly attested "EXCERPT" from the lost charter of Charles I., on which the prisoner had based his claims to the Stirling peerage! This "excerpt" was the instrument which proved to be the *first* article of indictment against the prisoner. Mr Banks gives, in the last-cited letter, the following account of this truly wonderful instrument. He found it in a parcel, which had been left at his hotel in Dublin, by some stranger, "a person with whom he had had no communications." But discovering an all-important indorsement upon it, verifying the

* Swinton, p. .civ.

authenticity of the document, and signed "*Thomas Conyers*, 10th July 1723," he returned to Carlow, which he had visited on the preceding occasion, and found out a Mrs Fairclough, who had some knowledge of the family of Conyers; and Mr Banks was at length led to believe, that this mysterious parcel had come from her husband, who had gone from Carlow, and whom he represented to be a disreputable person. "Fairclough most probably sent the parcel to me without any communication, that his name might not be brought forward, and he be thereby exposed to questions or investigations as to the Conyers' concerns, which he might not choose to answer. Such are my surmises. However, the 'excerpt' is certainly of great importance, as the identity of its having once belonged to Mr Conyers, who had the original charter of Novodamus," [the indorsement stated, that "*the original charter* was at present in his keeping"] "is so well proven and established." He had come to this conclusion, from an alleged interview with the Inspector of Franks at the General Post-Office, Carlow, to whom he showed the indorsement, and who compared the signature with the undoubted signature of Conyers, particularly that affixed to his will. "I think," added Mr Banks, "I have been very fortunate." His discovery, however, did but realise an anticipation which he had formed, and conveyed to his employer a year before, during his former visit to Ireland, viz., on the 23d April 1828: "I am in great hopes to trace Conyers' family; which if I do, and find his representatives, his papers might mention when, and to whom he gave the charter; and, not improbably, even a copy might be found amongst them."* A month afterwards, Mr Banks wrote two letters to Mr Lockhart, a Writer to the Signet at Edinburgh, who had been professionally engaged by the prisoner in the preceding April, which the prisoner's counsel vainly endeavoured to get admitted in evidence, without calling Mr Banks,

* Swinton, Additional Appendix, p. xcii.

though he was alive and within reach, and the counsel for the crown challenged the prisoner's counsel to call him. This, however, was declined, on the alleged ground that, in 1834–5, the intercourse and friendship between the prisoner and Mr Banks had been terminated through a quarrel.* The first of these two letters, dated the 10th April 1829, contained the following passages:† "I must observe that, during my stay in Ireland, I was very fortunate in some points of high consequence, all particularly confirmatory, as well of his lordship's descent, as of the identity of the charter of *Novodamus;* an original excerpt from which I have had put into my hands, of a most undoubted nature and authenticity. * * * I consider what I have so unexpectedly met with to be of very estimable service, as I should think it could amply prove the tenor of the original charter." The second letter, of the 17th April 1829, contained the following:—"As to the excerpt I so unexpectedly got in Ireland, it appears to have been either taken by, or to have belonged to, Mr Conyers, who had the original charter, for *his initials are on the back of it;* and these initials I have had examined with his original writing to several documents in the several courts at Dublin. Having made a copy of this excerpt, I also send it for your perusal, that you may judge how far it may be adequate to maintain the application for a new charter before the Lord Advocate, or to sustain an action *to prove the tenor* in the Court of Session at Edinburgh."‡

Within a month's time, viz., in the ensuing May, this memorable "excerpt" was in the hands of Mr Lockhart; who, on the 12th of the ensuing October, commenced an action at Edinburgh, for the purpose of "*proving the tenor,*" as it is called, of the original though lost charter, of which this alleged excerpt had been discovered. The action was opposed by the crown lawyers; and as the

* Swinton, Additional Appendix, pp. 106, 110, 178.

† Ibid. p. cvi.

‡ Ibid. Preface, p. xii.

prisoner had nothing but this "excerpt" to rely upon, adducing no evidence of his propinquity to the grantee of the charter, the suit was dismissed for want of title, on the 4th March 1830. A second similar attempt followed the same fate, on the 2d March 1833; and these two were the only efforts made by the prisoner to use this capital instrument of evidence, the "excerpt," for the purpose of proving his rights of succession to both the honours and estates of the Stirling family. All this while, however, he was strenuously endeavouring also to establish his *pedigree;* for which purpose he availed himself of certain methods of legal procedure in Scotland, appearing to us so absurd in their nature, and dangerous in the facilities afforded by them for fraud, as to have become, says Mr Swinton, "for some time a subject of very general complaint in Scotland."* Any claimant of a right of succession there, has, it seems, only to obtain, as a matter of course, a precept to the sheriff to summon an inquest to try the alleged right; and if there be no opponent claiming precisely in the same character, nothing can be heard against the claimant! Evidence of any description is admitted; and the inquest finds, upon oath, that the claimant is entitled to the character which he seeks to establish! And beyond all this, if their proceedings should continue unchallenged for twenty years, said the Solicitor-General,† it would not have been possible to set aside or annul them! Surely "the amending hand," which Lord Coke prays may be "blessed," is here required in Scotland! By means of this precious process, the prisoner procured himself, on the 11th October 1830, to be declared nearest lawful heir, as GREAT-GREAT-GREAT-GRANDSON of William first Earl of Stirling. On this occasion he produced, among his documentary evidence, a copy of the affidavit of Henry Hovenden, already referred to, and also of another by a *Sara Lyners*, dated the 17th January 1722, of which more anon. Within a

* Swinton, Preface, p. xiv. 13. † Ibid. p. 195.

few months' time, again, he was, on the 2d July 1831, declared heir in the Nova Scotian and Canadian possessions of the first Earl!—a fact which, a few days afterwards, namely, on the 12th July ensuing, he formally communicated to the public authorities there, and inhabitants, by way of proclamation,* in terms almost befitting a sovereign newly restored to his dominions. While thus intrepidly urging on his way in the law courts of Scotland, he seized every opportunity of personally exercising the rights of the peerage. On the 2d September 1830, he voted, under protest made by the Earl of Rosebery, but not seconded, at the election of representative peers at Holyrood; again, on the 3d June 1831, but under a protest formally entered by the Duke of Buccleuch and Lord Lauderdale.† On the 29th August 1831, he petitioned for leave to do homage at the coronation, as hereditary-lieutenant of Nova Scotia; created several baronets in right of such lieutenancy, one of whom was his agent Mr Banks, to whom he also assigned 16,000 acres of land in Nova Scotia, but who resigned the rank after his quarrel with the prisoner in 1834–5; and finally, on the 25th January 1838, forwarded to Lord Melbourne a solemn protest, as hereditary-lieutenant of her Majesty in the provinces of Nova Scotia, including New Brunswick, and Upper and Lower Canada, against the appointment of the late Earl of Durham as Governor-General of the colony. That this was at all events a bold and decisive line of operations, apparently indicating supreme confi-

* Swinton, 2d Appendix, p. lxxxiii.

† On the 25th June 1847, was passed an Act (10 and 11 Vict. c. 52) entitled, "An Act for the correction of certain abuses which have frequently prevailed at the election of Representative Peers for Scotland," which recited that divers of the peerages of Scotland have from time to time become dormant or extinct, and frequent abuses have prevailed by persons assuming such peerages, and voting in respect thereof at such elections, to which peerages such persons had no right. It proceeds to enact that no title standing in the authentic list of the Scottish Peerage, entered in the Roll of Peers by order of the House of Lords on the 12th February 1708, in right of which title no vote has been given since the year 1800, shall be called over at an election, without an order of the House of Lords.

fidence in the validity of his pretensions, no one will doubt; and it renders deeply interesting the inquiry on which we are about to enter.

In the meantime, however, a question may occur,—Whence could be derived the funds requisite for carrying on these expensive, extensive, and complicated operations, in different and distant parts of the world? In the year 1829, the prisoner appears to have quitted Worcester, in distress, and came to London, where he established himself in lodgings at the corner of Jermyn Street and Regent Street. While there, again, as was reluctantly testified by a witness at the trial,* he was "in great distress for money, unable to pay for his lodgings; and he acknowledged that he had left his butcher's bill at Worcester unpaid, and that his family were in great distress there." Such, however, were the results of his confident and enterprising energy, such the reliance placed on his representations of success, in enforcing his claims in America, and the *éclat* which he derived from frequently and publicly asserting and exercising the rights of the peerage,—that in about eighteen months' time he appears to have succeeded in raising from one agent alone, on the faith of his prospects, no less a sum, though at enormous rates of interest, than £13,000. He now brought up his family to town, established them in fashionable quarters, and lived expensively; and also opened an office in Parliament Street, whence he issued advertisements for the sale of territories in Canada, and debentures on his American possessions!

Let us now, however, inspect the machinery by which he originally proposed and attempted to raise himself from obscurity to distinction, from extreme poverty to vast wealth, to ally himself to aristocracy, and indeed become one of its prominent members.

The proposition which he undertook to prove, as has been seen, was, that he was the great-great-great-grandson of the first Earl of Stirling. We shall now place be-

* Swinton, Second Appendix, p. 165.

fore our readers so much only of the various pedigrees as is necessary to trace, and render interesting to follow, the operations attributed to the prisoner:—

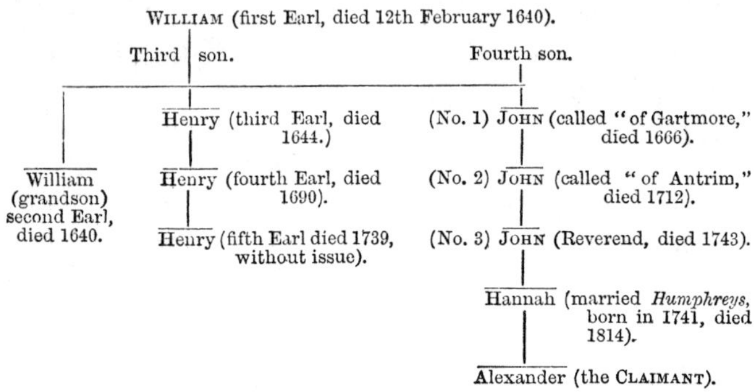


Here, it will be observed, we have three *Henrys*, in immediate succession, Earls of Stirling, and three *Johns;* which Henrys and Johns were respectively and successively brothers, first cousins, and second cousins; and one naturally asks, Why did not John (No. 3), the claimant's grandfather, at once take up the earldom, on the death, without issue, of his second cousin, Henry the fifth earl, whom he survived four years? A second observation arising on the above pedigree is, that the claimant derives title through a female descent—*Hannah*, his mother, claiming to do so by means of the irrecoverable but sweeping charter of *Novodamus*. The reader will bear in mind that there are, as we have already seen,* two patents of nobility to the Stirling family, respectively dated the 4th September 1630, and the 14th June 1633, giving the titles, first of Viscount, then of Earl, "to him and HIS HEIRS-MALE for ever, bearing the name and arms of Alexander." To establish his right under these patents, the prisoner must of course have proved that he was heir-male of the first Earl of Stirling. That would

* *Ante*, p. 185.

have been a matter of mere pedigree—showing himself the last of an unbroken succession of males. But the prisoner set up a case of a totally different nature; and it was this:—that the first earl "being," to quote from a "statement of William Gordon," hereafter referred to, "under great dejection of spirit, after losing three of his sons, who had given him the brightest hopes; and fearing, from the declining state of health of two of y^e^ survivors, that his honours might at no dist^t^. period pass to a collateral branch of his family, RESIGNED his titles and estates into the king's hands; who, by a charter under the great seal, bearing date the 7th Dec. 1639, (*i.e.*, two months only before the earl's death,) conferred them DE NOVO ['*de novo dedit*'] upon him and the heirs-male of his bodye: which failing, [the whole case hinges on this clause] to y^e^ ELDEST HEIRS-FEMALE WITHOUT DIVISION OF THE LAST OF SUCH HEIRS-MALE hereafter succeeding to the titles, honours, and dignities aforesaid, and to the HEIRS-MALE to be procreated of the bodys of such heirs-female." * "Note"—continued Mr Gordon—"I have not met with this charter in our publick records; but from a marginal reference to y^e^ 57 volume of y^e^ Reg^r^. of the G^t^. Seal, w^h^. I noticed while I was taking y^e^ foregoing clause of limitation from *Mr James Hay's* transcript, I am led to conclude that y^e^ charter was entered in a part of that vol. where several leaves are now awanting. Be my conjecture true or false, little importeth, however, since the original charter is at this time [14th January 1723] in y^e^ possession of *Thos. Conyers*, Esq^e^. of Catherclaigh, in y^e^ kingdom of Ireland, who will no doubt let you have inspection thereof, and, for aught we know, may further be willing to give it up to you, as it can be of no use to him." On the back of this document, in the alleged handwriting of "*the Reverend John Alexander*," was found "No. 3, from Mr W. Gordon, Edinb. 14th Jan^y^. 1723. Rec^d^. 27th." And at the foot of the "Statement" is the following "Attestation:"

* Swinton, Additional Appendix, pp. lxxxix., xc.

—"I have compared the limitations copyed on the other side in English by Mr William Gordon, with those cont[d]. in the original charter of the 7th Dec. 1639, at present in my keeping; and for Mr Alexander's satisfaction, I do hereby certifye that the said Wm. Gordon has given a true and faithful translation of the clause by which the estates and titles of Lord Stirling are limited in the aforesaid charter, and descend to the heirs therein mentioned. Witness my hand, this 10th day of July 1723. Thomas Conyers." Thus the prisoner's case was, to prove the existence of this all-important charter of "*Novodamus*," as it was called, operating so great a change in the destination of the honours of the Stirling family; and then that he, by his descent, satisfied its conditions. But this original charter itself, he declared from the first, was not forthcoming; and not only was it lost or destroyed, but also the official record of it in the Register of the Great Seal; and his reliance was placed on the next best procurable evidence of its existence, afforded (after proof of the loss or the destruction of the original) by authentic quotations from its essential provisions, by the persons who had made such quotations from the original; but above all by the famous EXCERPT of the charter, so fortunately discovered in Ireland by Mr Banks. What cogent evidence, however, was requisite to establish such critical facts! and what courageous confidence must he have had in the merits of his case, who undertook to dare the lynx-eyed scrutiny to which his "proofs" would be inevitably exposed!

Divested of all technicalities and superfluous statements, the following is the first public formal account of the matter given by the prisoner, in the former of the two actions already alluded to, brought by him in 1829, to establish or "prove the tenor" of the original charter. His prayer was, "That it might be declared and decerned that the charter was in form following, [setting it out in the original Latin—and pretty Latinity it is—according to the excerpts,] and that such 'decree' should be in all respects as valid and effectual a document to the pursuer (the prisoner) in all cases, causes, and questions whatsoever, as the original charter of *Novodamus*, if extant and found, would be, notwithstanding the same has been lost and is amissing, and cannot now be discovered."*

After setting out at length the various original and undoubted patents of nobility and charters to the first Earl of Stirling, the "summons" proceeded to recite his resignation, for the purpose of a re-grant, of his titles and honours, and the new charter of Novodamus, accordingly, of the 7th December 1639, with the new limitations. These stated the successive descents of the title to the fifth earl, who died without issue; after which, substantially the following curious narrative was given, and which is well worthy of attentive consideration, as affording a key to much of what follows. The Reverend John Alexander, the grandfather of the prisoner, (John No. 3,) being at this time *heir-presumptive* to the earldom, proceeded, in the year 1722, to collect the evidence of his right of succession. This, it will be observed, was after his second cousin, the last earl, had enjoyed the peerage and estates for thirty-two years—doubtless without having alive, at that time, any issue to succeed him; which is obviously intended to account for the heir-presumptive being then on the look-out after his own rights. One should have thought, reverting to the state of the pedigree already given, that all was simple and straightforward enough, as in an ordinary case of succession to a peerage. But the reverend grandfather of the prisoner is represented to have taken some peculiar steps in 1722. He employed an Edinburgh *expert* in genealogy, the Mr William Gordon of whom we have already heard, to "collect the evidence of the rights of succession, and draw out a statement of the descent." Mr Gordon set about his task; and early

* Swinton, Appendix, pp. vii., viii.

in 1723 transmitted to his employer a translation of the limitations in the charter of Novodamus, of the 9th December 1639, but made from only a copy of it; stating that the original was in the hands of a Mr THOMAS CONYERS, Master Extraordinary in Chancery in Ireland. On this, the heir-presumptive employed an Irish professional man, skilled in such matters, a Mr Hovenden, to make further inquiry in Ireland. He went, accordingly, to this Mr Thomas Conyers on the 10th July 1723, *who allowed him to see the original charter*, which he "most minutely examined," and found to agree with the account of it which had been supplied to him by Mr Gordon. The heir-presumptive (John No. 3) afterwards succeeded in getting possession of this same original charter, which, on his death in 1743, came into the hands of his widow, who shortly afterwards went to England, and settled at Birmingham. About the year 1758, however (that is, nineteen years after the death of the fifth earl, and fifteen years after the death of her husband), the Reverend John Alexander, according to the prisoner's case, must have been for four years *de jure* the sixth earl, and died such! This invaluable charter, the foundation of the family honours, having been carefully and secretly kept by the *de jure* countess, was feloniously stolen from her by one of her servants, who had been bribed to do so by the William Alexander of America, who was then laying claim to the title.* This gentleman having thus obtained possession of it, entered into an agreement of partition of the family estates with two nephews of the fifth earl living in England, obtained the charter from their hands, and thereupon assumed the title, and, after a time, either suppressed or destroyed the charter! The claimant (the prisoner) had publicly advertised and offered a reward for the discovery of the missing charter, but in vain; and, as a forlorn hope, caused inquiries to be made in America, among the persons into whose hands the papers, &c., of

* *Ante*, p. 186.

the aforesaid Mr William Alexander had come in the year 1806. These persons swore (in America) that all his papers had been "sent to auction *en masse*," prior to the year 1812, and that "among them were a number of large parchments," and that, though diligent search had been made for them, none could then be found or heard of. The claimant next averred that the original charter had been duly registered in the Register of the Great Seal, at Edinburgh, but that the record of it "had perished or disappeared" in consequence of the loss—a matter of public notoriety—of a part of the Register, as had been officially testified by the Lords of Council and Session to the House of Lords, on the 27th February 1760. For these reasons, "it was necessary, in order to supply the place of the said charter of Novodamus, that THE TENOR of it should be proved," as prayed for;* that the claimant "was possessed of AN ABRIDGED COPY OR ABSTRACT of the said charter," which could be produced in court with the summons; that such copy or abstract was authenticated by the said Thomas Conyers, who had the original charter in his keeping; and the same, and other documents offered, are sufficient evidence for proving the existence and tenor of the said charter."

It may be here as well to give some notion of what is called in Scotland a charter of "Novodamus," and which we find, in our limited knowledge of the subject, some difficulty in squaring precisely, in point of character, with the tenor of the instrument put forward as such by the prisoner, as indicated in a former page.† A charter of *Novo*damus does not, in spite of its name, necessarily imply the existence of a former charter, but may be equally an original or a renewed grant. Everything comprised by it is held to be effectually conveyed to the donee, though he may have had no antecedent title to it. The true nature of the charter of Novodamus, however, is, when the superior, whether the crown or a subject,

* *Ante*, p. 190. † *Ante*, p. 195.

really *re*-grants the matters therein contained, to remedy any defect or flaw in the former grant; or where the grantee seeks to avoid burthens chargeable in respect of "casualties," *i. e.*, emoluments fallen due to the superior.* It may be well to bear in mind this attempted explanation, when hereafter adverting to one or two clauses in the famous "Excerpt-charter of Novodamus." When the fact is adverted to of the prisoner having, as long before as the years 1815 or 1816, consulted Mr Corrie, his family solicitor, a respectable professional man, who, as we have seen, had been the confidential adviser and trustee of the prisoner's father, on the subject of his claim to the earldom, and then acknowledged to him that "he had *no documents*, or no *effectual* documents, to support his claims;" and that it was not till ten or eleven years afterwards that we have any trace of his movements or proceedings; when, in 1826, he produced the affidavit of Hovenden, the statement of Gordon, and the certificate of Conyers, and, three years afterwards, the memorable "excerpt" charter, of which he had heard for the first time from Mr Banks in March 1829; when all this is borne in mind together, the above narrative affords matter for curious speculation, especially as to the state of facts existing in 1815, and the developments of the ensuing ten years. We must, however, hasten on.

The crown lawyers of Scotland were at length startled by the persevering energy, system, and success, which characterised and attended the movements of the prisoner, and the results to which they were leading. In the year 1833, therefore, they resolved to undertake the task of demolishing the entire fabric of his proofs; and, on the 15th of January, in that year, commenced formidable proceedings, denominated as those of "*Reductive-Improbation*," having for their object to obtain a solemn judicial declaration that everything done by the prisoner, in the prosecution of his claim, was null and void, and, as such,

* Erskine's *Institutes*, book ii. title iii. sec. 23.

should be rescinded and annulled; that his vouchers were fabricated, and that he was not the great-great-great-grandson of the first Earl of Stirling, and had no pretensions to assume the name or title, or exercise the rights appertaining to it. Thus, at length, challenged to mortal encounter, the prisoner brought forward, in support of his claim, several witnesses, as well as documentary evidence, among which were the affidavits of Henry Hovenden and Sara Lyner, aforementioned; but the celebrated "*excerpt*" having, as we have seen, been twice rejected by the courts in former proceedings, did not make its appearance in this new and serious stage of the proceedings. It appears to have been a very protracted inquiry—three years having elapsed between the commencement of it, in January 1833, and the delivery of the Lord Ordinary's (Cockburn) interlocutory judgment, at the close of December 1836.

The object of the prisoner in that inquiry was to prove the pedigree, as it appears in a previous page*—that is, to connect the *three John Alexanders* there set forth, in the relationship of father, son, and grandson; and the object of his opponents, of course, was to disprove such relationship. Judging solely from the materials placed before us by Mr Swinton, and not familiar with the details of Scotch legal proceedings, we are astonished at the time taken to demolish the most flimsy structure of pedigree proof we ever remember to have seen—always excepting in the droll page of the novelist. In the English courts, half a day would have sufficed for the purpose. Nay, we question whether any member of the Bar, with any legal reputation to lose or endanger, would have seriously offered, or at least pressed on a judge and jury, such evidence as was tendered, and long and solemnly canvassed, by the Scottish courts in this instance: we are speaking, of course, without the advantage of having the full proceedings before us.

* *Ante*, p. 194.

Yet we are bound to say that the judgment pronounced by the Lord Ordinary* is exceedingly able and convincing, and characterised by a courteous and dignified gravity, pregnant with indications of suppressed severity of comment on the audacity which could have offered such materials for judicial exposition. The case stood briefly thus, according to his important and decisive judgment:—It was admitted by the crown lawyers that the prisoner was the lawful son of Hannah Alexander, and that she was the daughter of the Reverend John Alexander, said to have died in 1743; but they strenuously denied its having been proved that he was the son of John (No. 2) of Antrim, or that this last was the son of John (No. 1) of Gartmore, the fourth son of the first Earl of Stirling. "*The whole of the defender's case*," said the Lord Ordinary, emphatically, "*depends upon the genuineness of these two descents.*" In attacking that case, the crown lawyers proved incontestably, at starting, that John of Gartmore (so called because he had married Agnes Graham, the heiress of Gartmore), had issue by her a *daughter* only! Unless, therefore, *as intimated by the Lord Ordinary during the progress of the case*, and coincided in by the prisoner's counsel, he contracted a SECOND MARRIAGE, the whole case fell to the ground. The lucky suggestion would appear to have been eagerly snatched at; and it was asserted that there had been such a second marriage. Of such marriage, however, not a tittle of evidence was offered, except inferentially, from the supposed proofs of his having had a son! "The fact of the second marriage," said the Lord Ordinary, "is not even attempted to be established by any direct or separate evidence." This seemed like laying the axe at the root of the tree. Next came the Lord Ordinary to the proof of "the *filiation* of the two Johns," consisting of the two affidavits of Sara Lyner and Hovenden, a tomb-stone inscription, and the examination of two very old female

* Swinton, Appendix, p. 22.

witnesses. First, as to the affidavits, even admitting them to be genuine, they seemed liable to almost every conceivable objection to their admissibility: made, not by relatives or connexions, but by total strangers to the family, of whose means of knowledge nothing was known! in no judicial cause! before no opponent capable of questioning and testing their truth, under circumstances "with which," said the Lord Ordinary, "we are not in the slightest degree acquainted!" made, not *post litem*, but *post controversiam motam!* They might have been voluntary affidavits, and made for fraudulent purposes! The Lord Ordinary, notwithstanding, deemed it advisable, on the whole, not to reject them *in limine*, as inadmissible, but to admit them for the purpose of considering their credit and efficacy. The affidavit of Sara Lyner was so ludicrously deficient in all formal attributes of authenticity and attestation, that "it was difficult to imagine any document introduced into a case with poorer recommendations." The affidavit of Hovenden presented itself in an infinitely more questionable shape; for, though professing to have been sworn before, and to bear the signature of, one "J. Pocklington," admitted by the crown lawyers to have been a Baron of the Exchequer in Ireland in 1723, and attested by Hovenden, whose signature purported to be again attested by a notary-public, they averred that the paper on which the body of the affidavit was written had been originally *covered with some other writing*, constituting the affidavit really sworn before Baron Pocklington; and which had been chemically removed, to make way for the existing affidavit. "The evidence of this charge of fabrication," said the Lord Ordinary, "which is not directed against the defender (*i. e.*, the prisoner) personally, consists of the appearance of the paper, and the uncontradicted testimony of Dr Fyfe and Dr Gregory, two gentlemen of undoubted character and skill in chemistry." "The Lord Ordinary," he continues, in a forbearing tone, "is very unwilling to hold this painful charge to be legally established,* and therefore carries the result no further than this—that the paper is exposed to a degree of suspicion which makes it unsafe to rely on this document." Having thus tolerated the reception of these two disgraced documents, let us see what they contained. That of Sara Lyner stated that she was eighty-four years old; nursed the mother of the Rev. John Alexander (John No. 3) when he was born; and that he was the son of John of Antrim (No. 2), in whose family she had lived twenty years. But how did she connect John of Antrim with John of Gartmore? How pass over this great gulf? She said that *her mother* had lived in the service of Lord Montgomery; and while there, no date being given, Mr John Alexander *of Gartmore*, a son of the Lord Stirline, in Scotland, came to see my lord, and brought with him his only son—who was—Mr John Alexander of Antrim! This is the whole scope of the affidavit—the unexplained *assertion*, or conjecture, of that solitary witness—"he brought with him his only son, and that son was—John of Antrim!" The second affidavit is one which, if true, settled the whole matter compendiously, completely, and conclusively, in favour of the prisoner. Mr Hovenden commenced by the invaluable statement, that he was "intimately acquainted with the reverend minister, John Alexander, grandson, and only male representative of John Alexander of Gartmore, the fourth son of William, first Earl of Stirling, in Scotland;"—which said John Alexander was formerly of Antrim; "but was then (16th July 1723) dwelling in Warwickshire, in Great Britain!" It was to establish, as facts, the above neat little course of descent, that this affidavit had been offered in evidence: but the above pregnant sentence formed only an introductory statement, the body of the affidavit consisting of an account of its deponent having been informed by the said Rev. John Alexander (John No. 3) that the original

* Neither of these affidavits formed an article of charge in the indictments against the prisoner.

charter of the earldom was in the possession of Thomas Conyers; to whom the deponent went at the particular desire of Mr Alexander, on the 10th July 1723, and was shown the original charter, in Latin, dated the 7th December 1639: and then followed "a faithful translation of the clause" which operated that signal change in the original destination, under which the prisoner claimed. And, finally, there was indorsed, or subscribed, to their affidavit, the following memorandum, purporting to be by a son of the aforesaid Thomas Conyers:—

"I willingly bear testimony to the truth of this statement, and the written affidavit. Lord Stirling's charter was trusted to my late father in troublous times, by y[e] dec[d] Mary, Countesse of Mr Alexander, without the present Earl's consent.

"Carlow, 20th July 1723.
"THOS. CONYERS."

By "the present Earl," was meant the fifth and last Earl of Stirling—who survived the year in which this affidavit purported to have been made, sixteen years! It is pertinent here, with a view to subsequent elucidation, to remind the reader of another similar attestation, by this Mr "Thomas Conyers," to the accuracy of Mr William Gordon's abstract of the same clause of limitation in the charter in question.

As this affidavit was put forward before the Lord Ordinary only for the sake of its statement of pedigree, he despatched it on the same ground as that on which he had disposed of the affidavit of Sara Lyner—viz., as only a general assertion by a stranger to the family, with no circumstance stated in support of that assertion. So much for the affidavits. Then comes some tombstone evidence.

"Tombstones," said the Lord Ordinary, with a sort of subdued sarcasm, "have sometimes gone far to decide pedigrees; but probably none were ever founded on, in circumstances like the one relied on by the defender;" and the reader will probably be of the same opinion. The evidence consisted of an alleged inscription on a tombstone in the churchyard at Newtown-lands, in Ireland; which inscription, quoth the Lord Ordinary, drily, "is very strong in the defender's [the prisoner's] favour; *as strong as if it had been composed for this very case!*" The reader will bear in mind this observation, as we shall hereafter have occasion to present him, in full splendour, with this "Inscription." Suffice it to say, for the present, that the tombstone which bore it was confessedly not in existence; the copy relied on was alleged to have been inscribed on a page in a Bible, which also was confessedly not in existence! And the shape in which the copy was presented was—a piece of paper, purporting to have been that page in that Bible! The alleged leaf was headed thus:—"Inscription on my grandfather's [John No. 1—of Gartmore] tomb, at Newton: copied for me by Mr Hum. Lyttleton." Who this last gentleman was, no one knew: no one proved his handwriting—but *we* shall shortly hear something not a little curious about him. And the only evidence in support of this all-important document was a sort of certificate by four persons—that "this leaf, *taken out of* poor *John's* bible, is put up, with the other family papers, for my son *Benjamin*. Done this 16 Dec. 1766, in the presence of my friends, who, at my request, have subscribed their names as witnesses!" The absurdity of all this is cuttingly exposed by the Lord Ordinary. It was then sought to corroborate this alleged "copy" by showing that there really had been such a tombstone: and how, thinks the reader? By the evidence of a pauper eighty years old, the widow of a mason, who, forty-four years before, had *told her* that he had seen a tombstone in the floor of the old church, with the words, "John Alexander, Esq., Antrim," upon it; and that he had built this stone into the walls of the church for better preservation. If so, it was safe and visible in the wall at the time of his telling her that fact—viz., in 1792: and that fact was directly and conclusively disproved by evidence!

Finally, the old pauper aforesaid, and another elderly woman, were called to speak to statements concerning the fact of relationship in dispute, exceeding in absurdity even what has gone before—strangers' hearsay, upon hearsay, upon hearsay! For instance, one of them, a stranger, says—"*I* heard my *grandmother* say, that *she* heard *her father* say! that the said John of Antrim was *come* of the Alexander from Scotland, and was *nearly* related to the Earl of Mount Alexander, in Ireland. I heard my *grandmother* also say that *she* had heard from *her father*, that John of Gartmore was—the Honourable John Alexander, and was the father of John of Antrim!" *

"On the whole," concludes the Lord Ordinary, "he is of opinion that the evidence, whether considered in its separate parts, or as a whole, is utterly insufficient to sustain the verdicts. And it is impossible not to be struck with the number of collateral facts by which, if the claim be well founded, the proof might have been strengthened, but in which there is a total absence of evidence." The Lord Ordinary decreed accordingly, leaving the claimant to the Stirling peerage prostrate. Bitter, indeed, must have been his mortification and disappointment, at the blight thus fallen upon the fond hopes of so many years, rendering all his anxieties and exertions utterly bootless.

But how little he must have dreamed of the wonderful events which a very few months, nay, weeks, were to produce! They may have appeared to him like two direct and very special interpositions of Providence in his behalf!

It will have been remembered that the Lord Ordinary emphatically declared the two great gaps in the pedigree proof to be—the Rev. John Alexander's (John No. 3) being the son of John of Antrim (John No. 2); and John of Antrim's being the son of John of Gartmore

* Swinton, Appendix, p. xxix.

(John No. 1). This decree was pronounced on the 10th December 1836; and on the 8th day after that disastrous event, viz., on the 18th December 1836, pressed by pecuniary difficulties, and the vindictiveness of his enemies, the prisoner says he went to France, under a feigned name, and lived in great seclusion in or near Paris, till the 15th August 1837, when he returned to Scotland, to vote at the election of Scotch Peers. During that otherwise cheerless interval, occurred, in April and July, the two signal discoveries above alluded to. We shall give his own summary of the results thus obtained, quoting from the official "Minute" given in by him to the court on the 15th Nov. 1837, in the name of his two eminent counsel.

"The defender has lately come to the knowledge of various documents which tend very materially to strengthen the evidence of propinquity, in regard to THE TWO DESCENTS referred to by the Lord Ordinary. By these newly-discovered documents he trusts he will be able to establish that John Alexander of Gartmore (John No. 1),* after he had lost his wife, Agnes Graham, heiress of Gartmore, married, as his second wife, Elizabeth Maxwell, of Londonderry, by whom he had an only son, JOHN, who died at Derry in 1665–6. That this son John (John No. 2), son of John of Gartmore, received his early education at Londonderry; was afterwards sent to a German university; and, after being many years abroad, settled at *Antrim;* married Mary Hamilton, of Bangor; had by her one son, John (John No. 3) and two daughters; died on the 19th April 1712, and was buried at Newtown. That Mr Livingston, an old friend of the family, wrote the *Inscription* † to his memory, which was on the tombstone at Newtown-lands; and that Mr Lyttleton's copy of it was known in 1765. That the said John Alexander of Antrim (John No. 2) had encouraged the taste of his son (John No. 3) for the ministry

* Refer to the Pedigree, *ante,* p. 194.

† *Post,* p. 221.

of the Church of Scotland; and that the said son, who was the Rev. John Alexander, died at Dublin on the 1st November 1743."*

These decisive facts were sought to be substantiated by two classes of documents, of an equally remarkable character, respectively finding their way to the prisoner anonymously, in April and July 1837 — the one in London, the other at Paris.

I. Mr Eugene Alexander, the third son of the prisoner, happening, towards the close of April 1837, to call at Messrs De Porquet and Co.'s, booksellers in London, who had been occasionally employed by the prisoner, was informed by them that they had just received by the twopenny-pòst, a packet addressed to them, which inclosed another, addressed, "The Right Hon. the Earl of Stirling," accompanied by the following note, addressed to them, in a lady's hand, without disguise:—"Mrs Innes Smyth's compliments to Messrs De Porquet and Co. She had fully intended calling in Tavistock Street, when she arrived in town yesterday from Staffordshire; but another commission she had to execute having prevented her, she is induced to send the inclosed packet to them by the twopenny post, with her particular request that they will forward it *instantly* to the Earl of Stirling, or any member of his lordship's family, whose residence may be known to them.—Hackney, April 19."—Who "Mrs Innes Smyth" was, neither the prisoner nor any of his family could discover; and she remains to this hour, for aught we can gather to the contrary, utterly unknown, having come like a shadow, and so departed. Mr Alexander seems to have been not a little flustered by the occurrence; and having immediately consulted some solicitors, he and they went to a notary-public the next morning, and in his presence opened the packet addressed to his father; when they discovered another packet, cased in parchment, on which was written, "Some of my wife's family papers." On seeing this, he instantly exclaimed,

* Swinton, Appendix, p. xxxi.

"That is my grandfather's handwriting!" "This inner packet," continued his son, in writing to his father, "was sealed with three black seals, all the same impression—evidently my grandfather's seals — not like those *we* have." Accompanying this inner parchment packet was the following mysterious note:—"The enclosed was in a small cash-box, which was stolen from the late William Humphreys, Esq., at the time of his removing from Digleth House, Birmingham, to Fair Hill. The person who committed the theft was a young man in a situation in trade which placed him above suspicion. Fear of detection, and other circumstances, caused the box to be carefully put away, and it was forgot that the packet of papers was left in it. This discovery has been made since the death of the person alluded to, which took place last month. His family, being now certain that the son of Mr Humphreys is the Lord Stirling who has lately published a narrative of his case, they have requested a lady going to London to leave the packet at his lordship's publishers, a channel for its conveyance pointed out by the book itself, and which they hope is quite safe. His lordship will perceive that the seals have never been broken. The family of the deceased, for obvious reasons, must remain unknown. They make this reparation; but cannot be expected to court disgrace and infamy.—April 17, 1837."*—"The sheet of paper on which this was written," said young Mr Alexander, "is a mourning one, with a deep black edge round, owing to the death of the thief."† The inner packet was then taken to a proctor, and opened by young Mr Alexander in the presence of four witnesses, and proved to contain five documents, all bearing most decisively, and indeed conclusively, on that precise part of the prisoner's case pronounced by the Lord Ordinary to have been defective! One was a genealogical tree, purporting to have been made out by a "Thos. Campbell,"

* Swinton, p. 19. † Ibid. Appendix, p. xliii.

on the 15th April 1759; and, to be sure, it was calculated to settle the whole matter: for it set out the two marriages of John of Gartmore, the second being with "Elizabeth Maxwell of Londonderry;" that by this second wife he had a son, John, "who married Mary Hamilton of Bangor, and settled at Antrim, after living many years in Germany—died 1712—buried at Newtown." That this John of Antrim had a son, "John, sixth Earl of Stirling (*de jure*)," and died at Dublin, 1st November 1743; and that this *de jure* sixth Earl of Stirling had four children; the eldest, "John, born at Dublin, 1736, heir to the titles and estates;" the second, Benjamin; the third, Mary; the fourth, "Hannah, born at Dublin in 1741." And this inestimable document bore the following inscription:—"Part of the genealogical tree of the Alexanders of Menstry, Earls of Stirling in Scotland, showing only the fourth and now" [*i. e.*, 1759, being twenty years after the death of the fifth earl, and sixteen years after that of the *de jure* sixth earl] "existing branch. Reduced to pocket size from the large emblazoned tree, in the possession of Mrs Alexander, of King Street, Birmingham, by me, Thos. Campbell, April 15, 1759." The next enclosure consisted of a letter from the above Benjamin to his elder brother, the Rev. John (both uncles of the prisoner). Benjamin spoke, in this letter, about the missing tombstone; its place, however, being supplied by "Mr Lyttleton's copy, which can be proved;" about "Campbell's copy of grandfather A.'s portrait being very like;" that a curious memorandum was pasted at the back, "from which it appears that our grandfather [*i. e.*, John of Antrim] received his early education at Londonderry, under the watchful eye of Mr MAXWELL, his MATERNAL grandsire. At the age of sixteen, the dowager-countess wished him to be sent to Glasgow College; but at last it was thought better for him to go to a German University. He attained high distinction as a scholar, remained many years abroad, and visited foreign courts. Yr. affe. bro. BENJAMIN

Alexander. Lond. 20 Aug. 1765. To Rev. Mr Alexander, Birmingham." A second letter was to the same person, from one "A. E. Baillie," dated 16th September 1765. He also alludes to the missing tombstone. "But I shall be ready," he proceeds, "to come forward, if you want me. I was about twenty-one when I attended y$^{r}$ grandfr.'s funeral [*i. e.*, John of Antrim], Mr Livingston, a very old friend of y$^{r}$ family, wrote y$^{e}$ inscription, w$^{h}$ y$^{e}$ claimant from America got destroyed. I always heard that y$^{r}$ great-grandf$^{r.}$ y$^{e}$ Honble. Mr Alexander (who was known in the country as Mr Alexander of Gartmoir), died at Derry; but for y$^{e}$ destruction of y$^{e}$ parish registers in y$^{e}$ North by y$^{e}$ Papists, during y$^{e}$ civil war from 1689 to 1692, you mit have got y$^{e}$ Certifs. you want." The above letters, thus first brought to light in April 1837, after "fifty years" had elapsed since the alleged theft of the packet containing them, became, when connected with the statements made in the affidavit of Eliza Pountney, the prisoner's sister, on the 27th of January 1826, deeply significant. We allude to her observations respecting her two uncles, John and Benjamin, and their intention to have claimed the peerage, but for their "dying in their prime;" and, on comparing dates, it will be found that the one (John) is alleged to have died in 1765, the year in which the above letters were addressed to him; and the other (Benjamin) three years afterwards—respectively in their twenty-ninth and thirty-first years! To return, however, to the mysterious black-sealed packet—it contained also "a beautiful miniature painting of John of Antrim." "The contents of the parchment packet must, I suppose," continued the son, in writing to his father, "have remained untouched (if it was put up just before the removal to Fairhill) fifty years, which accounts for the admirable state of preservation it is in. The thief never dared break the seals." The prisoner stated in his minute, "that these seals were identical with that on a letter which was in evidence, of the Rev. John Alexander

(John No. 3); that the impressions of both must have been made with the same seal." *

Such were the contents of "the DE PORQUET PACKET," as it may be called, of which the prisoner, when required by the court, on his lodging them in evidence, to state how he came by them, solemnly "declared that he never had any knowledge of the existence or contents of these documents until he heard that the packet had been transmitted to Messrs De Porquet, as above mentioned." †

It is also right here to apprise the reader, and recommend him to weigh the fact, that Mr Corrie, the solicitor already mentioned, whose veracity no one attempted to impeach, distinctly proved, at the trial of the prisoner, that the words, "some of my wife's family papers," on the outside of the packet, were really in the handwriting of the prisoner's father; and that the latter had told him, at Fairhill, in 1796-8, or 1797, that he had *lost valuable documents* at the time he removed from Digleth to Fairhill, since called "The Larches." ‡—So much for what we may, for distinction's sake, designate No. 1, the *English* windfall. Let us now proceed to No.

II. The *French* windfall. Here will be found accumulated wonders upon wonders!

The prisoner's wife, it has been seen, had been an intimate friend of Mademoiselle le Normand of Paris since the year 1812; and she kept up her correspondence with that lady, according to the prisoner's statement to the Court, up to the period of the pending investigations before the Scottish Courts. The prisoner had, he said, been frequently advised to prosecute inquiries after evidence in France; and his wife had made application on that subject to, amongst others, Mademoiselle le Normand, then upwards of seventy years old, having an extensive literary connexion, and facilities for acquiring information from public offices. She promised her assistance. The prisoner, having quitted England on the 18th

* Swinton, p. xxxii. † Ibid. p. xxxv. ‡ Ibid. p. 181.

December 1836, arrived at Paris on the 21st of that month. On the 12th of the ensuing July he waited upon her; and she told him "that she had received a document," to quote his own account of the matter, "which might be of importance to him; and, after conversing for some time about his family, she drew from under a heap of papers a packet, and showed to him its contents—an old map of Canada, with a great number of documents written on or pasted against the back of it, 'all relating to his family.'" "Various inquiries were afterwards made by her, for the purpose of tracing the individuals in whose custody the document had been previously preserved, but without effect." She said that this map, in its now state, had come into her possession on the 11th of July 1837, and was accompanied by an anonymous letter in French, dated the 10th of July 1837, of which the following is a translation:—

"I have just heard, Mademoiselle, that you take a lively interest in the success of an Englishman, who claims, as a descendant of the Earl of Stirling, the inheritance of his ancestor in America. If the autographs which I have the honour of sending you can insure his success, I shall be delighted to have found an opportunity, by rendering him a service, of gratifying you, and at the same time discharging a small portion of the obligations which I owe to you. I regret, however, that the duties of an office which I at present hold do not permit me to make myself known in this affair of Lord Stirling's. You, who know a great deal about it, will feel no surprise that a man in office (*qu'un homme en place*) should not dare to interfere in it openly. I have already stated that I am under obligations to you. Yes, Mademoiselle, I am, and more than once have I had the advantage of consulting you: even at the time when I was menaced with a signal disgrace, it was you who saved me, by a salutary *éclaircissement* seasonably given. You have not obliged an ungrateful man. On all occasions, I do justice to your talents; and to you, while I live, I shall be devoted and grateful. You may well imagine that I purchased this old map of Canada solely on account of the autographs, which are very curious. The note on the margin of Mallet's note (in the right corner) is said to be Louis the Fifteenth's. The autographs of Fénélon and Flechier are no less precious; and the dealer, who sold me the map in 1819,* assured me that it had belonged to Louis XVI., which is probable enough, from what I have just said of his grandfather's marginal note. The dealer lived, in 1819, on the Quai Voltaire, but since that time many changes have taken place, *and his name has escaped me.* Receive, Mademoiselle, the homage of the distinguished sentiments which I have vowed to you, and which you so well deserve.—M. *Versailles*, 10*th July* 1837.

"I confide this packet to trustworthy persons. They will go to consult you: do not be surprised to find it on some table or chair, in your study."

This mysterious "M," equally with the mysterious "Mrs Innes Smyth," has hitherto (as far as we know) remained altogether undiscovered; and the prisoner solemnly declared "that he never knew of the existence, or contents, of the several documents on the map of Canada, until he saw the map itself in the hands of Mademoiselle le Normand, in July 1837; that he had never dreamed of seeking in France the document illustrative of his own pedigree; and it was with the greatest surprise that he afterwards learned that those documents, now produced, had been discovered, and were calculated to throw light on that pedigree; and, in fact, no one was more surprised."† We doubt whether a more extraordinary document, or series of documents, than this map, with its accompaniments, has ever, either before or since, challenged deliberate judicial investigation.

"In consequence of the cession," said the prisoner,‡ "as is alleged, of Nova Scotia to France, by the Treaty of Breda, in 1667, and its subsequent recovery by Great

* *Vide post*, p. 264. † Swinton, Appendix, p. xxxviii.
‡ Ibid. xxx. p. vi.

Britain in 1690, and in consequence of the stipulations in regard to it in the Treaty of Ryswick in 1697, everything connected with the possession of that country became a matter of much interest at the Court of France. The grants to the Earl of Stirling thus came to be well known, and the effect of them much canvassed. Influenced by these considerations, he was induced to direct anxious searches to be made in France, for any documents that might throw light on the family of Stirling.* It appears from these documents," continued the prisoner, briefly but correctly indicating their general character and tendency, "that a Monsieur Mallet wished to obtain information in England as to the actual state of the descendants of William, Earl of Stirling; but that, having died suddenly, one of his friends — a M. Brossette — applied to FENELON, Archbishop of Cambray, for the wished-for information; and that the Archbishop, knowing the intimacy that subsisted between the Marchioness de Lambert and Mr John Alexander of Antrim, applied to her on the subject: that she accordingly wrote to him, who, in return, sent her a full communication as to the family history: that this letter was transmitted to her by the Archbishop, who forwarded it to M. Brossette."

Anxious to avail himself of this important new evidence, the prisoner, having previously prevailed on Madlle. le Normand to procure attestations of the hand-writings of the different parties, sent over his son, Charles Alexander, from Edinburgh to Paris, for the purpose of receiving the precious documents, and bringing them over in safety to this country. They were delivered to him by Madlle. le Normand on the 8th November 1837: on that day he quitted Paris for Scotland, and a week afterwards—viz., on the 15th November, 1837 — the existence of these documents, as well as of the De Porquet packet, and an outline of the points they were to prove, was formally certified, and they were laid on the table of the Court of

* Swinton, Appendix, p. xxxii.

Session at Edinburgh: and a sensation they were well calculated to produce.

The map purported to bear date (and it is an all-important one) A. D. 1703, and bore the following printed heading—"Carte du Canada, ou de la Nouvelle France, par Guillaume Delisle," the most celebrated geographer of his day. With the exception of one of the two documents *pasted* on the back of the map—that in English—all the remaining indorsements were in French, and every word of them deserves weighing. We shall take them in the order in which they appeared in the indictment.

I. First came the note, or memorandum, signed "Ph. Mallet," dated "Lyons, 4th August, 1706. During my residence in Acadia in 1702, my curiosity was excited by what I was told of an ancient charter, preserved in the archives of that province. It is the *Charter* of Confirmation, or *De novo damus*, of date 7th December 1639, by which Charles I. of England renewed, in favour of William, Earl of Stirling, the titles and dignities which he had previously conferred upon him, and all the grants of land which he had made to him from 1621, in Scotland and America. My friend Lacroix gave me a copy of it, which, before my departure, I took the precaution of having duly attested. From this authentic document I am now about to present some extracts (translated into French for such as do not understand Latin), in order that every person who opens this map of our American possessions may form an idea of the vast extent of territory which was granted by the King of England to one of his subjects. If the fate of war, or any other event, should return New France and Acadia under the dominion of the English, the family of Stirling would possess these two provinces, as well as New England, within the boundaries assigned by the charter. The order of succession to this inheritance is as follows:—" and then followed a fuller quotation from the limitations by way of *Novo damus*, than even those given by Gordon and Hovenden, and certified by Conyers.* The memorandum thus concludes:—"Thus the King of England has given to the Earl, and has secured to his descendants in perpetuity, enough of land to found a powerful empire in America."

II. Memorandum subscribed to the above, signed "Caron Saint Estienne," and dated "Lyons, 6th April 1707."

"The above note is precious. I can certify that it gives in few words an extremely correct idea of the wonderful charter in question. As to the copy of it, it is attested by the keeper of the records (l'archiviste) and the Acadian witnesses, and must be in entire conformity with the register of Port Royal. While at Quebec, I had heard of the grants to the Earl of Stirling; but my friend M. Mallet was the first who procured me a perusal of the charter. This extraordinary document extends over fifty pages of writing, and the Latin anything but classical; still, as a Canadian, somewhat interested in its contents, I am bound to say that I read it from end to end with as much curiosity as satisfaction. The late M. Mallet was a man whose good qualities and rare understanding make us regret a death which snatched him so suddenly from his friends. He had foreseen that the copy would not make the charter known in France: hence he carried the idea of writing, on one of the beautiful maps of Guillaume Delisle, a note which all the world could read with interest. Had he lived long enough he would have added to this interest: for he wished to obtain information in England as to the then situation of the descendants of the earl who had obtained the charter; and all the information which he might have received respecting them, he would have transferred to this very map. But, after all, with the two documents which he has left to us, no person in France can question the existence of such a charter."

III. Memorandum, also subscribed to that of M. Mallet, signed "*Esprit, Ev. de Nismes,*" [*i. e.* Esprit

* *Ante*, p. 196.

Flechier, Bishop of Nismes] and dated Nismes, 3d June 1707.

"I read lately, at the house of Monsieur Sartre, at Caveirac, the copy of the Earl of Stirling's charter. In it I remarked many curious particulars, mixed up with a great many uninteresting details. I think, therefore, that the greatest obligations are due to M. Mallet, for having, by the above note, enabled the French public to judge of the extent and importance of the grants made to that Scottish nobleman. I also find that he has translated the most essential clauses of the charter; and in translating them into French, he has given them with great fidelity. M. Caron Saint Estienne has asked me to bear this testimony. I do so with the greatest pleasure."

IV. Letter from "John Alexander, of Antrim" [John No. 2], to the Marchioness de Lambert.

"Antrim, *27th August* 1707.

"I cannot express to you, madam, how sensible I am of the honour of your remembrance. My sincere thanks are due also to Monsieur de Cambray, since he, by facilitating the journey of my friend M. Hovenden, was the means of my being so quickly put in possession of your letter, and the copy which you have been good enough to send to me of the note respecting my grandfather's charter. The questions which you ask of me I shall endeavour to answer to the best of my ability. I am not, as you suppose, heir to the family titles. The present head of our family is Henry, fifth Earl of Stirling, descended from the third son of my grandfather. He resides within a few miles of London; has no children; but has brothers, of whom the eldest is heir-presumptive. Of the first son no descendants survive, except the issue of his daughters. The second son died without issue. My father was the fourth son; his first wife was an heiress of the house of Gartmore, in Scotland; my mother, of the Maxwell family, was his second wife. But though he had daughters by his first wife, he never had any sons but me. To complete this family genealogy, I must tell you, madam, that my wife is a cadette of the Hamilton family, a ducal house in Scotland; and that she has borne me a son called John, after my father and myself, and two daughters. I have, at present, so little idea of the possibility of the title and estates of Stirling devolving on my children, that I have encouraged my son in his inclination for the ministry of our Church of Scotland; and with that view he is now prosecuting his studies at the university of Leyden, in Holland.

"I shall preserve with care the interesting note of M. Mallet. The charter was at one time registered in Scotland, as well as in Acadia; but during the civil war, and under the usurpation of Cromwell, boxes containing a portion of the records of that kingdom were lost during a storm at sea; and, according to the ancient tradition of our family, the register in which this charter was recorded was among the number of those that perished. Such, madam, is all "[!]" that I can say in reply to your questions; for it is impossible, in this country of Ireland, to obtain any other information with regard to the registered charter. I believe that my grandmother" [the widow of the first earl] "gave the original charter, which she brought from Scotland when she came to take up her abode in Ireland, to her son-in-law, Lord Montgomery, in order that he might preserve it carefully in Castle Comber, where he resided. I shall ascertain what this family may have done with it; and I shall have the honour of acquainting you with any discovery which I may make. I shall never forget, madam, your kindness towards me, or the charms of the society which I have always enjoyed at your house. While I live, I shall not cease to be attached to you, by the most respectful devotion.

"JOHN ALEXANDER."

V. Memorandum authenticating the above by FENELON, Archbishop of Cambray!

"The friends of the late Mr Ph. Mallet will doubtless

read with great interest this letter of a grandson of the Earl of Stirling's. M. Cholet, of Lyons, setting out to-day, 16*th October* 1707, on his way home, will have the honour of delivering it to M. Brossette, on the part of Madame de Lambert. To authenticate it, I have written and signed this marginal note. FR. AR. DUC DE CAMBRAY."

The above letter of "John Alexander of Antrim," with Fénélon's marginal authentication, was *pasted* on the back of the map; as also was a portion of the envelope of the letter with the seal upon it of the aforesaid John of Antrim.

VI. Inscription on the tablet erected to the memory of John of Antrim (John No. 2).

"HERE LIETH THE BODY OF
JOHN ALEXANDER, ESQUIRE,
LATE OF ANTRIM,
THE ONLY SON OF THE HONOURABLE JOHN ALEXANDER.
HE WAS THE FOURTH SON OF THAT MOST ILLUSTRIOUS
AND FAMOUS STATESMAN,
WILLIAM EARL OF STERLINE,
PRINCIPAL SECRETARY FOR SCOTLAND:
WHO HAD THE SINGULAR MERIT OF PLANTING AT HIS
SOLE, EXPENSE THE FIRST COLONIE IN
NOVA SCOTIA.
HE MARRY'D MARY, ELDEST DAUGHTER OF THE
REV. MR HAMILTON OF BANGOR,
BY WHOM HE HAD ISSUE AN SON, JOHN, WHO
AT THIS PRESENT TIME IS THE PRESBYTERIAN MINISTER
AT STRATFORD-ON-AVON, IN ENGLAND,
AND TWO DAUGHTERS,
MARY, WHO SURVIVES, AND ELIZABETH, WIFE OF
JOHN M. SKINNER, ESQ., WHO DIED 7 JAN. $17\frac{10}{11}$,
LEAVING THREE CHILDREN.
HE WAS A MAN OF SUCH ENDOWMENTS AS ADDED
LUSTRE TO HIS NOBLE DESCENT, AND WAS UNIVERSALLY
RESPECTED FOR HIS PIETY AND BENEVOLENCE.
HE WAS THE BEST OF HUSBANDS:
AS A FATHER MOST INDULGENT: AS A FRIEND
WARM, SINCERE, AND FAITHFUL.
HE DEPARTED THIS LIFE
AT TEMPLE PATRICK, IN THE COUNTY OF ANTRIM.
ON THE 19TH DAY OF APRIL 1712."

The above was written in imitation of print, in small

capitals, and surrounded by an ornamental etching, or bordering, as if to represent the shape of the tablet. On the margin was written :—

"This is a faithfull copy of the Inscription to the Memory of John Alexander, Esquire, upon the Tablet over his Tomb, at Newtoun-Ardes, Co. of Down, Ireland.

"W. C. GORDON, Jun.

"Stratford-upon-Avon, *Oct.* 6, 1723."

This inscription and attestation were pasted on the back of the map; and adjoining it was the following corroborative attestation, forming

VII. Memorandum, written on the back, but without any date or signature.

"This inscription has been communicated by Madame de Lambert. Since the death of Mr Alexander in 1712" (John of Antrim), "this lady has not ceased to bestow on the son of this distinguished man marks of her goodwill and friendship. This son is favourably known in England as a Protestant clergyman, and a learned philologist. In the knowledge of Oriental languages, he is almost without a rival. He is at the head of a college for the education of young clergymen, established at Stratford, in the county of Warwick."

VIII., and finally, came a royal autograph, adjoining Memorandum No. I.,—*i. e.*, that of Ph. Mallett—in the alleged handwriting, bold and flowing, of Louis XV.! as follows :—

"This note is worthy of some attention, under present circumstances; but let the copy of the original charter be sent to me." *

Such was the "French windfall," as we have termed it: a staggering accumulation of proposed proofs such as, when examined, might perhaps not unreasonably excite the astonishment, and then, in some degree, the suspicions

* "Cette note est digne de quelque attention dans les cérconstances presentes—mais qu'on m'envoie la copie de la charte origènale." [Observe the spelling of the words—"*cérconstances,*" "*origènale.*"]

of the Scottish legal authorities.—As we have seen, the De Porquet and Le Normand packets of documents were placed before the Court of Session on the 15th of November 1837, on behalf of the prisoner. During the ensuing twelvemonth, interlocutory investigations, we apprehend, were being carried on; the result being, that on the 14th of November 1838, the Lords of Session ordered the prisoner "to give in, within fourteen days, an articulate condescendence of the facts and circumstances how he came to the knowledge of the documents in question, and how they came into his possession." * In obedience to this order (we know not whether it be an order of course), he duly gave into court substantially the account which has been incorporated into the foregoing narrative. Growing still more dissatisfied with the aspect and position of the prisoner's case, especially in relation to these additional proofs, and not satisfied by the articulate condescendence which he had already given in, the Lords of Session, on the 11th of December, ordered "the *unusual* proceeding," as Mr Swinton himself characterises it, † of a personal "judicial examination" of the prisoner. He therefore came before the Second Division of the Court of Session, on the 18th December 1838, and was subjected to a lengthened and searching series of questions by the Lord Advocate. We presume that the Court had power to take this "unusual" step, as it may well be termed, which, be it observed, was in the course of a merely *civil* proceeding, as far as we understand the matter; and (speaking with the utmost deference and respect towards the Scottish judicial authorities) it does seem an extraordinary stretch of power, to call one of the parties to a civil suit before the Court, and subject him, *nolentem volentem*, to a highly criminating course of examination, afterwards to be made available on prosecution—and that, too, without any caution that his answers might be used against him, nor any intimation that he need not answer unless he chose.

* Swinton, Appendix, p. 34.

† Ibid. Pref. xvii.

This "judicial declaration" is given at length by Mr Swinton,* and after a formal entry begins thus:—"Compeared Alexander Earl of Stirling, and interrogated by the Lord-Advocate, if he had read the condescendence given in, in his name? Declares, that he has. Interrogated, if he desires to make any additions, or alterations, on that condescendence? Declares, that he is ready to make any further explanations that may be asked." And then commences an able and acute examination, with the critical question—"When he was first made acquainted with the note issued by Lord Cockburn, dated 10th December 1836?"—proceeding with his journey to France;—enquiring how he spent his time there, and particularly respecting his intercourse with old Mademoiselle le Normand; his pecuniary obligations to her; the securities he had given her; what she said on delivering to him the memorable map of Canada—particularly whether she told him whom she suspected to have sent it to her: as to which, he said, "she had never told him." On this the court interposed, and asked—"Who he himself suspects to be the person by whom the document had been sent? Declares that he cannot venture to name that person, being of such exalted rank as to make such a declaration on his part unsafe and improper, without positive proof. That he neither can, nor dare do more, having only strong suspicions on the subject." † He was closely questioned as to his wife's intercourse with Mademoiselle le Normand; and as to the first tidings he received concerning the De Porquet papers. He was then asked several questions respecting the alleged robbery of his father in 1793–4, when he removed from Digleth House to Fairhill. Declares, "that he has heard his father mention that he had lost a cash-box containing some hundred pounds, but never heard him say anything of papers," ‡ which seems a striking and candid answer. Among the remaining questions and answers, are the following:—

* Swinton, Appendix, p. 37. † Ibid. p. 39. ‡ Ibid. p. 41.

"Interrogated, whether he ever heard, before the reception of the packet from Messrs De Porquet, that John Alexander, fourth son of the first Earl of Stirling, had been married a second time, after having been first married to a daughter of Graham of Gartmore? Declares, *he never had;* but he suspected it, as a general conclusion drawn by him and his friends from other facts in the case. He had never before heard that John Alexander had been married to a lady of the name of Maxwell, as connected with his family." This, again, is worthy of much consideration.

Shortly after this examination, the prisoner was apprehended on the charge of forgery; and almost immediately, viz., 14th February 1839, underwent another close examination by the Sheriff Substitute, but only after giving him the caution usual in England—that it was optional with him to answer, and that, if he did answer, what he said might be used in evidence against him. Four days afterwards, viz., on the 18th February 1839, he was subjected to a second lengthened examination; and finally to a third, on the 6th of March 1839; but on this last occasion he gave only one answer to the few but important questions put to him—"That, by his agent's advice, he declines to answer any questions;" and well he, or any one similarly situated, honourably might!

He was committed for trial, which was ordered to take place on the 3d April 1839, but, at the instance of the prisoner's counsel, was postponed till the 29th of that month.

The Indictment was necessarily long, and founded on three classes of alleged forgeries: first, the excerpt charter of *Novodamus;* secondly, the De Porquet packet of papers; lastly, the Le Normand packet of papers—all of which the prisoner was charged with having forged, or having used and uttered, knowing them to have been forged. The indictment runs not, as in England, in the third person, but in the second, as addressed to the prisoner, personally, throughout: *e. g.*, "Alexander Humphreys, or Alexander, pretending to be Earl of Stirling, you are indicted and accused, at the instance of John Archibald Murray, Esq., her Majesty's Advocate, for her Majesty's interest, that," &c. All its allegations are direct and simple, and divested of technical verbiage. We shall now endeavour to present the reader with an intelligible account of an intensely-interesting trial; one which must have been listened to, from first to last, with breathless interest.

"ALEXANDER HUMPHREYS, or Alexander, *pretending* to be Earl of Stirling," said Lord Meadowbank,* addressing the prisoner, on his being first placed at the bar, "you have been served with an indictment charging you with the crimes of forgery, and of feloniously using and uttering, as genuine, certain documents therein described, and alleged to have been forged and fabricated, you knowing them to be so. Are you guilty, or not guilty?"

"Not guilty, my Lord," replied the prisoner, standing beside his friend, Colonel D'Aguilar. But now occurred the question, how was he to be tried? As a peer of Scotland, or as a commoner? If as a peer, the court before whom he stood was incompetent to try him; for he was entitled, by the Treaty of Union, as a peer of Scotland, to be tried as peers of Great Britain are tried—viz., in the Court of the Lord High Steward; and the mode of procedure is that prescribed in 1825 by Statute 6 Geo. iv. c. 66, which required the Scottish judges to be summoned and to sit with the English judges, and according to the law of Scotland. This privilege, however, as will be presently seen, the prisoner waived. Then came another question: was he to be tried as a "*landed* man?" by which is meant a landed proprietor. It is an ancient

* The duty here performed by the President of the Court, is in England discharged by an officer of the court called the clerk of Arraigns.

privilege of landed men, by the Scotch law, that they should be tried only by their peers, *i. e.*, their brother landed proprietors. In process of time, however, this right has been so far modified as to entitle the prisoner to a *majority* only of his landed brethren. This right also, as will shortly be seen, the prisoner waived—having probably no pretence to the possession of any lands in Scotland, except such as he claimed as Earl of Stirling. To meet any possible difficulty, however, on this score, two lists of assize had been prepared—respectively consisting of "*landed men* and common jurors," and "*special* jurors and common jurors:" the former to be adopted "if the said Alexander Humphreys claimed, and was entitled to, the privilege of a landed man;" the latter, "if he did not claim, or was not entitled to, the privilege of a landed man."

After the prisoner had pleaded not guilty, the clerk in court read aloud the "defences" which, according to the procedure in Scotland, had been lodged in court for the prisoner, signed by his two counsel. They were entitled "Defences for Alexander Alexander, *Earl of Stirling*,* against the indictment at the instance of her Majesty's Advocate."

These defences were comprised in two paragraphs. The first stated that, as Lord Cockburn's interlocutor, though not final, had decided against the prisoner's claim to be the heir of the Earl of Stirling,† "he was advised that he was not in a condition to plead the privilege of peerage; but was bound to acknowledge the competency of that court to proceed under the indictment before it." The second proceeded thus:—

"The panel pleads not guilty of the libel generally; and, even particularly,‡ he denies that he had the slight-

* This was subsequently altered to "*claiming to be* Earl of Stirling."—Swinton, p. 48.

† *Ante*, p. 207 *et seq.*

‡ This is widely different from the course adopted in English courts. On the substance of the indictment being read to the prisoner, unless he plead

est ground to suspect that all, or any, of the documents libelled on were forged or fabricated. He produced them under legal advice, in the belief of their being genuine, and useful for the support of his interest."*

A third paragraph consisted of an application to postpone the trial, on the ground that the prisoner was not prepared for it, "as *one of his counsel* and his agent had gone to London and Paris to make inquiry as to several of the witnesses for the Crown, and such further investigation as might be necessary for his defence." The words which we have placed in italics indicate a course of procedure at variance with that adopted at the English Bar.

As soon as these defences had been read, the prisoner's counsel rose and said, "My lords, I do not mean to claim for the panel the privilege of a landed man; nor do we intend to state any objections to the relevancy of the indictment." By "relevancy," a technical term in Scotch law, is signified "the justice and sufficiency of the matters stated in the indictment, to warrant a decree in the terms asked;"† and, according to the criminal law of Scotland, this objection must be taken, if at all, before the trial. If it be not, the prisoner cannot make it the subject of arrest of judgment by the court, but must refer it to the law advisers of the crown, after the sentence has been pronounced by them, to have such weight attached to it as may be deemed proper, with a view to pardon or mitigation of punishment. ‡

guilty, or demur to the legal sufficiency of the indictment, on the face of it, he pleads simply Not Guilty; which throws on the prosecutor the whole *onus* of proving his case, and gives the prisoner the right of offering every defence he has, except those arising out of a previous acquittal, conviction, or pardon, in respect of the same charge. These must be specially pleaded.

* If this be the usual course in Scotland, it seems nugatory, as being only a detailed repetition of Not Guilty, with an intimation of the exculpating evidence intended to be relied on.

† Bell's *Dictionary of the Law of Scotland,* p. 844. In civil cases this rule is reversed.—*Id. ib.*

‡ Alison's *Practice of the Criminal Law of Scotland,* p. 651.

"Let the relevancy of the indictment be determined," said the Solicitor-General, "by your lordships pronouncing the usual interlocutor."

LORD MEADOWBANK. — "Alexander Humphreys, or Alexander, attend to the interlocutor of the court," which the clerk read as follows:—

"The Lords Commissioners of Justiciary find the libel RELEVANT to infer the pains of law, but allow the panel a proof in exculpation and alleviation; and in respect that the panel has by his counsel waived his right, if he any have, to be tried by a jury, of which the majority shall consist of landed men, remit the panel, with the libel as found relevant, to the knowledge of the *ordinary assize*."

Lists of all the witnesses and documentary proofs, on both sides, were, as it would appear, interchanged; and the trial having been postponed from the 3d to the 29th April 1839, on the latter day it commenced—not, however, as in England, with a preliminary statement on the part of the prosecutor of the course of expected proof, but with the evidence itself in detail. After that on both sides had been adduced, the counsel for the crown addressed the jury, and then the counsel for the prisoner; after which Lord Meadowbank summed up. We beg to say that we think the English course of procedure greatly preferable to the Scottish, in commencing the trial with a temperate and lucid statement of the case intended to be made out by the crown, enabling both the court and the jury, but especially the latter, to obtain an early clue through the labyrinth of oral and documentary proof, to see the drift of it, and appreciate, in going along, the significance of what is being done. In the present case, for instance, the jury, with the exception of the scanty gleam of light afforded by the indictment read to them by the officer of the court, with the defences, were plunged *instanter* into a series of details of somewhat complicated legal proceedings, and legal and other documents; the Solicitor-

General feeling the necessity many times of interposing, to intimate that "the object of *this* or *that* evidence was to show so and so," &c. &c. And, indeed, if the jury really saw their way with only middling clearness through the evidence, *as it was beiny adduced*, they were a far shrewder and more experienced jury than it has been our fate to see for many a long year, even at Guildhall, or Westminster, where juries have long been celebrated for their discretion and acuteness. In the present case, a half-hour's calm preliminary statement, by the Solicitor-General, of the points of the charge, and the application to them of the evidence, would have greatly assisted the jury, possibly even the court, and, long afterwards, let us sorrowfully add, ourselves. In despair we leaped out of the intricate evidence into the speeches of counsel, and the summing up of the judge, afterwards recurring to the evidence and appendices. At length we found ourselves on sure ground, and in a clear atmosphere; and grudged not the effort we had made to overcome the obstacles of which we have been complaining, and also the difficult technicalities of Scottish criminal law procedure.

It will be recollected that the indictment embraced three distinct classes of alleged forgeries; the excerpt charter of *Novodamus*, the Le Normand packet, and the De Porquet packet. To establish the "using" and "uttering" of these instruments, evidence was given of their having been adduced, on the part of the prisoner, in the various Scottish courts in which he had from time to time asserted, and endeavoured to maintain, his claims. Lord Cockburn's important judgment of the 10th December 1836 was also put in evidence; with the examinations of the prisoner, some of his correspondence, and the instruments charged by the indictments to be forgeries. Let us take these last in their order; and—

I. THE EXCERPT CHARTER OF *Novodamus* OF THE 7TH DECEMBER 1639. Was this a genuine or a forged document? The acute and learned scrutiny to which it was subjected, elicited remarkable and decisive results. We know, from the documents printed by Mr Swinton, a little more than was disclosed to the Court—namely, that the mysterious discovery of this "excerpt" was communicated to the prisoner from Ireland by his indefatigable agent, Mr Banks, on the 17th March 1829. All that was proved before the Court was, that the prisoner delivered it, in that year, to his law-agents, who immediately commenced proceedings in the Scotch courts to "*prove its tenor*." Let it be observed, that "this most suspicious scrap of writing," as the Solicitor-General styled it,* professed to be only an "excerpt" of a lost charter of King Charles I., dated the 7th December 1639 —not an entire copy, but only "an abridged copy!" and the exigencies of the prisoner's case had required that *that* identical excerpt should have been in existence as long ago as the year 1723,† since it bore an indorsement‡ by "Thomas Conyers," attesting its authenticity, dated the 10th July 1723. It will be impossible, however, to appreciate the force of the delicate but decisive evidence brought to bear upon this unlucky document, unless we have a distinct idea of the different stages of progress through which a royal charter would have to pass in the year 1639. They were explained at the trial by several learned and experienced officials; and we have taken some pains to clear away technicalities, and present their evidence briefly and popularly. The stages, then, through which a royal charter had at that time to pass, were three.

*First* came the "SIGNATURE." This was not, as the word would ordinarily import, and in England, a mere name signed, or mark, but an entire document, constituting the foundation of the proposed charter, and containing its essential elements. It was drawn up in English, by a Writer to the Signet, and brought by him, on a given day, to a Baron of the Exchequer to be examined, in order to ascertain that it was correct, especially as to the

* Swinton, p. 196. † *Ante*, p. 198, *et passim*. ‡ *Ante*, p. 199.

*reddendo*, or annual feu-money due to the Crown. On being satisfied of its accuracy, the Baron marked the signature as "revised;" and in due time the sign-manual was affixed to it. It was then complete; was recorded in the Exchequer Record; and retained by the Keeper of the Signet. There were subscribed to it only the date, and the words, "At Whitehall, the day of ."

*Secondly*, Warranted by the possession of this revised "signature," the Keeper of the Signet issued a "*Precept to the Privy Seal*," which was simply a Latin translation of the English signature, and was recorded in the Privy Seal Office. That office then issued this precept to the Great Seal; and it is to be noted that this Privy Seal Precept had subscribed to it the words, "PER SIGNETUM," which seems to be an abbreviation of the words, "*per* preceptum datum sub *signeto* nostro."

*Thirdly*, As soon as the Privy Seal Precept had reached the Chancery Office, the functionaries there drew up formally, and *in extenso*, THE CHARTER, which was sealed with the Great Seal; the Privy Seal Precept on which it was grounded, either remaining in the Chancery Office, or being lodged in the General Records of Scotland. This completed Charter, alone, had a testing clause; and it was the Privy Seal Precept only which bore, as we have seen, the words "*per signetum*."

See, then, the origin, progress, and completion of a Royal Charter in 1639—SIGNATURE; PRIVY SEAL PRECEPT; CHARTER; each having its appropriate depository or record—the Signet Office, the Privy Seal Office, the Great Seal Office; to which, indeed, may be added a fourth, the COMPTROLLER OF EXCHEQUER'S REGISTER; where also was recorded every instrument of the above description, to enable that officer to account to the Crown for the feu-duties. These four old registers, or records, are all completed from periods long anterior to the year 1639, down to the present day, with the exception of a *hiatus* of twelve leaves at the commencement of the fifty-seventh volume of the Great Seal Record; but the contents of these twelve leaves were clearly ascertainable from the indexes of other records. "It is the boast of this country," said Lord Meadowbank, in summing up, to the jury,* "and always has been, that its registers have been kept with a regularity unknown elsewhere."

If, therefore, there had ever been such a charter as that of which the document under consideration professed to be an excerpt, that charter ought to have been found *in every one of the four* records or registers above mentioned.† Add to this, that William Earl of Stirling was himself, at the time, the Keeper of the Signet,‡ and also, "a man of talent, and attentive to his own interests—not likely to have received grants of such unusual importance as those contained in the charter in question, without seeing them properly carried through the seals."§

Now for the Excerpt itself, and its physical aspect. It was written on several single leaves of paper, not numbered, apparently cut recently out of some book, and stitched together, the outside leaf being brought round and stitched down on the remaining leaves. The colour was a uniform deep brown—equally so underneath the margin covered over at the stitching. There were ruled red lines round the pages. The writing appeared "fresh" —at all events, not so old as the paper; and was not in a Scotch chancery-hand, or any hand used in the Register Office, but like that used in engrossing deeds in England and Ireland. The language of the excerpt was Latin—but such Latin!—and it extended to about thirty English common-law folios, containing seventy-two words each. At the beginning of the charter, on the right-hand side, were the abbreviations, "REG. MAG. SIG. LIB. LVII."—*i. e.*, "*Registrum Magni Sigilli, Liber LVII.*"

The only portion of the excerpt with which we shall trouble the reader *in extenso*, is the conclusion—the test-

* Swinton, p. 309.
† Per Lord Meadowbank, *Id. ib.*
‡ Ibid. p. 84.
§ Ibid. p. 94.

ing part—which, especially the part in Italics, is worthy of the utmost attention; and we adopt the translation used at the trial.—" Witnesses: *the most reverend father in Christ and our well-beloved councillor, John, by the mercy of God Archbishop of St Andrews, Primate and Metropolitan of our kingdom of Scotland, our chancellor;* our well-beloved cousins and councillors, James, Marquis of Hamilton; Earl of Arran and Cambridge; Lord Avon and Innerdaile; Robert, Earl of Roxburghe; Lord Ker, of Cesford and Casertoun, Keeper of our Privy Seal; our beloved familiar councillors, Sir John Hay of Barro, Clerk of our Rolls, Register and Council; John Hamiltoun of Orbestoun, our Justice-Clerk; and John Scott of Scotstarvet, Director of our Chancery, Knights. At our Court of Quhythall, the 7*th day of the month of December, in the year of God* 1639, *and of our reign the* 15*th year.*

" [ GRATIS ]

" *Per Signetum.*"

On the back of this document was written—" Excerpt from the original charter to William, Earl of Stirling, 7th December 1639. T. C." [*i. e.*, Thomas Conyers.] This indorsement was also alleged in the indictment to be a forgery. Here, then, we have an " excerpt " or " abridged copy " of a royal charter, dated the 7th December 1639, granted by King Charles I. to one of his most distinguished subjects, conferring high dignities and vast possessions; a charter yielded to the anxious importunity of the Earl in his old age, " when labouring under great dejection of spirits, after losing three of his sons, who had given him the highest hopes, and fearing, from the declining health of two of the survivors, that his honours might, at no distant period, pass to a collateral branch of his family." * And this earl, too, the head of the office in which the charter originated.

Now, behold, FIRST, that the records of every one of the four departments above mentioned—viz., the Signature

* *Ante*, p. 195.

Record, the Comptroller of the Exchequer's Record, the Privy Seal Record, and the Great Seal Record—had been rigorously searched, *and not the faintest trace of such an instrument appeared in any of them!*—it being sworn that had it ever existed, it must have been found in ALL! "This might possibly have been accounted for," said the Solicitor-General,* "had there been but one register only; more especially if a blank had occurred in that register through the obliteration, imperfection, or loss of a volume, or part of a volume. But where there are four independent registers, and these all concurring to supply, in the fullest details, the necessary evidence as to all other charters" [of which various instances were proved at the trial], "and when you find that this charter is not recorded in any one of them, it is quite impossible to believe—it would really be asking too much of credulity itself, to believe—that such a document could ever have existed." If this instrument were the handiwork of a forger, it may be reasonable to suppose him capable of appreciating the efficacy of the negative evidence which might be brought against him, and to endeavour to supply it. This brings us, SECONDLY, to the memorandum in the margin of the first page of the excerpt—*i.e., Reg. Mag. Sig. Lib. LVII.* —which meant that the charter itself was to have been found "in the fifty-seventh volume of the Register (or Record) of the Great Seal." We have already seen,† that, in point of fact, twelve leaves, at the beginning *of that volume* were amissing; and the suggestion, or rather assertion, of the prisoner, when he commenced his legal proceedings to prove the tenor of the missing charter, was, that it was to have been found in one of these twelve leaves, "which had perished or disappeared—that being a matter of public notoriety, and was so observed by the Lords of Council and Session in their return of 27th February 1740, to an order of the House of Lords of the 12th June 1719, respecting the state of the Peerage in Scot-

* Swinton, p. 205. † *Ante*, p. 199.

land."* Here, then, are only *twelve* leaves missing; and on referring to one of the writings indorsed on the map of Canada, in the Le Normand packet, the writer stated he had *seen* the charter, and "it extended over *fifty* pages of writing."† On this subject, Lord Meadowbank proposed the following question to the jury:—"Putting aside the evidence of this index, could you have believed, when there is no evidence or trace of this charter in the volume where it should be found, that it could, *out of its place*, have been crammed into the twelve pages that are lost, when the prisoner's own evidence tells you the charter extended to fifty-eight?"‡ To proceed, however—What will the reader suppose was proved at the trial? First, two ancient indexes of the missing twelve pages of vol. lvii. were produced, unerringly indicating the charters which had stood recorded there, and among which was *not* the charter in question, but only those of date *subsequent* to the year 1639; while all the charters of that year 1639 stood regularly recorded in the previous—the fifty-sixth volume; and among them, also, was *not* to be found the charter in question. Mr George Robertson, one of the joint keepers of the records, thus certified on oath:—"I have searched the principal record of the fifty-seventh volume of the Great Seal Register, and at the beginning of the said fifty-seventh volume, twelve leaves have been destroyed or lost. The charters originally recorded in these missing leaves are, however, ascertained with precision from two ancient indexes of the Great Seal Record. I have examined these, and can state as the result, that the twelve leaves now lost did not contain any charter, diploma, patent, nor other grant, in favour of William, Earl of Stirling, nor of any Earl of Stirling, nor of any person of the name of Alexander." Still further, however, the words on the margin, "*Reg. Mag. Sig.*

* *Ante*, p. 199. Swinton, App., p. vii. † *Ante*, p. 236.

‡ Swinton, p. 311. This seems a slight inaccuracy, on the part of the learned Judge, of fifty-*eight* instead of fifty.

*Lib. LVII.,"* purported to have been written there by the framer of the excerpt, in the year 1723; and three experienced official gentlemen declared their confident opinion, that no such style of marking was coeval with the making of the excerpt itself. It was established at the trial that this mode of referring to the Great Seal Records was *quite a modern one*, commencing with the year 1806 only; a fact proved by the very author of the arrangement, and his assistant; by whom, in the latter year, the records were rebound, and the titles made uniform, for facility of reference, in lieu of the loose and discordant methods of reference till then in use! Other experienced officials proved that till the year 1806 no such mode of reference as "*Reg. Mag. Sig.*" existed, and they gave specimens of the former mode: *e. g.* "*Chart. in Archivis*," appeared in a law book of 1763; and in a subsequent edition, in the year 1813, the reference was altered to "*Mag. Sig.*" If, therefore, the "excerpt" were a modern forgery, it would almost appear as if the fabricator, aware of the missing leaves of vol. lvii., but not knowing *how very recent was the abbreviated lettering on the back*—"Reg. Mag. Sig."—had taken it for granted that it was coeval with the original formation of the volume, or at least had been there for a century—viz., since 1723. But if this reference, "*Reg. Mag. Sig. Lib. LVII.*," were a forgery, it must have been a very modern one, necessarily *later* than the year 1806, the date of Mr Thomson's rebinding of the record, and changing the titling. We have seen, however, that the prisoner had accompanied his father to France in the year 1802, and did not return to England till 1814; and in the subsequent year told his own agent, Mr Corrie, that he had no documents to support his claim. Is it a fair inference from these dates that, down to at least the year 1815, the famous excerpt was not in existence—or at least unknown to the prisoner? So much for the negative evidence that any such genuine document as the alleged charter of 7th December 1639 had ever existed. But,

THIRDLY, the excerpt itself seemed to furnish a conspicuous and glaring demonstration of spuriousness; we allude to the alleged attestation of the charter by ARCHBISHOP SPOTTISWOODE, in the capacity of "OUR CHANCELLOR" of the kingdom, and as such, keeper of the Great Seal. Now Spottiswoode, the Archbishop of St Andrews, was undoubtedly for a considerable period Chancellor of Scotland; and his name is found in the records as an official witness to all charters from the crown, passing the Great Seal of Scotland during the time that he held it. In the excerpt charter, he appears in that capacity at the alleged date of the instrument—viz., the 7th December 1639; but, lo! not only had he ceased to be Chancellor on the 13th November 1638, *but he had actually died on the 26th November* 1639—that is, eleven days before that on which he was made to attest the alleged Charter of Novodamus! These facts were proved beyond all doubt, both directly and collaterally: as, for instance, by an instrument of a nature similar to that before the court, dated only four days afterwards—namely, the 11th December 1639—a charter in favour of the city of Edinburgh, and attested, &c., not by "John, Archbishop and Chancellor," but by his successor, the Marquis of Hamilton,—whose appointment on the 13th November 1638 was proved,—and this very "William Earl of Stirling and Canada," and others: all of whom were also witnesses, on the same day, to another charter to Heriot's Hospital. Here, then, was a great charter, making under the Great Seal magnificent grants to a Scottish nobleman, and attested by a non-existent Chancellor, whose temporary successor had been installed in office thirteen months previous to the date of the charter! Mr Swinton acutely points out* the source of this blunder, assuming the excerpt to be altogether a forgery. Archbishop Spottiswoode, as has been seen, ceased to be Chancellor on the 13th November 1638, and died on the

* *Pref.* p. xxi.

26th of the ensuing November—*i. e.*, eleven days before the date of the alleged charter. Now, from the date of the Archbishop's resignation, till the appointment of the Earl of Loudon as Chancellor in 1641, the Great Seal was in commission, the head commissioner being the Marquis of Hamilton. But it singularly happens, that, in the catalogues of the Scottish Chancellors appended to Spottiswoode's History, and other works, the list during the reign of Charles I. and the Commonwealth, is given as follows:—

"1622, George Hay, Earl of Kinnoul.
"1635, John Spottiswood, Archbishop of St Andrews.
"1641, John Campbell, Earl of Loudon.
"1660, William Cunninghame, Earl of Glencairne."

——no mention being made, nor any notice taken, of the interval between the resignation of the Archbishop and the appointment of the Earl of Loudon. From this it may be inferred that the fabricator of the document, if it were fabricated, took it for granted that from 1635 to 1641, and consequently in the year 1639, falling within that interval, the Archbishop was Chancellor of Scotland. But again—Is there any reason assignable for the supposed fabricator having pitched on the particular date of 9th December 1639? Yes! In Crawford's Life of the Archbishop, the death of that prelate is erroneously alleged to have occurred on the 27th *December* 1639!—*i. e.*, just eighteen days after the completion of the alleged charter.*

FOURTHLY, there was apparently another great blot pointed out by the crown lawyers. Immediately after the above-mentioned *testing clause*, followed the words "*Gratis.*—PER SIGNETUM."† Now, it has been seen that the testing clause is the conclusion of only a com-

* Swinton, p. 209.

† When the precept issues in favour of a Writer to the Signet, or of the Keeper of the Signet (as Lord Stirling then was), the precept passes the signet *gratis:* and that word is written at the bottom.—Swinton, p. 84.

pleted charter. This "excerpt," therefore, if taken from any document, must have been taken from a completed charter. It could not have been taken from the Signature, nor the Signet Precept, nor the Privy Seal Precept, for in none of these instruments could such a clause appear. But in addition to this testing clause, appear the words "*Per Signetum!*" which are never to be found in any charter at all, but only in the Privy Seal Precept! So that here was a document containing, on the one hand, words (the testing clause) which are to be found in only a completed charter, and which could not exist in a Privy Seal Precept; and, on the other hand, certain other words (*Per Signetum*) never to be found in a completed charter, but only in a Privy Seal Precept! It was accordingly sworn unhesitatingly by all the professional witnesses, even on the strength of these conclusive elements of intrinsic evidence alone, that the document before the court could not be an excerpt, or copy, of any authentic writ of any description whatever, known in the law of Scotland. There seems some little force in the Solicitor-General's observation on this part of the case: "Gentlemen, is there not here, then, the clearest and most satisfactory evidence that this is not, and cannot be, an excerpt from any real or genuine document? There is an incongruity about it, which shows it could not have been copied from any document that ever existed. The writer of it, whoever he was, may have had a sort of glimmering of what it ought to have been; but still, in his ignorance, he has made a monster of it. It is utterly impossible, looking merely to the intrinsic evidence, that it could be the document which it professes to be."

FIFTHLY, Not satisfied with these vigorous assaults upon the genuineness and authenticity of this unfortunate document, the Scotch lawyers detected, as they considered, several serious intrinsic evidences of spuriousness. *First*, the alleged charter professed to convey estates which had never belonged to the Scottish crown—viz., lands, provinces, and territorial rights in New England. "It is not possible," said Lord Meadowbank, and the professional witnesses supported him, "that a charter granted by a king of Scotland could convey, or be granted, as if it had conveyed, any property not belonging to the crown of Scotland. That such a SIGNATURE should have passed the Barons of Exchequer, and their officers, is beyond all belief:" for it must be remembered, that the "Signature" is, in its first stage towards a charter, submitted to a Baron of Exchequer, to be "revised," before the sign-manual is affixed to it. This is, undoubtedly, a fact lending great weight to any really inconsistent or objectionable provisions in the "Signature," or subsequent charter. *Secondly*, In crown charters of resignation, to which that in question professed to belong, it was proved that the *dates* of the resignation were "invariably given:" here were none—and this objection also must have escaped the somnolent Baron of the Exchequer of 1639. *Thirdly*, The "charter" stated a resignation to have been made by a grandson of the Earl of Stirling, in the Earl's lifetime; which resignation the grandson had no title to make; and till he had, *having* nothing, he could resign nothing according to the law of Scotland;* and such could never have passed the Exchequer. *Fourthly*, The alleged charter professed to convey the titles and dignities of the earldom; the Earl professed to resign his earldom, which the king, by that deed, was made to reconvey, with precedency from the date of the first grant. "This," said Lord Meadowbank, and the evidence supported him, "I believe to be altogether unprecedented. It was totally unnecessary—the precedency conveyed, following as a matter of course. I have seen many such grants, and never such a dignity reconveyed, with such a stipulation." *Fifthly*, While the invariable practice, in royal charters to peers, is

* *Qui non habet ille non dat*, is also a rule of English law, subject to certain important exceptions.

to address the one concerned as "*consanguineus* noster," and never to give that title to a commoner, the alleged charter in question twice applied that title to Alexander, the son of the peer (consequently a commoner), and *not* to the Earl himself!

LASTLY, As to the structure and aspect of the "Excerpt." It had red lines round the margin, which, said the principal witness, Mr Thomson, the deputy-clerk register, "were not introduced till the year 1780: at least it has not come under my notice at an earlier period." Then, again, three gentlemen, "the most experienced," said Lord Meadowbank, "as to old writings that are to be found here or anywhere else," stated that, on looking at the document, they had at first sight not the least doubt or difficulty in saying, that they did not believe it to be genuine, but of *recent fabrication.* One of them, the Mr Thomson above mentioned, declared that the paper was older than the ink in which the words on the face of it were written; that where the paper was folded over and stiched down, it was of the same tinge with the body of the paper which had been exposed to the air, and which could not be, had it been folded for any length of time. Here it must have been so folded for at least a century. That the "excerpt" appeared to consist of separate leaves recently cut from a book—all of them half-sheets detached from each other; and that where, under the cover, the paper should have been whiter, through non-exposure to the atmosphere, it was not of a different colour from the rest of it. Two eminent professors of chemistry were engaged by the Court to make experiments on a portion of the paper, in order to ascertain whether the dark colour of the paper was the natural result of age, or of artificial means used to obtain that result. The "doctors," however, "differed;" and their evidence, therefore, was properly discarded from the case. As to the character of the handwriting, one of the most experienced of the professional witnesses, Mr Mackenzie, a Writer to the Signet of thirty-six years' standing, made, in the opinion of Lord Meadowbank, "a very striking remark:" that the writing was in a peculiar hand, in imitation of old hand, which was altogether different from the Chancery hand in which charters in Scotland are written; that he had never before seen a copy made like the one in question, in old hand; and that a person sitting down to make a copy of such a charter, would do it in the running-hand of the country where it was written. "It is my duty to observe to you," said Lord Meadowbank, "that impressions made by such appearances," as the above, "on the minds of persons of skill, at first sight, are often of great weight. I leave this part of the case with this single observation—that the impression of these witnesses, when they first saw it, was to the prejudice of the genuineness of this document, as an excerpt from a genuine charter. Whether it was a writing somewhat older, or only thirty years old, seems to be very little to the purpose; but they said it appeared to be a document of recent formation—that that was the first impression made upon their minds, when it was submitted to their inspection." The Solicitor-General had thus closed *his* remarks on the subject of the above excerpt charter: "These considerations make the absence of all explanation as to the history of this document a most suspicious circumstance in the prisoner's case; so much so, with submission, that the possession of the deed must be accounted for by the prisoner in some way or other, before he can shake himself free from the charge that is now made against him."

The following is the substance of the answer to this portion of the case, offered by his eloquent and ingenious advocate. Unable to struggle against the bulk of the professional evidence tending to impeach the genuineness of the excerpt, and to disprove the existence of the alleged charter from which it was taken, Mr Robertson admitted that there were the great distinctions which had been alleged, between a completed charter and the instrument which preceded it; that the words "*per signetum*" could not properly appear on a completed charter; that the document under consideration purported to be an excerpt of such completed charter; that the abbreviations "*Reg. Mag. Sig. Lib. LVII.*" could not appear on an excerpt of the date assigned by the prisoner to that which he had brought forward before the Scottish Courts; that it was proved that no such charter as that of the 9th Dec. 1639 was entered on record; and that Archbishop Spottiswoode could not have attested such an instrument, having undoubtedly ceased to be chancellor, and died previously to its date. BUT, he said, there was a vast difference between a genuine, though erroneous copy, and a forged principal; and also between a forgery, if such it were, so palpable as to challenge everybody's notice, and one so skilfully executed as to have been capable of deceiving all the Scottish law functionaries, and the prisoner's own law advisers, and himself, for a period of ten years, during which it had been courting examination, without forgery having been suggested till that prosecution. But *was* the excerpt proved to be a forgery? The statement, in the Lord Ordinary's judgment, relating to Hovenden's affidavit, showed that there was evidence, or something like it, in that proceeding, to establish the existence of the excerpt in 1723. The document was not a *copy* of the alleged charter, but only an excerpt or *extract;* and so might be explained the absence of some matters which would be in the original. And as to the admitted *errors*, the excerpt was made in Ireland, not in Scotland; was "an old *Irish* bungled copy"—a "blundering *Irish* extract"—"an *Irish* excerpt of a copy of a deed"—"an *Irish* copy." The marking "*Reg. Mag. Sig. Lib. LVII.*" in the margin may have been an *ex post facto* addition by some third person, who may be the person who had invented the story of Cromwell carrying off the records of Scotland. "*Consanguineus* noster," and the attestation of the Archbishop, were both Irish blunders. "And on such evidence," said Mr Robertson, "this bungled excerpt is to be held proved to be a deliberate forgery!"* Before leaving this part of the case, let us remind the reader of the fact that it was Mr Thomas Christopher Banks who, according to his own letter, discovered this challenged "excerpt" in Ireland, and transmitted it to the prisoner; that the prisoner's counsel elicited at the trial that this Mr Thomas Christopher Banks had been seen, by a witness, alive, at Edinburgh, *a few weeks before the trial, and at the office of the crown solicitor;* and that Mr Banks was not called as a witness by either side.

Was then this "excerpt charter" a forgery, or a genuine document? The reader has before him the same materials for forming a judgment which were presented to the Edinburgh jury. Let us proceed now to—

II. The Le Normand Packet—*i. e.*, the French evidence. It now lies before us, in the large *fac-simile*, nearly a yard square (one prepared for use at the trial), prefixed to Mr Swinton's report, representing eight different inscriptions, or indorsements, on the back of an old French map of Canada. Six of them, be it especially observed, are written on the paper itself of the map, and two on two other pieces of paper, afterwards pasted on the back of the map. We beg to repeat emphatically an observation already made,† that we doubt whether such an extraordinary document, or series of documents, as this map, with its accompaniments, has ever, before or since, challenged deliberate judicial investigation. It is at once fearful and ludicrous to regard these documents as forgeries, really *expected by their fabricators to be received as genuine*, and, as such, intrepidly submitted to competent scrutiny. So, at least, we own it would have appeared to ourselves; but, after all, there is nothing like a jury for deciding upon conflicting testi-

* *Ante*, p. 188. † *Ante*, p. 215.

mony. We cordially concur in the following admirable observations of Lord Brougham, delivered on an important occasion, when he was sitting as Lord Chancellor:* "The best tribunal for investigating contested facts is a jury of twelve men of various habits of thinking, of various characters of understanding, of various kinds of feeling, of moral feeling—all of which circumstances enter deeply into the capacity of such individuals. * * * The diversity of the minds of the jury, even if they are taken without any experience as jurors, their various habits of thinking and feeling, and their diversity of cast of understanding, and their discussing the matter among themselves, and the very fact of their not being lawyers, their not being professional men, and believing as men believe, and *acting* on their belief, in the ordinary affairs of life, give them a capacity of aiding the court in their eliciting of truth, which no single judge, be he ever so largely gifted with mental endowments, be he ever so learned with respect to past experience in such matters, can possess." Without presuming therefore to express, or even to suggest or insinuate, anything like dissatisfaction with the conclusions arrived at by the jury with reference to the class of facts now before us, but more fully laid before them, we request the reader to imagine himself a juryman, under a sacred obligation to resist prejudice and guard against first impressions.

It is proper to remind the reader that the essence of the prisoner's pedigree, as he endeavoured to establish it before Lord Cockburn, consisted of proof that the Rev. John Alexander (John No. 3)† was the son of John of Antrim (John No. 2); and that this John No. 2 was the son of John of Gartmore (John No. 1). "The whole of the case," said Lord Cockburn on the 3d December 1836, "depends upon the genuineness of these two descents."‡ And his judgment, as has been seen, demo-

* Starkie on Evidence, vol. i., p. 8, note G, 3d ed.

† See the Pedigree, *ante*, p. 194.

‡ Swinton, Appendix, p. xxiii.

lished the case which had been set up before him; for he pronounced "that the evidence, whether considered in its separate parts or as a whole, was utterly insufficient."* Now, if the writings on the back of the map were genuine and authentic, they exactly established, beyond all possibility of cavilling, the case which it was the prisoner's grand object to establish; going, moreover, far beyond the exigencies springing out of the adverse judgment of Lord Cockburn. For, first, those writings were designed to demonstrate not only that John No. 3 was son of John No. 2, and he son of John No. 1; but also, secondly, that the ORIGINAL CHARTER OF NOVODAMUS, of the 9th December 1639, was bodily in existence in the archives of Canada in the year 1702—as indubitably attested by those who had seen, and examined it, and made copies and extracts from it!—as testified by right reverend, noble, and royal personages, two very eminent bishops, a marchioness, and a king of France—all under their own hands. These singular writings, eight in number, have already been given *in extenso* and *verbatim*, but translated into English,† and we hope that the reader will take the trouble of referring to, and carefully reading them before he proceeds further with the present paper. We promise him that his trouble shall be amply repaid, by disclosures which he will then, and then only, be able fully to appreciate.

I. FIRST comes the statement, written on the back of the map, of a certain "M. MALLET," supposed to be a Canadian French gentleman, who simply makes the memorandum in question, without signing it, or mentioning his own name, but heading it, "*Lyons*, 4th August 1706." He states that in the year 1702 he was residing in Acadia [Nova Scotia]. "His curiosity had been excited by what he was told of an '*ancient*' charter, preserved in the archives of that province—it is the charter of confirmation, *De Novo Damus*, of date 9th December 1639." He says, "My friend Lacroix gave me

* Swinton, Appendix, p. xxix.

† *Ante*, pp. 217–222.

a copy of it, which I took the precaution of having duly attested. From this authentic document I am about to present some extracts, in order that every person who opens this map [the one in question] of our American possessions, may form an idea of the vast extent of territory which was granted by the King of England to one of his subjects. If the fate of war, or any other event, should replace New France and Acadia under the dominion of the English, the family of Stirling would possess these two provinces, as well as New England"— and then he quotes the "passages," as from the original charter. He proceeds, "The order of succession! to this inheritance is as follows:" and gives the entire of the new limitations of the alleged charter, *in extenso!* concluding, "Thus the King of England has given to the Earl, and has secured to his descendants in perpetuity, enough of land to found a powerful empire in America." So much for M. Mallet. Opposite his important memorandum was the following autograph memorandum (forming No. 8 in our series) of LOUIS XV! "This note is worthy of some attention, under present circumstances; but let THE COPY of the original charter be sent to me." Subjoined to M. Mallet's memorandum was another—

II. Signed "CARON SAINT ESTIENNE," and dated "*Lyons*, 6th April 1707," announcing the sudden death of "the aforesaid M. Mallet," whose loss was, it seems, an irreparable one to his friends, from his "good qualities and rare understanding." He it was who "first procured M. Saint Estienne a perusal of the charter—an extraordinary document extending over fifty pages," and the "unclassical Latin" of which shocked that accomplished reader. He says that "the above note of M. Mallet is *precious*—giving in few words an extremely correct idea of the wonderful charter in question." "As to the *copy*," which M. Mallet had "taken the precaution of having duly attested," M. Estienne informs us by whom it had been attested—viz., by the Keeper of the Records, and the

Acadian witnesses, and it (the copy) must be in entire conformity with the register of Port Royal." "M. Mallet had foreseen," observes his friend St Estienne, "that the copy would not make the charter known in France, hence he conceived the idea of writing, ON ONE OF THE BEAUTIFUL MAPS OF GUILLAUME DE L'ISLE, a note which all the world may read with interest. Had he lived long enough"—poor soul—"he could have added to this interest; for he wished to obtain information in England as to the then situation of the descendants of the earl who had obtained the charter; and all the information which he might have received respecting them, he would have transferred to this very map." M. St Estienne, however, concludes with the consolatory assurance, "But, after all, with the two documents" [*i. e.*, the duly attested copy, and his own memorandum on the map] "which he has left to us, no person in France can question the existence of such a charter." Here, then, were two gentlemen who had been actually favoured with a sight of the *ipsissima charta;* had obtained a copy of it from a third, M. Lacroix, himself, doubtless, similarly privileged; had taken the precaution of having that copy officially attested; and had given accurate extracts of its essential provisions. We are, however, under still further obligations to the solicitous vigilance of St Estienne; for two months afterwards he procured no less a person than Flechier, the Bishop of Nismes, to add the sanction of his eminent name to the authenticity of his—St Estienne's—memorandum. Accordingly, the obliging Bishop wrote on the map the following certificate:—

III. Signed "Esprit, Ev. de Nismes," [*i. e.*, Esprit Flechier, Bishop of Nismes] and dated "Nismes, 3d June 1707." The Bishop had been shown by St Estienne the "copy" of the charter, and thus chronicles the event. "I read lately, at the house of Monsieur Sartre, at Caveyrac, the copy of the Earl of Stirling's charter. In it I remarked many curious particulars, mixed up with a great many uninteresting details;" "I think, therefore, that the greatest obligations are due to M. Mallet for having, by the above note, enabled the French public to judge of the extent and importance of the grant made to the Scottish nobleman. I also find that he has extracted the most essential clauses of the charter; and, in translating them into French, he has given them with great fidelity. Monsieur Caron St Estienne has asked me to bear this testimony. I do so with the greatest pleasure." Courteous and venerable Bishop of Nismes! But you must now make your exit, for an archbishop approaches, and that no less a personage than the great, the good, the justly revered FENELON, Archbishop of Cambray; who, in the ensuing autumn, viz., on the 16th October 1707, on the solicitation doubtless of St Estienne, and other zealous friends of the excellent deceased M. Mallet, condescended to write the following memorandum round the margin of a letter presented to him for that purpose, and forming No.—

IV. "The friends of the late Mr Ph. Mallet will doubtless read with great interest this letter of a *grandson of the Earl of Stirling's!* M. Cholet, of Lyons, setting out to-day, 16th October 1707, on his way home, will have the honour of delivering it to M. Brossette, on the part of Madame de Lambert. To authenticate it, I have written and signed this marginal note. FR. AR. DUC DE CAMBRAY." *Nec Deus intersit,* says our ancient astute adviser, *nisi dignus vindice nodus.* Who, thinks the reader, was the writer of the letter thus solemnly authenticated by so distinguished a witness? Who but (the very man of all others on earth that was wanted) JOHN OF ANTRIM, John No. 2, John Alexander, grandson of the first Earl of Stirling! But proceeding, we have,

V. A letter of John Alexander, dated "Antrim, 27th August 1707,"—*i. e.*, five years only before his death —addressed to a certain Marchioness de Lambert, a lady of fashion, whose splendid hospitalities he therein commemorates. He thanks her ladyship for having, through the good-natured interposition of the Archbishop, favoured him so soon with a copy of "the note respecting '*my grandfather's* charter.'" "I shall preserve with care the interesting note of M. Mallet. The charter was at one time registered in Scotland, as well as in Acadia: but during the civil war, and under the usurpation of Cromwell, boxes containing a portion of the records of that kingdom were lost during a storm at sea; and, according to THE ANCIENT TRADITION of our family, the REGISTER in which this charter was RECORDED was amongst the number of those that perished! Such, madam, is all that I can say in reply to your questions; for it is impossible, in this country of Ireland, to obtain any other information with regard to the registered charter. I believe that MY GRANDMOTHER" [*i.e.*, the first countess] "gave the ORIGINAL CHARTER (which she brought from Scotland, when she came to take up her abode in Ireland) to her son-in-law, Lord Montgomery, in order that he might preserve it carefully in Castle Comber, where he resided. I shall ascertain what this family have done with it; and I shall have the honour of acquainting you with any discovery which I may make." He proceeded to give a remarkably neat and succinct account of that state of the pedigree which the Lord Ordinary had so ruthlessly annihilated; particularly explaining that John of Gartmore (John No. 1) had had a second wife, named Maxwell, "the mother" of the communicative writer. The benevolent and indefatigable Marchioness de Lambert seems to have pushed her inquiries, even after the death of her correspondent; for we find, constituting No.—

VI. A memorandum, though without signature or date, showing that "this lady had not ceased to bestow on the son," the Rev. John Alexander (John No. 3), "of this distinguished man" (John No. 2), "marks of her good-will and friendship. This son is favourably known in

England as a Protestant clergyman, and a learned philologist. He is at the head of a college for the education of young clergymen, established at Stratford, in the county of Warwick." But this memorandum contained, as the first sentence, one of infinite significance—"THIS INSCRIPTION has been communicated by Madame de Lambert!" And that was document

VI. Forming the inscription on the tombstone of John of Antrim,* whom it stated to be "the best of husbands, the most indulgent of fathers; as a friend warm, sincere, faithful; a man of such endowments, &c.; and universally respected for his piety and benevolence." But what was vastly more to the purpose, as far as concerned his descendants, he was also the only son of the Hon. John Alexander! who "was the fourth son of William Earl of Stirling!" and "married Mary, eldest daughter of the Rev. Mr Hamilton of Bangor, by whom he had issue a son, John, who "at this present time is the Presbyterian minister at Stratford-on-Avon, in England." There could not be a doubt as to these facts, seeing that a certain "W. C. Gordon, junior," of Stratford-on-Avon, certified, on the margin of a copy of the inscription, that it "was a faithful copy!" Here, however, occurred a somewhat disagreeable fact. The figure "7" in the date, "Oct. 6th, 1723," was originally a figure "8" [*i.e.*, 1823] "made into a 7." This swore Mr Lizars; on which "*a juryman* asks, Has there been an *erasure?*—*A.* No. It has been a different figure, corrected, and made into a 7. *Lord Meadowbank.*—Look at it again, Mr Lizars. Are you sure it has not been a blot? *The witness* (having carefully examined the document with a glass).—No, my lord, it has been decidedly a figure. There are both the top and middle of a figure here, my lord."

Such were the documents indorsed on and attached to the map of Canada; and a perusal of them suggests a

* See it *in extenso, ante*, p. 221.

few questions. *First*, According to them, the original charter of the 7th December 1639 was, in the year 1702, in Acadia, "in the archives there." How did it get thither, and why was it sent? According to another part of the prisoner's case before the Lord Ordinary, the first earl, grievously dejected by the death of three of his sons, and fearing, from the declining health of two of the survivors, that his honours might, at no distant period, pass to a collateral branch of the family, obtained the new charter in question in 1639. This charter conveyed large estates in Scotland, as well as in America: "but," as Lord Meadowbank observed, "while the former were within reach, and easily accessible, those in Canada and the State of Maine, being" [*then, i. e.* in 1639, the original grants having been made in 1626 and 1628] "in the hands of the French, were altogether out of the reach of the grantees! In these circumstances, you are required to believe that the earl, in place of retaining this charter in Scotland, and getting it recorded and perfected *there*, where he might have got something by it, carried it to Canada, and had it recorded, where he could get nothing; and where, except as a matter of curiosity to men like Monsieur Mallet and his friend Lacroix, it was altogether a piece of waste paper. I again put it to you, is it credible that, if the earl had really got such a charter, and had wished to *change the destination* of his estates—and we know that he was a person of no ordinary talents—he would have omitted taking means for preserving in his own country, the evidence of what he had done?"

But, *secondly*, again, the original charter was, in 1702, in Nova Scotia. Now we have seen that, in 1723, this "original charter" was, on the 10th July 1723, in Ireland, in the hands of a Mr Thomas Conyers, of Carlow, who "permitted" Mr Hovenden "to see it, and he did most minutely examine the contents:" and on the 20th of that month, in the same year, the son of the aforesaid

Conyers certified that that charter "had been trusted to his late father, in troublesome times, by the deceased Mary, Countess of Mount Alexander." At that time the fifth earl was living. When, then, did the charter return from Acadia to Scotland, and go thence to Ireland? According to the letter of John of Antrim on the map, his grandmother, the first countess, took it to Ireland to her son-in-law, Lord Montgomery, to be taken care of. That son-in-law died in 1670. What did he do with it? Did he send it to Canada?—and why? What were the three Earls of Stirling about, that they did not get possession of this document, the very foundation of their fortunes and honours? It goes, however, to Canada in 1702; is back again, and in Ireland, at all events, in 1723; and then gets placed in uncomfortable circumstances, and encounters queer adventures. It found its way into the hands of the Rev. John Alexander (John No. 3), *in the lifetime of the fifth* Earl of Stirling; and on his death, in 1743, it found itself in the hands of his widow, who took it to Birmingham when she went to reside there; whence it was stolen, in 1758, by an emissary of the then claimant of the peerage, William Alexander, who took it off to America, and either suppressed or destroyed it, the latest trace of it existing in 1806 or 1812, when it was presumably destroyed. All this was the original official statement of his case, by the prisoner himself, in 1829, in the process of "proving the tenor."

*Thirdly*, In 1702, this M. Mallet speaks of the charter as "an *ancient* one;" whereas it was then only sixty-three years old—its date being 1639.

*Fourthly*, It having been thus a dead letter for sixty-three years, owing to the altered ownership of the territories included in it—they having become the undisputed property of France, and so continued for half a century afterwards, namely, till General Wolff's conquest of Quebec in 1760; yet we have a forecasting Frenchman, in 1702, represented as calmly speculating, in the year 1702, without anything to suggest such an idea, on the possibility of the territories being reconquered from France by the English, and in that event the charter becoming an object of great interest!

*Fifthly*, We have him also giving himself very particular concern with the *limitations* and family destinations of the tenures of the foreign grantees claiming under this "*ancient*" dead letter—then a mere useless piece of parchment, likely to attract the eye and attention of none but some exceedingly inquisitive antiquarian. Who was this M. Mallet? There is no suggestion that he was acquainted with any member of the family, or had ever been concerned in any way with them. Why, then, should he feel it necessary to "take the precaution" of having the copy which he had made "duly attested?" Who, again, was Lacroix? What was there *then* to interest any one in France or America in the fortunes of the noble Scottish family of the Alexanders? Why was it to be expected that "all the world would read with interest" the note which M. Mallet had so quietly written on his map, and then committed to his bureau?

*Sixthly*, In 1702, 1706, and 1707, Acadia was in the hands of the French, and consequently its archives or registers were under their control; and a copy of any instrument deposited there could be easily obtained. Why, then, was not the command of Louis XV. obeyed, and a copy procured for his Majesty? Again, what became of the solemnly-attested copy spoken of by M. Mallet, Lacroix, and St Estienne? No account whatever is given of it, nor any reason why it was necessary to set such store by a brief epitome of one or two of the clauses to be found in that copy! Why, therefore, was the "Note" of M. Mallet so "*precious*," when those interested in the matter to which it related could have so easily seen the original of which it spoke, and obtained a *verbatim* copy of the whole? The "Note" of M. Mallet might, indeed, be precious in the eyes of his suddenly-bereaved survivors, as an autograph memento of their deceased friend, but not otherwise.

*Seventhly*, Why should there be, in 1707, in the family of John of Antrim, a tradition, and that, too, an "ancient" one—*i. e.*, forty or fifty years old—concerning the loss of the record of a copy of the charter, *when the original* was in existence in the archives of Acadia?

*Lastly*, Why is the great shade of the author of *Telemachus* evoked? Simply to "*authenticate*" the letter of John Alexander to the Marchioness de Lambert, to whom that letter was then on its way!—This much for the intrinsic indication of genuineness or spuriousness, afforded by the indorsements on the map of Canada, which we have hitherto been considering.

We have now, however, to record as remarkable an incident as ever occurred in the course of a judicial inquiry.—As already stated, one of the two documents *pasted* on the back of the map, was the alleged tombstone inscription. As the map was lying on the table of the densely crowded court, owing to either the heat, or some other cause, one of the corners of the paper on which the inscription was written, curled up a little—just far enough to disclose some writing underneath it, on the back of the map. On the attention of the Solicitor-General being directed to the circumstance, he immediately applied to the court for its permission to Mr Lizars, the eminent engraver, then present, to detach from the map the paper on which the tombstone inscription was written. Having been duly sworn, he withdrew for that purpose, and soon afterwards returned, having executed his mission very skilfully, without injury to either paper. That on which the inscription was written, proved to be itself a portion of another copy of the map of Canada, and the writing *which it covered* was as follows, but in French:—

"There has just been shown to me *a letter of Fénélon* written in 1698, having reference to this grandson of Lord Stirling, who was in France during that year, and with regard to whom he expresses himself as follows:—'I request that you will see this amiable and good Irishman, Mr John Alexander, whose acquaintance I made some years ago. He is a man of real merit, and whom every one sees with pleasure *at court*, and in the best circles of the capital.' These were the initials, as far as they are legible, 'E. Sh.'" This was represented by the Solicitor-General as palpably an inchoate abortive forgery; and Lord Meadowbank pointed out to the jury the evident and partially successful effort which had been made to *tear off* that portion of the surface of the map on which the above had been written. That effort failing, said he, "the only precaution that remained, to prevent its appearing, was to cover it over; for which purpose the parties used the inscription. But then the apprehension of its appearing, if the map were held between the light and the eye, seems to have come across the minds of the parties engaged in the operation, and hence, with a very singular degree of foresight, expertness, and precaution, they used for their cover that by which the eye of the inquirer might be misled in his investigation; for you have seen that the lines and words of the map forming the *back* of the inscription were exactly such as would naturally fall in with those on the *front* of the map of Canada, from which the extract from the pretended letter of Fenelon had refused to be separated. Accordingly the invention, it would appear, had proved hitherto most successful; for though this map had been examined over and over again by persons of the first skill and talent, and scrutinised with the most minute attention, the writing which was thus covered up escaped detection, till, by the extreme heat of the court-house yesterday, or some other cause of a similar nature, a corner of the inscription separated from the map, and revealed to our observation that which was hidden below. Gentlemen, it is for you to consider the *effect* of this revelation; but I must fairly tell you, that, in the whole course of my experience, I have never seen more clear and satisfactory evidence than has hereby been unexpectedly afforded, of the progress of a palpable and impudent forgery." The reader will bear in mind these observations, against the time when we apprise him of the finding of the jury. The reason suggested by Lord Meadowbank for the abandonment and concealment of the sub-inscription was, that it was of such a nature as could not acquire credit from any one, as Fénélon was therein made to speak as if he were a courtier, familiar with the gay scenes of the court and the capital; whereas it was notorious that he lived more at his diocese than at Paris. Mr Lizars stated that this newly discovered writing did not resemble that of the leter signed "John Alexander." "How the crown counsel would have chuckled," said the prisoner's counsel to the jury, "if the marvellous new discovery had resembled that of Mallet or Alexander!" And that was his only remark on the subject. To us the handwriting of these three manuscripts appears certainly different: all those on the map, indeed, appear different; but an obvious suggestion occurs, that, if they were really forgeries, those perpetrating them may have taken the precaution of employing distinct writers.—Let us now come to the *extrinsic* evidence, to determine the genuineness or spuriousness of these multifarious writings. First, as to the ink and character of the writings. Two eminent French witnesses (MM. Teulet, joint-secretary of the archives of the kingdom of France, and Jacobs, geographical engraver attached to the Institute of France at Paris), peculiarly conversant with the art of making *fac-similes* of ancient writings, solemnly and confidently pronounced their opinions that all the documents on the back of the map were false; that they were written with ink generally used for that purpose—viz., a composition of China ink, yellow and carmine, or red; and the paper afforded visible indications of little red splashings, or spottings, the result of accidents in using that composition.

" *Q.*—M. Teulet, from what you know, are you of opinion that these writings on the back of the map are authentic writings of the dates they bear?

" *A.*—I have considered them; and say, on my conscience, that all the writings on the back of that map are false."

" *Q.*—To M. Jacobs.—Forming a judgment from the ink alone, and the appearance of the writing itself, is it your opinion that these are genuine or false documents—documents of the dates they bear?

" *A.*—I should think them false."

Mr Lizars also stated that " there was a very great resemblance between the ink in the writing signed 'Ph. Mallet' and the letter signed 'John Alexander,' and it was " like common water paint." He said that " if he were to make any conjecture, it would be that the ink was composed of sepia and amber." But on being asked —" Suppose the ink were made of a mixture of China ink, yellow and carmine, might the carmine come out at the edge?" He answered—" It would be sure to do it: a bungler only would use such a mixture, as the carmine would certainly precipitate: it were much better to use sepia and amber." This gentleman also stated that he had compared the writings on the back of the map with those of the prisoner and Mademoiselle le Normand, but found no resemblance between them. He also stated, that he thought the writings in question *genuine*, and written in a natural, not a feigned hand.

We come now, however, to an astounding fact, rendering all such speculations and surmises superfluous. It will have been observed that all the writings on the back of the map, by Mallet, Estienne, John Alexander, Bishop Flechier, and Archbishop Fénélon, bore date in the years 1706 and 1707; that of Mallet only being in the former year. What will the reader say on being told that it was proved beyond all possible doubt at the trial, that *the map on which these various indorsements were written, was posi-*

*tively not in existence till eleven years afterwards—viz.,* 1718*; and, moreover, that Bishop Flechier had died in* 1711, *and Archbishop Fénêlon in* 1715? Proof so complete and crushing as that establishing these facts, scarcely ever before came under our notice; and the circumstance which had led to this result would have ensnared the most cautiously astute into the belief, that the true date of the map's coming into existence was that which it appeared to bear—viz., 1703—and with relation to, and in consistency with which, all the above five dates would seem to have been selected and adjusted.

Guillaume de l'Isle was the greatest French geographer of his day, and his maps were held in the highest repute for their accuracy and beauty. Amongst others was an elaborate one of Canada: and the copy of that on which the memorable indorsements were made, bore the following printed description, or title, on the back. We give it *verbatim et literatim*, and beg particular attention to the vacant space following the name Guillaume De l'Isle, which is indicated by brackets, and the italic words "*et Premier Geographe du Roy*" in the line but one following, and which is unduly close to the one before, as we shall endeavour to represent :—

"Carte<br>
Du Canada<br>
ou de la<br>
Nouvelle France<br>
et des Decouvertes qui y ont été faites<br>
dressée sur plusieurs Observations<br>
et sur un grand nombre de Relations imprimées ou manuscrites<br>
Par Guillaume De l'Isle [                    ]<br>
de l'Academie Royale des Sciences<br>
*et Premier Geographe du Roy*<br>
A Paris<br>
chez l'Auteur sur le Quai de l'Horloge à l'Aigle d'Or<br>
avec Privilege de sa Maj[te] pour 20 ans<br>
1703."

The date at the foot, "1703," and which would seem to

have so cruelly misled the gentlemen who had prepared the indorsements on the map, was the date, not of the publication of that edition of the map, but of the *original* publication, from which dated the twenty years' copyright granted by the king as above stated. When that impression of the map was originally printed, in the year 1703, the printed title varied from the above, by having the word "*Géographe*" occupying the vacant space above-contained in brackets; and by the absence of the line "*et premier Géographe du Roy*," so evidently interposed subsequently between the preceding and subsequent lines. And the fact was, that on the 24th August 1718, fifteen years after the original publication of the map, De l'Isle had received the high appointment of "PREMIER Géographe du Roi." M. Teulet, one of the keepers of the "Register of the Secretary of State" in France, a "register of the greatest possible authenticity,"—"the *only* register of authentic documents in which the commission of Guillaume De l'Isle could be found," produced an "extract made after the most authentic manner in France, certified by the keeper of the register, and by the seal of the archives of France,"—an "extract which would have all possible authenticity in a court of justice in France," and which extract M. Teulet "had compared twice over, word for word, and letter for letter, with the record," and swore that "it was correct." The extract was as follows:—

"Du vingt quatre Aoust mil sept cent dix huit

"Brevet de Premier Géographe du Roy pour l S^r. De l'Isle." The entry runs thus in English:—

"*This day* (24th August 1718) the king being in Paris, having authentic proofs of the profound erudition of the S. Guillaume de l'Isle, *of the Royal Academy of Sciences*, in the great number of geographical works which he has executed for his Majesty's use, and which have been received with general approbation by the public, his Majesty, by the advice," &c. &c., "wishing to attach him more particularly to his Majesty's service by a title of honour, which may procure him at the same time the means of continuing works of such usefulness, has declared, and declares, wishes, and enjoins, that the said S. de l'Isle be *henceforward* [' DORESNAVANT '] his first geographer," &c. &c. This appointment was signed by the king, and countersigned by the secretary of state. It was distinctly sworn by M. Teulet and M. Jacobs, than whom there could not have been higher authorities on such a subject, that they had carefully examined the map in question—and that, till the 24th August 1718, there never was a map of De l'Isle thrown off having on its face the title of "Premier Géographe du Roi;" but that, *after* that date, this designation was invariably added to his name;—and though the period of printing was later than 1718, it was necessary to retain the original date of the map, 1703, *in order to secure the copyright;* because the privilege of printing it, as recited on the map, extended to only twenty years from the time of the map being originally published. Thus was clearly and most satisfactorily explained the erasure of the word "Géographe" after the name of Guillaume de l'Isle, and the contemporaneous interpolation of the new title of dignity—*Premier géographe du Roy*—between the next line and the one following. All the three witnesses (MM. Teulet, Jacobs, and Mr Lizars) swore, and gave conclusive reasons for doing so, that the same copperplate was used in making the engravings—that De l'Isle was in the habit of retouching his plates, and making alterations in them from time to time; and great numbers of his plates were produced, showing that, in the maps dated anterior to 1718, the words "Premier Géographe du Roy" were *interpolated;* and in the one before the court, the interpolated line was much "fresher" than the rest of the inscription. In those subsequent to 1718 there was "no such interpolation, the words being always regular with the other part of the title." In addition to this, it was proved, that the word "Géographe" had been mechanically effaced from the copper; for, on carefully examining the under side of the copper, there were "evident traces of hammering, which had been done to fill up the spaces where the words had been effaced."

Nothing could be more lucid and decisive than the evidence given by the eminent M. Teulet on these points; the result being a downright demonstration, as far as the nature of the case admitted of demonstration, that the copy of the map in question could not have been, and was not, in existence, till after the 24th August 1718. The prisoner's counsel, fearfully pressed by these considerations, frankly—but necessarily—admitted, that "if the map were not in existence till 1718, the writings on it purporting to be dated prior to 1718 were forgeries." But he contended, that, though "he should be ashamed to deny that there were *strong reasons* for supposing the fact to be so, there was not *conclusive* evidence that the copy of the map in question was not in existence till 1718; for the Crown had not proved a search of the Records of France prior to 1718, and it might be, that the commission which had been proved, was not the *first* in favour of De l'Isle—there might have been a previous one." "But this," said Lord Meadowbank, unanswerably, "was a strange supposition, refuted by the patent proved before the jury. Had any *former grant* existed, it must have been there referred to; notice of it could not have been omitted." One other suggestion was offered, faintly, from a sense of its hopelessness; that the alterations on the title of the map might have been effected by the use of double plates; the additional line having been inserted by a second impression *on the same sheet of paper* Such a process, however, could not have *effaced* the word "Géographe," or effected the changes which appeared in the statement of De l'Isle's residence—the words "à l'Aigle d'Or" being manifestly engraven on the site of only partially-obliterated previous letters. That this, in point of fact, had been the process, was distinctly sworn to by those who had seen the original plate.

Before quitting this part of the case, we shall quote a critical section of the evidence given by the Crown —that of Pierre François Joseph Leguix, a print and map seller at Paris, whom the prisoner's counsel made a desperate attempt to exclude from the witness-box. He said, "My print-shop is in the Quai Voltaire, Paris. I remember *in the winter of* 1836-7* a person coming frequently to my shop in search of maps. I think he was an Englishman. The maps he sought for were maps of Canada. He came during the length of five or six weeks. I sold him several maps of Canada. He wished to get one map of a particular date. *It was the date of* 1703. I sold him a map of 1703. It was procured by me after considerable search. He came to my shop no more after getting that map. It was similar to this [the one in question]. There were no writings then on the back of it. He did not explain who he was, nor say why he wished to have that map. He inquired chiefly for a map of 1703.

"*Q.* (by the Counsel for the Crown)—'*Have you seen the prisoner before?*'

"*A.*—'*Yes.*'

"*Q.*—'*It was not he?*'

"*A.*—'*No, Sir.*'"†

What a moment for the prisoner, whether guilty or innocent!

In a letter written to the prisoner by Mademoiselle le Normand, dated Paris, 8th January 1839, occurs the following passage (read in evidence at the trial), which may possibly relate to the facts above deposed to. "Seulement *on a découvert l'homme du Quai;* on veut le faire partir pour l'Ecosse; il déclare que voilà 18 mois il a vendu une Carte du Canada à un Anglais, qui plusieurs fois est venu chez lui, on lui a dit: le reconnaitriez-vous? *je le crois.*"

Finally, M. Teulet proved that Fénélon, Archbishop of Cambray, died at five o'clock in the morning of the 7th

† *Ante*, p. 215. * Swinton, pp. 143-4.

February 1715; by the following examined extract from the Register of the Chapter of Cambray—"*Feria* 2, *die* vii *Januarii* 1715.—*Hodie circa quintam matutinam obiit illustrissimus Dominus Franciscus de Salignac de la Mothe Fenelon, Archiepiscopus et Dux Cameracensis, sacri Romani Imperii Princeps, Comes Cameracensis, etc. Requiescat in pace.*"*

The death of Flechier, Bishop of Nismes, in 1711, was also proved by M. Teulet, who produced an examined copy of letters patent for the installation of the successor of Flechier, dated the 26th February 1711; and one of the witnesses, M. de Pages, stated that the Bishop died in the year 1710. Notwithstanding, however, this evidence, M. de Pages (a nephew of the Marqüis de Valfour, and attached to the Historical department in the King's Library, and possessing some little familiarity with ancient manuscripts), having brought over some alleged writings of Louis XV. and Flechier, said, "that the writing on the map attributed to Louis was *exactly like* the specimens of his writing which the witness had brought;" and of that attributed to Flechier he observed, "I think it is the same as the writing of his which I produce." On this, one of the judges (Lord Moncrieff) put this acute question:—

"*Q.*—'If you were assured that that map had no existence till 1718, would you still say that the writing on it was Flechier's?'

"*A.*—'Wherever it might be placed, I find it conformable to the writing of Flechier.'

"*Lord Moncrieff to the Interpreter.*—'Remind him that he said that Flechier ceased to be Bishop of Nismes in 1710, and then ask him the question again.' [This was done.]

"*A.*—'It would be not the less like.'

Lord Meadowbank, it may be observed in passing, re-

* Swinton, App. lviii.

garded the writings brought over by M. de Pages as "important," and handed them to the jury, on their retiring to consider their verdict.

The signatures of Louis, Fénélon, and Flechier were attempted to be proved also by certificates from M. Daunou, M. Villenave, and other eminent French antiquaries; but as they were living, such certificates were of course rejected. If these writings, then, *were* forgeries, they must have been most skilfully executed; and, in fact, the question as to their genuineness or spuriousness excited, as we learn from Mr Swinton, great interest and much discussion in Paris. It may also be here mentioned, as a somewhat singular circumstance, that, a few years previously to this trial, as we also learn from Mr Swinton, a series of portraits and autographs of illustrious Frenchmen, published by Delpech (Quai Voltaire, Paris), contained *fac-similes* of the writing of Louis XV., Fénélon, and Flechier, exactly resembling the writings on the map attributed to them;—and in the specimen given in that work, of the writing of Louis XV., which was taken from the collection of M. Villenave above-mentioned, occur the very *two expressions*, and *similarly spelled*, which are found on the map—"les c*e*rconstances presentes"—and "or*e*g*e*nale." Mr Swinton speaks of this coincidence as "remarkable;" but to us it appears not at all so. What is easier than to conceive that, if the writings on the map were forgeries, the fabricator had before him at the time these very fac-similes, and astutely determined to introduce the expressions in question, with the peculiar spelling?

Let us now recur for a moment to the excerpt charter of the 7th February 1639. On the assumption that it was a forgery, *what becomes of the writings on the map of De l'Isle?* They then speak of, they are bottomed on, a document of which there is no earthly trace whatever, except in a forged extract! If the excerpt be annihilated, so is the charter! And if so,—in the name of holy truth and ordinary common sense, how comes it, but by a double forgery, that we find on the map of De l'Isle, produced for the first time in 1837, *all the essential elements of that charter*, as far as sufficed to further the interests of the prisoner—viz., the altered destination of the titles and property, set forth *verbatim et literatim*, in conformity with the terms of the forged excerpt? "How, but through the evidence of one in the possession of this first forgery of the charter," asked the Solicitor-General,* "could the persons who executed the second arrive at such a close and perfect correspondence with the terms and effect of the former, as has been exhibited through the whole contents of the last?"

The prisoner's counsel said, in defence of this serious section of the charge—the map is not pretended to have been forged; nor is the date "1703" false. Who Ph. Mallet, or Caron St Estienne, was, "at the distance of one hundred and thirty years, no one could tell. Flechier was alive in 1707, and therefore *might* have written the note attributed to him in that year; and so with Fénélon." "Now, gentlemen," said Mr Robertson, "what is the case of the crown on the map? I think it rests entirely on the appointment of De l'Isle as *premier géographe du Roi*," which was unquestionably the true—the inevitable—issue on which to put the case; and he proceeded to contend, on grounds which we have already indicated in passing, that the crown had not established the act of forgery, by clear, irrefragable, irresistible proof.

What, then, says the considerate reader, we ask, as we did in the former instance—were these writings on the map of Canada, any or all of them, genuine, or spurious?

III. The De Porquet Packet. With every disposition to treat this item of evidence with the gravity and impartiality befitting quasi-judicial investigation, we ac-

* Swinton, p. 237.

knowledge feeling extreme difficulty in doing so. To us, as English lawyers, intense would seem the simplicity of those expecting any rational being to give credit for an instant to the contents of this astonishing packet, as genuine. Two months after the judgment of the Lord Ordinary, pointing out the fatal flaw in the prisoner's pedigree, (viz., the non-proof of two particular steps in that pedigree—that John No. 3 descended from John No. 2, and the latter from No. 1), a sensitive and conscientious thief died—viz., in March 1837—in the exact nick of time, having kept by him till that sad event a packet which he had purloined from his employer in 1798,* *i. e., for forty years;* and which packet contained four family documents, of vital moment, applying themselves with miraculous exactness to the deficiency in the pedigree aforesaid! We are here stating shortly, but correctly, the effect of a document under this head of the charge, set forth in the indictment. That document we gave *verbatim* in a former part of this paper.† Messrs De Porquet, London booksellers, received a packet by the penny post, on opening which they found one addressed to Lord Stirling, accompanied by a note from a "*Mrs Innes Smyth*" (of whom no one has hitherto seen, heard, or known anything whatever), requesting them to send it to his lordship; whose son happening in the month of April 1837—*i. e.*, a few weeks after the opportune death of the mysterious thief—to call at Messrs De Porquet, they gave him the packet addressed to his father. Instead of forwarding it to him, the young gentleman instantly took it to his solicitors; and after an exciting colloquy as to what this packet might contain (the idea never occurring to him that it would be the proper formal course to send it off to his parent according to its address), it is arranged that they should go on the ensuing morning to a notary public, and open the packet in his presence!

* *Ante*, p. 210. † *Ante*, p. 209.

This was done; on which they discovered the interesting document above referred to, explaining the theft of the packet which it accompanied, cased in parchment, sealed with three black seals, "evidently," said the young Alexander, in his letter to the prisoner, "my grandfather's seals—not like those *we* have;" and with the following words, also instantly recognised as being in his grandfather's handwriting, on the packet—"*Some of my wife's family papers*"—that wife being the prisoner's mother, Hannah, daughter of John No. 3 (the Rev. John Alexander), the "person of such great humility, and so perfectly unostentatious," according to her daughter's statement,* "that she did not take upon herself the title of countess, though she often told her children that they had noble blood in their veins; that she had two brothers, '*John*' and '*Benjamin*,' who had fully intended assuming their peerage honours, but for their premature death, *unmarried*, whereby she," the lady aforesaid, "believed herself the last of the family of Alexander who were entitled to be Earls of Stirling!" The sheet of paper accompanying this mystic parchment packet had a black border, "owing to the death of the thief!"—who "had never dared to break the seals," the threefold seals of the packet, "which accounts for the admirable state of preservation" in which the contents were after this forty years' interval! † This inner packet the modest notary felt to be of too solemn a character to be opened in his presence; and recommended its being taken for that purpose to a functionary of commensurate solemnity—to wit, a proctor. ‡ This was done; and they were closeted with the proctor five hours; and in his presence—and that "of four witnesses"—the young gentleman ventured to cut the parchment over the middle black seal—and there appeared four enclosures which completely settled the business in favour of the claimant of the Stirling peerage.

* *Ante*, p. 209.

† *Ante*, pp. 210-12.

‡ Swinton, p. 263.

Never was anything so beautiful in aptitude. *First*, was a genealogical tree—thus

"JOHN
Eldest Son, born at Dublin, 1736, *heir to the title and estates* (*!*)

BENJAMIN,
Second Son, born at Dublin in 1737.

MARY,
Eldest Daughter, born at Dublin, 1733.

HANNAH,
Second Daughter, born at Dublin in 1741.

JOHN
*Sixth Earl of Stirling*, (*de jure*), died at Dublin, Nov. 1st, 1743, buried there.

MARY,
Eldest Daughter, born 1683, died unmarried.

ELIZABETH,
born 1685, died 1711, leaving issue.

JOHN,
Married MARY HAMILTON of Bangor; *settled at Antrim! after living many years in Germany!* Died 1712. Buried at Newtown.

JANET,
*only surviving child of the heiress of Gartmore!*

JOHN,
Fourth Son—marry'd (1.) *Agnes Graham*, the heiress of Gartmore! (2.) *Elizabeth Maxwell!* of Londonderry; settled in Ireland in 1646; died 1665.

WILLIAM,
1st Earl of Stirling—born 1580—m: Janet Erskine. Had issue, 7 sons and 3 daurs. Died 1640. Buried at Stirling."

"Part
Of the Genealogical Tree
of the
Alexanders of Menstry,
Earls of Stirling in Scotland,
*Shewing*
*only the Fourth and now existing branch* (*!*)
Reduced to pocket size, from the Large Emblazoned Tree in the possession of Mrs Alexander, of King St., Birm.
By me,
Thomas Campbell,
April 15, 1759."

*Secondly*, came a letter from the above-mentioned "Benjamin" to the above-mentioned "John," his elder brother (John No. 3), speaking of the tombstone, and giving many interesting particulars concerning *John of Antrim*—his portrait, his education at Londonderry under his *maternal* grandsire, Maxwell! his travels abroad, and "visiting foreign courts," (as indeed Fénélon would seem to have testified, as well as the aforesaid John himself, on Madlle. Le Normand's map). *Thirdly*, a letter to the same "John" (No. 3) from a certain "A. E. Baillie," certifying as to the missing tombstone, who had written the inscription given at length in Madlle. Le Normand's map, and assuring "John No. 3" that the writer had "always heard that *your great-grandfather*, *the Hon. Mr Alexander* (who was known in the county as *Mr Alexander of Garmore*), died at Derry, but 'the Papists of the north' had unfortunately destroyed the parish registers." *Lastly*, "a beautiful miniature painting of *John of Antrim!*"

Such were the contents of the De Porquet packet; and we must here add, that the superscription on the parchment, "Some of my wife's family papers," was clearly proved to be really the handwriting of the prisoner's father.

The Solicitor-General, partly from the intrinsic preposterous absurdity of this whole transaction, and partly from his extended and able analysis of the two former heads of evidence, dealt rather summarily with the De Porquet packet. "This packet, too," he observed, "was received through the post-office. We have not, therefore, had the same means of tracing these documents as we possessed in regard to the map." * His commentary, however, though brief, was cutting, particularly on the "absurd solemnity" of the "opening" of the packet by the prisoner's son, the "death of the thief in the very nick of time," and the mysterious unknown "Mrs Innes Smyth." "I admit," said he, "that there is no *direct* evidence as to these English documents. But it must be taken into account how closely the whole case is here riveted and dovetailed together; so that I think the documents produced are all parts and portions of the grand machinery of forgery which has been set agoing here, to meet the effect of the Lord Ordinary's interlocutor setting aside the panel's title." †

The prisoner's counsel dealt still more briefly with this part of the case. The little that he did say,

* Swinton, p. 263. † *Ib.* p. 265.

however, was excellently said. He dwelt on the proof that the superscription, "Some of my wife's family papers,"* had been proved to be genuine. "Yet a verdict of forgery is demanded on that paper, and all the documents contained in that parcel are said to be forged —the one, because we have proved it to be genuine; the others, because the crown has proved—nothing at all. That is the plain English of it, gentlemen, and I leave it in your hands." †

Lord Meadowbank dealt with this portion of the case at considerably greater length, and very carefully. He remarked on the absurd improbability of so notable a discovery being made at the precise moment of difficulty, and in the manner alleged, by the son of the prisoner—a packet full of most critical documents, sent anonymously —exactly as in the case of the Le Normand packet, in both respects—the one in April, the other in July next, after the Lord Ordinary's judgment had indicated the *hiatus* in the proof which these two windfalls *exactly filled up*. The two letters enclosed in it—viz., from Benjamin Alexander to his brother John (No. 3), and from "A. E. Baillie" to the same person — Lord Meadowbank regarded as "deserving the most serious consideration of the jury, not so much for the sake of the letters themselves, as from being a part of that great mass of evidence which bore upon the whole question of the authenticity of these various productions." ‡ He remarked strongly on young Alexander's letter announcing to his father the discovery of the packet—his going to a notary and proctor to have it opened, instead of at once sending it on to his father. "For aught his son is supposed to have known, or could possibly tell, it was strictly confidential to his father, and he had no right to make any conjectures as to the contents of it. Did you ever hear a more extraordinary story than he tells? I leave it to you to

* This superscription was charged in the indictment as a forgery.

† Swinton, pp. 293, 294.

‡ *Ib.* p. 324.

consider whether such a proceeding can be accounted for on any rational principle. Did you ever hear of such a thing as this being done before? For my own part, the proceeding is altogether incomprehensible upon any supposition but one—and that is, upon the notion *that the contents of the packet were not unknown to some of the performers in the drama, before ever it* [the packet] *entered the shop of De Porquet.*" Lord Meadowbank laid great stress on the following certainly significant passage in this letter, relating to the "*inscription*" mentioned in the two letters of "Benjamin Alexander" and "A. E. Baillie:"—"You will see that the inscription is *now made a good document, being confirmed* by the letters of B. Alexander and A. E. Baillie. The cause is enrolled to be heard on the 31st day of May." The son was writing on the 23d April. "The better to appreciate this letter," continued Lord Meadowbank, "let me recall your recollection to the map of Canada. You have thus three letters, and that inscription confirming *another inscription* (as stated in young Alexander's letter) *fixed on the map;* and if you do not hold the map or the papers upon it to be genuine, you will consider how the two sets of papers are affected by each other—the one produced at the same moment to confirm that which had been produced before." As for the superscription, "Some of my wife's family papers," the "writing on the cover," said Lord Meadowbank, "may be genuine, while the documents said to be contained in it may be forged; original enclosures may have been withdrawn, and others substituted."—"If you have arrived at the conclusion that the documents at the back of the old map are forgeries (and how you are to do otherwise it is difficult for me to imagine), I think you will not find it very easy to disconnect this reference to the inscription, and to the alleged genealogy of the persons with whom it was the object of the prisoner to connect himself, from these documents, or to entertain any reasonable doubt that both are in *pari casu*—were fabricated with the view of bolstering up one another, and must be alike liable to the imputation of forgery: both sets of documents were exactly calculated for making up those defects in the chain of evidence pointed out by the Lord Ordinary. I shall conclude what I have to say upon this matter with an observation which will have occurred to yourselves — that if you hold the *excerpt charter* a forgery, and that the documents written and pasted upon the back of the map are forgeries, it will be difficult for you not to hold that this must affect in a most material degree the evidence relating to the *other* documents, which the public prosecutor avers to be also forgeries. In other words, if you are satisfied that the proof is clear that *any* of these sets of documents are forged, but that the evidence with respect to others is not so conclusive, you will have to make up your minds whether, considering that the whole are so connected with and bear upon each other, there can be any good reason for fixing a character upon the one which must not also belong to the other."

We have been thus particular in laying before the reader the observations of Lord Meadowbank on this last portion of the case, chiefly because of the result at which the jury arrived. It seems to us not a little singular that one material enclosure in the De Porquet packet escaped the notice of both the counsel for the crown and the prisoner, and also the judge: we allude to the Genealogical Tree, professed to be certified by "Thos. Campbell, 15th April 1759," and forming one of the charges in the indictment. If this be really a forgery, it seems one of extraordinary impudence.

Again, then, as in the two former instances, we ask the reader, weighing well the evidence, and particularly the above observations upon it of Lord Meadowbank, to say *Ay* or *No* to the question, Were the documents contained in the De Porquet packet genuine or spurious? Bearing in mind that all three were the contributions of anonymous informants—the excerpt charter, sent to Mr Banks by—he knew not whom; the Le Normand papers, by—an exceedingly mysterious and exalted personage; and the De Porquet packet, by—a third mysterious unknown: the first sent to the confidential agent of the prisoner in Ireland; the second to one of his oldest and most confidential friends at Paris; the third to his bookseller in London. It may also be worth mentioning that neither Mr Banks, nor Mademoiselle le Normand, nor either of the prisoner's sons, nor his sister, "Lady Eliza Pountney," was called as a witness by the prisoner, nor by the crown.

There remains to be determined, however, a question of infinite moment to the prisoner—whether, in the event of the foregoing documents, or any of them, being pronounced forgeries, he was guilty of having either forged them, or used and uttered any of them, knowing them to have been forged? "This," said Lord Meadowbank, with an air of deepening solemnity, "is the heaviest part of the charge against the panel; and I assure you, gentlemen, that in the whole course of my life, I never addressed a jury with greater anxiety than I do at present."

Let us pause, however, for a moment, to see how this grave question was respectively dealt with by the counsel for the crown, and for the prisoner.

I. The Solicitor-General, it will be observed, according to the Scottish mode of criminal procedure, had only one opportunity of addressing the jury—and that after the whole evidence on both sides had been laid before them, and immediately *before* the speech by the prisoner's counsel. In England, the counsel for the crown speaks also only once, but that before the evidence has been adduced, unless the prisoner call evidence—in which event the counsel for the crown "has the last word," as it is called, "to the jury." This difference may perhaps account for the earnestness with which the Solicitor-General, in the case before us, appears to have "pressed for a conviction"—such is the phrase used on such occasions in England. We are bound, however, to say that, in our opinion, the Solicitor-General did not exhibit any undue or unseemly eagerness; nor approach even towards unfairness, or exaggeration, misrepresentation, or suppression.—The prisoner, said he, is at all events, *de facto*, the utterer of these various documents, and the presumption is always against the utterer—especially when, as in the present case, these documents were calculated to advance his own direct personal interest exclusively. The *onus* lay on him to prove that he innocently uttered, having been deceived by others. Could the jury, in the face of such a marvellous coincidence of times, of means, of objects, believe that a number of different persons were concerned in promoting the prisoner's objects and interests, and he all the while profoundly ignorant of what was being done? The documents are all proved forgeries; and these he utters, and for the advancement of his own interests alone! In the agony of his difficulty—the crisis of his fate—he goes to France clandestinely, and is proved to have been in constant intercourse with Mademoiselle le Normand, and to have incurred immense pecuniary liabilities to her at that very period; giving, however, a most contradictory account of his relations and transactions with her! Up to the hour of his trial, he had given no explanation whatever of his doings at Paris, whither he went immediately after Lord Cockburn's adverse judgment, and returned so shortly after the discovery of the Le Normand and the De Porquet packets! And Leguix is found selling a map of Canada, of 1703, exactly at the time of the prisoner's being at Paris; and Mademoiselle le Normand writes to him—"They have found the man on the quay!"

II. The prisoner's counsel made an ingenious, eloquent, and judicious address—very brief, and directed vigorously and steadily towards the strong parts of the defence, leaving untouched the formidable points arising out of the prisoner's correspondence with Mademoiselle le Normand,

and the conflicting accounts of his movements and transactions given in his judicial examinations. All the forgeries, said he, are charged on, or supposed to be, the act of *one man*—the prisoner; yet not only does no single witness trace the faintest resemblance, in any of the alleged forgeries, to the handwriting of the prisoner, or Mademoiselle le Normand, but an able witness for the crown, Mr Lizars, negatives such a fact. Well might the prisoner be deceived, if the documents *were* forgeries, when his counsel, his agents, the Lord Advocate, and the Judge Ordinary, every one concerned during the ten years' litigation, were so deceived, and never once suspected it. Why did not the crown produce Mademoiselle le Normand? And as to the purchase of the old map of Canada from Leguix, on the Quai Voltaire, he explicitly stated that the prisoner was *not* the man! But there was no evidence of the forgery, and therefore the guilty knowledge, using, and uttering, fell to the ground. If even there were doubts on the subject, the prisoner was clearly entitled to the benefit of them: his character "was everything;" for he had received as high as man could give. In an early part of his address, Mr Robertson averred that he saw in the countenances of the jury "the cheering light of an acquittal—so that he could almost stop *there;*" and his last sentence was one which would be deemed highly objectionable on the part of counsel, under such circumstances, in England—"*On my conscience I believe him innocent of the crimes here charged*, and to have been merely the dupe of the designing, and the prey of the unworthy!"* So solemn an expression of belief could not, of course, have been made by a gentleman if he were not sincere; but it is certainly not a part of the duty of counsel to make such protestations; and in doing so he trespasses beyond his province upon that of others, and that one the confines of which ought to be most jealously and sacredly guarded—we mean the province of the witness, and that of the jury.

* Swinton, pp. 333–4.

Bating a little wilful blindness to ugly facts, which is occasionally to be found elsewhere than in Scotland, the address of Mr Robertson was as fair as can be expected from a prisoner's advocate, and calculated to make a strong impression upon the jury.

III. Lord Meadowbank's summing up was long and elaborate; stern and uncompromising from first to last, in the expression of a hostile view of the whole case, as against the prisoner, but still not, in our judgment, straining the proved facts. It is the charge of an upright yet severe judge, not ambitious of replying to the prisoner's counsel, but vigorously expressing his own conscientious opinions.

It is evident that Lord Meadowbank regarded the advantage derived by the prisoner from the presence in the dock of his distinguished friend Colonel D'Aguilar, and also from the flattering testimony to character which he had received, as likely to prove a disturbing force to the jury in forming their estimate of the case. He therefore, in the first instance, addressed himself with an evident air of anxiety to this section of the evidence. "That of Colonel D'Aguilar," said he, "of the gallant officer now seated with the panel at the bar,* was not more creditable to the panel than it was to the witness. It proved that his feelings of obligation, long ago conferred, had not been obliterated by the lapse of time; and it was given with an earnestness which, if it told on your minds as it did on mine, must have been by you felt as most deeply affecting. * * * But in weighing this evidence to the character of the prisoner, you must attend to what that proof really amounts to."† He proceeded to point out the chasm of thirty years in their *personal* intercourse; and then exhibited, in lively colours, by way of set-off, the conduct of the prisoner in raising large sums

* Such a thing would not be allowed in England, except, probably, under very special circumstances. *We* never witnessed anything of the kind.

† Swinton, pp. 333–4.

of money on false representations as to his resources—"raising a sum of £13,000 on bonds granted by him for £50,000. All this, gentlemen, is, to say the least of it, a most discreditable proceeding on the part of a person bearing the high character which has been given the prisoner. It is for you, gentlemen, to consider if the evidence which has been given as to the character he once bore, be or be not counterbalanced by these disreputable proceedings at a later period."*

The "evidence of the prisoner having *uttered the whole* of the instruments and documents charged in the indictment to be forgeries, has not been called in question by the prisoner's counsel, he not having said one word on the subject. For my own part, I see no ground for disputing that the whole were uttered by the prisoner, and I shall content myself with referring to the evidence of the official witnesses, who received them from the agents of the prisoner; who again, in so producing, and so delivering them, acted under his authority, and were the mere instruments for carrying into effect those acts for which he alone can be responsible." Shortly afterwards, Lord Meadowbank gave a blighting summary of undisputed facts.

On the 10th December 1836, the Lord Ordinary issued his note, pointing out the evidence that was deficient: "The prisoner admits that he left the country immediately afterwards, and went to Paris. Where he went to then, he does not tell; under what name he went, he does not tell; where he got his passport has not been discovered, because he concealed the name under which he travelled. He continued in Paris till the ensuing August, when he returned, as he says, to Scotland, to be present at the peers' election, and there he voted. He then despatched his son to Paris, and *he* returned with the map (which you are *now*, in considering the case in this view, to assume to be a fabrication) in the month of Octo-

* Swinton, pp. 335–6.

ber, having all these documents written or pasted upon it." Lord Meadowbank proceeded to point out a circumstance "of the last importance to this branch of the case," which "had been lost sight of by the prisoner's counsel, and had not attracted the attention of the counsel for the crown." And certainly the judge was right. This was the "circumstance" in question. One of the documents pasted on the back of the map was a portion of the envelope in which the supposed letter of John of Antrim (John No. 2) had been enclosed; and on this envelope was the impression of a *seal.* Now, in the prisoner's judicial examination before the Lord Ordinary (the step admitted by Mr Swinton to have been "unusual"), he was shown the parchment packet contained in the De Porquet packet, indorsed, "Some of my wife's family papers;" and the seal attached "was an impression of his *grandfather's seal* (John No. 3); he had not seen that seal later than the year 1825; it is in the possession of my sister, Lady Elizabeth Pountney." The judge then pointed out to the jury a fact which he had himself discovered, that the impression of the seal on this packet and that on the envelope on the map *were identical*—a fact, indeed, which the prisoner himself had admitted in another part of his examination. "Now, gentlemen," continued Lord Meadowbank, "supposing there was not another tittle of evidence in the case to connect the prisoner with these proceedings, see what this amounts to. You find a link in his pedigree wanting in December 1836. Immediately after this has been pointed out, he is in Paris, and stays there till August. During this short interval he is brought into immediate and close connection with this mass of fabrications, of fabrications of no earthly use or moment to any human being but himself, and having among them *the impression of that seal which he admits to be in the possession of his own sister.* Gentlemen, suppose that the name of Mademoiselle le Normand had never been heard of in this case, I leave it to you to consider, whether the irresistible inference be not, that that seal could have been appended only by the person in possession of it, and, at least, that that person was within his own domestic circle!"

Next followed some weighty remarks on the evidence of Leguix as to the purchase by an Englishman, in the winter of 1836–7, of the map of Canada of 1703; and then Lord Meadowbank pointed out certainly a serious contradiction in the prisoner's statements, under his different "examinations," as to the period of his becoming acquainted with Lord Cockburn's judgment of December 1836. When first examined, on the 18th December 1838, in answer to the direct question when he first knew of that judgment, he declared that "it was not till the month of *March* or *April* following [*i.e.*, 1837], that he was made acquainted with that or any part of his lordship's judgment or proceedings, *except as to their general import*, which he had learned from a letter addressed to him by his own family." Then he was asked whether he had not been made acquainted with Lord Cockburn's judgment in the same month of December in which it was pronounced. He declared "that *he had not*, and even *then* [*i.e.*, 18th December 1838], he knew nothing of the particulars of that judgment. On the 14th February, 1839, however, on being again examined before the sheriff, he declared that, when in Paris, in March or April 1837, he heard that Lord Cockburn had pronounced an unfavourable judgment in his case; and *at that time a copy of the printed papers of the judgment and of the note* was sent him by his family from Edinburgh, and until that time he was not aware that Lord Cockburn had formed an unfavourable opinion of his case!" "Here are declarations of the prisoner, contradictory on matters as to which there could be no error in point of recollection,—an important contradiction, and one testifying a desire of concealment of the truth, which, in all cases like this, has ever been deemed greatly to affect the innocence or guilt of a party." Again, "if these declarations establish the prisoner's knowledge of what had been done by Lord Cockburn, you are bound to consider whether that knowledge does not materially affect the evidence of the fabrication of these documents, as having been known to him, to whom alone they could be useful."

Then Lord Meadowbank came to the prisoner's visits to Mademoiselle le Normand—his having trafficked with her as far back as 1812, since which time he said, "she had been in the constant habit of advancing money to himself and his wife;" and yet her existence, even, was not known to his most intimate friends! Then he admits that he and his wife "desire her to institute a search for documents and charters to support his claims;" that he had never dreamed of searching *in France* for documents illustrative of his own pedigree; and it was with the greatest surprise he afterwards learned that they had been discovered! Then Lord Meadowbank contrasted the prisoner's statements as to the paucity of his visits to this old lady with the evidence of one Beaubis, the porter at the hotel where she resided, and who stated that the prisoner "saw her *every night*." Infinitely more serious, however, were the conflicting answers given by the prisoner, as to the nature and amount of his pecuniary liabilities to Mademoiselle le Normand, which Lord Meadowbank pronounced to be "a mass of contradictions." At one time he stated that he had given her his bond for *four hundred thousand francs!*—then only two bonds for 100,000 francs each, sent by him to her in 1837!—"payable, palpably, on the event of his succeeding in his claims on the Earldom of Stirling. This," continued Lord Meadowbank, "perhaps affords a pretty good key for solving the mystery of the interest that this woman has taken in these productions!" Having adverted to various portions of this old lady's correspondence with the prisoner, which had been seized at his house—certainly containing matters pregnant with violent suspicion—Lord Meadowbank said, "These are the circumstances from which you are to infer, or not, the guilty knowledge of the panel, and of his being, or not, art and part in the forgery of these documents. Remember, it is not said or proved that he forged them with his own hand; the question is, whether he had a knowledge of the forgeries that were going on at Paris during his stay there. * * * You will judge whether his obligation to Mademoiselle le Normand for 400,000 or 200,000 francs was or was not given for the fabrication of that document. And in looking to that document itself [*i. e.*, the map with its indorsements], you will see his statement as to *the seal* on the back of it; and consider whether he be not thereby brought into immediate contact with the fabrication of that document, in consequence of the impression of the seal on its back, which he admits was in the possession of a member of his family." Lord Meadowbank proceeded to advert briefly to "the exculpatory evidence," and said that the fact of the fabricated excerpt charter having escaped the notice of the Lord Ordinary, and also of Mr Lockhart, was "no doubt a strong circumstance in favour of the prisoner," if that excerpt had been *the only* case against him; but it was altogether a different matter when regard was had to the great number of other documents alleged to have been forged, or knowingly uttered as forged, by the prisoner. "Gentlemen," said Lord Meadowbank, "the prisoner may have been a dupe in all these transactions; but you have it clearly made out that the only person who enjoyed the fruits of the imposition, was the prisoner himself! Gentlemen, I have now laid before you the whole case as it occurs to me. I have never bestowed more pains upon any case than I have upon this; and in none have I ever summed up the evidence with greater pain. Our business is to do justice, and you, in particular, have to weigh the evidence calmly and deliberately; and, should you doubt of that evidence being sufficient to bring the present charge home to the prisoner, to give him the full benefit of that doubt.* But, to entitle you to do so, these doubts must be well considered, and the circumstances on which they are founded, deliberately weighed. To doubts that are not reasonable, you have no right whatever to yield. You are not entitled to require from the prosecutor *direct proof* of the facts laid in his charge. The circumstances laid in evidence must be put together; and it is your duty, then, to consider what is the reasonable inference to be drawn from the whole of them: in short, whether it be possible to explain them upon grounds consistent with the innocence of the party accused; or whether, on the contrary, they do not necessarily lead to a result directly the reverse."

The jury, thus charged with their solemn responsibility, withdrew to consider their verdict; and as they were absent for FIVE HOURS, we have time to ask the reader what would have been *his* decision, as one of that jury, on this remarkable case?

*First*, Were any, or all, of these documents forgeries?

*Secondly*, If they were, did the prisoner forge them?

*Thirdly*, If forgeries, though not by the prisoner, did he use and utter them with a guilty knowledge of their being forgeries?

As a specimen of the impassioned style in which Scottish counsel can address the jury on behalf of a prisoner, we present the reader with Mr (now Lord) Robertson's peroration, as subsequently revised by himself.

"Gentlemen, in a case of doubtful evidence, which this

* "Giving the prisoner the benefit of a doubt," is a common judicial expression, but not a happy or exact one. A prisoner has a right to insist on a case being so clearly proved against him, as to exclude all reasonable doubt; and if the evidence do not come up to that point, then he has a RIGHT to require the jury *to hold the case unproved*. In Scotland, the verdict "Not Proven" exactly meets the case of defective proof. In such a case, the only verdict which an English jury can pronounce is, Not Guilty—*i. e.*, they can "*not*" say that, "according to the evidence," the prisoner is "*Guilty*." It will be well to have in mind these observations in considering the verdict pronounced in the case now under the reader's consideration.

is, character is everything. You have heard the character given of my client, at both the beginning and end of his career. And you have seen it — a moral spectacle unexampled in the annals of a court of justice — in the conduct of the gallant officer who now sits beside him, and whom I should be proud to call *my* friend. You heard, gentlemen, yesterday, the testimony given by that gallant officer, in strains of manly eloquence, in behalf of the associate of his boyhood, and the correspondent of his riper years. With the spirit of a British officer, and the pride and generosity of a British gentleman—not like the cold world turning his back upon his friend in the day of his perplexity and distress, but recollecting what had passed betwixt them in early youth, and seeing with interest the rising friendship of their children—he thought of nothing but how he could comfort him in his hour of danger. He saw his frail bark tossed among the breakers; he rushed to its succour, and he will bring it in safety to the desired haven. The contemplation of that spectacle, gentlemen, was a requital to me for all my anxieties here, and must have been equally gratifying to you; and the embrace which these two men shall have, when this trial is over, and they quit that bar together, as I feel they shall, is a pleasure that I envy that gallant officer more than all the treasures of wealth, or the laurel that adorns his brow. Gentlemen, do not think of the character of the panel as a light thing. I fully anticipate his acquittal at your hands, from this heavy charge, as being as certain as that I am now addressing you. When I look back on the life of this unfortunate man, I see nothing but anxious days of heart-sickening hope, and sleepless nights of feverish rest, disturbed and chequered by golden dreams that were speedily dissipated by the rays of the morning sun—a rising family, taught to look on nobility and wealth as their birthright, yet seeing nothing but penury and distress before them—calling to their parent for bread, and lo, he has nothing to give them but a stone—

> 'Lo! Poverty to fill the band
> That numbs the soul with icy hand,
> And slow consuming age.'

And when I look forward to the future, I trust I see a prospect that his mind shall be directed to pursuits more solid, and to the attainment of objects more consolatory and enduring. Let the visionary coronet be plucked from his bewildered brow—let the prospects of wealth and of courtly titles and honours vanish into air; but oh, gentlemen, leave him that best and highest title of nobility—his good name; let his character remain to solace him on retiring from the fatigues and bustle of this vain and transitory world. Gentlemen, I am one of those who venerate the memory of the illustrious dead—of those whose prejudices, feelings, and principles, unite in admiration of hereditary rank and high title, conferred as the reward of patriotism and virtue upon those whose names adorn the page of history, and who are enrolled amidst the nobles of the land: and I also venerate those of more recent name, who, from their valour, their piety, or their learning, have been added to grace that august assembly. But without truth, integrity, and honour, titles and distinctions are worse than nothing. Without these, the glitter of the coronet hath no splendour in my eye—the rustling of the silken robe hath no music in my ear. On the tarnished ermine I trample with contempt. Do not, gentlemen, add to the pangs of this man more than he deserves. Leave him in possession of that character which he has hitherto enjoyed, as his only solace under his heavy trials. Leave him that, without which the crown itself is but a bauble, and the sceptre a toy; for, *in my conscience I believe him innocent of the crimes here charged*, and to have been merely the dupe of the designing, and the prey of the unworthy."

That Mr Robertson made the assertion printed in Italics truly, cannot be doubted; but, in doing so, as we have already stated, he far exceeded his duty as an advocate, as that duty is understood in England, though there have been exceptions. At best, with an intelligent jury, such asseverations are rejected as worthless, coming as they do from one whose judgment is so biassed and warped; and we should lament to see the practice prevail, for it is a highly reprehensible and mischievous one. The judge, in the case before us, made no observation, however, on the matter; and there we shall leave it.

His charge, of which we have already given a summary, occupies fifty-four pages of the Report. It commenced by anxiously calling the attention of the jury to "the real merits of the case which they had been empanneled to try. * * * The thing *you* have to do with," said he, "is the charge against the panel of the forgery of one particular document" [*i.e.*, the alleged excerpt charter of Charles I. in 1639], "and of others of a minor description, alleged to have been fabricated by him, or by others with his knowledge; and all of which he is charged with having uttered, knowing them to be forged." Lord Meadowbank's commentary may be characterised as lucid, elaborate, and crushing. His own view of the case glares through every sentence, most ominously for the prisoner; and perhaps may be regarded as a little too much like a reply to the speech of the prisoner's counsel. At the same time, after carefully weighing it, we see nothing seriously to find fault with; for the facts are stated fairly, and the comments on them are such as a judge was entitled to make, for the guidance of the jury. If we were to venture criticism, it would be, that we do not see on the report, corrected by the judge, that clear categorical statement of the questions for the jury, which are usual with the English judges. In England, the jury would probably have been told, at the close of the charge, to consider whether the prisoner forged all, or any, of the instruments charged in the indictment? Or, if not, whether he uttered any of them, knowing them to be forged? The verdict, however, which will be presently seen, showed that the judge and the jury had sufficiently understood each other.

At length, after their long absence from court—a torturing five hours' absence—the return of the jury is announced: the four judges resume their seats with stern gravity and expectation: the agitated prisoner, still accompanied by his chivalrous friend, Colonel D'Aguilar, appears at the bar: the anxious crowd is hushed into silence: and the chancellor (or foreman) delivers in the following verdict:—

I. "The jury UNANIMOUSLY find it proved that the *excerpt charter is a forged document;* and, BY A MAJORITY,* find it NOT PROVEN that the panel FORGED the said document, or is guilty art or part thereof, or that he UTTERED it, knowing it to be forged."†

II. "UNANIMOUSLY find it proved that the *documents on the map are forged;* and by A MAJORITY find it NOT PROVEN that the panel FORGED the said documents, or is guilty art and part thereof, or that he UTTERED them, knowing them to be forged."

III. "UNANIMOUSLY find it NOT PROVEN that the documents contained in De Porquet's packet are forged; or were uttered by the panel as genuine, knowing them to be forged."

IV. "UNANIMOUSLY find it NOT PROVEN that the copy letter to Le Normand,‡ in the fifth and last charge of the indictment, is either forged, or was uttered by the panel as genuine, knowing it to be forged."

As soon as the chancellor of the jury had finished delivering the above verdict, the prisoner swooned, and was

* In Scotland, the verdict in a criminal case is according to a majority of the jury; in a civil case they must be unanimous.

† Here arose a burst of applause from the audience, in consequence of which the court immediately ordered the gallery to be cleared.

‡ This was the anonymous letter to Madlle. le Normand, dated the 10th July 1837, accompanying the map professed to have been left with her so mysteriously on the ensuing day. See it *in extenso, ante,* p. 214.

carried out of court insensible. On one of his counsel certifying to the court, on the authority of a medical gentleman in attendance on him, the continued indisposition of the prisoner, and that it would be dangerous to bring him back into court, his further attendance was dispensed with, the Public Prosecutor consenting; and as soon as the verdict had been formally approved of and recorded, the court pronounced the following sentence:—

"The Lords Commissioners of Justiciary, in respect of the foregoing verdict of assize, assoilzie the panel *simpliciter*, and dismiss him from the Bar."

By the law of Scotland, a verdict of "*Not Proven*" has the same effect as a verdict of "*Not Guilty*," with reference to liability to a second or subsequent trial on the same charge.

Thus ended, on Friday the 3d May 1839, this extraordinary trial, than which we know none more so on record.

The jury unanimously find, it will be observed, that the document forming the foundation of the prisoner's claim to the Stirling peerage, *i.e.*, the Excerpt Charter of Charles I., is a forged document. If it be so, there is an end of the prisoner's claims for ever; but we are disposed to think that in point of law it is still open to him to offer that document in evidence, in support of his claims to the peerage, if he should be so advised: in other words, that he is not stopped by the above verdict from doing so. The point of that verdict was, that the prisoner was not proved guilty of forging, or uttering the Excerpt Charter, knowing it to have been forged; and their adding that the document was forged, has no legal effect, as a finding. It is only the statement, by the jury, of their opinion—one of the premises from which they had deduced their inference. If fresh evidence of genuineness could be adduced, it would be admissible; and even as to such evidence as was offered in the Scottish court, another to a different conclusion as to the validity of the alleged charter. It appears to us, however, that this is hopeless —for in all our experience we never saw an instrument so annihilated by evidence of spuriousness.

The same observations are applicable to the second class of instruments—the documents on the map. With the other two, viz., the documents in the De Porquet packet, and the letter to Le Normand, the jury deal differently; unanimously finding them not proven to have been forged. This also is a matter of mere gratuitous statement on the part of the jury; no more establishing the validity of these latter, than their other statement legally impugned that of the former.—If all or any of these instruments be really forged, it could not have been by any one possessing any knowledge of the law of evidence, or in the least degree acquainted with the innumerable liabilities to detection afforded by even the most cunning of their contrivances. The prisoner was, by a majority of his jury, as to two of the charges, and unanimously as to the other two, relieved by the verdict of not proven, from the heavy criminal liability which it had been sought to attach to him. There seems to have been no suggestion on the part of the prosecution that the prisoner's own hand forged a single letter of any of the instruments which the jury believed forged. Practically, the one great question in the case on the evidence really was—did the prisoner utter any of the instruments, knowing them to have been forged? Of that question the jury were the sole judges; and it may be, that after lengthened deliberation, and much difference of opinion, as indicated by the verdict, they adopted the suggestion of his eloquent counsel, that the prisoner "had been merely the dupe of the designing, and the prey of the unworthy." By this we conceive to be meant, that, believing himself to be entitled to the earldom, in his eagerness to establish his rights, he might have innocently held out such splendid expectations to those who assisted him, as induced *them* to resort to forgery. This, if true, is based on a low estimate of his understanding; but it is that proposed by his own eloquent and zealous counsel. As far as the evidence goes, we ourselves entertain not a shadow of doubt that every one of the instruments mentioned in the indictment is spurious, but leave the reader to draw his own conclusion as to whether the prisoner was wholly innocent, or wholly guilty, of forging, or uttering, all, or any, of the instruments in question, knowing them to have been forged. The prisoner is in the meanwhile entitled to the full benefit of the verdict of *Not Proven*, as to every part of the charge.

We have bestowed no small pains on presenting a faithful and clear statement of this extraordinary case, on account of its great public importance and interest; and because it affords an excellent exercise for the young student in jurisprudence. In conclusion, we have to express our obligations to the learned and accomplished reporter of the case, Professor Swinton, for the fulness and fidelity with which he appears to have placed it before us. The *fac-similes* of all the documents greatly add to the value of the report; and we advise both English and Scotch law students to expend a few shillings in the purchase of that report.

## NOTE.

In the Obituary of the *Times* of Monday the 13th November 1854, appeared the following, while these sheets were passing through the press:—

"On the 30th September, at Greenwich, in the 90th year of his age, THOMAS CHRISTOPHER BANKS, BARONET OF NOVA SCOTIA, and Knight of the Holy Order of St John of Jerusalem, LAW GENEALOGIST, and ANTIQUARIAN.

# MODERN STATE TRIALS.*

## No. IV.

## DUELLING: AND, "WHAT'S IN A NAME?"

Is, or is not, a trial in this country for DUELLING, to be regarded as a Farce, following a Tragedy? There are those who say that it is; but we are not of the number. Such trials often greatly excite the public mind, and array opinions and prejudices against each other, in such a manner as to disturb and derange the judgment. Then more or less is expected from the law, and its administration, than is right. If the heated public should have prepared itself for a conviction, loud and violent is its reclamation against an acquittal; especially if it have been brought about by what are styled technical objections, and *vice versâ*. They forget, under the impetuous impulses of a sense of rough natural justice, that settled rules of legal procedure must be observed indifferently on all occasions, if even-handed justice is to be administered in a court of justice. How did these rules come to be settled? They are the results of centuries of experience—of ten thousand observed instances of the advantage, nay, the absolute necessity, for adhering to them. If it could be imagined with any, even the slightest foundation of truth, that those sworn to decide according to the law and the facts had wilfully shut their eyes to the one or

* *Blackwood's Magazine*, December 1850.

the other; or, either directly or indirectly, connived at an evasion of the letter or a violation of the spirit of the law, in order to secure a particular result; then there is certainly no power in language adequate fitly to denounce so deliberate and awful a perjury, so monstrous an outrage on the administration of justice.

*Bonâ fide* duels are always lamentable affairs, happen under whatever circumstances they may: especially when attended by loss of life, or serious personal injury—occurring, too, in a highly civilised and Christian country like ours. They properly arouse the grief and indignation of every thoughtful and virtuous member of the community; whom, however, they also satisfy as to the great practical difficulty of dealing with such cases. While the law of the land is clear on the subject as the sun at noonday, alike unquestionable and unquestioned, there yet exist, in almost every detected duel, far greater difficulties than are suspected by the public, in bringing to justice the guilty actors. First of all, it must be borne in mind how deep an interest they have in cutting off all means of future evidence, by intrusting a knowledge of the affair to the fewest persons necessary for carrying it out, and by selecting scenes remote from observation. Then, again, let it be remembered that both principals and seconds, and all others present aiding and abetting, have incurred heavy criminal liability; are liable to be indicted for murder, as principals or accessories; and, consequently, none of them can be compelled to furnish any evidence which may even *tend* to criminate himself. This great rule of criminal law has doubtless operated as an indirect encouragement to duelling; but how is this difficulty to be encountered? Must the rule be abrogated?

Assuming, however, the existence of evidence, and that it is satisfactorily adduced before the jury, it then becomes the duty of the judge and the jury to act in accordance with their oaths: the former to lay down the aw distinctly and unequivocally; the latter to find their verdict conscientiously according to the principles of law so laid down, as applicable to the proved facts of the case. If a conviction ensue, the judge must then pronounce the sentence of the law; when it depends upon the discretion and firmness of the executive whether that sentence shall be carried into effect. Take the case of a fatal duel, conducted with unimpeachable "fairness," as far as concerns the practice of duelling—and that the prisoner had received cruel provocation from his deceased opponent, who had obstinately refused retractation or apology. What is to be the decision of the executive? What will be its moral effect, as an encouragement or discouragement of duelling? Will it operate as a tacit recognition, to any extent, of the practice of duelling, as at all events a necessary evil, and denuded of moral turpitude? These are questions by no means of easy solution.

In the present constitution of society in this country, a Christian community, duelling is a practice environed with difficulties, whichever way it may be approached by its most discreet and resolute opponents. We must deal with men and things as they are, at the same time that we would make them what we think they ought to be. How many professing Christians, men of otherwise pure and virtuous lives, have gone out deliberately to take the life of an opponent, or expose or sacrifice their own; solely, it may be, from a puerile notion that their *honour* required the committing of the crime! "It is not one of the least evils of this system," it has been well observed, "that the word *honour*, which, rightly understood, denotes all that is truly noble and virtuous, should be prostituted as a pretext for gratifying the most malignant of human passions, *or as a cover for that moral cowardice—the fear of being thought afraid.*" This is one of the chiefest roots of the poisonous tree: and can human laws kill it? We think they can. If the legislature were really intent upon annihilating duelling, its members would long ago have acted on the suggestion of

Addison—that, "if every one who fought a duel were to stand in the pillory, it would quickly diminish the number of these imaginary men of honour, and put an end to so absurd a practice." If men will fight for a little stake, let them be made into little men, by enduring a degrading punishment; if for a great stake, that is to say, the gratification of malignant passions, let them be treated as great criminals, and die the felon's death, or live his life. Let justice be really blind in all such cases, her sword descending upon noble and ignoble of station alike.

We acknowledge that there is one aspect of the practice of duelling, which somewhat perplexes the moralist: for it cannot be denied or doubted, that duelling operates as a great preventive check to ruffian insolence and violence—as a potent auxiliary in preserving the necessary restraints and the courtesies of society. "It must be admitted," says Robertson, "that to this absurd custom we must ascribe, in some degree, the extraordinary gentleness and complaisance of modern manners, and that respectful attention of one man to another, which at present renders the social intercourse of life far more agreeable and decent than among the most civilised nations of antiquity." How many a viper-tongued slanderer's lips have been sealed by the dread of a bullet! How many an insolent inclination to personal violence has been checked—how many a truculent heart has sickened before the prospect of a "leaden breakfast!" Take a single case, which is really embarrassing to the candid opponent of duelling—an insult offered, by either words or deeds, to the character or person of a lady whom one is bound to protect—an injury beyond all legal cognisance, and perpetrated by one occupying the station of a gentleman. To one who does not bow under the paramount influence of religion, the harassing question occurs, What is to be done? Cases may be easily imagined in which it would be idle to say, "treat the offence and the offender with contempt—leave them to the contempt of society;" where such a course would only add to the poignancy of the wrong or insult, and invite aggravation and repetition. Let the outraged lady be imagined one's own wife, or daughter, or sister! "Is the wrong to be perpetrated with impunity?" asks the upholder of duelling. "What would you do?" retorts his opponent; "will you deliberately take the life of the offender, and give him an opportunity of taking yours?* Is that your notion of *punishment* or *satisfaction?* What will be the effect of an example such as this upon society at large? Is every one to be at liberty to do the like? thus deliberately to ignore the law of God and of man?"

Duelling is, in truth, generally the resource of the weak-minded, the vain, the vindictive, or the cowardly; and it is not right to ask society to be liberal in its allowances for the wrong-doings of its less worthy members. There are, nevertheless, cases in which persons have found themselves involved in duels, under circumstances pregnant with extenuation in the eyes of even the hardest moralist; and such as warrant the executive, when the majesty of the law has been vindicated, and its authority recognised, in mitigating or remitting the punishment due to an acknowledged violation of the law.

The law of the land is better able to vindicate really outraged character and honour than may be imagined by many foolish hot-blooded persons, who give or accept "hostile messages." It is armed with ample powers of compensation and punishment, as may be easily ascertained by those who can satisfy it that they have been

* In one of Dr Johnson's various conversations with Boswell and others, on the subject of duelling, he said, "A man is sufficiently punished [for an injury] by being called out, and subjected to the risk that is in a duel. But," continues Boswell, "on my suggesting that *the injured person* is equally subjected to risk, he fairly owned he could not explain the rationality of duelling." It will be remembered that, in previous conversations, the doctor had endeavoured to do so, by various unsatisfactory and sophistical reasons; and one of his arguments, recorded by Boswell, was quoted by the counsel of Mr Stuart, when tried for having shot in a duel Sir Alexander Boswell, the eldest son of Boswell!

the victims of deliberate and wanton insult and injury. Little more than a year ago, one gentleman thought proper to write to some naval and military friends of another, most offensive imputations upon his honour. When apprised of this, he instantly wrote to demand that his traducer should either prove the truth of his assertions, or unequivocally retract and apologise for them. Both alternatives were contemptuously refused, on which the injured party brought an action for libel against his traducer; who, unable to justify, and unwilling to apologise, allowed the case to go before a jury. On their learning the true nature of the affair, and being reminded by counsel, that they were appealed to as a jury of twelve gentlemen, to vindicate the honour of an unoffending gentleman, they gave such heavy damages (£500) as soon brought his infuriate opponent to his senses, and elicited an unequivocal retractation, and as ample an apology as could have been desired. A few instances of this kind would soon satisfy the most sceptical of the potency of the law in cases too often deemed beyond its reach, and of the effective reality of its redress in cases of wounded honour. Who could lightly esteem being solemnly and publicly branded, by its *fiat*, as a liar and a slanderer—its blighting sentence remaining permanently on record? He who would regard such a circumstance with indifference surely is not worth shooting, or running the risk of being shot by, or of being hanged or transported for shooting or attempting to shoot! If a person of distinguished station or character receive an insult or an injury of such a nature, as not to admit of being treated with silent contempt, it becomes his duty to society to set an example of magnanimous reliance on the protection of the laws of his country, and reverence for the laws of God. Against one thing, however, every one should be constantly on his guard—the entertaining and cherishing that false overweening estimate of personal dignity and importance, which predisposes too many to take offence, and then hurry to revenge it!

According to the law of England, as already stated, a death caused by duelling, though in the "fairest" possible manner, is clearly murder, to all intents and purposes whatsoever. In the year 1846, the majority of the Criminal Law Commissioners suggested a change in this law, recommending that, where two persons agree to fight, and a contest ensues, and one of them is killed, the homicide should be extenuated. The reasons on which this suggestion was founded appear to us of a very unsatisfactory nature; and one of the Commissioners, the late Mr Starkie, altogether dissented from the views of his brethren, embodying his reasons in an able and convincing protest or counter-statement. "Whilst," he observes, at its close, "as it seems to me, little good could be expected from the proposed alteration, it might be productive of much harm in a *moral* point of view. It would be understood to manifest an alteration in the opinion of the Legislature as to the heinousness of the crime of homicide, and of course tend to diminish the efficacy of the law against it." We entirely concur in the following remarks of Mr Townsend, in one of the best expressed passages in his book:*

"Founded on the law of God, the law of the land should remain clear and stringent, that whoever kills in a deliberate duel, commits murder. The sanctity of human life would be impaired, were this denunciation lessened, and the forfeit, for expediency's sake, commuted. The very good to be obtained by the compromise with 'codes of honour' would be temporary; for arguments of hardship, as the consequences of conviction, and appeals to compassion against a *gentleman* being adjudged guilty of felony, and transported, it might be for life, would equally tickle the ears of credulous jurors, and be list-

* Modern State Trials.

ened to with as much avidity as the present topic of capital punishment. Let the law maintain its own independent straightforward path, *irretortis oculis*, and, be the fluctuations in fashionable feeling what they may, continue, in its austere regard for life, unchanged and unchangeable." *

Thus stands the matter. The Legislature, therefore, not having ventured to interfere with the law, which must be administered with rigorous faithfulness, by those to whom that severe and responsible duty has been entrusted, God forbid that there should ever be coquetting with an oath on these occasions!

We have no hesitation in saying that our English Judges, as far as our experience and inquiries have gone, invariably lay down the law, in these cases, with clearness and unfaltering firmness. The only approach towards a departure from this rule of right, is one which we trust has no other foundation than an erroneous report of what fell from Baron Hotham at Maidstone, in the year 1794, in trying a Mr Purefoy, who shot his late commanding officer, Colonel Roper. That judge, according to Mr Townsend, † who also intimates a hope that the judge has been incorrectly reported, concluded his summing up, which produced, as might have been expected, an instant acquittal, by the following extraordinary passage:—

"It is now a painful duty which jointly belongs to us; it is mine to lay down the law, and yours to apply it to the facts before you. The oath by which I am bound obliges me to say that homicide, after a due interval left for consideration, amounts to murder. The laws of England, in their utmost lenity and allowance for human frailty, extend their compassion only to sudden and momentary frays; and then, if the blood has not had time to cool, or the reason to return, the result is termed manslaughter. Such is the law of the land, which, un-

* Townsend, vol. i. pp. 170-171. † Ibid., pp. 154-5.

doubtedly, the unfortunate gentleman at the bar has violated, *though he has acted in conformity to the laws of honour.* His whole demeanour in the duel, according to the witness whom you are most to believe, Colonel Stanwix, was *that of perfect honour and perfect humanity.* Such is the law, and such are the facts. *If you cannot reconcile the latter to your consciences,* you must return a verdict of guilty. But if the contrary, *though the acquittal may trench on the rigid rules of the law, yet the verdict will be lovely in the sight both of God and man.*"

If Baron Hotham really uttered this language, he was totally unfit to administer justice, and should have been removed from the Bench. Mr Townsend, in one place, observes that Baron Hotham "must have allowed his kindly feelings to master his judgment;" and in another, cites the case as "a very *famous* (*!*) one, being the first of those occasions on which judges admitted, from the bench, the necessity and expediency of juries tempering the law, where, by a stern necessity, they have held themselves bound by it;" that is, in plain English, where judges advised juries to violate their oaths, in order to defeat the just administration of the law. We know no parallel to this "famous" case, except that of Justice Fletcher, a judge in Ireland, in the year 1812; who, as we learn from Mr Phillips' interesting *Memoirs of Curran,* thus addressed an Irish jury, in a trial for murder occasioned in a duel: "Gentlemen, it is my business to lay down the law to you, and I shall do so. Where two people go out to fight a duel, and one of them falls, the law says it is murder. And I tell you, by law it *is* murder; but, at the same time, *a fairer duel I never heard of in the whole coorse* [*sic*] *of my life!*" The prisoners were, of course, immediately acquitted.

Mr Townsend states, that "the long series of judicial annals has not been darkened by a single conviction for murder, in the case of a duel fairly fought." * If this be

* Townsend, vol. i. p. 152.

a correct statement, which we greatly doubt, it argues either a signal deficiency of evidence in every case, or a perverse disregard of duty by either judges or juries, or both. We repeat it, and do so, anxiously desirous of giving every degree of publicity in our power to the fact, that our judges discharge their duties on these occasions with unwavering firmness. We shall give two or three modern and interesting instances.

The late eminent Mr Justice Buller tried a clergyman, the Reverend Bennet Allen,* and his second, for killing a Mr Dulany, in a duel, fought at ten o'clock at night, in Hyde Park, at the distance of eight yards: the reverend duellist had actually put on his spectacles, in order to see his man! Mr Justice Buller told the jury that "they were bound to adhere to the law, as to which there never," he continued, "has been a doubt. In the case of a deliberate duel, if one person be killed, it is murder in the person killing him. Of that proposition of law, there is not, there never has been, the smallest doubt. Sitting here, it is my duty to tell you what the law is, which I have done in explicit terms; and we must not suffer it to be frittered away, by any false or fantastical notions of honour." Here the judge did his duty: but the jury seem, according to Mr Townsend, who doubtless spoke after having duly examined the facts of the case, "to have temporised between their consciences and wishes, by acquitting the second, and finding the principal guilty of manslaughter."

Mr Justice Patteson, in trying the seconds for murder, in the case of the fatal duel between Dr Hennis and Sir John Jeffcott, who shot the former, thus plainly put the matter to the jury: "Whether duelling ought to be tolerated in this land, I say nothing. It is no question for any *jury* at all. The law of the land does not tolerate it. I repeat that, if you are satisfied on this evidence, that the three gentlemen went out to Haddon, knowing that Sir John Jeffcott and Dr Hennis were about to fight a

* Townsend, vol. i. p. 162.

duel there, without heat or irritation, but deliberately aiding and assisting the affair, on a point of honour, after vainly endeavouring to effect an amicable arrangement, I cannot tell you, in point of law, that it is anything short of murder." The jury at once acquitted the prisoners! *

In the year 1838, a young man named Mirfin was shot in a duel at Wimbledon, by a young man named Elliott, twenty-five years of age, under deplorable and aggravated circumstances. The former had been a linen-draper! in Tottenham Court Road; and, together with the latter, seemed to have led the dissolute life, for some time, of men about town. The duel arose out of a quarrel which had occurred in a certain scene of nightly infamy near Piccadilly! Two young men named Young and Webber, respectively only twenty-four and twenty-six years of age, were tried for the wilful murder of Mirfin. They had not acted as seconds of the survivor, but had accompanied him and his second to the scene of action. The chief witness was a surgeon, who detailed with a deadly simplicity and matter-of-fact air, the whole particulars of the duel, at which he was present; and produced such an effect on the jury that, on delivering their verdict, they expressed the "horror" with which they had heard his evidence and regarded his conduct, and their regret that he had not himself been put upon his trial for murder. The reader shall have an opportunity of judging for himself on the subject, from a portion of the evidence given by this person. †

"After the pistols were loaded, Mr Elliot and Mr Mirfin were placed on their ground, and a pistol was delivered to each. I then went and stood seven or eight paces from them, with the two seconds. I looked at the principals. The word to fire was given by Mr Elliott's second: he said, 'Gentlemen, are you ready?—*Stop!*' That was the agreed signal for firing: they were to fire

* Townsend, vol. i. p. 163.

† Regina *v.* Young. 8 Carrington and Payne, 644.

instantly on the last word 'stop' being uttered, and not before. They fired together immediately on the signal. After they had fired, I observed that *the ball had passed through the crown of Mr Mirfin's hat:* I saw something fly up in the air: I saw a portion of the crown just raised at the moment. As soon as they had fired, the seconds interfered. I and they were standing together. They moved towards the principals, who remained in their places. Some conversation took place between the principals and seconds, and then between the seconds themselves—which lasted for a few minutes only. Mr Mirfin insisted on a second shot. He spoke loud enough for all present to hear. I stood within seven or eight paces of him, and could hear every word he said. I was intent looking at his hat—I saw the ball had passed through it. I could hear that the conversation was with a view to reconcile the parties; but Mr Mirfin would not hear of any reconciliation. I believe Mr Elliot would have made a verbal apology; but Mr Mirfin would accept nothing but a written apology, and insisted on a second shot. After he had made this statement, another pistol was delivered to each. They next left their ground. I told Mr Mirfin that his hat had been shot through, and he took it off and looked at it, and said nothing, but replaced it on his head. The second pistols were Mr Mirfin's, and were fired at a signal exactly similar to the former one. Mr Elliott fired first, but not till after the signal had been given. I distinctly heard the sound of his pistol, immediately after the word had been given; and Mr Mirfin's shot was fired almost immediately. I think his pistol was discharged after he had received the fatal shot. I think he felt the wound previous to his firing off his pistol. He did not sufficiently raise his hand. His ball struck the ground. He was in the act of bringing his pistol to the level, when he fired. After both shots had been fired, I looked at each of the men, and did not, at first, perceive that either was injured.

Mr Mirfin walked towards me about six paces, I think, with his left hand on his right side, and I think also, the pistol still in his right hand. I think he gave it to me. He advanced towards me, saying, 'I am wounded.' I asked him where; he looked towards the wound and raised his fingers, showing me where he was wounded, but without speaking. I said, 'I am exceedingly sorry to hear it: good bye! God bless you!' He replied, '*Good bye, old fellow!*' I then assisted him to lie on the grass. He did not fall immediately. I undid his pea-jacket and waistcoat, and pulled up his shirt, and probed the wound. The other persons were standing by. Mr Mirfin's second walked up, and asked if the wound were fatal. I said it was a very fatal wound. Mr Elliott and his second said nothing, merely looking on. Mr Broughton asked me again, after I had probed the wound, whether it was fatal. I said it was. He asked, 'What shall we do?' I replied, 'The sooner you leave the ground the better, and I will wait.' They all three left the ground together. Mr Mirfin died within ten minutes. I did not speak to him after this. I saw I could be of no service to him, and did not wish to fatigue him by saying anything to him. I examined the body after I had got it home, and discovered a small wound not quite the size of a (bird's?) egg, between the fifth and sixth ribs."

We have given these details in all their sickening simplicity and utter hideousness, because they are worth a world of comment on the nature and tendency of Affairs of Honour.

The trial came on before the late Baron Vaughan, and the present Baron Alderson, at the Old Bailey, on the 22d Sept. 1838; and the former thus laid down the law to the jury: "When, upon a previous arrangement, and after there has been time for the blood to cool, two persons meet with deadly weapons, and one of them is killed, he who occasions the death is guilty of murder; and the seconds are also equally guilty. The question then is, did the prisoners give their aid and assistance by their countenance and encouragement of the principals, in this contest? Though neither of the prisoners acted as second, still, if either sustained the principal by his advice *or his presence*—or, if you think he went down for the purpose of encouraging and forwarding the unlawful conflict, although he did not say or do anything, yet if he were present, and was assisting and encouraging at the moment when the pistol was fired, he will be guilty of the offence of wilful murder. Questions have arisen as to how far the second of a party killed in a duel is liable to an indictment for the murder of the deceased: I am clearly of opinion that he is."

The prisoners were convicted; but under the special circumstances of the case—for there existed, in the evidence, considerable doubt as to the part taken in the murderous affair by the prisoners, or even whether they, in fact, took *any* part in it—sentence of death was not passed, but only ordered to be recorded against them; and they were afterwards sentenced to a lengthened term of imprisonment. Mr Townsend does not seem to have been aware of this case, as he makes no allusion to it.

We ourselves were present at a remarkable trial for duelling, twenty-four years ago,* at the Old Bailey, before the late excellent and very learned Justice Bayley, on which occasion he also laid down the rule of law respecting duelling, with uncompromising firmness and straightforwardness. This was the case of a militia officer, who had shot, in a duel in France, a young officer in the army; and a clergyman, the brother of the deceased, made strenuous and persevering efforts to bring the survivor to trial. The latter continued, for some time after the duel, in France; and possibly under the impression, then a natural one, that he could not be tried in this country for a duel fought in a foreign country not under

* On Saturday the 9th October 1830.

the British crown, he came to England; where he was instantly arrested, under Stat. 9 Geo. IV. c. 31, § 7, which had been passed only two or three years previously, viz., in 1828, and might consequently well escape the notice of a non-professional person. That act authorises the trial, in England, under a special Commission, issued under the Great Seal, of any British subject charged with having committed any murder or manslaughter abroad, whether within or without the British dominions, as if such crimes had been committed in England. The prisoner was admitted to bail, to meet the charge, and, having duly surrendered, took his place at the bar of the Old Bailey, at nine o'clock on a Saturday morning.

He was a man apparently approaching middle age, of gentlemanly appearance, his features indicating determination of character; but they wore an expression of manifest anxiety and apprehension as he entered the dock, and, looking down, beheld immediately beneath him, the brother of the man whom he had shot, and through whose ceaseless activity he was then placed on trial for his life as a murderer. He was to be tried, moreover, by an uncompromising judge—stern and exact in administering the law, and animated by pure religious spirit, but, withal, thoroughly humane. Throughout the whole of that agitating day, the prisoner stood firm as a rock, sometimes his arms folded, at others his hands resting on the bar; while his eyes were fixed intently on the judge, the witnesses, or the counsel; every now and then glancing with gloomy inquisitiveness at the jury and the judge. His lips were from first to last firmly compressed. A considerable number of witnesses was called for both the prosecution and the defence; who gave conflicting testimony as to the circumstances under which the parties had fired at each other. The unhappy deceased, a very young man, was shot through the neck, and died, shortly afterwards, on the ground. The prisoner's witnesses, who had seen the duel, denied that he had fired irregularly. As counsel were not at that time allowed to address the jury for the defence, the prisoner spoke himself at considerable length, alleging himself, and truly, to have been the challenged party, and denying that he had been guilty of any unfairness, or had entertained any ill-will towards the deceased. As the case stood, however, it looked black enough to those who knew the law, and the character of the judge who sat to administer it. That venerable person began his summing-up to the jury about seven o'clock in the evening, and the scene can never be effaced from our memory. The court was extremely crowded; the lights burned brightly, exhibiting anxious faces in every direction: but what a striking figure was the central one—that of the prisoner! Immediately over his head was a mirror, so placed as to reflect his face and figure vividly, especially to the jury. A few moments after the judge had commenced his charge, we observed the Ordinary of Newgate glide into court, the late Rev. Dr Cotton, in full canonicals, and with flowing white hair, having a picturesquely venerable and ominous appearance, and take his seat near to, but a little behind, the judge. It was then usual* for the Ordinary to be present at the close of capital cases, in order to add a solemn "amen" to the prayer with which the sentence of death concluded—that "God would have mercy on the soul" of the condemned. "Gentlemen of the jury," commenced Mr Justice Bayley, amidst profound silence, "we have heard several times during the course of this trial, of the law of honour; but I will now tell you what is the law of the land, which is all that you and I have to do with. It is this: that if two persons go out with deadly weapons, intending to use them against each other, and do use them, and death ensue, that is—murder, wilful murder." He paused for a moment, as if to give the jury time to appreciate the dread significance of his opening. As soon as he had

* Such is believed to be still the case.

uttered the last two words, the prisoner's cheek was instantaneously blanched. We were eyeing him intently at the moment, and shall never forget it. He stood, however, with rigid erectness, gazing apparently with mingled anger and fear at the judge, whom he felt to be uttering his death-warrant; and after a while bent his eyes on the jury, from whom they wandered scarce a moment during that momentous summing-up—one which, with every word, was letting fall around him, as he must have felt, the curtain of death. "The law of honour," said the judge, towards the close of his charge, "is an imposture—a wicked imposture, when set against the law of the land, and the law of God Almighty, claiming the right to take away human life. I tell you, who sit there to discharge a sworn duty, that a fatal duel is malicious homicide—and *that* is wilful murder." The jury retired to consider their verdict; and the judge at the same time quitted the court till his presence should be required again. The prisoner, however, continued standing at the bar almost motionless as a statue. After a considerable absence the jury returned into court. The prisoner eyed them, as one by one they re-entered their box, with a solicitude dismal to behold, and the irrepressible quivering of his upper lip indicated mortal agitation. The verdict, however, was—Not Guilty; on which the prisoner heaved a heavy sigh, passing his hand slowly over his damp forehead, bowed slightly, but rather sternly to the jury, and was then removed from the bar, and released from custody.*

* Owing to the length of time which had elapsed since this case was tried, nearly a quarter of a century, the author, trusting solely to memory, erroneously stated certain incidents to have been supposed to attend the duel, which led the survivor to challenge the correctness of the statements in a court of law. At the suggestion of the court, who stated that the article in question was evidently written with a high moral object, and that there was no pretence for imputing more than *bonâ fide* mistake, the matter at once terminated by an ample apology.

The decision of the court on that occasion, and the interesting and important point of law submitted to it, has been much canvassed; and, it is said, has

It is now, however, time to return to Mr Townsend's volumes, where we find two trials for duelling. One is that of the late Mr Stuart, who killed Sir Alexander Boswell, in Scotland, on the 26th March 1822, in a duel conducted with undisputed regularity and fairness. The other is that of the Earl of Cardigan, who fought and wounded Captain Harvey Tuckett, but not mortally, in a duel, on the 12th September 1840. This trial is one of remarkable interest, in every point of view; and we shall take some pains in bringing it distinctly and intelligibly before our readers.

About five o'clock on the afternoon of Saturday, the 12th September 1840, a person named Daun, a miller, together with his wife and son, observed from the stage of their mill, on Wimbledon Common, two carriages approaching it from opposite directions, and at once suspected what was about to take place. Two gentlemen first quitted the carriages, each with a pistol-case, duly loaded a brace of pistols, and stepped out twelve paces; on which two other gentlemen, the Earl of Cardigan and Captain Tuckett, came up from their respective carriages, and took their stations at the points indicated. To each was given a pistol; the other two persons withdrew to a

been disapproved of by very high authority. The question was, whether an action for damages can be maintained by the survivor, in a fatal duel, against any one who, in giving an account of the duel, alleges it to have been supposed accompanied by circumstances at variance with the ordinary notions of fairness or honour on such occasions? It was argued for the defendant, "that the libel resolved itself into a charge of murder;—that there are no degrees of murder;—that there is no such thing known to law as a '*fair*' murder; and that there can be no such distinction as a '*fair*' or a '*foul*' duel, when it ends fatally." It was also contended, that no action for libel lies for anything written against a person touching his conduct in an illegal transaction, according to the cases of Yrisarri *v.* Clement, 3 Bing. Cas. 432, and Hunt *v.* Bell, 1 Bing. 1. The court said, however, "that the libel, in substance, charged that the plantiff was guilty of murder, under circumstances of grave and malignant aggravation; and the justification states simply, that the plaintiff committed murder, by killing his antagonist in a duel!" "If the libel go further, and state something besides the murder, which is injurious to the plaintiff's character, it is clear upon every principle of the law of libel, that that must be justified as well as the rest, or the defence fails."—11*th Common Bench Reports,* pp. 128, 130.

little distance; the word, to fire, was uttered, and immediately followed by an ineffectual discharge of both pistols. The principals remained at their posts; a second brace of pistols was given them; again both fired, and Captain Tuckett fell, wounded in the small of the back—bleeding profusely, but, as it proved, not from a mortal, or even dangerous wound. Thus the aristocratic affair of *honour* was more fortunate in its issue than that plebeian one in which, two or three years before, the young linen-draper Mirfin had received his mortal "satisfaction." Lord Cardigan's second was Captain Douglas, and Captain Wainwright was that of Captain Tuckett. The whole affair of the duel had been witnessed by the miller, who was also a constable, and his wife and son, standing on the stage of the windmill. The moment that Captain Tuckett fell, the miller and his son quitted their post of observation, ran up to the scene of action, and intimated to all the parties that they must consider themselves in his custody. How much better would it have been if the interference had taken place before the offence had been committed! It was the plain duty of the constable to have hastened to the spot the moment he saw preparations for committing an offence, and so have prevented it. Lord Cardigan still held in his right hand the pistol with which he had fired; and there lay on the ground two pistol-cases, one of them bearing the earl's coronet. Captain Tuckett lay on the ground, his second, Captain Wainwright kneeling beside him, supporting him; while Sir James Anderson, a surgeon, who had attended them to the field, was examining the wound. One of these three entreated the constable to allow the wounded gentleman to be removed to his own house, giving a solemn pledge that, on his recovery, he should attend before the magistrate. At the same time one of them took out a card, on which was printed, "Captain Harvey Tuckett, No. 13 Hamilton Place, New Road," and wrote in pencil, on the back of the card, the words, "Captain H.

Wainwright." Who gave this card remains, on the evidence, a mystery; nor did it appear whether Lord Cardigan saw the card given, or knew what was printed or written on it, or heard what was said. As almost the whole interest of the trial, and also its unexpected issue, turned upon the identity of the wounded duellist, and the exquisite adroitness and vigilance of the late Sir William Follett, the earl's counsel, in dealing with this card, and the circumstances attending its delivery to the constable, the reader will find his account in noting these circumstances accurately. On the constable's receiving the card, and the pledge above mentioned, he allowed those who had given it to depart. The conduct of the Earl of Cardigan was undoubtedly distinguished throughout by soldierly straightforwardness and frankness. He went direct, with Captain Douglas, to the Wandsworth Police Station, and tapping at the door, the inspector presented himself, and asked what was wanted. "I am a prisoner, I believe," said Lord Cardigan. "Indeed, sir! on what account?" asked the surprised inspector, as Lord Cardigan entered the station-house. "I have been fighting a duel," said his lordship, "and hit my man—but not seriously, I believe—slightly—merely a graze across the back"—drawing his hand across his own back, to indicate the region where he believed his ball had struck Captain Tuckett. Lord Cardigan then turned to Captain Douglas, and said, "This gentleman also is a prisoner —my second, Captain Douglas." He then took several cards out of his right breast-pocket, and handed one of them to the inspector. It bore the words, "The Earl of Cardigan, 11th Dragoons." On reading the name, the inspector said, "I hope the duel was not with Captain Reynolds?"—alluding to the notorious disputes between his lordship and that officer, and which led to a court-martial on the latter. Lord Cardigan "stood up erect," said the inspector, in giving his evidence, and seemed to reject the notion with the utmost disdain: saying, "Oh no, by no means!—do you suppose I would fight with one of my own officers?"* He duly appeared before the magistrates, and was bound over in heavy recognisances to appear whenever his presence should be required. He did so, from time to time. As soon as Captain Tuckett had sufficiently recovered, he also made his appearance at the police-office, *and gave his name.* The affair had by this time attracted much public attention, chiefly, there can be little doubt, from the unpopularity of the Earl of Cardigan; the newspapers teeming with accounts of his alleged discourteous and oppressive treatment of the officers under his command. The prosecution of Lord Cardigan was loudly called for; it being alleged that the high rank of the offender imperiously demanded that even-handed justice should be dealt to him. Mr Townsend speaks of this demand for prosecution as "a very pitiful manifestation of popular rancour and spleen."† "As the duel," he adds, "had been fairly fought, and the code of honour satisfied, without loss of life, it seemed strange that the first unsheathing of the statute should be directed against a high-spirited and gallant nobleman, who had been exposed to violent prejudice and popular clamour; and the prosecution seemed justly obnoxious to the supposition that it originated in party malevolence, and not in respect to the law." *We* never shared in the hostility here spoken of as existing towards the gallant nobleman in question. Our political opinions are also his; and we are disposed to believe that he has been the victim of much misrepresentation and injustice. We have always regarded him, moreover, as a first-rate Bri-

* In opening the case against Lord Cardigan, at the bar of the House of Lords, the Attorney-General (now Lord Campbell), of course speaking from erroneous instructions, imputed to Lord Cardigan the utterance of a most unbecoming and offensive expression,—"Do you think I would *condescend* to fight with one of my own officers?" We are satisfied that no such language could have fallen from a British officer; and the evidence shows that it did not in point of fact.

† Vol. i. p. 210.

tish officer;* we desire, nevertheless, to be understood as vindicating the call for judicial inquiry into the transaction to which Lord Cardigan and his opponent, with their seconds, were parties, if that transaction had been of a criminal character. Only three or four years previously, two young men had been tried and convicted of wilful murder, for having only been present at the duel which cost one of the principals (Mirfin) his life. If Captain Tuckett had been killed, Lord Cardigan would clearly have been guilty of wilful murder; that is beyond all question, if the law of England be not a dead letter, and those who affect to set it in motion be not guilty of a mockery of justice. If, therefore, a peer of the realm, a member of the supreme court of judicature in the kingdom, had really been guilty of a conspicuous and grave violation of the law, which all are required to obey with implicit reverence, those who demanded inquiry ought to have been given credit for acting on public grounds. The peer should not escape, where the plebeian would be condemned. Let us see, then, how stood, and how stands the law on this momentous subject—for momentous it is.

In the first place, let it be understood that *the mere challenging*, whether verbally or in writing, to fight a duel, and the mere *carrying* any such challenge, is such a high misdemeanour, punishable by fine and imprisonment, according to the circumstances of the particular case. This offence consists in the provoking or inciting others to commit a breach of the peace; but may also be regarded in a much more serious light—namely, as an attempt to commit or provoke others to commit a felony, —the felony of wilful murder. In the present case, a challenge had been sent and accepted: those who had done so, met, and fired deliberately at each other with deadly weapons, at only a few paces' distance. They fired twice; the first time innocuously; the second time, one

* He is now (October 1854) gallantly engaged with our army in the East.

of them was wounded. Every single step was here highly criminal; the earlier ones as misdemeanours, the later ones as felonies; the last indeed a capital felony, for which, beyond all question, the life of Lord Cardigan had become forfeited to the outraged law of the land. This we will shortly show, for the consolation of all future duellists. By the common law of the land, no personal violence, unattended by death, amounted to more than a misdemeanour. In the year 1722, was passed "the Black Act," * which, amongst various enactments levelled at the class of offenders who caused the passing of the statute, contains this brief general one. "If any person shall wilfully and maliciously *shoot at* any person, in any dwelling-house, *or other place*, he shall be adjudged guilty of felony, and suffer death." This was the first statute which made the mere act of shooting wilfully and maliciously at another, without reference to the result, felony. Subsequent statutes, respectively known as Lord Ellenborough's and Lord Lansdowne's Acts, made it a capital offence to shoot at another with intent to murder, or do grievous bodily harm, provided the death which might be occasioned would amount to murder. Though the matter had never become the subject of judicial decision, it had been suggested by a late eminent writer on the criminal law,† that, where an ineffectual interchange of shots took place in a duel, both parties might be deemed guilty of the offence of maliciously shooting, within one of these acts, passed in the year 1803 (43 Geo. III. c. 58), and the seconds also, as principals in the second degree. In the year 1837, however, was passed the Statute of the 1st Victoria, c. 85, which we advise every intending duellist

* It was called "the Waltham Black Act," as occasioned by the devastations committed near Waltham, in Hampshire, by persons disguised, and with *blackened* faces—"who seem," says Blackstone, "to have resembled the followers of Robert Hood, who in the reign of Richard I. committed such great outrages on the borders of England and Scotland."—4 Black. Com. 245.

† The late Mr Chitty.

to consult deliberately, before committing himself to its meshes. It enacts first (§ 2), that "whoever shall *wound* any person, or by any means whatsoever cause to any person any bodily injury dangerous to life, with intent to commit murder, shall be guilty of felony, and suffer death." Again, secondly (by § 3), whosoever shall shoot at any person, or, by drawing a trigger, or in any other manner, attempt to discharge any kind of loaded arms at any person, with intent to commit the crime of murder, shall, *although no bodily injury be inflicted*, be guilty of FELONY, and liable to be transported for life, or for any term not less than fifteen years, or imprisoned for any term not exceeding three years, at the discretion of the court." Lastly, thirdly (by § 4), "Whoever shall maliciously shoot at any person, or, by drawing a trigger, or in any other manner, attempt to discharge any kind of loaded arms at any person, or wound any person, with intent to maim, disfigure, or disable, *or to do some other grievous bodily harm* to such person, shall be guilty of felony, and liable to the same punishment contained in the previous section."

Blackstone, following Hawkins, thus lays down the law in the case of duelling: "Express malice is, where one, with a sedate deliberate mind, and formed design, doth kill another,—which formed design is evidenced by external circumstances, discovering that inward intention, —as lying in wait, antecedent menaces, former grudges, and concerted schemes to do him some grievous bodily harm. *This takes in the case of deliberate duelling, where both parties meet avowedly with an intent to murder; thinking it their duty as gentlemen, and claiming it as their right, to wanton with their own lives and those of their fellow-creatures, without any warrant or authority from any power either divine or human, but in direct contradiction to the laws of both God and man, and therefore the law has justly fixed the crime and punishment of murder on them, and on* *their seconds also*."* This passage may be said to reflect a somewhat ghastly light on the three sections of the statute law given above, such as must have startled the Earl of Cardigan and his advisers, as soon as they found that he had been made the subject of *bonâ fide* prosecution under that statute. We affirm unhesitatingly, and no lawyer will deny, that the facts relating to the duel, as they appear above stated, brought Lord Cardigan's case within every one of these three sections—as clearly within the first, rendering the offence capital, as within the other two, declaring it felony punishable with transportation. This the Attorney-General himself stated to the House of Lords, in opening the case against the prisoner: "The present indictment might have been framed on the *capital* charge." *A wound had been inflicted*, which constituted one branch of the capital offence; but "the prosecutor had, very properly, restricted the charge to firing with *an intent*, without alleging that a bodily injury *dangerous to life* had been inflicted."† The indictment was founded on the third and fourth sections alone; charging, in the first count, a shooting with *intent* to murder; in the second, to maim and disable; in the third, to do some grievous bodily harm. Indictments were preferred before the grand jury, at the Central Criminal Court, against both principals, and both seconds. The grand jury ignored those against Captain Tuckett and his second, but "found" those against Lord Cardigan and his second. As probably the same evidence, precisely, was laid before the grand jury in both cases, it is certainly difficult to account for the totally different results, except on the supposition that the grand jury suffered themselves to be influenced by feelings of commiseration for the party who had been wounded by one who had escaped unhurt. Lord Cardigan was reputed to be "a dead shot," and was certainly very unpopular; but there was no pretence whatever for saying that he had acted otherwise than

* 4 Black. Com. p. 199.

† 1 Townsend, pp. 215, 216.

with rigorous fairness in his encounter with Captain Tuckett, who, for all the grand jury could tell, was as "dead a shot" as the Earl. We would, however, fain hope that this secret-sworn inquest were not obnoxious to the censures which Mr Townsend* and others have levelled at them in this matter. On the bill being found, Lord Cardigan, of course, claimed his right to be tried by his peers—(*i. e.*, *pares*, *æquales*)—a right which he possessed in common with every fellow-subject; and the indictment was removed by *certiorari*, to be tried before the House of Peers in full Parliament.

The court of the Lord High Steward of Great Britain is one instituted for the trial of a Peer indicted for treason, or felony, or misprision of either;† but when the trial takes place during the session of Parliament, as was the case on the present occasion, it is before the High Court of Parliament. A Lord High Steward is appointed in either case; but in the latter he officiates, not as the supreme judge in matters of law, as he would be in a trial during the recess, but as speaker, or chairman, having an equal voice with his brother peers, in matters of both law and fact.

This was the first time that duelling had been made the subject of prosecution under the statutes against shooting with intent to kill, maim, disable, or do grievous bodily harm; and the position of the Earl of Cardigan had suddenly become perilous in the extreme, and doubtless occasioned the gravest apprehensions to himself and his advisers. If his case should be held to fall within the statute in question, not only was he liable to transportation for life,—and he knew that the House of Peers would firmly do its duty, especially conscious as it was that upon it were fixed the eyes of the whole country,—but what would be the effect of *a conviction of felony* on his property? Four days after the trial, it was stated in

* 1 Townsend, p. 210.

† For misdemeanor, a peer has no such privilege, but must be tried by a jury.

the *Times* newspaper,* and has not been, as far as we know, contradicted, that "such had been the doubts as to the issue of the trial, entertained by Lord Cardigan and his legal advisers, that his lordship, to prevent the whole of his property being forfeited to the crown, executed, some time before, a deed of gift, assigning over the whole of his valuable possessions to Viscount Curzon, the eldest son of Earl Howe, who had married a sister of the Earl of Cardigan. It is stated that the legal expenses of this transfer of property, arising from fines on copyholds and the enormous stamp-duties, amounted to about £10,000; and as the deed of transfer was said to have been enrolled in due form, in the event of an acquittal the immense expenditure would have to be again incurred, in order to effect a re-transfer." So serious a matter, even in a pecuniary point of view, has now become the fighting a duel, to a nobleman or gentleman of fortune; who are recommended, consequently, not to fight in a hurry—at all events, till they shall have had an opportunity of taking the best advice of counsel learned in the law, as to all the liabilities and incidents which they are about to encounter. The deed of transfer in question, if executed at all, had probably been executed before it was known to Lord Cardigan and his advisers, that it was not intended to indict him for a capital offence, under the second section of stat. 1 Vict. c. 85, and that he could not, consequently, be attainted. Even, however, as the case stood, if he had been convicted of the felony with which he was charged, the validity of his expensive attempt to obviate the legal effect of that conviction upon his large property would have been gravely questionable, had the law advisers of the crown felt it their duty to impugn the transaction.

The House of Lords presented, on the morning of Tuesday the 16th February 1841, an imposing appearance. Lord Denman, the Chief Justice of the Queen's

* 20th February 1841.

Bench had been appointed, by commission from the Queen, *pro hâc vice*, Lord High Steward."* The judges were in attendance in their state robes, and took their seats on the woolsack. The peers were attired in their robes, such of them as were knights also wearing the collars of their respective orders. The Lord Chancellor, Lord Cottenham, was absent, through illness; but there were, independently of the Lord High Steward, no fewer than five law lords present—Lords Lyndhurst, Brougham, Wynford, Abinger, and Langdale. The side galleries were filled with ladies; and the scene was one of great solemnity and magnificence. The Lord High Steward having made reverences to the throne, to which he had been conducted by the state officer, the Garter King-at-Arms bearing the sceptre, and the Gentleman Usher of the Black Rod the Lord Steward's staff, took his seat on the chair of state placed on the upper step but one of the throne. The necessary formalities of reading the commission, the writ of *certiorari*, and indictment, having been gone through, the Lord High Steward ordered proclamation to be made to the Yeoman Usher of the Black Rod to "bring James Thomas, Earl of Cardigan, to the bar." This was quickly complied with; the Earl, accompanied by the officer above mentioned, appearing at the bar, dressed in plain clothes. As he approached, he made three "reverences," and knelt, till directed by the Lord High Steward to rise. He again made three reverences, respectively to the Lord High Steward, and his brother peers on each side of the house, they returning his courtesy. He was then conducted to a stool within the bar near his counsel. His demeanour was calm and dignified, and he had a very soldierly bearing. He was then in his forty-fourth year. The Lord High Steward's deep impressive tones were then heard, as he thus ad-

* The mode of appointing this high officer, and of constituting the court, will be found explained at length in Blackstone's Commentaries.—Vol. iv. p. 259, *et seq.*

dressed the noble prisoner: "My Lord Cardigan, your lordship stands at the bar charged with the offence of firing with a loaded pistol at Harvey Garnett Phipps Tuckett, with intent to murder him; in a second count, you are charged with firing with intent to maim and disable him; and in a third count, you are charged with firing with intent to do him some grievous bodily harm. Your lordship will now be arraigned on that indictment." The reader will bear in mind that in each count Captain Tuckett's name was given as "Harvey *Garnett Phipps* Tuckett."

The Earl was then arraigned in the usual manner, by the Deputy Clerk of the Crown, in the Queen's Bench, who thus proceeded:—

"How say you, my Lord, are you guilty of the felony with which you stand charged, or not guilty?

"EARL OF CARDIGAN.—Not guilty, my lords.

"DEPUTY CLERK OF THE CROWN.—How will your lordship be tried?

"EARL OF CARDIGAN.—By my peers.

"DEPUTY CLERK OF THE CROWN.—God send your lordship a good deliverance."

The Earl, then, by leave of the house, sate down, uncovered: and after the usual proclamation had been made for all persons to come forward and give evidence, the Lord Steward, with the leave of the House, descended from his seat on the throne, and took his seat at the table. The Counsel for the Crown were the Attorney-General, the present Lord Campbell, and Mr Waddington, now the permanent Under Secretary of State; and for the prisoner, Sir William Follett, Mr Serjeant Wrangham, and the late Mr Adolphus. It has been said, and is indeed intimated by Mr Townsend, that, imperturbable as was the self-possession of Sir William Follett, on this occasion he exhibited unusual indication of an oppressive sense of responsibility. Both facts, indeed, and law were so "dead" against his noble client, and the consequences of conviction so serious and alarming, that nothing was left for him but to watch with lynx-eyed acuteness, in order to see that nothing but rigorously exact legal proof was adduced against his client.

The opening address of the Attorney-General was clear and temperate; faithfully stating the law which he charged Lord Cardigan with having violated, and the facts constituting the violation. He reminded the House that sixty-four years had elapsed since a similar trial had taken place—that of Lord Byron for killing his opponent in a duel. "I am rejoiced, my Lords, to think," continued the Attorney-General, in terms which immediately occasioned great observation, "that the charge against the noble prisoner at the bar *does not imply any degree of moral turpitude:* and that, if he should be found guilty, the conviction will reflect no discredit upon the illustrious order to which he belongs. But, my Lords, it seems to me that he has been clearly guilty of a breach of the statute law of the realm, which this and all other courts of justice are bound to respect and enforce. Your lordships are not sitting here as a court of honour, or as a branch of the legislature, but as a court of justice, bound by the rules of law, and under a sanction as sacred as that of an oath. * * * Your lordships are aware that the noble earl is in the army—Lieutenant-colonel of the 11th Hussars; and I have no doubt that, on this occasion, he only complied with what he thought necessary to the usages of society. But, under these circumstances, though it would have been considered, if death had ensued, *a great calamity, and not a great crime*—though moralists of the highest authority have defended duelling—it remains for your lordships to consider what duelling is by the law of England." After quoting from the known great authorities, Hale, Hawkins, Foster, and Blackstone, proving that a death by duelling was wilful murder, the Attorney-General correctly observed—"It necessarily follows, from this definition of murder, that the *first count* of the indictment is [that is, he expected it would be] completely proved. The only supposition, my Lords, by which the case can be reduced to one of *manslaughter* would be that Lord Cardigan and Captain Tuckett *casually* met at Wimbledon Common—that they *suddenly* quarrelled—and that, while their blood was up, they fought. But your lordships can hardly strain the facts so far as to suppose that this was a casual meeting, when you find that each was supplied with his second—that each had a brace of pistols—and that the whole affair was conducted according to the forms and solemnities observed when a deliberate duel is fought." Could anything be more clear and cogent? "Then, my Lords, with regard to the second and third counts of the indictment, I know not what defence can possibly be suggested; because, even if there had been this casual meeting, contrary to all probability and all the circumstances of the case—if it would only, had death ensued, have amounted to the crime of manslaughter—that would be no defence to the second and third counts of the indictment, as has been expressly decided* by the fifteen judges of England."

Such was the opening of the Attorney-General—such as must have left not a single crevice through which a glimpse of hope could be caught. The words of the Act of Parliament could not have applied more exactly to the facts of the case, as our readers must see, even if the Act had been expressly framed to meet these particular facts! The miller of Wimbledon, his wife and son, had witnessed the whole affair—the arrival of the parties on the ground, and the double interchange of shots. Lord Cardigan, on the spot, and at the police office, in plain terms voluntarily avowed who he was, what he had done, and who had been his second; the inspector of the police station being present to prove such avowal. Sir James Anderson, the

* Anonymous. 2 Moody's Criminal Cases, p. 40.

surgeon, who had also seen the duel, and accompanied Captain Tuckett home, was in attendance as a witness. The miller, who had received Captain Tuckett's card, went, a week afterwards, to the residence mentioned in the card, and asked for, and saw, Captain Tuckett. It would seem as though the wit of man could not suggest how these facts could be evaded, or how they could fail of being proved!

Yet the case totally broke down; the whole prosecution crumbled into pieces, under the subtle and watchful dexterity of the consummate advocate to whom Lord Cardigan had committed his almost hopeless case. What does the reader suppose to have been the fatal flaw? Positively, neither more nor less than this: that the prosecution could not prove THE IDENTITY OF CAPTAIN TUCKETT! Each of the three counts in the indictment charged Lord Cardigan with having fired at Harvey *Garnett Phipps* Tuckett. That was his real name, but it became impossible to prove the fact; and, without such proof, the prisoner was, beyond all question, entitled to an acquittal. A man cannot be indicted for firing at A B, and convicted of firing at C D. If Captain Tuckett had been called, he could, of course, have instantly disposed of the difficulty; and it is said that that gentleman was actually in, or near, the House of Lords; but the Attorney-General explained that he could not call that gentleman, nor his second, because, though the bill against them had been ignored by the grand jury, "they were still liable to be tried," and therefore "it would not be decorous to summon them to give evidence which might afterwards be turned against themselves." And as for Captain Wainwright, he was in the situation of his noble fellow-prisoner, as a true bill had been found against him at the Central Criminal Court. What, then, shall be said against calling Sir James Anderson? Fortunately for himself and for Lord Cardigan, he was in a position to be tried himself on a charge of having been present, aiding and assisting at the commission of a felony. On this gentleman being sworn, the Lord High Steward thus cautioned him, as he was bound to do in the case of any witness similarly situated:

"Sir James Anderson, With the permission of the House, I think it my duty to inform you, after the opening we have heard made by the Attorney-General of the facts of the case, that you are not bound to answer any question *which may tend to criminate yourself.*" Doubtless, Sir James Anderson expected nothing less, and had come to the House of Lords perfectly at his ease. Therefore he came like a shadow, and so departed. Thus "had he his entrance and his exit":—

"ATTORNEY-GENERAL—Of what profession are you?

"*A.*—I am a physician.

"*Q.*—Where do you live?

"*A.*—New Burlington Street.

"*Q.*—Are you acquainted with Captain Tuckett?

"*A.*—I must decline answering that.

"*Q.*—Were you on Wimbledon Common on the 12th September last?

"*A.*—I must decline answering that also!

"*Q.*—Were you on that day called in to attend any gentleman that was wounded?

"*A.*—I am sorry to decline that again!

"*Q.*—Can you tell me where Captain Tuckett lives?

"*A.*—I must decline answering the question!

"*Q.*—Has he a house in London?

"SIR WILLIAM FOLLETT.—He 'declines to answer the question.'

"*A.*—I have already said that I decline answering the question.

"ATTORNEY-GENERAL.—Where did you last see Captain Tuckett?

"SIR WILLIAM FOLLETT.—We [the counsel for the prisoner] have no *right,* my Lords, to interfere in this case;* But, the witness having several times declined to answer the question, I apprehend that it is not regular for the Attorney-General, by circuitous questions, to endeavour to get him to answer.

"ATTORNEY-GENERAL.—I have never pressed him in any question I have put. [*To Sir James Anderson*]—Do you decline any question whatever respecting Captain Tuckett?

"*A.*—*Any* question which may 'tend to criminate' myself.

"*Q.*—And you consider that answering any question respecting Captain Tuckett *may* tend to criminate yourself?

"*A.*—It is possible that it would.

"*Q.*—And on that ground you decline?

"*A.*—Yes.†

"ATTORNEY-GENERAL. [*to the House*]—Then, unless your Lordships wish to ask any questions of the witness, he may withdraw.

"The witness was directed to withdraw."

Here, then, were four avenues through which light might have been thrown on a transaction which was the subject of such solemn and dignified inquiry by the most

* The meaning of this observation is, that the privilege of not answering questions tending to criminate the witness belongs to the witness, and not to the parties; wherefore the objection to such questions ought to come from the witness, and not from the counsel for either of the parties. It is rather the duty of the judge to interfere, in order to apprise the witness of his right, in time. See the next note.

† The point here resolved came before the Court of Common Pleas, in November 1852, in the case of *Fisher v Ronald*, 12 Common Bench Reports 762; where the right claimed in the text as that of a witness, was amply vindicated by unanimous court. Mr Justice Maule referred to the case now under discussion: "In Lord Cardigan's case the witnesses were cautioned *before they claimed their privilege*. I do not know that a judge would do wrong if he were to caution a witness before *every answer*. . . . The witness may be conscious that there was evidence against him *which his answer might render complete*. . . . I think the judge is bound by the witness' oath: otherwise, you may exhaust all possibilities consistent with a man's innocence, and so convict him of even murder." "We must allow the witness," said the Chief Justice, "to judge for himself, or he would be made to criminate himself entirely."

illustrious judicial assembly in the world, carefully closed: Sir James Anderson, Captain Tuckett, Captain Douglas, and Captain Wainwright. It will be further observed that Lord Cardigan, in his frank avowal at the police station, had happened not to mention the name of the gentleman whom he had fought and wounded; an omission probably altogether accidental, for his Lordship seems to have been in a humour of signal yet becoming and characteristic frankness.

The sole question in this celebrated case thus became one of identity. The indictment charging Lord Cardigan with having fired at one *Harvey Garnett Phipps Tuckett*, it became the duty of the prosecutors to prove that the prisoner fired at a person *bearing these names;* for, as we have seen, all those names were used in each count. There might have been counts varying the names, so as to meet the evidence which might be reflected, especially calling him "Harvey Tuckett." Why this was not done, does not appear.* There was abundant evidence that Lord Cardigan had fired at and wounded a Captain Harvey Tuckett; but this might be a person totally different from him named in the indictment. The skill and vigilance of the prisoner's counsel were visible in tripping up his opponents whenever they approached inconveniently near his client. There is no reason to believe that Lord Cardigan's counsel were aware of there being the slightest difficulty, on the part of the prosecution, in proving the identity of the wounded man with the one specified in the indictment; but at the very first start, Sir William Follett perceived a faint possible advantage, and never for an instant lost sight of it.

* By a recent Act (Stat. 12 and 15 Vict. c. 100, § 1), passed August 1851, the count may amend variances between statements in the indictment, and the evidence in, amongst others, the figure or description of the person alleged to be injured by the offender—or the Christian and surname, or either, of any one named in the indictment, if it be not "material to the merits of the case;" by which is meant the substantial defence to the charge. The prisoner, however, is not to be "prejudiced in his defence on such merit," by the amendment. The trial can be postponed, and be before the same, or a different ury.

"You tell us," said the counsel for the prosecution, examining the first witness—the miller, "that you saw the pistols fired a second time: did you observe whether either of the shots took effect?

"*A.*—I thought Captain Tuckett was wounded—or, at least, the other gentleman: *I did not know who it was.*

"*Q.*—You thought that the gentleman, whom you afterwards knew to be Captain Tuckett, was wounded?

"*A.*—Yes.

"*Q.*—Did you see what that gentleman did with his pistol, after the second shots were fired?

"*A.*—No.

"*Q.*—You did not see whether he held it in his hand, or what he did with it?

"*A.*—Which are you alluding to?

"*Q.*—I am speaking of Captain Tuckett.

"SIR WILLIAM FOLLETT.—He has said he did not know who it was!"

Here was a stumble by the prosecutors, which their wary adversary never allowed them to recover. The miller then stated the giving of the card of address of "Captain Harvey Tuckett, 13 Hamilton Place, New Road," and produced it; but Sir William Follett objected to its being read in evidence against Lord Cardigan without evidence that he had seen it given, and was aware of what it was: and such evidence was not forthcoming. The Attorney-General then withdrew the card for the present, and asked the miller whether, on receiving it, he allowed the wounded gentleman to go; to which the answer was "Yes."—"In consequence of receiving this card, did you afterwards call at a particular house?" (meaning the house mentioned on the card, but which Sir William Follett had succeeded in excluding, for the present, from evidence). Sir William Follett objected that the question was a leading one, and it was not pressed. The witness then stated that, a week afterwards, he called at No. 13 Hamilton Place; asked for "Captain Tuckett."

"*Q.*—Whom did you see?

"*A.*—Captain Harvey Tuckett.

"*Q.*—Did you speak to him?

"*A.*—I did.

"SIR WILLIAM FOLLETT.—I wish you would put your questions differently!

"ATTORNEY-GENERAL.—We ask him whom he saw.

"SIR WILLIAM FOLLETT.—He does not know Captain Harvey Tuckett, I suppose.

"*Q.*—Did you speak to him?

"*A.*—I did."

The Attorney-General then tendered the card in evidence: and Sir William Follett, ignorant of what was written on it (for the Attorney-General had not specified in stating the case), objected to its being received. On this a very ingenious and elaborate argument ensued between him and the Attorney-General, whether this card was or was not admissible in evidence, at all events in that stage of the case. The latter insisted on the affirmative, on the ground that the card had been given to the constable in Lord Cardigan's presence, and the constable had afterwards gone to the address specified in the card. It was therefore a part of the *res gestæ.* "No," answered Sir William Follett; "it does not appear who it was that gave this card, or that Lord Cardigan saw it, nor that he knew what was written on it. The Attorney-General is trying to prove an important fact in the case, by an apparent *admission* of Lord Cardigan; whereas he is not shown to have had any cognisance whatever of the fact which he is supposed to have admitted!" The Lord High Steward said that, at all events, the House would postpone for the present its decision as to the admissibility of the card. "Whether the Attorney-General," said Sir William Follett, "will have any other evidence to prove who it was that had given the card, or to connect the card with the Earl, is another question"—which doubtless occasioned no little anxiety to the Earl and his astute counsel.

The next witnesses were the miller's wife and son, who were cross-examined by Sir William Follett irritably and severely, but ineffectually. They did not, nevertheless, appear to carry the case much farther than had the miller. Then came Mr Busain, the police inspector, who gave evidence of the facts already stated in connection with his name, in the Earl's avowal that he had just fought a duel, and hit his man. On his being asked a very critical question, viz., as to Captain Tuckett's having called at the magistrate's office *and given his name*, Sir William Follett anxiously and hastily interposed—"was Lord Cardigan present then and there?" to which the answer was, "No, he was not." Sir William Follett therefore succeeded in excluding what Captain Tuckett had said on calling at the magistrate's office, and thus again "averted the decisive stroke."*

Then the Attorney-General called a Mr Matthew, a chemist in the Poultry, in whose house "Captain Tuckett" occupied rooms for business. Mr Matthew said that Captain Tuckett lived at "No. 13, Hamilton Place, New Road." He was then asked the Christian names of Captain Tuckett. On this, Sir William Follett interposed, and having elicited the fact that the witness had never been at the house No. 13, Hamilton Place, New Road, objected to the witness being asked the Christian names of the gentleman who had lodged with the witness in the Poultry! This objection, however, was overruled; but on the question being put, it turned out that the only names by which the witness knew his lodger were "Harvey Tuckett!" As a last resource, the Attorney-General called Mr Codd, an army agent, who paid "Captain Tuckett," of the "11th Light Dra-

* Townsend, vol. i. p. 229.

goons," his half-pay, *and knew his name to be "Harvey Garnet Phipps Tuckett!"* But the witness added that he used to pay the money at his own house in Fludyer Street, Westminster, and had never seen Captain Tuckett except there, and at an insurance office! Again was the Earl of Cardigan's star in the ascendant. How could the prosecutor connect the half-pay officer spoken of by this witness, with the Captain Tuckett shot by Lord Cardigan, and afterwards seen wounded in Hamilton Place?

The case was brought, at length, pretty nearly to a stand-still. "Is *that* your case, Mr Attorney?" inquired Lord Brougham; on which the Attorney-General pressed for the decision of the House as to the admissibility in evidence of the card which had been delivered by one of the parties on the ground to the constable.

"LORD HIGH STEWARD.—You object to its being received, Sir William Follett?

"SIR WILLIAM FOLLETT.—Certainly, my lord: and I should wish to address your lordships, if any doubt is entertained on the subject.

"LORD HIGH STEWARD.—Their lordships are ready to hear your objection.

"SIR WILLIAM FOLLETT (to the Attorney-General). —Will you let me look at the card?"

The card was handed to Sir William Follett, who, on examining it, addressing the Lord High Steward, said calmly and resolutely—"My lord, I do not think it necessary to object to this card being read." And, indeed, he had no need to do so; for, as the reader must see, it did not advance the case a single hair's-breadth. [The card, it will be recollected, had, in print, the words, "Captain *Harvey Tuckett*, No. 13, Hamilton Place, New Road;" and there were written in pencil, on the back, the words, "Captain H. Wainwright."] With this evidence before them, it seems extraordinary that no counts should have been inserted, omitting the words, "Garnet

Phipps"—when it might have appeared conclusively that Captain Tuckett was usually known by the name of Harvey Tuckett, which would have sufficed.

"Is *that* your case, Mr Attorney?" inquired Sir William Follett, with mingled anxiety and hope. "That, my lords, is the case on the part of the prosecution," said the Attorney-General:—on which, turning to the High Steward with a confident exulting air, Sir William Follett "submitted to their lordships that no case had been made out, requiring an answer from the prisoner at the bar."

Into what a minute point this great case had dwindled! "There is no evidence whatever to prove," said Sir William Follett, "that the person at whom the noble Earl is charged to have shot, on the 12th September last, was Harvey Garnett Phipps Tuckett—the name contained in every count of the indictment. The evidence would rather lead to a contrary presumption, if presumption could be entertained in such a case; but it is incumbent on the prosecutor to give positive evidence of the identity of the person named in the indictment with the person against whom the offence is alleged to have been committed. * * * Is there anything before your lordships to identify the Captain Tuckett spoken of by the army agent, Mr Codd, with the person who is said to have been at Wimbledon Common on the 12th September last? There is nothing whatever."—"If there be the smallest *scintilla* of evidence," answered the Attorney-General, "the prosecution cannot be stopped on this ground; and there is abundant evidence from which it may be inferred that the person wounded in this duel was—Harvey Garnett Phipps Tuckett. We prove that the wounded gentleman was *a* 'Captain Tuckett;'—that it was 'Captain *Harvey* Tuckett;' that the wounded Captain Tuckett lived at 13 Hamilton Place, New Road. Is there any doubt that it was *that* Captain Tuckett who had taken the premises in the

Poultry? When he did so, he gave a reference to No. 13 Hamilton Place, New Road. Is it not an irresistible evidence, then, that the Captain Tuckett of the Poultry and of Hamilton Place, and who fought with Lord Cardigan, was one and the same person? There is only one other stage—that this Captain Tuckett is the Captain Tuckett of whom Mr Codd speaks. Is there not cogent evidence to prove the identity here? Would any person, out of a court of justice, for a moment doubt the identity here? If not, can this House undertake to say *that there is not a scintilla* of evidence of identity before it?" "What we object," said Sir William Follett, in reply, "is this—that Mr Codd, who says he knows *a* Captain Tuckett who bears the names mentioned in the indictment, gave no *scintilla* of evidence to connect that individual with the gentleman who was on Wimbledon Common on the 12th September last. It depended altogether on Mr Codd to give such proof—and that proof he wholly failed to give. Your Lordships are now sitting as judges, to decide solely on the evidence which has been laid before you. The Attorney-General says that the card afforded *one* of the Christian names—'*Harvey* Tuckett;' but is that proof that the person mentioned in that card is the 'Harvey *Garnett Phipps* Tuckett' mentioned in this indictment? There may be two, or ten, or fifty persons named 'Harvey Tuckett.' I ask your Lordships, sitting as judges on a criminal case, and looking at the evidence alone—disregarding surmise, conjecture, and what you may have heard out of doors—whether there is any evidence to prove that the gentleman wounded on Wimbledon Common bears the name and surname of 'Harvey Garnett Phipps Tuckett?'"

The Lord High Steward, during the deliberation of the House with closed doors, delivered a luminous and convincing exposition of the legal merits of the case before the House:—

"There is an absolute want of circumstances to connect the individual at whom the pistol was fired, and who afterwards was seen wounded in Hamilton Place, with the half-pay officer known to Mr Codd as bearing the names set forth in the indictment on which your Lordships are sitting in judgment; for the mere fact of the wounded person bearing *some* of the names used by the half-pay officer, is no proof that the former and the latter are the same; and the representation by that officer of his having held a commission in the same regiment of which Lord Cardigan told the policeman that he himself was colonel (which, coupled with the actual receipt of half-pay, may sufficiently prove that fact), cannot, I apprehend, be turned into a presumption that those two individuals would meet in hostile array. Here are two distinct lines of testimony, and they never meet in the same point."

* * * * *

"No fact (*i. e.*, of identity) is easier of proof in its own nature; and numerous witnesses are always at hand to establish it, with respect to any person conversant with society. In the present case, the simplest means were accessible. If those who conduct the prosecution had obtained your Lordships' order for the appearance at your bar of Captain Tuckett, and if the witnesses of the duel had deposed to his being the man who left the field after receiving Lord Cardigan's shot, Mr Codd might have been asked whether that was the gentleman whom he knew by the four names set forth in the indictment. His answer in the affirmative would have been too conclusive on the point to admit of the present objection being taken.

"Several other methods of proof will readily suggest themselves to your Lordships' minds. Even if obstacles had been imposed by distance of time and place, by the poverty of those seeking to enforce the law, by the death of witnesses, or other casualties, it cannot be doubted that the accused must have had the benefit of the failure of proof, however occasioned; and here, where none of those causes can account for the deficiency, it seems too much to require that your Lordships should volunteer the presumption of a fact which, if true, might have been made clear and manifest to every man's understanding by the shortest process. Your Lordships were informed that no persons out of doors could hesitate, on the proof now given, to decide that the identity is well made out. Permit me, my Lords, to say, that you are to decide for yourselves upon the proofs brought before you, and that nothing can be conceived more dangerous to the interests of justice, than for a judicial body to indulge in any speculations on what may possibly be said or thought by others who have not heard the same evidence, nor act with the same responsibility, nor (possibly) confine their attention to the evidence actually adduced. Your Lordships," continued the Lord High Steward, "sitting in this High Court of Parliament, with the functions of a judge and a jury, I have stated my own views, as an individual member of the court, of the question by you to be considered, discussed, and decided. Though I have commenced the debate, it cannot be necessary for me to disclaim the purpose of dictating my own opinion, which is respectfully laid before you with the hope of eliciting those of the House at large. If any other duty be cast upon me, or if there be any more convenient course to be pursued, I shall be greatly indebted to any of your Lordships who will be so kind as to instruct me in it. In the absence," continued the noble Lord, "of any other suggestion, I venture to declare my own judgment, grounded on the reasons briefly submitted, that the Earl of Cardigan is entitled to be declared NOT GUILTY." * This was followed by the unanimous declaration of "Not Guilty," —pronounced successively "upon my honour"—by every peer present, beginning with the junior baron. The only variation of the form occurred in the case of

* Townsend, pp. 239–241.

the Duke of Cleveland, who said—instead of "not guilty, upon my honour"—"not guilty, *legally*, upon my honour." The white staff of the Lord High Steward was then broken in two; and so was dissolved the first—may it be the last—commission, during the present century, for the trial of a peer on a charge of felony.

Lord Denman's reasons for recommending an acquittal were unanswerable, and by special direction of the House of Lords, though not in conformity with precedent,* were published, to enable the country to judge of the grounds on which the House had proceeded. The result, however, so contrary to that which had been expected, excited no little indignation; and the *bona fides*, even of those who conducted the prosecution, was very sternly questioned. It was insinuated by some of the most powerful organs of public opinion, that the prosecution had been taken up unwillingly, and with not even ordinary precautions to secure the ends of justice. "We ask," said the *Times*, "whether the law officers of the Crown had no foresight to anticipate, or no disposition to provide against, a conclusion so unsatisfactory? Is any man capable of believing that if some tailor, or linen-draper, had been indicted at the Old Bailey for the crime of stealing—or that he, having an honour to vindicate equally with noble lords, pistolled and wounded one of his companions—does any man believe that, in such a case, we should have heard of any miscarriage, or of any name that could not be proved? Oh no! there would then have been precautions in abundance—there would have been no loophole left—there would have been no lack of friends and relatives carefully subpœnaed to prove all the Christian names of the necessary party."

We ourselves have reflected frequently on the result of this trial; and the points which have occurred to us are two. *First*, Why was not Captain Tuckett summoned to the bar of the House of Lords—if merely to be pointed

* Townsend, p. 238.

out to the witnesses to see if they could identify him? The miller could have been required to look at him, and been then asked—"Is that the person whom you saw lying wounded on the common?"—and Mr Codd could then have been also required to look at Captain Tuckett, and say—"Is that the gentleman to whom you used to pay half-pay as Captain Tuckett of the 11th Light Dragoons, and whose name you knew to be Harvey Garnett Phipps Tuckett?" On both these witnesses answering these questions in the affirmative, it would have required a thousand times even Sir William Follett's ingenuity to suggest a further doubt on the point of identity. This was the course which the Lord High Steward plainly pointed at, in his address to his brother peers, as that which might have been adopted. *Secondly*, Why was not the name of Captain Tuckett varied in various counts of the indictment, so as to meet not every probable, but every possible doubt and difficulty? If in one count he had been called "Harvey Tuckett," it would have sufficed to meet the evidence actually adduced; and the other counts might have respectively described him as "Harvey Garnett Phipps Tuckett"—"Harvey Garnett Tuckett"—"Harvey Phipps Tuckett"—"Garnett Tuckett"—"Phipps Tuckett"—even adding to these other combinations of the four names in which Captain Tuckett rejoiced. To dispose first of this latter point—we verily believe that, up to the moment when the question of identity was started, the counsel for the prosecution, and their clients, believed that the proof of identity was a matter of course. The indictment had been preferred before the Grand Jury at the Central Criminal Court; and was doubtless framed, in the ordinary course, by the clerk of indictments, from the depositions—in which might have appeared all the four names of Captain Tuckett, without any intimation of doubt or difficulty as to the fact of those being his names, or as to proof that they were. Possibly the clerk had before him a positive statement that Mr Codd, the army agent, who paid Captain Tuckett his half-pay, could clearly prove that his name was "Harvey Garnett Phipps Tuckett;" and that, if so, it was a needless and expensive encumbering of the record to insert counts aimed at only imaginary difficulties. The indictment having once gone before the Grand Jury, and been returned a true bill, no alteration could have been made in it, especially after it had been removed by *certiorari.* * * * Doubtless the brief of the counsel for the prosecution would contain the evidence of Mr Codd, in as direct and positive a form as could be imagined; and they would regard him, as the army-agent of Captain Tuckett, as peculiarly qualified to prove his real names. When the difficulty had been started, we know of no degree of ingenuity that could have been exhibited by counsel, exceeding that of the Attorney-General, in his contests on the point with Sir William Follett. All experienced practical lawyers will acknowledge the probability that the solution of the question here proposed is the true one. It is easy to be wise after the result. A blot is not a blot, until it has been *hit.*

Adverting again to the absence of any effort to produce Captain Tuckett at the bar of the House of Lords, be it observed that there is no evidence that he was in attendance, or that he could have been met with, at the exact moment when his presence was required. It may have been, that no order of the House had been obtained for his attendance, only because it had not been thought necessary; that no difficulty was anticipated, which his attendance could solve; and in the absence of direct legal compulsion, Captain Tuckett may have felt it a point of honour not to volunteer himself as a witness against his brother duellist. We can also readily believe that the counsel for the prosecution were anxious to conduct a perfectly novel case—the first instance on record of an attempt to bring a non-fatal duel under the category of felony, with its alarming incidents and consequences—with unusual liberality, and not to exhibit anything like a vindictive pressure upon the accused. They knew, besides, that Captain Tuckett was himself liable, at that moment, to be placed in the same situation as Lord Cardigan; and that it would have been idle to call before the House of Lords a witness who would come armed with a right to decline answering any question which he believed might even *tend* to criminate himself.

It must also be borne in mind that the Attorney-General boldly avowed, before the House of Lords, that he regarded the act with which Lord Cardigan stood charged as one devoid of "any degree of moral turpitude," and that "a conviction would attach no discredit to the illustrious order to which he belonged." These observations, proceeding from an Attorney-General on a solemn official occasion, became, a few days afterwards, the subject of grave discussion and censure in the House of Lords. But even the excellent Earl of Mountcashel thus pointed at the practical hardship of Lord Cardigan's position—"An officer in the army receives an affront. His brother officers expect he shall go out. If he do, he encounters the pains and penalties of the statute 1 Victoria c. 85; if he refuse, he is obnoxious to the contempt of his brother officers."* It was, certainly, not to be expected that an Attorney-General, entertaining and avowing the views of duelling which he did—and having to deal with a nobleman bearing her Majesty's commission, who was placed

* 1 Townsend, p. 211. Lord Campbell has included his opening address in Lord Cardigan's case among his published "Speeches," and thus deprecates the censures which had been past upon him: "I was much hurt by an accusation that my address contained a defence of duelling, and had a tendency to encourage that practice. Nothing could be further from my intention. * * * I continue to think that to engage in a duel, which cannot be declined without infamy, and which is not occasioned by any offence given by the party whose conduct is under discussion, whether he accepted or sent the challenge, though

in the dilemma indicated by Lord Mountcashel, and had fought his duel "fairly," and unattended by fatal consequences—should have been as eagle-eyed a prosecutor as if he had had to deal with a man, gentle or simple, military or civil, who had shamefully provoked, and as disgracefully fought, a fatal duel.

Had Lord Cardigan been convicted, he would still have had a *chance* of escaping the serious personal consequences, by claiming that absurd and unjust privilege of the peerage of which Lords Mohun, Warwick, and Byron, in past times, had respectively availed themselves, immediately on their having been convicted, in cases of fatal duels, of manslaughter. This privilege had been confirmed by statute, 1st Edward VI. c. 12, § 14, which was passed in the year 1547, and consisted in enabling a lord of parliament and peer of the realm to have benefit of clergy for a first conviction of felony—that is to say, to escape the penal consequences of conviction, on simply alleging that he was a peer, and praying the benefit of that act! In 1827, however, by one of the statutes which effected so salutary a reform of our criminal law (statute 7th and 8th Geo. IV. c. 28, § 6), it was enacted as follows,—that "benefit of clergy, with respect to persons convicted of felony, shall be abolished." It had been intended, by this section, to repeal that of the 1st Edward VI. c. 12, § 14; but serious doubts were entertained, during the pendency of Lord Cardigan's trial, whether that intention had been effectuated. We offer no opinion on the point, which would have been argued, of course,

contrary to the law of the land, is an act free from moral turpitude. * * * I consider that to fight a duel must always be a great calamity, but it is not always, necessarily, a great crime." Fully acknowledging the difficulties of the subject, we publicly and solemnly disclaim participation in these opinions, for reasons already laid before our readers. We give Lord Campbell full credit for the purity of his motives, and the sincerity of his convictions; but we must withhold our concurrence from opinions which ignore *moral* turpitude in a breach of THE LAW OF GOD.

with desperate pertinacity, and commensurate learning and ingenuity, had the occasion for such an exhibition arisen. To extinguish, however, all possible doubt, and prevent any future failure of justice, an act was passed in the same session during which Lord Cardigan was tried (statute 4th and 5th Vict. c. 22, 2d June 1841), asserting that "doubts had been entertained" whether, notwithstanding the statute of 1827, that of 1547 "might not, for some purposes, still remain in force." The statute of 1841 had but one section, which declared the 1st Edward VI. c. 12, § 14, to be "thenceforth repealed, and utterly void, and no longer of any effect;" and enacted that "every lord of parliament, or peer of the realm having place in parliament, against whom any indictment for felony may be found, shall plead to such indictment, and shall, upon conviction, be liable to the same punishment as any other of her Majesty's subjects are, or may be, liable upon conviction for such felony."

Thus stands the law of DUELLING, alike for lord and commoner; whom we trust we have satisfied of the alarming responsibilities entailed upon those who may choose to perpetrate these outrages upon the laws of their country.

In closing this paper, and taking leave of a painfully interesting topic, he would fain express a hope, and also a belief, that a better feeling on the subject of duelling is gaining ground, in this country, than has existed for centuries. There is growing up a spirit of dignified submission to the law of man, based as it is on the law of God, which totally prohibits these unholy exhibitions of murderous malevolence. A truer estimate is formed of the nature of HONOUR—one which forbids alike the offering, and the resenting, of insults. The following noble paragraph, recently introduced into the Articles of War, is worthy of being written in letters of gold—of being exhibited (with suitable variation of expression) in every place of public resort, and in every possible manner brought under the notice of men of the world, and the youths in our public schools:—

"We hereby declare our approbation," says her most gracious Majesty,* "of the conduct of all those who, having had the misfortune of giving offence to, or of injuring, or of insulting others, shall frankly explain, apologise, or offer redress for the same; or who, having had the misfortune of receiving offence, injury, or insult from another, shall cordially accept frank explanation, apology, or redress for the same; or who, if such explanations, apology, or redress, are refused to be made or accepted, and the friends of the parties shall have failed to adjust the difference, shall entrust the matter to be dealt with by the commanding officer of the regiment, or detachment, fort, or garrison; and we accordingly acquit of disgrace, or opinion of disadvantage, all officers who, being willing to make or accept such redress, refuse to accept challenges, as they will only have acted as is suitable to the character of honourable men, and done their duty as good soldiers, who subject themselves to discipline."

There speaks the Queen of England!

The following is the stringent Article of War† on the subject of duelling:—

"Every officer who shall give, send, convey, or promote a challenge; or who shall accept any challenge to fight a duel with another officer; or who shall assist as a second at a duel; or who, being privy to an intention to fight a duel, shall not take active measures to prevent such duel; or who shall upbraid another for refusing or for not giving a challenge; or who shall reject, or advise the rejection of, a reasonable proposition made for the honourable adjustment of a difference, shall be liable, if convicted by a general court-martial, to be cashiered, or suffer such other punishment as the court may award.

* Articles of War, Art. 17.

† Art. 101.

"In the event of an officer being brought to a court-martial for having assisted as a second in a duel, if it shall appear that such officer had strenuously exerted himself to effect an adjustment of the difference, on terms consistent with the honour of both the parties, and shall have failed, through the unwillingness of the adverse parties to accept terms of honourable accommodation, then our will and pleasure is, that such officer shall suffer such punishment, other than cashiering, as the court may award."

# MODERN STATE TRIALS.*

## No. V.

## THE MURDERED GLASGOW COTTON-SPINNER; AND THE TRIALS OF DANIEL O'CONNELL AND WILLIAM SMITH O'BRIEN.

WITH this part we propose to conclude the short series which we have founded on Mr Townsend's "Modern State Trials." They are fifteen in number, of which we have selected for illustration *five*:—one for murder, that of Daniel M'Naughten; two for high treason, those of Frost and Oxford; one for wounding in a duel, that of the Earl of Cardigan; and one for forgery, that of Alexander Humphreys, or Alexander. Each of these possesses points of permanent interest, which we have taken no small pains to bring out clearly and popularly,—always keeping in view, moreover, the objects which we proposed to ourselves at the outset. A subordinate one was to contrast the trials taking place in England, Scotland, and Ireland, as exhibiting some of their respective peculiarities of criminal procedure, and the characteristics of their respective judges and advocates. Of the entire series in Mr Townsend's volume, there are ten English, three Scottish, and two Irish trials—those of Daniel O'Connell and his companions in 1843-4, for treasonable conspiracy, and Smith O'Brien in 1848, for high treason. We

* *Blackwood's Magazine*, June 1851.

intend, in this paper, to indicate the most interesting features of another Scottish, and the two Irish cases.

I. The "trial of Hunter and four others, at Glasgow, on January the 3d, 1838, and seven following days, for conspiracy and murder," is reported at considerable length by Mr Townsend, but by no means more fully than is justified by the extraordinary nature of the case, and the striking incidents developed at the trial.*

A little after eleven o'clock on the night of Saturday the 22d July 1837, a poor fellow named John Smith, an industrious cotton-spinner of Glasgow, was returning home, accompanied by his wife, after making a few purchases for their Sabbath's dinner. A minute or two after quitting a butcher's shop, he suddenly fell in the street, mortally wounded, having been shot in the back. One bullet had passed through his arm, and the other severed the spinal cord! In his dying declaration, the next day, he stated that "he was unable to say who had shot him, and had no suspicion who had done so, nor had he heard any footsteps behind him before having been shot;" "that he was convinced that it was on account of his having taken work from his employers, Messrs Houldsworth and Sons, that he had been shot last night:" "all this he depones to be the truth, as the deponent shall answer to God." The following touching description of this barbarous transaction was given by Mr Robertson, the counsel for the individual by whom it was alleged that the act of murder had been committed. "It was a murder perpetrated on this poor man, who had finished his week of labour in the toilsome occupation to which Providence had destined him; and who was entitled to lay his head for one night on his peaceful pillow, and

* Mr Townsend's account of this trial is taken, as was that of Alexander, mainly, if not altogether, from an elaborate report, published in an octavo volume, by Mr Swinton, in the year 1838; though in this instance, also, no allusion is made to the fact—doubtless from inadvertence.

look forward to the return of that day when even the weary artisan is entitled to repose of body, and rest of mind, that he may dedicate to his God one day of the week, and pass some hours without bodily fatigue, if not without mental solicitude. At that moment the cowardly assassin, lurking behind, draws the fatal trigger, which hurries this honest and toil-worn artisan, in a very few hours, to the presence of the God who made him, and terminates his earthly course of toil and care." This was carrying into the heart of Glasgow an atrocity such as are so frightfully familiar to us as happening in Ireland. The murdered man's offence was—having taken work from his employers at a lower rate of wages than his companions chose to accept, and who had consequently "struck work." Six hundred pounds reward (five hundred by the master cotton-spinners of Glasgow, and one hundred by Government) were immediately offered for the discovery of the assassin, but in vain.

This murder formed, says Mr Townsend, the crowning act of other desperate enormities recurring during different strikes in the cotton trade, and which had been attributed to the same gigantic conspiracy—the "Association of Turn-out Spinners"—whose leaders had hitherto remained undetected. For presuming to work at reduced rates of wages, men had been fired at and wounded in open day, on the Green, in Glasgow, in the presence of scores of fellow-labourers, none of whom would protect the assailed, or inform against the murderous miscreants who had so attacked them! To deter masters from taking fresh hands, fire-balls were thrown into the mills; and canisters ignited, full of blazing combustibles, flung into the bed-rooms of private dwellings! The houses of workmen were invaded at dead of night, and the inmates forced to take an oath that they would discontinue work, for the future, on pain of death! A woman was brutally beaten to death in her own house, having been mistaken for her daughter, who had presumed to take the forbidden work! Vitriol was thrown on a poor fellow guilty of the same offence, and he died in horrible tortures: but though the ruffian perpetrator of the outrage was fortunately detected and executed, his companions were not deterred from prosecuting their career of cruelty and crime. The masters were compelled to wear masks, to protect them from the vitriol thrown at their faces! and were accustomed to receive letters threatening horrible modes of death, if they did not yield to the demands of their men! These deeds of atrocity and blood, which had for *twenty years* disgraced Scotland—sober, well-educated Scotland—Scotland in the nineteenth century—were traced, at length, to the infamous association which has been mentioned, having ramifications in the three kingdoms, comprehending hundreds of thousands of workmen. At the will of a secret and self-elected body of fifteen men, these trades-unions perpetrated systematic acts of tyranny almost incredible, and entailing incalculable misery on their victims; "who all," said Mr (now Sir Archibald) Alison, (whose noble conduct in this affair we shall have speedily to notice,) "got deeply into debt, if they had any credit; and, if they had none, sank into such habits of idleness, profligacy, and intemperance, that great numbers have been permanently rendered mere nuisances and burdens to society. The cotton-spinners' strike alone instantly threw six or seven thousand women and children out of employment for a long period: eight thousand human beings were retained in a state of destitution and wretchedness for four months—merely at the pleasure of fifteen men!" The total loss entailed on the county of Lanarkshire alone, by these various strikes, was half a million sterling! Between twenty and thirty thousand young persons of both sexes were thrown into compulsory idleness for many months: the funds for their support grew rapidly less and less; each week they sank into deeper penury; and the starving pauper rushed desperately and recklessly into crime. The prisons were crowded with ten times their ordinary number; fever and other deadly diseases crept stealthily in the rear of "combination," and gleaned a copious harvest of death in the weakened victims of enforced want. Such effects must ever be produced by such causes.

On the murder of Smith being officially reported to Mr Alison, the Sheriff of Lanarkshire, he resolved, "come what come might," to crush the destructive combination which had occasioned it; and, accompanied by Captain Miller and a strong police force, he boldly burst into the committee-room of the association, at ten o'clock on a Saturday night, four days after the death of Smith; and the result was the capture of fifteen of the ringleaders, together with all their books and papers. He thus described the scene, not as Mr Townsend erroneously supposes, in his evidence at the trial, but on a subsequent occasion, and in a quasi-official capacity. Though sinking all allusion to himself, every word of his eulogy tells really as strongly upon himself as on Captain Miller; and we are delighted by the opportunity of doing an act of mere justice, by bringing conspicuously forward this instance of gallant daring.

"My lords, when I recollect Captain Miller's conduct when he entered the committee-room of the conspirators, and reflect on the moment when I stood beside him in the middle of the apartment, as he beckoned them out one by one, till the whole fifteen were delivered over to the police on the outside, with as calm a manner and resolute a voice as if he were now discharging his ordinary duty in this court; and when I call to mind the character and proved deeds of the conspiracy, and recollect that every room in the house was then also crowded with conspirators, and that hundreds of the association thronged the streets, almost within call, I cannot but regard his conduct on the occasion as one of the most remarkable instances on record of that moral resolution which is at once the shield of innocence and the bridle of crime, and which, paralysing guilt by the ascendency of courage, proves its own safeguard by the awe which it inspires."

The effect of this enterprise was decisive, great, and consolatory. It palsied the energies of the entire confederacy. Early in the ensuing week the strike was at an end: the deluded, miserable, beggared followers of such wicked leaders, after four months of suffering and privation, returned to their work; and life and property were once again safe from molestation, and have ever since so continued. The captives were detained in custody till the ensuing January, when the five prisoners in the case before us were put upon their trial. A few witnesses, tempted by the reward, and relying on the protection of Government from the vindictiveness likely to be developed by their disclosures, came forward to throw light on the nature, character, and proceedings of the association. Great preparations were made on both sides for this important trial, after nearly half a year's interval. A thousand pounds were subscribed by the working-men towards the expense of the defence, for which five of the most eminent advocates were retained; the Crown being represented by the Lord-Advocate, the Solicitor-General, and two other leading advocates. The indictment extended over twenty-six quarto pages; and ninety-one witnesses were summoned!

The prisoners were charged with *a conspiracy* to keep up wages by molesting other workmen, and the perpetration of acts of violence to the persons and property of masters and workmen. They were further charged in the Criminal Letters,* which gave a long narrative of the

* There are two methods of criminal procedure in Scotland—by Indictment, and by Criminal Letters; "which," says Mr Alison (*Pract. of the Crim. Law*, p. 211), "though different in form, are the same in substance." The "Indictment" is at the instance of the Lord-Advocate alone, and runs in his name; Criminal Letters proceed in the Sovereign's name. In so far as concerns the trial, there is no practical difference between the two methods of procedure. In the case before us, Mr Townsend speaks in one place of the Criminal Letters as "the Indictment" (p. 230), having probably failed to notice the distinction between the two forms of procedure.

atrocities that had been perpetrated for twenty years, with conspiring to burn mills, to set fire to private dwellings, and to murder Smith by the hands of one of the prisoners, M'Lean. It is not our intention to give a detailed account of the trial, which was necessarily troublesome and harassing, from the extent and multiplicity of the circumstances requiring to be brought distinctly under the notice of the jury, in order that a real "conspiracy" might be established, and the parts borne in it proved as against the prisoners respectively charged with it. "The whole defence," says Mr Townsend, "was founded in fraud, and supported by perjury." * Mr Duncan M'Neill, now [1854] the Lord Justice-General, defended four of the prisoners, and very ably and powerfully—though in this instance, contrary to Mr Townsend's wont, he is unaccountably niggard of his praise. He says briefly that the defence "was shrewd, plain, forcible, and pathetic;" which last expression does not appear to us properly to characterise the strain of vigorous eloquence which was really poured forth before the jury. Mr M'Neill's peroration was at once sober and deeply impressive. Mr Robertson appears to have figured very favourably in the eyes of Mr Townsend. He "commenced his eloquent oration by," &c.; "The accomplished orator denounced," &c.; "In his peculiar vein of banter and pleasantry, he ridiculed," &c. After giving copious extracts from this speech, Mr Townsend deals somewhat unceremoniously with the "very minute and elaborate summing up of the Lord Justice-Clerk, which occupied thirteen hours," but which Mr Townsend disposes of in nearly as many lines. "He let the jury clearly infer, as the intimation of his opinion, that the minor conspiracy, charged as having been to keep up wages by threats, intimidation, and acts of illegal violence to the persons of masters and workmen, was proved; but that the heavier conspiracy—to keep up the price of labour by fire-raising and murder—was *not* fully proved." * * * A case of greater

* Townsend, p. 196.

public importance has seldom or never been brought before a jury. After an absence of five hours, the jury returned with a verdict which, we presume, was in full conformity with the summing up: "My lords, the jury have, by a majority, found the charges Nos. 1, 2, 3, and 10, against all the panels, proven: and they have unanimously found the rest of the charges not proven." Mr Townsend has forgotten to give any account of the different heads of charge, so that, as we have not Mr Swinton's report before us, we cannot appreciate the precise effect of this report of the finding. It was, however, followed immediately—"between eleven and twelve o'clock at night"—by "most impressive statements of the reasons for passing so serious a sentence" as that of transportation for seven years.

On this trial we have two or three observations to offer. *First*, the prisoners were allowed twenty-five peremptory challenges to the jury—an indulgence which would not have been granted them in England, where peremptory challenges are allowed in cases of felony alone, not in misdemeanors; a distinction, however, unknown to the law of Scotland, where all offences are denominated "*crimes*" only. Our general readers may like to know that there are two kinds of challenges: *peremptory*—*i. e.*, an objection to a man's serving as a juror, made *simpliciter*, without assigning any reason for it; and *for cause*—*i. e.*, a challenge assigning the ground or reason on which it proceeds. This distinction exists also in Scotland. By stat. 3 George IV. c. 85, the prosecutor and the prisoner have each *five* peremptory challenges; and where Mr Townsend speaks of the prisoners having been allowed twenty-five peremptory challenges, we presume he must, if aware of this statute, mean that each of the five prisoners exercised his full statutory right of peremptory challenge.

*Secondly*, the sentence was one of transportation, on conviction for that which in England would be regarded as only a misdemeanor at common law. In England this punishment can in no case be inflicted, except where expressly imposed by statute; but there is no such distinction in Scotland, where the common law empowers the judges to pass this or any other sentence, applicable in their discretion, to the quality of the offence of which the prisoner may have been convicted. The common law of England punishes even the most aggravated misdemeanor by either fine and imprisonment, or by both. Lord Brougham, in the House of Lords, endeavoured to urge on the Government a mitigation of punishment, on the ground that in England only three months' imprisonment would have been inflicted. With due deference, however, we concur with Mr Townsend in regarding this ground as totally untenable. Besides, in aggravated cases of misdemeanor, two years is a common period of imprisonment; and there is nothing to prevent the infliction of three or four years, or even longer imprisonment, according to the discretion of the judges trying the case.

*Thirdly*, according to Mr Townsend, there exists in the Scottish courts "a strange and irrational rule, that no question can be asked in *re-examination!*" And he states that, in this trial, it was owing to the operation of this rule, "that the guilt of actual participation in the murder could not be brought home to the prisoners!" and also that "the formation of the infamous Secret Committee was left in doubt."* Mr Townsend, however, has unintentionally aggravated the defective state of the law, as it stood at the period of this trial. It was then fully competent to re-examine a witness, to any legitimate extent, after his cross-examination had been completed, but not to recall him for that purpose after he had quitted the witness-box, and heard the evidence of other witnesses. It was *this* rule which had such a deleterious operation in the case before us; and the rule has been since relaxed by the legislature,† at the instance, we believe, of Lord Rutherfurd. From another part of Mr Townsend's account of the case,‡ it appears distinctly that a witness, "*on his re-examination*"

* Vol. ii. p. 160. † By the Act 3d and 4th Vict. c. 59. ‡ P. 186.

gave a most important explanation of an answer which had been elicited on cross-examination.

*Fourthly*, English lawyers will be greatly astonished at finding the gossipping account of what she had casually seen of the alleged murder, given by a woman, since dead, to an acquaintance, gravely received in evidence at the mouth of that acquaintance without any objection made, though "it turned the nicely-poised scales in favour of M'Lean,"* the principal prisoner, to whom was strongly imputed the very act of the murder! The witness was a cotton-spinner, who said that the woman in question had died of a fever since the death of Smith (the murdered man). The witness, having heard her say that she had seen Smith shot, went to her, asked her if such was the fact, and, if so, what sort of man it was, when she replied, "A little set man, with dark moleskin clothes." This evidence was mightily relied on by the prisoners' counsel, who had elicited this portion of the evidence on cross-examination; and was allowed to call the wife of the witness to give *her* version of what she had heard the deceased woman say—"That he was a little man, with dark dirty moleskin clothes, and below the common size of men!" In commenting on this evidence, Mr Robertson suddenly called upon his client in the dock to stand up: he instantly did so, and proved a taller man than any of the other prisoners! † We have looked through Mr Alison's

* Townsend, vol. ii. p. 188.

† This gives Mr Townsend occasion to mention a curious incident which, he says, occurred some years ago in an English trial, on the Western Circuit. It was a case of theft; and the prisoner's guilt was deemed to have been brought home to him by the foot-marks of two feet, traced from the place of the theft to his dwelling. His counsel had, to the surprise of all in court, cross-examined minutely as to these foot-marks, their length and breadth, and the depth of the impressions: and at the close of the case for the prosecution, laughed the case out of court, by desiring the prisoner to show his nether extremities to the jury. He had a *wooden leg!* Can this be true? Is it conceivable that those conducting the prosecution were not aware of the circumstance of the prisoner having a wooden leg? How could it have escaped the notice of those who arrested the prisoner, who had had him in custody ever since; and of the committing magistrates?

section on Evidence, in his *Practice of the Criminal Law of Scotland*, and see nothing to sanction the reception of such evidence; for which, we repeat, we are totally unable to account.

*Lastly*, it will be observed, that the verdict of Guilty was that of a majority only of the jury; and as it proved to have been one of eight to seven—*viz.*, a majority of *one* only—on that circumstance was founded an urgent appeal to Government and to Parliament for a remission of sentence, backed by a memorial to the Queen from the prisoners' counsel, and a petition from the *minority* of the jury, stating that, in their opinion, none of the charges were proved! Lord Melbourne strongly resisted the application made by Lord Brougham in the House of Lords; taking the opportunity of remarking, on the illustration afforded by the cause assigned for it, of "the inconvenience of the law of Scotland in not requiring *unanimity.* If they were to reflect on the length of time the jury took to consider their verdict, and the time they were out, and make these circumstances raise a presumption for attacking the verdict, there would be no end of such proceedings." * Thus much for two Scottish trials. Turn we now to

II. Two Irish trials — and those, moreover, really "*State* trials," and of the first magnitude: those of the late Daniel O'Connell and his eight companions, in 1843–4, for treasonable conspiracy; and of Smith O'Brien, in 1848, for high treason. These are the only two Irish trials in the collection; and, but for the length to which this series of papers has unexpectedly extended, we should make the former of the two the subject of an entire article, for it possesses many features of vivid and enduring interest, in the eyes equally of political and forensic readers.

There was something grand and ominous in the position

* Hansard, 3d Series, vol. ii. p. 938.

of affairs in Ireland, which led to the prosecution of the late Daniel O'Connell and his companions, in the year 1843–4. That consummate veteran agitator had been suffered, by a sagacious and powerful Government, to proceed step by step in his treasonable conspiracy to dismember the British empire, up to a point when the bloody outbreak of civil war seemed inevitable. That he was never in earnest in agitating for a repeal of the Union, and never dreamed of being able to effect it, was the opinion of the great majority of thinking persons, whose attention had been directed to his character and movements. He heartlessly adopted it as an expedient for maintaining his political ascendency, and securing splendid pecuniary resources from his credulous and confiding fellow-countrymen. *They* believed him in earnest; that he was honestly earning his income; and paid him accordingly, cheerfully and punctually. He told them that, as fear alone had extorted Roman Catholic Emancipation, so fear alone could, and would, extort a repeal of the Union; and that he would guarantee success, provided the people trusted to him steadfastly and implicitly. At length, on the 2d January 1843, he ventured solemnly to declare that the repeal year had commenced—that, before it closed, the accursed link which bound Ireland in forced and fraudulent union to Great Britain would be snapped asunder. Keeping skilfully within the letter of the law, and relying on the proverbial caution and forbearance of Sir Robert Peel and the Duke of Wellington, Mr O'Connell at length appeared to act upon his own avowed convictions, by taking steps to secure the great result "of all his political labours—the emancipation of Ireland." His monster meetings, twenty or thirty in number, held in different parts of Ireland—some attended, as he boasted, and as was generally believed, by hundreds of thousands of enthusiastic and unanimous fellow-countrymen—appeared at length to have convinced him either that success was within reach, or that he *must* really proceed upon that assumption.

A mixture of feelings—of anxiety, of fear, of intoxicated vanity, of excitement that left no interval for calm reflection—seems at length to have overpowered his prudence, and confused his natural clearsightedness. He suffered a quasi-coronation amidst hundreds of thousands of future willing subjects; and at length boldly sanctioned the organization of his myriad adherents in military fashion. Foreign Governments looked on at the apparent irresolute inaction of the British authorities with amazement; and great numbers of persons in this country began to entertain dire apprehensions, and to regard the silence and inaction of the Government as at once inexplicable and inexcusable. Parliament separated in the autumn of 1843, leaving affairs, with mingled confidence and solicitude, in the hands of Ministers. A tremendous responsibility indeed was theirs; for immediately afterwards, matters assumed an infinitely more alarming aspect. The meetings were held with increasing frequency, attended by vastly augmented numbers, and characterised by speeches, arrangements, and plans for the future, of dangerous audacity. On the first of October a meeting was held at Mullaghmast, attended, as Mr O'Connell himself publicly declared shortly afterwards, by *a million of persons!*—the lowest calculation, by independent military observers, placing them at a quarter of a million! Mr O'Connell stated at that meeting, "I choose this place for the meeting, because it was the precise spot on which English treachery, and false Irish treachery, consummated a massacre unequalled in the world, until the massacre of the Mamelukes by Mehemet Ali!" Another meeting was appointed to be held a week afterwards—on the 8th October—of a still more decisive character; an article relating to it in the *Pilot*, one of Mr O'Connell's newspaper organs, being headed, "*The Battle of Clontarf—the Repeal Year!*" The language of Mr O'Connell himself was characterised by greatly augmented audacity; and the well-affected in Ireland, as well as everywhere in Great Britain, looked on daily with hourly increasing anxiety and wonder, at the course which might have been, or might be, adopted by Government to meet this tremendous exigency. They were somewhat reassured, however, by the vast military preparations going on in Ireland, directed by THE DUKE; and which he, and indeed all men knew, would have been personally supported even to the point of death, by every Englishman, Scotchman, and Irishman, capable of bearing arms and shedding his blood as a loyal subject of Queen Victoria.

That these military preparations filled with dismay all those even most vain-glorious among the Irish disaffected, is undoubted; but they did not prevent their uttering loud notes of warlike defiance. But how long was this fearful and sickening suspense to last? Every post from Ireland was expected to bring intelligence that civil war had commenced. The Lord-Lieutenant and Lord-Chancellor of Ireland (Lord de Grey, and Sir Edward Sugden, now Lord St Leonards) came over to England to consult with the Government, and returned on Friday the 6th October—ten days only before the dreaded Clontarf gathering on the ensuing Sunday—and immediately held a Privy Council at Dublin Castle, the result of which was looked for in an agony of excitement and apprehension by all parties: the general expectation being that the intended meeting would be declared by proclamation illegal and treasonable—and probably Mr O'Connell and his companions arrested on a charge of high treason. In the mean time, their adherents were pouring in hourly from Liverpool and the remotest quarters of Ireland; simultaneously with ammunition, artillery, and regiments of infantry and cavalry, forwarded by the Government. Threats were heard of *foreign intervention* on behalf of those "struggling for freedom!"

Friday evening passed, and no sign was seen from

Dublin Castle. On Saturday the 7th October, Mr O'Connell and his companions of the Repeal Association met in council at the Corn Exchange, to concert measures which might be rendered necessary by any movement from the Castle, where the Privy Council re-assembled early in the same morning. The morning wore away, leaving Mr O'Connell and his companions, in short, everybody in Dublin, on the very tenterhooks of agitation and anxiety; and the impending crisis was undoubtedly fraught with the possibility of frightful results. An inflamed and half-maddened population was hurrying from all parts of Ireland, to attend a meeting which might at any moment be pronounced illegal, and prevented necessarily by bloodshed and slaughter. At length, at half-past three o'clock that afternoon, appeared a printed PROCLAMATION, prohibiting the meeting on the ensuing morning; and within an hour afterwards, a counter notice, couched in the language of a rival "Proclamation," was issued by Mr O'Connell, imploring those who read it to abstain from attending the meeting, and to use their utmost exertions to prevent others from doing so. Desperate efforts were made by his emissaries to give effect to this missive, and with success. The site of the intended meeting was pre-occupied by the military, and the awful consequences of a collision between them and the innumerable dupes of designing demagogues were averted. During the ensuing week additional troops poured into Dublin, and overwhelming preparations were made against any outbreak. Every one then looked for the instant arrest of Mr O'Connell, and the leading members of the Repeal Association, on the charge of high treason, or at least sedition: it being alleged that Government had at length obtained sufficient evidence to justify such a procedure, and had waited no longer than till the moment of their becoming possessed of it, to act with decision. Owing to their overpowering demonstration of strength, and also to the incessant and passionate entreaties of Mr O'Connell, doubtless then feeling himself in mortal peril, no breach whatever of the peace occurred. Early in the ensuing week he received official intimation that he would be required to give bail to answer Informations for "conspiracy and other misdemeanors;" and on Saturday he was required to attend at the house of one of the judges, where he gave the requisite bail, and was then set at liberty; doubtless secretly overjoyed at finding himself rated no higher an offender than a misdemeanant.

The country justly reposed confidence in the consummate administrative ability, and the experienced sagacity, which distinguished the Government of that day; and the calm resolution with which Sir Robert Peel withstood the importunities of both Parliament and the public to adopt strong legislative and executive measures, in proud reliance on the energy of the common law to deal with the prodigious exigency which had risen, was truly admirable. "I am resolved," was his memorable declaration, "to walk in the light of the constitution. If I find the law of the land incapable of dealing effectually with the case, I will not hesitate to ask for greater powers from the Legislature." Would that a similar spirit had actuated him in every other subsequent State emergency! As soon as the course which he had resolved upon had become known to the country, it occasioned intense anxiety. Had he thoroughly considered the nature of the proceedings on which so much thenceforth depended? Were his legal functionaries in Ireland equal to the occasion—one of almost unprecedented magnitude? Could a fair and firm jury be reasonably expected to be got together? And what a desperate evil would be a miscarriage! one likely to affect the tranquillity of Europe! What a prosecution! One against infuriate myriads, represented by nine men, the chief of whom had devised and developed the enormous confederacy, and was noted for his successful astuteness in baffling legal proceedings! But the Government had a first-rate Attorney and Solicitor-General, as well as experienced and very able legal subordinates; they did not despair of finding an honest, patriotic, and independent spirit in Irish jurymen; and felt "thrice armed" in having "their quarrel just."

As soon as Mr O'Connell felt himself entangled in the meshes of the law, he issued earnest solicitations to the Irish people to violate "no law,"—not to be "guilty of any tumult or disturbance," nor be "tempted to break the peace; but to act peaceably, quietly, and legally,"—and then "the attempt upon *their liberties!* must fail." Then he addressed himself to his personal difficulties, not magnanimously, but with a pettifogging pusillanimity calculated to wither the eagerest and fondest sympathy with misfortune. As for ourselves, the contrast between his previous mighty demonstrations, and his subsequent conduct under criminal prosecution, frequently brought to our recollection the lines of old Creech—

"That all may laugh to see that glaring light,
Which lately shone so fierce and bright,
End in a stink at last, and vanish into night!"

In this "monster prosecution" everything was on a commensurate scale. There were twenty-eight counsel engaged! The indictment filled fifty-eight closely printed folio pages, having to deal, in distinct detail, with as many "overt acts," in the shape principally of seditious orations and documents, committed during the greater part of the year 1843. The grand jury took five days to consider whether they should find "a true bill." The Attorney-General,* without throwing away a word, or wandering from his point for a moment, occupied eleven hours in opening the case. The counsel for the defendants, and Mr O'Connell himself, spoke for eight successive days! The Solicitor-General† occupied two days and five hours with his incomparable "reply;" and the Lord Chief-Justice's‡ luminous "charge" consumed a day and a half! The jury took only five

* Now Sir T. B. C. Smith, Master of the Rolls, in Ireland.

† Mr Serjeant Green. ‡ Mr Pennefather.

hours to agree to their verdict of Guilty, and three or four more to adjust it to the eleven counts of the indictment; and finally, the trial lasted for nearly a month—namely, from the 16th of January to the 12th of February.

The interval between that day and the 30th of May was spent in desperate but fruitless efforts to obtain a new trial, and move in arrest of judgment; which was—a fine of £2000, and imprisonment for twelve calendar months. On the 14th June the defendants sued out a writ of error to the House of Lords. On the 7th September the appeal was allowed, judgment arrested, and the prisoners set at liberty! To adopt the terse account of Mr Townsend—"By a lucky combination of an *indictment* partly bad, a *verdict* partly bad, and a *judgment* partly bad, the prisoners escaped"—to the scandal of lawyers, and the amazement and chagrin of the country at large. We were among those who failed to perceive the convincing force of the reasonings which led to the reversal of judgment in this case; and we made the decision of the House of Lords the subject of an elaborate, dispassionate, and respectful examination in *Blackwood's Magazine*, in the ensuing month of November.* We remain of that opinion, and adhere to the reasons for it there assigned. Let us, however, recur to the commencement of the proceedings, which were contested foot to foot, and inch by inch, with a kind of ludicrous desperation—with an unheard-of pertinacity. A brief enumeration will amuse even general readers.

*First*, The Informations, on reaching the accused, proved to have been sworn to by Mr Bond Hughes, a Government short-hand writer: a gentleman of unquestionable honour and veracity, who had been engaged officially to take notes of what was said at the various public meetings which led to the prosecution. He appeared publicly and avowedly in the capacity of Govern-

* The O'Connell Case—Was the Judgment rightly Reversed? No. cccxlix., pp. 539–569.

ment reporter, treating others, and being treated, with uniform courtesy. He performed his harassing duties, as was ultimately acknowledged on all hands, with exemplary fidelity. But behold! The instant that the Informations fell under the lynx-eyed defendants and their friends and advisers, they discovered that Mr Hughes had made a mistake in including Richard Barrett, one of the prisoners, among those present at a meeting, and a dinner, on the 8th October; whereas it seemed that he really had not been at either. Upon this, Informations for wilful and corrupt perjury! were forthwith preferred against the luckless stenographist, "it being considered as a providential circumstance"—piously says one of the elaborate printed reports now before us—"that he should have thus tripped at the very outset!" Mr M'Donogh, Q.C., one of the counsel for the accused, attended before the magistrates to urge their reception of the Informations. They, however, recommended him to apply to the Commission; and the Commission refused to interfere. As soon, accordingly, as Mr Justice Burton had charged the grand jury, in the O'Connell case, on the first day of Michaelmas term, Mr M'Donogh, after the jury had retired, applied to the court for an order, in the nature of a Mandamus to the magistrates, compelling them to receive the Informations. On the ensuing day, various affidavits in support of the application were made by seven of the defendants; and on a subsequent day, Mr M'Donogh made another vigorous effort to obtain a Mandamus, but in vain—the court, however, giving him leave to prefer the charge to the grand jury, as soon as they should have disposed of the great matter then before them. No further proceedings, however, were attempted, and the cruel and absurd charge fell to the ground.

*Secondly*, While deliberating on the bill, the grand jury came into court, to ask that a mere clerical error in one of the counts—the name of "Tierney" being used by mistake for "Tyrrel"—should be altered by the officer of the court: an application quite a matter of course. It was, however, strongly opposed by the counsel for Tyrrel! but ultimately overruled, at the instance of the Attorney-General, on the obvious ground that, in such a stage of the proceedings, no third person could interfere between the Crown and the Grand Jury. At length they found a "true bill," on which it became in law an *Indictment*—but not before one of the grand jurors had exclaimed aloud, "I beg leave to express my dissent from that bill, as one of the jurors!"

*Thirdly*, On the defendants appearing in court, after the finding of the indictment, according to their recognisances, and being required by the Attorney-General, under statute 6 Geo. III. c. 4 § 1, to plead in four days' time, the counsel for the prisoners *seriatim* applied to the court to order that the four days should run, not from that moment, but only from the delivery of copies of the indictment. After considerable discussion, the Attorney-General waived the point, consenting to give copies of the indictment immediately, and to reckon the commencement of the four days from the ensuing one.

*Fourthly*, Application was made the next day for liberty to compare the copies of the indictment with the original, that the defendants, before pleading, might be assured of the correctness of such certified copies. The Lord Chief-Justice thought this a reasonable application, and granted it; and then it was demanded that the time to plead should run only from the time of delivering the *compared* copies.

*Fifthly*, Then was demanded a copy of the indorsements on the indictment, including *the names of the witnesses*, which was refused unanimously by the court, after full argument.

*Sixthly*, Next was demanded a copy of the *caption** of

* By the "caption" of an indictment, is meant merely the *style or preamble*, which is superadded to the indictment, when the whole record is ultimately made up in form. The caption is no part of the indictment; and, when this

the indictment,—a point strongly urged by counsel in elaborate arguments, and decided in the negative by the majority of the court, Mr Justice Perrin dissenting. By this time the last day for pleading to the indictment had arrived, on which all the defendants, instead of pleading Not Guilty, handed in separate pleas *in abatement*—*i. e.*, dilatory pleas; on the ground that four witnesses before the grand jury had not been previously sworn *in open court*, according to statute 56 Geo. III. c. 87. The Attorney-General objected to the pleas being received at all at that stage, which was too late. The court, however, ruled otherwise, on which the Attorney-General handed in demurrers to the pleas, which were argued ably and elaborately on both sides. The court, in equally elaborate judgments, unanimously decided against the pleas in abatement.

*Seventhly*, The Attorney-General then required the defendants to plead *instanter*. This, again, was opposed very earnestly, but ineffectually; and at length, after ineffectual objections, the defendants were forced to hand in pleas of Not Guilty. But was the quiver of preliminary objections exhausted? Oh, no!

*Eighthly*, When the Attorney-General moved to have a trial at bar, and to fix it for the 11th December, he was encountered by voluminous affidavits, and motions to postpone the trial till the 15th January, on the ground that the jury-lists, then deemed objectionable by the defendants, would by that time have been revised. The Attorney-General yielded, on which the defendants insisted on a further postponement till the 1st February. This, however, after argument, was refused, and the trial ordered to take place on the former day.

*Ninthly*, On the ensuing morning, it will scarcely be believed that a renewed application was made for a list of

application was made, was notoriously not in existence. There was, in fact, no pretence whatever for the application, and we cannot appreciate the reason which induced the dissent of Mr Justice Perrin from the rest of the court.

the names of the witnesses indorsed on the back of the indictment! Again the old question was elaborately argued, on professedly new grounds, on both sides, and again the judges delivered judgments *seriatim* as before, and with the like result. A rule was then obtained by the Attorney-General for a special jury.

The battle-field was now to be looked for in another quarter—the Recorder's Court; where the jury-lists to be in force during the ensuing year were to be made out,—or rather the existing one revised; the great struggle on the part of those representing the accused being to introduce the names of as many Roman Catholics as possible. The fight was furious for an entire fortnight!

Then the battle was transferred to the Crown Office on the 3d, 4th, and 5th January, where both parties, with their counsel, attended, for the purpose of "striking" the special jury—*i. e.*, reducing it to twenty-four names, by each party striking out one alternately; and the result was, as might have been expected, from the preponderating numbers of Protestants on the jury lists, that those twenty-four were such. The object of the Crown officers had been only the legitimate one, of rejecting all persons whom they had reason to believe disqualified for dispassionately acting as jurymen, from sharing the extreme political opinions of the defendants, on the subject of repealing the Union. At the opening of Hilary Term, on the 12th January, occurred the next obstructive step of the defendants, which we shall call, resuming our series—

*Tenthly*, An application to quash the panel of special jurors, or to add twenty-seven names to it, omitted on the alleged ground of fraud or mistake. This, also, the court overruled unanimously. At length, on Monday the 15th January, came the day of trial. After no little delay and difficulty, owing partly to various of the proposed jurymen endeavouring to avoid the perilous and harassing responsibility prepared for them, twelve gentlemen were got into the box. But then, behold!

*Eleventhly*, A long, elaborate *challenge to the array;* being in substance the same as number ten, unanimously disposed of against the accused three days previously! The Attorney-General instantly demurred to the challenge, supporting his demurrer with great promptitude and cogency of learning and ability; the whole matter was elaborately argued; and at length the Attorney-General was again victorious; one of the judges, however (Mr Justice Perrin), doubtfully dissenting from the rest of the court. Thus was consumed the whole of the first day! On the ensuing morning, fresh efforts to get themselves excused were made by some of those called into the box; and when one of them alleged old age and bad health, it was interesting to witness the zeal with which his liability to serve was insisted on by the counsel for the accused, owing to the chance it afforded them of defeating the proceedings, by the juryman's becoming unable to serve! They succeeded; and twelve jurymen having at length, after all this protracted struggle to prevent that "consummation devoutly to be" *deprecated* by the accused, been sworn, Mr Napier opened the pleadings, and Mr Attorney-General rose to state the case of the Crown. He performed his anxious and responsible duty admirably. What a position he must have felt to be his —with sixteen of his brethren, pen in hand, and ears erect, noting every topic, every word that fell from him —each surcharged with eager professional rivalry, anxiety to defeat him, and fierce political antagonism! And the pens of thirty expert short-hand writers transferring to paper every syllable that he uttered—to be indelibly recorded, to be universally disseminated, and scrutinised with the eye of fierce and jealous malignity! If ever man, placed in a similar position, exhibited powerful and well-trained faculties, it was the Attorney-General, on that momentous and memorable occasion. In short, this learned gentleman from first to last exhibited a wonderful exactness, minuteness, and comprehensiveness of legal knowledge, and readiness in using it—indomitable resolution, and unflagging vigilance. He depicted in his opening address, steadily and patiently, in strong but true colouring, the colossal conspiracy which he had so boldly undertaken to demolish by the unaided energies of the common law, *and did demolish;* for, though a technical objection ultimately secured a reversal of the judgment, it left the legal, moral, substantial merits of the case untouched, and the efficacy of the common law completely vindicated. The Solicitor-General's reply for the Crown was an exquisite specimen of legal logic throughout—uniformly temperate, courteous, and convincing; exhibiting a marvellous mastery of the facts, and lucidity of arrangement. What a vivid contrast is exhibited between its severe simplicity and sobriety—its unwavering directness of purpose—and the impassioned, imaginative, excursive addresses of the eight counsel to whom he had to reply! Some of these addresses exhibited merit of a high order. Those of Mr Shiel and Mr Whiteside appear to us pre-eminent as displays of rhetorical power, with this distinction* between the two: that the former appeared almost designedly unconnected with the evidence—with the legal merits of the case; while the latter appears that of a well-trained, eloquent, and accomplished lawyer, addressing himself discreetly and ingeniously to those facts which were susceptible of being favourably presented to the jury; and diverting attention from those of a different description, by elegant, feeling, and sometimes very powerful declamation. Several portions of his speech appear to us to justify the extraordinary sensation called forth by the delivery of them. Incomparably the best speech, in a legal point of view, delivered on behalf of the accused, was that of Mr Henn, who was subtle, ingenious, plaus-

* "How superior," says Mr Townsend (vol. ii. p. 515), "to the noisy gorgeous fireworks of Shiel, is the calm planetary light of the eloquent philosophical truths" enunciated by Mr Whiteside !

ible, and practical. If the intelligent jury were to be impressed favourably towards the prisoners, and desirous of seeing their way, according to law, towards an acquittal, Mr Henn went furthest in pointing out such a course to them. Towards the close of his address he disclaimed, with a quaint excess of modesty, the possession of intellect enough to discharge his duties. "I am not gifted with an intellect which would enable me to grasp the vast variety of facts, and the mass of evidence which has been laid before you in the case!"

Mr O'Connell's address was temperate and tame—disappointing all who have read it, as we understand was the case with those who heard it: a mere repetition of the topics which he had been in the habit of urging in Parliament and in public meetings, in favour of the repeal of the Union. He thus concluded:—"I leave the case to you; I deny that there is anything in it to stain me with a conspiracy; I reject with contempt the appellation. I have acted in the open day, in the presence of the Government, in the presence of the magistrates; nothing was secret, private, or concealed; there was nothing but what was exposed to the universal world." This sophism was thus conclusively disposed of by the Lord Chief-Justice (Mr Pennefather, one of the ablest lawyers that ever sate on the Irish bench):—"Gentlemen, it is a mistake in law to say, that in order to establish conspiracy, it is necessary to prove the existence either of *treachery* or of *secrecy*, in order to complete this charge. I do not mean to say, but rather the contrary, that very often both treachery and secrecy do not concur in the existence of various conspiracies; they are cognate to such an offence; but I deny altogether that it is the law of this country that the existence of one or other of such ingredients should be proved, in order to constitute the crime of conspiracy. Secrecy is very often involved in it; but, in my opinion, and so I put it to you, it is not a necessary ingredient in the charge of conspiracy. Nay, more, if secrecy were a necessary ingredient in the crime of conspiracy, the present alleged conspiracy might have been carried on from its beginning to its final consummation, and the parties could never have been stopped in their progress, or charged with a crime of that nature." *

The summing up of the Lord Chief-Justice was admirable throughout. Nothing could exceed the simplicity and accuracy with which he presented to the jury the true points of the bewildering complication of facts and reasoning with which they had been occupied so long. His own impressions of the case being strong and decisive, he presented them with unhesitating boldness and decision to the jury, without, at the same time, invading their province, or seeking to confuse its confines. The attempt subsequently made to impugn his impartiality, on the strength of a single ambiguous expression, "the gentlemen *of the other side*," [when speaking of the counsel for the accused,] was contemptible: it was one, justly observes Mr Townsend, "which a gesture, a nod of the head, or motion with the hand, might at once explain." The jury, after publicly expressing their embarrassment by the number and complexity of the issues which had been submitted to them—but which, we think, were presented as satisfactorily as the nature of the case would admit—returned a verdict of Guilty against *all* the defendants, on the last eight of the eleven counts of the indictment; against three of the defendants, including Daniel O'Connell, on the third count, and part of the first and second counts; and against four other of the defendants on parts of the first, second, and third counts. Had a verdict of Not Guilty been entered on those counts and parts of counts, in accordance with the real verdict of the jury, "all that exercise of forensic ingenuity," says Mr Townsend, "which afterwards perplexed the judges

* We quote, as in all the other references to this trial, the separate Report of it, by Messrs Armstrong and Shirley, (members of the Irish Bar), in 1844, pp. 808–9.

and divided the law lords, would have been stayed. *Sed Dîs aliter visum!*" Suffice it, for our present purpose, to say, that the judgment pronounced by the Irish Court of Queen's Bench was subsequently reversed by the decision of a majority of one—that is, of three judicial peers against two:*—the minority being supported by the overwhelming majority of the judges who had been called in to advise them, and only two† of whom had expressed the opinions subsequently adopted by the majority of the judicial peers. This judgment was arrested, however, on only *one point;* one arising necessarily after all the proceedings in the Irish courts had been completed, and founded on a mere matter of form, viz., the mode of entering the verdict on the record, and which was done, in conformity with the universally-understood practice, for a century and a half, in both the English and Irish courts!

This technical objection, of extremest shadowy tenuity, was suggested by the eminent English lawyers, Sir Thomas Wilde (since Lord Truro), Sir Fitzroy Kelly, Mr Peacock,‡ and the late Mr John William Smith. The point was this. Some of the eleven counts were bad in point of law, and others good; and instead of entering the verdict "guilty" and "not guilty" on the counts respectively applicable to the verdict, the verdict was entered *generally* "guilty;" and the formal entry of the sentence was "for *his offences* aforesaid"—which, looking only at the formal entry on the record, *might* be taken to indicate that the judge had been influenced, in awarding sentence, by bad as well as good counts! All the law lords, and all the judges, including the minority of two, were avowedly taken by surprise, when this objec-

* The late Lords Cottenham and Denman, and Lord Campbell, against the then Lord Chancellor Lyndhurst and Lord Brougham.

† Mr Baron Parke, and the late Mr Justice Coltman.

‡ Now [1854] the Fourth Member of the Legislative Council, in India. It was this gentleman who had suggested the point.

tion was started at the bar of the House of Lords; it had never been thought or heard of before; but it prevailed —and the prisoners were set at liberty, after having been confined, but very pleasantly, and with an extraordinary measure of indulgence, for three months. To prevent the recurrence of such a hardship as carrying into effect a sentence, in case of misdemeanor, pending a writ of error, a statute was passed (8 & 9 Vict. c. 68) in the ensuing session, "to stay execution of judgment for misdemeanors, *upon the parties giving bail in* error,"—a just remedial measure for an admitted wrong. Though the defendants were thus restored to their liberty, and relieved from the payment of fines, and the finding of securities for their good behaviour, and so far the result of this State Trial was nugatory, it was in reality most potent. It crushed the conspiracy at which it had been aimed; and demonstrated, in a way not to be misunderstood, and with resources not to be foolhardily hereafter undervalued, what the law can do again. The bubble of "Repeal" burst; and no one has been able to blow another. The arch-conspirator, Daniel O'Connell, received a blow from which he never recovered. He lost ground irrevocably in the estimation of his once credulous fellow-countrymen; though he affected, such was the hard necessity of the condition which he had imposed upon himself, to have still at heart the repeal of the Union, and made sickly and puny efforts to show that he was in earnest, and that success in the insane project was possible. He died not long afterwards; wherefore we shall say no more about him.

The only other Irish trial in Mr Townsend's collection, is that of William Smith O'Brien, in the autumn of 1848, for high treason. The occurrences which led to it, however, are too recent, and the course, incidents, and result of the trial too fresh in recollection, to admit of our dwelling upon it at any length. His conduct from first to last was calculated to excite emotions only of pity, contempt, and disgust; and while no one could entertain the slightest feelings of sympathy with him, it cannot be denied that, in his brief absurd campaign of treason, he showed personally a sense of gentlemanly feeling, of truth, and honour, which leads one to attribute his conduct, in a considerable measure, to intellectual deficiency. He seems to have been unable to see the absurdity of his schemes, or appreciate the personal risk he was running, and the moral enormity of his conduct. The country acted wisely, and with dignity, in exhibiting a contemptuous clemency in forbearing to take the life which he had so clearly forfeited. He had been taken in the very act of high treason—an act unequivocal and glaring, of literally "*levying war* against our lady the Queen, in her realm;" and his counsel must have been, indeed, at his wits' end to discover topics which might be urged on the jury without insulting their understanding. He adopted the only line open to him, and which was taken in Frost's case, as we explained in the first of these articles *—viz., to assert that the prisoner's object was not of a *general*, but a special and limited character—to effect, not a public national purpose, but a personal and selfish one. "This," observes Mr Townsend, graphically, "was the narrow ridge, scarcely sufficient for the foot to rest on; the frail, slight, ricketty plank over a yawning abyss, by which alone his counsel could hope to extricate their client; but his own speeches, letters, and acts rendered even this method of escape—rather, by the bye, an ignoble one—perfectly hopeless." The same desperate efforts were made by counsel, as in the cases of Frost and O'Connell, to secure the prisoner's escape by means of technical objections: applications to postpone the trial for non-delivery of lists of jurors and witnesses; a plea in

* *Ante*, p. 95.

abatement, founded on the same objection; a challenge to the array, on the ground of partiality in the sheriff—a charge, it need hardly be said, utterly groundless; and a claim to thirty-five peremptory challenges to the jury, according to the common law of England—a claim of course overruled. All, however, was ineffectual—as also was a subsequent writ of error to the House of Lords, argued with pertinacious zeal by four counsel. Sentence of death—the death of a traitor—was passed upon the prisoner; and on hearing that her Majesty had been graciously pleased to spare his life, on condition of his being transported for life,* this impracticable traitor positively argued that the Queen had no power to exercise this act of mercy! That her Majesty, however, had such a power, no lawyer doubted; but, to obviate all possible doubt on the subject, a declaratory act was immediately passed (Stat. 12 and 13 Vict. c. 27), entitled, "An Act to remove doubts concerning the transportation of offenders under judgment of death, to whom mercy may be extended, in Ireland."

We have little to remark on the conduct of this trial, as reported by Mr Townsend. We concur with him in saying, that it "combines the different elements of peculiarity" which distinguished the trial of O'Connell and his companions, and "all Irish State Trials." He forms a very different estimate of the merits of the addresses of counsel in this case. That of the Attorney-General, Mr Monaghan, "is a dry detail of most [un]interesting facts, unrelieved by style, and unadorned by a single grace of elocution;" while Mr Whiteside, for the defence, "redeemed the forensic honour of his country, and struck a key-note of national pathos which must have vibrated through the hearts of his hearers."

Before quitting this branch of the subject, we beg to

* Mr O'Brien has just [1854] received a pardon, conditional on his not returning to the United Kingdom; and is now on the Continent.

express our opinion that these Irish trials, but especially that of O'Connell and his companions, exhibit the Irish Bar in a very distinguished position in respect of their legal acquirements, and their prompt ability in applying these acquirements, as the exigencies of their cases demanded. Nor do we find any cause for censure in their repeated and strenuous efforts to defeat the cases against their clients, by availing themselves of every technical objection which could occur to skilful and practised lawyers. It was their bounden duty to do so—as was done by their English brethren in the case of Frost, and ought always to be done on behalf of clients who have intrusted their lives and liberties to their counsel, and rightfully insist on their seeing that the forms of law are in every respect strictly complied with. None but the most stupidly ignorant can deny the existence, or complain of the exercise of this right. "Technical objections," as they are called, are on such occasions only so many evidences of the existence of those time-hallowed and inestimable rules which secure the very existence of civil liberty, and constitute the essence of an enlightened and free jurisprudence. Let any one of our readers imagine *himself* in the position of an accused, being tried for a capital or any other serious offence—with his life, his honour, his liberty at stake, and believing himself the victim of an unjust accusation: what would *he* think of his counsel waiving all "technical objections?" He would accuse that counsel of ignorance, imbecility, or even collusion and corruption.

We think that the slight specimens which alone we have been able to give, in this brief series, of the mode of conducting criminal trials in England, Scotland, and Ireland, are such as reflect credit on the mode of administering criminal jurisprudence in this kingdom. As amongst ourselves, we can perceive peculiar excellences and peculiar defects in each of the three branches of legal practitioners; but all are distinguished by reverence for THE LAW OF THE LAND, and its judicial exponents; courtesy towards each other; and a vigilant, stern, and fearless spirit in guarding the liberty of the subject, when that liberty is in any degree endangered in the person of even the humblest fellow-subject, and on apparently the most trivial occasions.

It was our intention to have included in this paper a sketch of a great American trial for murder—that of the late Professor Webster, for the murder of Dr Parkman: a fearful occurrence—a black and dismal tragedy from beginning to end, exhibiting most remarkable indications, as it appears to us, of that overruling Providence which sometimes sees fit to allow its awful agency in human affairs to become visible to us. We have, however, now concluded the present series; but it is not impossible that we may take an early opportunity of giving some account of this extraordinary case, of which, even while we are writing, a Report has been courteously transmitted to us from America. All we shall at present say on the subject is, that the reply of Mr Clifford, for the prosecution, cannot be excelled in close and conclusive reasoning, conveyed in language equally elegant and forcible. Its effect, as a demonstration of the guilt of the accused, is fearful.

---

## NOTE.

A somewhat curious coincidence was connected with the receipt of the "Report" mentioned at the close of the preceding article. The latter was written in the month of May 1851; and the trial of Professor Webster had commenced on the 19th March 1850, and his execution occurred on the 30th of the ensuing August. The Author had made many ineffectual efforts to obtain an authentic report of the trial, in order to present an account of it in the concluding paper of the Series. Immediately after penning the paragraph in the text intimating this intention, he left home to make another effort, but in vain. On returning, however, to his chambers, he found a gentleman waiting his arrival, who introduced himself as the Rev. Dr Choules from the United States of America, and a friend of the Honourable J. H. Clifford, the Attorney-General of Massachusetts, "who had conducted the recent prosecution for murder against Dr Webster." Dr Choules then presented to the Author a large octavo volume, with numerous plates and fac-similes, entitled, "Report of the Case of John W. Webster, by George Bemis," (the junior counsel for the prosecution). The fly-leaf bore the words following:—

> "To the Author of the * * * Series of Articles in *Blackwood's Magazine*, entitled 'Modern State Trials,' with the best respects of John H. Clifford, Attorney-General of Massachusetts, New Bedford.
>
> "Mass., U. S. A., March 17, 1851.
>
> "Forwarded through the kindness of the Rev. Dr Choules of Newport, R. I."

Both these gentlemen were personally strangers to the Author; nor does he know how they came to identify him with the "Series of Articles" which were then appearing in *Blackwood's Magazine*. He begs to take this opportunity of returning cordial thanks to the Attorney-General of Massachusetts, for his courtesy and kindness: and of emphatically repeating the opinion, that while his conduct of the entire case was marked by great ability and discretion, his reply appears to the Author as clear and cogent as any that ever came under his notice.

It was only the pressure of his engagements that prevented the Author's fulfilling an intention, not yet definitively abandoned, of presenting to the readers of

*Blackwood's Magazine* a careful account of this great American trial. The circumstances attending the murder are invested with enthralling interest; and it has, to the eye of the moralist, some very hideous features. The efforts made by the prisoner—a man of intellect, learning, and high professional station—to avert suspicion, and escape from the awful consequences of crime, are positively sickening to read of. His idiosyncrasy, also, is a psychological study: and the net-work of circumstantial evidence in which he became inextricably enmeshed, will be regarded with watchful interest alike by lay and professional readers.

# THE MARTYR PATRIOTS:

(LIVY, BOOK XXVI. CHAPS. 13, 14.)

A POEM WHICH GAINED THE PRIZE FOR ENGLISH VERSE IN THE SENIOR HUMANITY CLASS OF THE UNIVERSITY OF EDINBURGH, SESSION 1827–8.

---

"Dulce et decorum est pro patriâ mori!"

---

'Tis sultry noon, Hesperia!—and the sun
Sits gleaming like a monarch on his throne;
Unfurls his dazzling standard in the sky,
And scatters living lustre from his eye;
Each fleecy cloud is bathed in golden light,
And, melting in the sunbeams, sinks from sight.
Yet, though serene and peaceful all on high,
Far other scenes, at Capua, meet the eye;
There, second Rome! thy glory's sun is set,
Thy fortunes darken at the frown of fate;
Ambition, blighted, marks thee for decay:
For Rome can bear no rival of her sway!
   Not Hannibal's strong arm avails thee now,
Defeat o'erclouds with shame his iron brow:
Baffled he quits with sullen ire thy wall,
To wreak his vengeance on the Capitol.
He leaves thee, Capua, to thy furious foes,
Oppress'd and fainting 'neath impending woes.
Wasted by ills without allay or cure,
All hope cut off,—destruction seal'd and sure!
   Crouching, like tigers, ere they seize their prey,
Rome's lowering legions round that city lay;
Each warrior's heart thick throbb'd with fierce delight

While flamed his falchion in the sunbeam bright;
While glanced his warlike eye, with eager pride,
O'er dense battalions ranged on every side,
While thundering rams assault the crashing wall,
And catapults their stony showers let fall.
Wild uproar all without, and deadly din,
Yet wilder uproars raged uncheck'd within;
Grief—wrath—despair—confusion—all combined
To shake and terrify each troubled mind;
Fierce clamorous outcries yell'd from every street,
And drove calm Legislation from her seat.
Lo! trembling rulers quit the helm of state,
And sternly wait at home their country's fate:
Deaf are the nobles to their people's calls,
Quailing in silence 'mid their marbled halls.
Ah! where is Wisdom now, or Valour where,
To check rebellion, or to soothe despair?
A thousand voices thousand schemes propose,
In vain attempt to mitigate their woes;
Wives—mothers—children—weep with ceaseless wail;
Reproachful thousands at their rulers rail,
Point to the senate-house untenanted,
And call down curses on each recreant head;
Till, maddening with their rage, they loudly swear
To drag from home each lurking senator.

Once more, thus urged, the unwilling Fathers meet,
And each resumes his long forsaken seat;
But now no noise of turbulent debate;
Each, fill'd with voiceless anguish, silent sate;
Their only eloquence a tearful sigh,
Lost in the echo of their people's cry.
Each at the other mournful glances cast,
Big with the bitterness of sorrows past,
And dire forebodings of yet coming woes,
Which mortal might may fruitlessly oppose:
Ah! wretched remnant of a ruin'd state,
Striving in vain to rise above your fate—
A state, alas! with nothing but the name—
Sad smould'ring emblems of expiring flame!

Slow, 'mid the silence, rose a senator,
His pale brow furrow'd with corroding care;
His manly bosom heaved the smother'd sigh,
While round his comrades glanced his gloomy eye.
Though melancholy majesty was there,
That once bright eye was dimm'd by deep despair.
As glares the eagle, of her young despoil'd,
Or lowering lion, of his victim foil'd,
So Virrius look'd with stern composure round,
On the full senate, sunk in grief profound:
Hush'd was each voice, each head expectant bow'd,
Like breathless nature 'neath the thunder cloud.
"Speak ye of yielding, Fathers, or of peace?
Are such the thoughts your timorous breasts that please?
Think ye, aside her fury laid, that Rome
Will leave us, rebels, to enjoy our home?
Think ye her bosom melts with mercy yet?
Can she so soon her wrongs forgive, forget,
Unmindful of the blood our swords have shed,
And yonder trenches fill'd with Roman dead?
We, who have join'd our cause with Hannibal,
And driven him headlong to her Capitol,
How can we hope her pardon yet to gain?
Fathers, that hope is frivolous and vain!
To former deeds your eye reverted turn,
If ye her deadly purpose would discern.
When Italy a foreign foe o'erspread,
And dreaded, hated Hannibal their head;
Heedless of him—of them—of aught beside,
To Capua's walls her vengeful legions hied.
Harass'd with famine, death, and every ill,
Firm to their purpose, here they linger still.
Though furious Hannibal assault their rear,
See still their dense battalions thronging near!
Pass'd the Vulturnus o'er, he fires the plains—
Not this from Capua's walls their force detains!
To their own Capitol his footsteps turn—
But lo, they laugh the menaced siege to scorn!
His standards flash beneath her very gate—
Here—at our walls—her consuls linger yet!

The lion for his young will bleed and die,
But Rome, infuriate, scorns her children's cry:
Their virgins, wives, and infants, weep in vain—
Their altars, temples, tombs, unwatch'd remain:
So fix'd to wreak their vengeance on our head,
And such their quenchless thirst of Capuan blood!
"How shall we grapple with such deadly foes?
How brave this torrent of o'erwhelming woes?
Say, Fathers, whither shall we look for aid?
Where are the spirits of our mighty dead?
Is there no god to bare for us his arm,
And from the clouds display his awful form—
Hurl the hot thunder from his reddening hand,*
And flash fierce lightnings o'er yon cruel band?
Alas! such aid we may not hope to see—
The gods have left us to our misery!
But, Fathers, cease to murmur at your doom,
There still is left an honourable tomb!
This grief-worn trunk shall never live to hear
Each scornful Roman's bitter taunt and jeer:
Yon haughty consuls never will I see
Exulting in ensanguined victory:
Never these limbs shall Roman fetters bind,
Dragg'd infamous the conqueror's car behind:
Nor shall these eyes behold their prison's gloom,
To wait in cold suspense a rebel's doom;
Ne'er writhe this back the blood-stain'd scourge beneath,
Ere summon'd forth to meet a shameful death:
Ne'er on this neck shall murderous axe descend;
They shall not break the soul they could not bend!
—Think ye these eyes shall see my country's fall,
Perish our lives, our liberties, our all?—
—Say, Fathers, can ye nobly dare to die,
Ere scenes so frightful meet your anguish'd eye?
For such as shrink not from a glorious end,
My tables now beneath a banquet bend:
One solemn cup our final feast shall close,
Oblivious antidote for all our woes:

* "——— rubente dexterâ."—Hor. Od. i. 2, 3.

In peaceful slumber seal our wearied eyes,
Reposing far beyond our enemies!
One funeral fire our bodies shall consume,
And heaven's own emblem* grace our noble doom:
So shall we all from every ill be freed,
And even our foes applaud the manly deed;
And Hannibal shall learn, too late, to prize
His brave, forsaken, and betray'd allies!"
Thus Virrius with unfaltering firmness spoke,
While not a sound the mournful silence broke:
Despair sate frowning on each gloomy brow,
Mingled with deep excitement's feverish glow.
His dread proposal gain'd applause from all,
But few had soul to answer to the call:
Some spoke of embassies, and some of peace,
Convinced that Rome would soon her fury cease:
Some silent sate in black despondency,
Lost and absorbed in speechless agony:
A steady few obey'd the stirring call,
And follow'd Virrius to his banquet hall.

'Twas eve—still eve; and in the western sky
The sun in slumber veil'd his glorious eye,
Though still the clouds his lingering lustre tinged,
Flush'd with rich crimson, and with silver fringed:
All nature's scenes serenely silent lay,
As though they sorrow'd for the parting day.
On Capua's walls a mournful light was shed,
As gilds a smile the features of the dead:
A beam of parting splendour—sad, though bright,
Doom'd soon to fade before a woful night;
A night, O Capua, on thy towers to fall,
Obscuring life, and liberty, and all!

Faint sunshine smiled upon a banquet hall,
Where sate, expectant of their country's fall,
Stern Virrius, and his fellow-senators;
No festive mirth, no wild carousal theirs!

* —— *πῦρ, τὸ τοῦ θείου σύμβολον ἁγιώτατον.*

A costly funeral feast the tables press'd,
The funeral feast of every death-doom'd guest;
Rich golden goblets of Etrurian shape
Sparkled with vintage of Falernian grape.
With fever'd lips the luscious draught they quaff.
But follows not the loud light-hearted laugh!
Its generous fumes each maddening brain excite,
And fill each eye with wild unnatural light.
Far other cup their mournful feast shall close,
Shedding forgetfulness and grim repose!
Deep, dark, and deadly as the Stygian stream,
Can draught like this such gorgeous cup beseem?
Mantles no blush its lurid surface o'er?
Oh, that such cup should stand such guests before!
Hush'd is each whisper, fix'd each languid eye;
Labours each bosom with the bursting sigh:
Each hectic cheek assumes an ashy hue,
Each brow is damp with drops of clammy dew:
Dim glistens on the board that ghastly cup:
Is there a hand that dares to take it up?
—Slowly outstretch'd is Virrius' steady arm;
With him no quivering muscle told alarm!
To his cold lips he raised the fatal draught,
And of its dread contents he calmly quaff'd:
To each the cup in dreary silence pass'd,
Till drain'd it to its deepest dregs, the last!
Lock'd hand in hand—in one last fond embrace,
Each gazing on the other's dying face,
For Capua gush'd their unavailing tears,
Though far, themselves, beyond its ills and fears!

Brightly and beautifully dawn'd the day,
Melting the early dews and mists away:
And gleams of trembling sunlight pierced a room,
Shrouded in dreary and unnatural gloom:
A sepulchre! with festive emblems spread!
Here, glittering cups, and there, the newly dead!
Here, burnt dim lamps with livid flickering ray,
As if in mockery of the rising day;

There, round rich viands sate a ghastly band,
Conjoin'd in rigid grasp each bloodless hand:
On each damp brow close clung the matted hair,
Shading the livid eye's unearthly stare:
Their lips with crimson foam were crested o'er,
Cold as the spray on ocean's surfy shore!*
No sound was heard within that dreary room,
But all was silent as the mould'ring tomb!
Ah, little reck'd the bright eye of the sun
The fearful sight he rose to look upon;
The forms he flung his golden radiance o'er,
The eyes that gladden'd in his beams no more!
—There, Capua! there, thy ruin'd greatness lay!
Well mightst thou weep in tears of blood that day!

—But hark! the crash of yonder mailed throng,
Which stately Roman consuls lead along:
The thundering tramp of prancing cavalry,
That shakes thy streets and walls, no longer free!
Hark! to the clangour of their martial peal,
See the fierce flashing of their burnish'd steel!
See how their standards flout the morning air,
While waves his silver plumes the Eagle there!
Ay!—triumph, Romans, o'er your prostrate foe:
Your might hath laid, at last, your rival low!
—Wave—wave your banners o'er her conquer'd walls,
And feast your troops in her deserted halls!
Summon her senators to meet their doom,
And bid your lictors with their axes come!
Speak with a voice the slumbering dead may hear:
Bid martyr'd Virrius at your call appear:
Start from the ashes of his funeral pyre,
With all his fellows in their robes of fire;
Then let your legions quail before his eye,
Whose noble soul disdain'd your tyranny,
Sublimely triumph'd o'er the ills of fate,
And fell, the last prop of a falling state!

* "And the foam of his gasping lay white on the turf,
But cold as the spray of the rock-beating surf."—BYRON.

# SPECULATORS AMONG THE STARS.*

"Whatever we talk, things are *as they are;* not as WE grant, dispute, or hope: depending on neither OUR affirmative nor negative, but upon the rate and value which GOD sets upon things."—JEREMY TAYLOR. †

LET us imagine one of our species, at an early period of its history, destitute of any artificial aid to the sense of sight, contemplating the aspect of things around him.

He perceives that, somehow or other, he lives upon a Something, apparently a flat surface, of indefinite extent in all directions from the spot where he stands, consisting of land and water, alternately visited with light and darkness, heat and cold; with a regular succession of seasons, somehow or other connected with the growth of vegetables of various kinds, suitable and unsuitable for his purposes, with beautiful flowers and magnificent forests: while the air, water, and earth, teem with insects, birds, fishes, and animals, which seem almost altogether at his command. There are also winds, dews, showers, mists, frost, snow, hail, thunderstorms, volcanoes, and earthquakes. He himself, equally with the vegetables and animals, passes through divers gradations, from birth to decay—from life

* *Blackwood's Magazine,* September and October 1854.

*Of the Plurality of Worlds: an Essay. Also a Dialogue on the same subject.* Second Edition. Parker and Son, 1854. [A third has since appeared, but we quote from the second.]

*More Worlds than One, the Creed of the Philosopher, and the Hope of the Christian.* By Sir DAVID BREWSTER, K.H., D.C.L. Murray, 1854. [Another Edition has since appeared, but we quote from the former one.]

*The Planets: Are they Inhabited Worlds?* Museum of Science and Art. By DIONYSIUS LARDNER, D.C.L., Chapters i., ii., iii., iv.; vols. i., ii., iii. Walton and Maberly, 1854.

† Works, vol. xi. p. 198. (Bishop Heber's Edition.)

to death: but during life, alike with the animals, alternately sleeping and waking, subject to vicissitudes of pain and pleasure, of health and disease:—but apparently, unlike them, capable of mental action of a high order, and moral feeling.

If he look beyond the locality on which all this takes place, he beholds a blazing body alternately visible and invisible, at regular intervals, and to which he attributes both light and heat; another luminous body brightly visible only at night, which it gently illuminates; and both these objects are occasionally subject to brief but portentous obscurations. During the night there also appear a great number of glittering white specks in the blue distance, which he calls stars; all he knows of them being, that they are beautiful objects in the dark; even contributing a little light, in the absence of the moon. Why, and how, he himself, and all these things, came to be as they are, he knows no more than the bird that is blithely carolling on the branch above him, but for a certain BOOK, which tells him that GOD ALMIGHTY made him, and everything he sees about him; the sun, the moon, the stars, the earth, with all the arrangements securing night and day, light and darkness, seasons, days, and years; forming *him*, in HIS IMAGE; giving him the earth for a dwelling, and dominion over everything that lives and breathes in it; adapting it exactly to his capacities and necessities, with countless arrangements for affording him happiness; and commanding him to be obedient to the will of his Maker. That the first Man and Woman placed on the earth became, nevertheless, almost immediately disobedient; whereby they incurred the anger of God, and their position became wofully changed for the worse. That God, nevertheless, loved man, formed in His own image, after His likeness, with such tenderness, that He devised means for his restoration, if he chose, to the favour which he had forfeited; and Himself visited the earth, vouchsafing to assume the form of that being whom He had *created in His image;* submitted to mockery, suffering, and death, on his behalf; rose again, and returned to heaven with the very body which He had assumed on earth. That though man's body must die and decay, equally with that of every animal, his shall rise again, and be rejoined by its spirit, to stand before the judgment-seat of God, to be judged in respect of the deeds done in the body, and be eternally miserable or happy, according to the righteous judgment then pronounced. This Book, moreover, tells him, with reference to the locality in which he exists, that all things shall not always remain as they are; but that the earth, and all that is in it, shall be burned up; that it, and the heaven, shall pass away with a great noise; that the elements shall melt with fervent heat; and that for those on whom a favourable doom shall have been pronounced in the day of judgment, there shall be a new heaven, and a new earth, wherein dwelleth righteousness. Believing all this, and his inner nature telling him that the law of action laid down in the Book is righteous, and exactly conformable to that nature, he endeavours to regulate his conduct by it, and dies, as dies generation after generation of his species, in calm and happy reliance on the Truth of that Book.

Ages pass away, and vast discoveries appear to be made, by the exercise of man's own thought and ingenuity, independently of any revelations contained in his Great Book. Whereas he had thought the earth stationary, he now finds it, the sun, and the moon, to be round bodies, each turning round on its own axis,—the earth once in twenty-four hours; that the earth also goes round the sun once in every year, the moon accompanying it, and at the same time turning round it once in every month; and that these are the means by which are caused light and darkness, night and day, heat and cold, and the various changes of the seasons! The stars, however, remain twinkling, the mere bright specks they ever appeared.

Let us now suppose our thoughtful observer's sight assisted by the aid of glass, in two ways: so as to place him, on the one hand, nearer to distant objects, and on the other, reveal objects close to him, the existence of which he had never suspected. In the latter case, his microscope exhibits an astounding spectacle: almost every atom turned, as it were, into a world, peopled with exquisitely-organised animal forms, adapted perfectly to the elements in which they are seen disporting themselves. In the former case, his telescope makes equally amazing revelations in an opposite direction. The heavens are swarming with splendid structures unseen to the naked eye: new planets are visible: others with rings, belts, and moons: and the stars seem to be resplendent suns, the centres of so many systems peopling infinitude; and these, moreover, obeying laws of motion the same as those existing in the system of which the earth forms part!

Well, says our overwhelmed observer, it is certainly late in the day to make these sublime and awful discoveries; but here they are, unless my instruments play me false, so that I am the victim of mere optical delusion; the boundless, numberless realms of insect life being only imaginary; and the stars really no suns or worlds at all, but simply the glittering spots, existing for purposes utterly inconceivable by me, which alone mankind has hitherto believed them. But if my telescope tell me truly, the little speck on which I live, is, in fact, but a grain of dust in the heavens, circling obscurely round a sun, itself a mere star, perhaps eclipsed in splendour by every other star in existence, each probably containing many more and greater planets circling about it than has our sun!

And about these matters THE BOOK is silent!

Pondering these discoveries, and assuming them to be real, our observer echoes the inquiry of our greatest living astronomer—"Now, *for what purpose* are we to suppose such magnificent bodies scattered through the abyss of space?"* And at length the grander one occurs—Are there human beings, or beings similar to myself, anywhere else than on this earth? On the sun, moon, planets, and their satellites? Nay, on all the other inconceivably numerous suns, planets, and satellites, in existence? He pauses, as though in a spasm of awe. But he may next, and rationally, ask, If it be so, *how does all this affect me?* Has it any practical bearing on the condition of a denizen of this earth?

If our bewildered inquirer unfortunately had at his elbow Thomas Paine, he would hear this blasphemous whisper: "The system of a plurality of worlds renders THE CHRISTIAN FAITH at once little and ridiculous, and scatters it in the mind, like feathers in the air. The two beliefs cannot be held together in the same mind; and he who thinks he believes both, has thought but little of either."† By this impious drivel is meant, that if this infinitude of systems be made by one God, who has peopled every orb as our own is peopled, with rational and moral inhabitants, it is absurd to suppose that He can have such a special regard for us, as the Scriptures assure us He has: that *He was made flesh, and dwelt among us:* lived with us, died for us, rose again for us; us, the insignificant occupants of this insignificant speck amidst the resplendent magnificence of the infinite universe!

Now, that such a notion is equally irreligious and unphilosophical, we trust no intelligent reader of ours requires to be persuaded; but that there are both friends and enemies of the Christian Faith, who respectively fear or believe otherwise, may be assumed; and hence the importance of viewing the matter soberly, by such light as we have,—as God has been pleased to vouchsafe to us. If we have little, we cannot help ourselves, but must gratefully and re-

* Hersch. *Astron.*, sec. 592.—[We quote from the first edition.]

† *Age of Reason.*

verently make the best use we can of it; assuring ourselves that there must be wise reasons for our omniscient Creator's having given us just as much light and means of knowledge as we have, and no more. He might have endowed us with faculties nearly akin to His own; He might have given us no more intelligence than the brutes that perish: but He has thought proper to act otherwise.

The attention of scientific persons, and those of a speculative character in religion, physics, and morals, has recently been recalled to the question, whether there are grounds for believing the heavenly bodies to be the habitations of rational beings, by the publication, eleven months ago, of a thin octavo volume of 279 pages, bearing no author's name, and modestly entitled, *Of the Plurality of Worlds: an Essay.* Internal evidence, however, seemed to point to a distinguished person at Cambridge as the author; a gentleman of great eminence as a mathematician, a logician, a divine, and a moralist—in short, to the Reverend Dr Whewell, the Master of Trinity College. The work was divided into numbered paragraphs, as is usual with that gentleman; peculiarities of spelling—*e. g.*, "offense," instead of "offence"—and of style and expression, are common to the *Essay* and the other works of the suspected author. We are not aware that up to the present time he has repudiated the work thus attributed to him. On the contrary, he has just published a *Dialogue*, by way of supplement to it, in which he and various classes of objectors are speakers; and on one of them telling him that one of his critics "repeatedly tries to connect his speculations with those of the author of *Vestiges of Creation*,"—a wild work of an infidel character,—he answers, "If he were to try to connect me with an *answer* to that work, which went through two editions, under the title of 'Indications of the Creator,' he would be nearer the mark; at least, I adopt the sentiments of this latter book." Now, this latter book was published, certainly not with Dr Whewell's name on the title-page, but by the publisher of all his other works, and entitled, "Indications of the Creator: Theological Extracts from Dr Whewell's History and Philosophy of Inductive Science." But whereas the "Essay" now before us is written by the present highly-gifted Master of Trinity, with the design of showing that "the belief of the planets and stars being inhabited is ill-founded; a notion taken up on insufficient grounds, and that the most recent astronomical discoveries point the other way;" the author declaring that these "views have long been in his mind, the convictions which they involve growing gradually deeper, through the effect of various trains of speculation;" it will be found, on referring to Dr Whewell's *Bridgewater Treatise*, published in 1833, that these views seem not then to have been entertained by him. In book iii. chap. 2, we find him speaking thus: "The earth, the globular body thus covered with life, is not the only globe in the universe. There are circling about our own sun six* other [bodies], so far as we can judge, perfectly analogous in their nature, besides our moon, and other bodies analogous to it. No one can resist the temptation to conjecture that these globes, some of them much larger than our own, are not dead and barren; that they are, like ours, occupied with life, organization, intelligence. To conjecture is all that we can do; yet even by the perception of such a possibility, our view of the domain of nature is enlarged and elevated." Speaking, again, of the stars, and supposing them suns, with planets revolving round them, he adds, "And these may, like our planet, be the seats of vegetable, animal, and rational life. We may thus have in the universe, worlds, no one knows how many, no one can guess how varied." And, finally, in the ensuing chapter, "On Man's Place in the Universe," he says: "We thus find, that a few of the shining spots which we see scattered on the face of the sky in such profusion, appear to be of the same nature as the earth; and may, perhaps, as analogy

* Neptune now [1854] constituting a seventh.

would suggest, be, like the earth, the habitations of organised beings." Undoubtedly these remarks are penned in a cautious and philosophic spirit; and upwards of twenty years' subsequent reflection, by the light of various splendid astronomical and geological discoveries during that interval, is now announced to have so far shaken Dr Whewell's faith in such "conjectures," as to induce him, "in all sincerity and simplicity," to submit "to the public the arguments, strong or weak," which had occurred to him on the subject; "and which, when he proceeded to write the *Essay*, assumed, by being fully unfolded, greater strength than he had expected." He is now disposed to regard a belief in the plurality of worlds "to have been really produced by a guess, lightly made at first, quite unsupported by subsequent discoveries, and *discountenanced* by the most recent observations, though too remote from knowledge to be either proved or disproved." And further, he thus indicates the grand scope of the entire inquiry: "I do not attempt to disprove the plurality of worlds, by taking for granted the truths of Revealed Religion; but I say that the teaching of Religion may, to a candid inquirer, suggest the wisdom of not taking for granted the Plurality of Worlds. Religion seems, at first sight at least, to represent Man's history and position as unique. Astronomy, some think, suggests the contrary. I examine the force of this latter suggestion, and it seems to me to amount to little or nothing." In the tenth and eleventh chapters of the *Essay*, Dr Whewell, it he be the author of it, thus speaks, in two passages (§§ 12, 20), which appear to us to indicate at once the spirit in which he offers his speculations, and his apprehension as to the reception with which they might meet. In the former, he owns that his "views are so different from those hitherto generally entertained, and considered as having a sort of religious dignity belonging to them, that we may fear, at first at least, they will appear to many rash and fanciful, and almost, as we have said, irreverent." In the latter he speaks thus:—

> "It is not to be denied that there may be a regret and disturbance naturally felt at having to give up our belief that the planets and the stars probably contain servants and worshippers of God. It must always be a matter of pain and trouble, to be urged with tenderness, and to be performed in time, to untwine our reverential religious sentiments from erroneous views of the constitution of the universe with which they have been involved. But the change once made, it is found that religion is uninjured, and reverence undiminished. And therefore we trust that the reader will receive with candour and patience the argument which we have to offer with reference to this view, or, rather, this sentiment."

In this tone of manly modesty is expressed the whole of this really remarkable work; but all competent readers will also be struck by the dignified consciousness of power associated with that modesty. These two characteristics have invested this book with a certain charm, in our eyes, which we cannot but thus avow, after having given his *Essay*, and the *Dialogue*, in which he deals with various objectors to his *Essay*, due consideration. A calm perusal of that *Dialogue*, by the way, may suggest to shrewd opponents the necessity of approaching the writer of it with caution.

Here, then, we have a man of first-rate intellectual power, a practised and skilful dialectician, formidably familiar with almost every department of physical science, in its latest and highest development; an eminent moral writer and academical teacher, and an orthodox clergyman in the Church of England, coming forward deliberately to commit himself to opinions which he acknowledges he does not publish "without some fear of giving offence:" —opinions at variance with those not only popularly held, but maintained by perhaps three-fourths of even scientific persons who have bestowed attention on the subject. Who can doubt his *right* to do so, especially in a calm and temperate spirit, as contradistinguished to one of arrogance and dogmatism? None but a fool would rush angrily forward, to encounter such an author with harsh and heated language, or derogatory and uncharitable insinuations and imputations. A philosophical and duly qualified opponent would act differently. He would say, In this age of free inquiry, no matter how bold and serious the attack on preconceptions and long-established opinion and belief, if it be made in a grave and manly spirit of inquiry and argument, and especially by one whose eminent character, qualifications, and position, entitle his suggestions and speculations to deliberate consideration — that deliberate consideration they must have. "I have presented," says the author, in his *Dialogue*, "gravely and calmly, the views and arguments which occurred to my mind, on a question which many persons think an interesting one; and if any one will introduce any other temper into the discussion of this question, with him I will hold no argument; if he write in a vehement and angry strain, I will have nothing to say to him." The essayist is here alluding to Sir David Brewster, the author of the second of the three works placed at the head of this article.—If, on the other hand, a man of great authority and reputation be unwise enough to run counter to opinions universally received, and that by persons of high scientific and literary reputation, merely as a sort of gladiatorial exercise, disturbing views rightly associated with religion and science, and with levity shaking the confidence of mankind in conclusions arrived at by the profoundest masters of science, he must take the consequences of being deemed presumptuous and trifling, and encounter the stern rebuke of those whom he is not entitled to treat with disrespect.

Now, a careful and unprejudiced perusal of this *Essay* has satisfied us concerning several things. It is written with uncommon ability. The author has an easy mastery of the English language, and these pages abound in vigorous and beautifully-exact expressions. From beginning to end, also, may be seen a subtle and guarded logic; a felicitous and masterly disposition of a vast and complicated subject; a thorough familiarity with the heights and depths of physics, divinity, and morals; and, above and infinitely beyond all, a reverent regard for the truths of revealed religion, and an earnest desire to advance its interests, by removing what, in the essayist's opinion, many deem a serious stumblingblock in the way of the devout Christian. That stumblingblock may be seen indicated in the audacious language which we have quoted from Thomas Paine. If this be the object which Dr Whewell has had in view,—and who will doubt it?—his title to respectful consideration is greatly enhanced. He must be given credit for having deliberately counted the cost of what he was about to do—the amount of censure, ridicule, and contempt which he might provoke. It seems that he has felt himself strong enough to make the experiment; and he almost immediately sees a distinguished contemporary, Sir David Brewster, quickly ascribing "his theories and speculations to no better feeling than a love of notoriety;"* who again stigmatises an argument of the essayist as "the most ingenious though shallow piece of sophistry which we have ever encountered in modern dialectics."†

That Dr Whewell offers us, in his *Essay* and *Dialogue*, his real views and opinions, and that they have been long and deeply considered, we implicitly believe, on his own statement that such is the case. It may nevertheless be, that he is the unconscious victim of an invincible love of paradox; and indeed Sir David Brewster unceremoniously characterises the essayist's conjectures concerning the fixed stars as "insulting to astronomy," and "ascribable only to some morbid condition of the mental powers, which feeds upon paradox, and delights in doing violence to sentiments deeply cherished, and to opinions universally believed."‡ It may be, again, that the essayist having once conceived what he regards as a happy idea on a great question, dwells upon it with such an eager fond-

* *More Worlds than One*, p. 199. † Ibid. p. 202. ‡ Ibid. p. 230.

ness as warps his judgment; that having committed himself to what he has seen to be a false position, he defends it desperately, with consummate logical adroitness. Or he may believe himself entitled to the credit of having demolished bold and vast theories, and plucked up by the roots an enormous fallacy. It may be so, or it may not; but Dr Whewell's is certainly a very bold attempt to swim against the splendid stream of modern astronomical speculation. He would say, however, Is it not as bold to *people* as to *depopulate* the starry structures? It is on you who do the former that the burthen of proof rests: you cannot see, or hear, inhabitants in other spheres; the Bible tells us nothing about them; and where, therefore, is the EVIDENCE on which you found your assertion, and would coerce me into a concurrence in your conclusions? I long for the production of sufficient evidence of so awful a fact, as that God has created all the starry bodies for the purpose of placing upon them beings in any degree like man: moral, intellectual, accountable beings, of an equal, higher, or lower degree of intelligence, consisting of that wondrous combination of matter and mind, body and soul, which constitutes *man*, existing in similar relations to the external world. The mere suggestion startles me, both as a man of science, and a Christian believer, on account of certain difficulties which appear to me greater than perhaps even you may have taken into account. But however this may be, I call upon you for proofs of so vast a fact as you allege to exist, or the best kind and greatest degree of evidence which may justify me in assenting to the existence of such a fact. We are dealing, moreover, he would observe, with facts, probabilities, improbabilities; and I repudiate any intrusion of sentiment or fancy. If God has told me that the fact exists, I receive it with reverence; and wonder at finding myself a member of so immense a family, from all communication with which he has been pleased to cut me off in my present stage of existence.

But if God has not told me the fact directly, and if I feel no religious obligation to hold the fact to exist or not to exist; I will regard the question as one both curious and interesting, and weigh carefully the reasons which you offer in support of your assertion. But will you, in return, weigh carefully the reasons I offer for asserting a fact which appears to me, however erroneously as you may think, of incalculably greater personal moment to me as a member of the human family,—namely, that "man's history and position are unique; that the earth is really the largest planetary body in the solar system, its domestic hearth, and the only WORLD in the universe"? I am quite as much startled at having to receive your notion, as you may be to entertain mine. My great engine of proof, says his opponent, is analogy: well, replies the other, there I will meet you; and the first grand point to settle is, whether there BE an analogy; * when that shall have been settled in the affirmative, we will, as carefully as possible, weigh the *amount* of it.

This is the point at issue between Dr Whewell and Sir David Brewster; who resolutely undertakes to demonstrate "More Worlds than One" to be the "creed of the philosopher, and the hope of the Christian." It is to be seen whether this eminent member of the scientific world, also a believer in the Christian religion, has undertaken a task to which he is equal. He must present such an amount of proof as will require the plurality of worlds to be accepted as his CREED, by a PHILOSOPHER; that is, by a Baconian—one accustomed to exact and patient investigation of facts, and inferences deducible from them; who rigorously rejects, as disturbing forces, all appeals to our hopes or wishes, our feelings or fancy.

There are two questions before us; to which we shall add, on our own account, a third. The first is that asked

* *Essay* (2d edition), p. 261.

in the year 1686 by the gifted and sprightly Fontenelle,* whom Voltaire pronounced the most universal genius which the age of Louis XIV. produced, and echoed in 1854 by Sir David Brewster: "Pourquoi non? Why should there *not* be a plurality of worlds?" The second is that asked by Dr Whewell: "Why *should* there be?" The third is our own: *And what if there be?*—a question of a directly practical tendency. We shall commence with the second, because it will bring Dr Whewell first on the field; as it was he who has so suddenly mooted this singular question. But we would at the outset entreat our readers, at all events our younger ones, to remember that we are dealing with a purely speculative subject, respecting which zealous partisans are apt to draw on their imaginations; to assert or deny the existence of analogy, on insufficient grounds; to overstrain or underrate its force; and lend to bare probabilities, or even pure possibilities, somewhat of the air of facts, where *facts* there are absolutely none.

I. *Why should there be* more worlds than one? "I do not pretend," says Dr Whewell, "to *disprove* the plurality of worlds, but I ask in vain for any argument that makes the doctrine *probable*." Astronomy no more reveals to us extra-terrestrial moral agents, than religion reveals to us extra-terrestrial plans of Divine government; and to remedy the assumption of moral agents in other worlds, by the assumption of some operation of the Divine plan in other worlds, is unauthorised and fanciful, and a violation of the humility, submission of mind, and spirit of reverence, which religion requires.† He considers Dr Chalmers's admission that astronomy offers strong analogies in favour of such opinions, "more than rash:" he regards such "analogies" as, "to say the least, greatly exaggerated; and by taking into account what astronomy really teaches us, and what we learn also from other

* Horace Walpole professed the reading of Fontenelle's book to have made him disbelieve in all revelation!—See the close of this paper.

† *Essay*, pp. 133, 134.

sciences," he will "attempt to reduce such analogies to their true value." We have seen him in the year 1833, expressing an opinion, very doubtfully,—with a "*perhaps*,"— that, "as analogy would suggest, a few of the heavenly bodies, appearing to be of the same nature as the earth, *may* be, like it, the seats of organised beings." He is now disposed to annihilate those analogies, so far as they are deemed sufficient to warrant such an immense conclusion. But that to which he is now disposed to come is equally immense, and, in the present state of popular opinion on the subject, startling. He says, "That the earth is inhabited, is not a reason for believing that the other planets are so, but for believing that they are *not* so."* Her orbit "is the temperate zone of the solar system, where only is the play of hot and cold, moist and dry, possible. * * * The earth is really the largest planetary body in the solar system; its domestic hearth; adjusted between the hot and fiery haze on one side, the cold and watery vapour on the other. This region only is fit to be a domestic hearth, a seat of habitation; in this region is placed the largest *solid* globe of our system; and on this globe, by a series of *creative* operations, entirely different from any of those which separated the solid from the vaporous, the cold from the hot, the moist from the dry, have been established, in succession, plants, and animals, and MAN. So that the habitation has been occupied; the domestic hearth has been surrounded by its family; the fitnesses so wonderfully combined have been employed, and the earth alone, of all the parts of the frame which revolve round the sun, has become a WORLD."†

Let us here point the reader's attention to two or three passages of Scripture, one of which he may possibly regard as very remarkable, with reference to the subject under consideration. "The heaven, even the heavens, are the Lord's; *but the earth hath He given to the children of men*."‡ "Thus saith God the Lord, He that created the

* *Essay*, pp. 299, 300. † Ibid. pp. 308, 309. ‡ Psalm cxv. 16.

heavens, and stretched them out; He that spread forth the earth, and that which cometh out of it; He that giveth breath unto the people *upon it*, and spirit to them that walk *therein*."* "I have made the earth, and created man *upon it;* I, even my hands, have stretched out the heavens, and all their host have I commanded. * * * Thus saith the Lord, that created the heavens; God himself, that formed the earth, and made it; He hath established it, He created it not in vain, He formed IT *to be inhabited:* I am the Lord; and there is none else."† Here the Psalmist speaks of both the heavens and the earth, saying of the latter, only, that He has *given it* to the children of men; while the inspired Prophet repeatedly speaks of the heavens and the earth, saying that God had given breath to the people upon *it*, and spirit to them that walk *therein;* that He had created man upon *it;* that He had created "the EARTH" not *in vain*, but formed "*it*" to be inhabited. It is not said that He formed the heavens to be inhabited, but the earth. Now, this latter passage Sir David Brewster has quoted as "a distinct declaration from the inspired prophet, that the earth would have been created IN VAIN, if it had not been formed to be inhabited; and hence, he continues, we‡ draw the conclusion, that as the Creator cannot be supposed to have made the worlds of our system, and those in the sidereal universe, in vain, *they* must have been formed *to be inhabited*."§ Is not this a huge "conclusion" to draw from these premises? And do not the words tend really the other way, to show that *the earth*, with its wondrous adaptations, would have been created in vain, if not to be inhabited; but that the heavens may be

* Isaiah xlii. 5.

† Isaiah xlv. 12, 18.

‡ Sir David Brewster's book is only an expansion of an article which he contributed to a Northern Quarterly Review; and he has forgotten to adapt its form to that of a professedly independent work, bearing its author's name on the title page. To this circumstance his watchful opponent, the essayist, makes sternly sarcastic reference in his *Dialogue*, pp. 83, 84 (Third Edition).

§ *More Worlds than One*, p. 17.

created for other purposes, of which man, in the present stage of existence, has not, nor can, and perhaps is *designed* not to have, any conception?

We have spoken of Sir David Brewster's drawing a huge conclusion from a passage of Scripture in support of his views of the question before us; but we have to present a still huger conclusion drawn by him from another glorious passage: "When I consider the heavens, the work of Thy fingers, the moon and the stars, which Thou hast ordained, what is man, that Thou art mindful of him, and the son of man, that Thou visitest him?" "This," says Sir David, "is a positive argument for a plurality of worlds! We cannot doubt that inspiration revealed to the Hebrew poet the magnitude, the distances, and the final cause of the glorious spheres which fixed his admiration. * * * He doubtless viewed these worlds as *teeming with life, physical and intellectual;* as globes which may have required millions of years for their preparation, exhibiting new forms of beings, new powers of mind, new conditions in the past, and new glories in the future!" In his *Dialogue*, Dr Whewell thus drily dismisses this extraordinary flight of his opponent: "That the Hebrew poet knew, or thought about, the plurality of worlds, is a fact hitherto unnoticed by the historians of astronomy; to their consideration I leave it."

Let us now, however, follow Dr Whewell in the development of his idea; bearing in mind his own impressive statement, in his preface, that, "while some of his philosophical conclusions appear to him to fall in, very remarkably, with certain points of religious doctrine, he is well aware that philosophy alone can do little in providing man with the consolations, hopes, supports, and convictions which religion offers; and he acknowledges it as a ground of deep gratitude to the Author of all Good, that man is not left to philosophy for those blessings, but has a fuller assurance of them by a more direct communication from Him."

---

"The two doctrines which we have here to weigh against each other," says Dr Whewell, "are the *plurality* of worlds, and the *unity* of the world;" and he "includes, as a necessary part of the conception of a 'WORLD,' a collection of intelligent creatures, where reside intelligence, perception of truth, recognition of moral law, and reverence for a Divine Creator and Governor." * His *Essay* branches into three great divisions, in disposing of the conjectural plurality of worlds, and suggesting the reality of the unity of the world. First, he considers the constitution of man; secondly, that of the earth which he inhabits, its adaptation, structure, and position; lastly, its neighbours in the heavens—the solar system to which it belongs, the fixed stars, and the nebulæ; and as to these, he declares that "a closer inquiry, *with increased means of observation*, gives no confirmation to the conjecture which certain aspects of the universe at first sight suggested to man, that there may be other bodies, like the earth, tenanted by other creatures like man; some characters of whose nature seem to remove or lessen the difficulties we may at first feel in regarding the earth as, in a *unique and special manner*, the field of God's providence and government." † This is not the order in which Dr Whewell proceeds, but it is that which, after carefully considering the entire scope of his work, we shall observe, in giving our readers such a brief and intelligible an account as we can, of this singularly bold *Essay*.

He commences with a beautiful sketch of the state of "Astronomical Discoveries," with which Dr Chalmers dealt in his celebrated Discourses; by no means understating the amount of them, with reference principally to the number of the heavenly bodies—"a countless host of worlds, arranged in planetary systems, having years and seasons, days and nights, as we have;" as to which, "it is at least a likely suggestion that they have also in-

* *Essay*, p. 359. † Ibid.

habitants; intelligent beings, who can reckon those days and years; who subsist on the fruits which the seasons bring forth, and have their daily and yearly occupations, according to their faculties." * IF this world be merely one of innumerable other worlds, all, like it, the workmanship of God; all the seats of life, like it, occupied by intelligent creatures, capable of will, law, obedience, disobedience, as man is,—to hold that it alone should have been the scene of God's care and kindness, and still more, of his special interposition, communication, and personal dealings with its individual inhabitants, in the way which religion teaches, is, the objector is conceived to maintain, in the highest degree extravagant, incredible, and absurd." † Such is, as we have seen, the assertion of Thomas Paine; and Dr Whewell proposes to discuss this vast speculative question, "not as an objection urged by an opponent, but rather as a difficulty felt by a friend of religion;" — "to examine rather how we can quiet the troubled and perplexed believer, than how we can triumph over the dogmatical and self-satisfied infidel." ‡ But let *our* reader note well, at starting, the above mighty "IF:" which he may regard as the comet's nucleus, drawing after it an enormous and dismaying train of consequences, sweeping into annihilation man's hopes, equally with his fears.

Dr Whewell gives a lucid and terse account of the scope of Dr Chalmers's eloquent declamation, his ingenious suggestions, and his astronomical or philosophical arguments, which he deems "of great weight; and, upon the whole, such as we may both assent to, as scientifically true, and accept as rationally persuasive. I think, however," continues Dr Whewell, "that there are other arguments, also drawn from scientific discoveries, which bear in a very important and striking manner upon the opinions in question, and which Chalmers has not referred to; and I conceive that there are philosophical views of another

* *Essay*, pp. 94, 95. † Ibid. pp. 98, 99. ‡ Ibid. p. 103.

kind, which, for those who desire, and will venture to regard the universe and its Creator in the wider and deeper relations which appear to be open to human speculation, may be a source of satisfaction." *

WHAT IS MAN? is the pregnant question of the royal Psalmist; and Dr Whewell gives an account of man at once ennobling and solemnising; in strict accordance, moreover, with revelation, and with those views of his moral and intellectual nature universally entertained by the believers in revealed religion. We know of none living entitled to speak with more authority on such subjects than Dr Whewell, as evidenced by his writings; and we think it impossible for any thoughtful person to read the portions of his Essay relating to this subject, without feelings of awe and reverence towards Him whose image we bear. Not that any new conditions of human nature are suggested, or any peculiarly original views of it presented; but our knowledge on the subject is, as it were, condensed into a focus, and then brought to bear upon the question, What is man, that his Maker should be mindful of him, and visit him? and thereby render the earth, in a unique and special manner, the field of God's providence and government?

Lord Bolingbroke objected to the Mosaic account of the creation, and "that man is made by Moses as the final end, if not of the whole creation, yet at least of our system;" but let us remember, that Moses also tells us that God determined "to make *man in Our image, after Our likeness;*" that God did, accordingly, create man in his own image; Moses, with special significance, twice asserting the fact that *in the image of God created He him;* and he tells us that, after the flood, God assigned this as a reason for visiting the crime of murder with death — Whoso sheddeth man's blood, by man shall his blood be shed; *for* in the image of God made he man. The full import of that awful and mysterious expression, "the

* *Essay*, p. 104.

image and likeness of God," though man, in his fallen state, may not know, yet it may have been known by Adam: and his descendants believe, that it consists in their Intellectual and Moral nature. The former is, in some measure, of the same nature as the Divine mind of the Creator;* the laws which man discovers in the creation must be laws known to God; those which man sees to be true, those of geometry, for instance, God also must see to be true. That there were, from the beginning, in the Creator's mind creative thoughts, is a doctrine involved in every intelligent view of creation: a doctrine which has recently received splendid illustration by a living "great discoverer in the field of natural knowledge." † Law implies a lawgiver, even when we do not see the object of the law; even as design implies a designer, when we do not see the object of the design. The laws of nature are the indications of the operation of the Divine mind, and are revealed to us, as such, by those operations of our own mind, by which we come to discover them. They are the utterances of the Creator, delivered in language which we can understand; and being thus *Language*, they are the utterances of an Intelligent Spirit. ‡

"If man, when he attains to a knowledge of such laws, is really admitted, in some degree, to the view with which the Creator himself beholds his creation; if we can gather, from the conditions of such knowledge, that his intellect partakes of the nature of the Divine intellect; if his mind, in its clearest and largest contemplation, harmonises with the Divine mind, — we have in this a reason which may well seem to us very powerful, why, even if the earth alone be the habitation of intelligent beings, still the great work of creation is not wasted. If God have placed on the earth a creature who can so far sympathise with Him (if we may venture upon the expression), who can raise his intellect into some accordance with the creative intellect; and that not once only, nor by few steps, but through an indefinite gradation of discoveries more and more comprehensive, more and more profound, each an advance, however slight, towards a Divine Insight; then, so far as

* *Essay*, p. 360. † Ibid. p. 360 (Professor Owen). ‡ Ibid. p. 362.

intellect alone, of which alone we are here speaking, can make man a worthy object of all the vast magnificence of creative power, we can hardly shrink from believing that he is so." *

Again. The earth is a scene of MORAL TRIAL. Man is subject to a moral law; and this moral law is a law of which God is the legislator—a law which man has the power of discovering, by the use of the faculties which God has given him. Now, the existence of a body of creatures, capable of such a law, of such a trial, and of such an elevation, as man is the subject, and has the power of, that is, of rising from one stage of virtue to another, by a gradual and successive purification and elevation of the desires, affections, and habits, in a degree, so far as we know, without limit; is, according to all we can conceive, infinitely more worthy of the Divine Power and Wisdom, in the creation of the universe, than any number of planets occupied by creatures having no such lot, no such law, no such capacities, and no such responsibilities. However imperfectly the moral law may be obeyed; however ill the greater part of mankind may respond to the appointment which places them here in a state of moral probation; however few there may be who use the capacities and means of their moral purification and elevation; still *that there is* such a plan in the creation, and that *any* respond to its appointments, is really a view of the universe which we can conceive to be suitable to the nature of God, because we can approve it, in virtue of the moral nature which He has given us. One school of moral discipline, one theatre of moral action, one arena of moral contests for the highest prizes, is a sufficient centre for innumerable hosts of stars and planets, globes of fire and earth, water and air, whether or not tenanted by corals and madrepores, fishes and creeping things. So great and majestic are those names of RIGHT and GOOD, DUTY and VIRTUE, that all mere material or animal existence is worthless in the comparison. * * * Man's moral

* *Essay*, pp. 364, 365.

progress is a progress towards a likeness with God; and such a progress, even more than a progress towards an intellectual likeness with God, may be conceived as rendering the soul of man fit to endure for ever with God, and therefore, as making this earth a preparatory stage of human souls, to fit them for eternity—a nursery of plants which are to be fully unfolded in a celestial garden. And if this moral life be really only the commencement of an infinite Divine plan beginning upon earth, and destined to endure for endless ages after our earthly life, we need no array of other worlds in the universe, to give sufficient dignity and majesty to the scheme of the Creator.

The author of the *Essay* then ascends to an infinitely greater and more awful altitude :—

"If by any act of the Divine government the number of those men should be much increased, who raise themselves towards the moral standard which God has appointed, and thus towards a likeness to God, and a prospect of a future eternal union with him; such an act of Divine government would do far more towards making the universe a scene in which God's goodness and greatness were largely displayed, than could be done by any amount of peopling of planets with creatures who were incapable of moral agency, or with creatures whose capacity for the development of their moral faculties was small, and would continue to be small, till such an act of Divine government was performed. The interposition of God, in the history of man, to remedy man's feebleness in moral and spiritual tasks, and to enable those who profit by the interposition to ascend towards a union with God, is an event entirely out of the range of those natural courses of events which belong to our subject: and to such an interposition, therefore, we must refer with great reserve; *using great caution that we do not mix up speculations and conjectures of our own with what has been revealed to man concerning such an interposition.** But this, it would seem, we may say, that such a Divine interposition for the moral and spiritual elevation of the human race, and for the encouragement and aid of those who seek the purification and elevation of their nature, and an eternal union with God, is far more suitable to the idea of a God of infinite goodness, purity, and

* We have placed these words in italics, in order to draw to them the reader's particular attention; for the "caution" here spoken of is never lost sight of by the author of the *Essay*.

greatness, than any supposed multiplication of a population, on our own planet, or on any other, not provided with *such* means of moral and spiritual progress. And if we were, instead of such a supposition, to imagine to ourselves, in other regions of the universe, a moral population purified and elevated without the aid, or need, of any such Divine interposition, the supposed possibility of such a moral race would make the sin and misery, which deform and sadden the aspect of our earth, appear more dark and dismal still. We should, therefore, it would seem, find no theological congruity, and no religious consolation, in the assumption of a plurality of worlds of moral beings; while, to place the seats of those worlds in the stars and the planets would be, as we have already shown, a step discountenanced by physical reasons; and discountenanced the more, the more the light of science is thrown upon it." *

Should it be urged, that if the creating *one* world of such creatures as man exalts so highly our views of the dignity and importance of the plan of creation, the belief in many such worlds must elevate still more our sentiments of admiration and reverence of the greatness and goodness of the Creator; and must be a belief, on that account, to be accepted and cherished by pious minds, Dr Whewell replies in the following weighty passage:—

"We cannot think ourselves authorised to assert cosmological doctrines, *selected arbitrarily by ourselves*, on the ground of their exalting our sentiments of admiration and reverence for the Deity, *when the weight of all the evidence which we can obtain respecting the constitution of the universe is against them.* It appears to me, that to discover one great scheme of moral and religious government, which is the spiritual centre of the universe, may well suffice for the religious sentiments of men in the present age; as in former ages, such a view of creation was sufficient to overwhelm men with feelings of awe, and gratitude, and love, and to make them confess, in the most emphatic language, that all such feelings were an inadequate response to the view of the scheme of Divine Providence which was revealed to them. The thousands of millions of inhabitants of the earth, to whom the effects of the Divine love extend, will not seem, to the greater part of religious persons, to need the addition of more, in order to fill our minds with vast and affecting contemplations, so far as we are capable of pursuing such contemplations. The possible extension of God's spiritual kingdom upon

* *Essay*, pp. 370, 371.

the earth will probably appear to them a far more interesting field of devout meditation than the possible addition to it of the inhabitants of distant stars, connected, in some unscrutable manner, with the Divine plan." *

"In this state of our knowledge," Dr Whewell subsequently adds, after recapitulating the whole course of the argument indicated by the lines above placed in italics, "and with such grounds of belief, to dwell upon the plurality of worlds of intellectual and moral creatures as a highly probable doctrine, must, we think, be held to be eminently rash and unphilosophical. On such a subject, where the evidences are so imperfect, and our power of estimating analogies so small, far be it from us to speak positively and dogmatically. And if any one holds the opinion, on *whatever* evidence, that there are other spheres of the Divine government than this earth, other spheres in which God has subjects and servants, other beings who do his will, and who, it may be, are connected with the moral and religious interests of man, we do not breathe a syllable against such a belief, but, on the contrary, regard it with a ready and respectful sympathy: it is a belief which finds an echo in pious and benevolent hearts, and is of itself an evidence of that religious and spiritual character in man, which is one of the points of our argument. * * * But it would be very rash and unadvised—a proceeding unwarranted, we think, by religion, and certainly at variance with all that science teaches—to place those other extra-human spheres of Divine government in the planets and in the stars. With regard to these bodies, if we reason at all, we must reason on *physical* grounds; we must suppose, as to a great extent we can prove, that the laws and properties of terrestrial matter and motion apply to them also. On such grounds it is as improbable that visitants from Jupiter, or from Sirius, can come to the earth, as that men can pass to those stars—as unlikely that inhabitants of those stars know and take an interest in human affairs, as that we can learn what they are doing. A belief in the Divine government of other races of spiritual creatures, besides the human race, and in Divine ministrations committed to such beings, cannot be connected with our physical and astronomical views of the nature of the stars and planets, without making a mixture altogether incongruous and incoherent—a mixture of what is material and what is spiritual, adverse alike to sound religion and to sound philosophy." †

Those possessing a competent acquaintance with the doctrines of theology, and ethical and metaphysical dis-

* *Essay*, pp. 371, 372. † Ibid. pp. 375, 376.

cussions, cannot, we think, read this necessarily faint and imperfect outline of what Dr Whewell has thus far advanced on the subject, without appreciating the circumspection and discretion with which he handles the critical subject which he here discusses. It is deeply suggestive to reflecting minds; who may be disposed to note with satisfaction how closely his doctrine, as thus far developed, quadrates with those of the Christian system. He has well reminded us, in the *Dialogue*, of a saying of Kant—that, "two things impressed him with awe: the starry heavens without him, and *the Moral Principle within;*" and the current of his reflections impels the reflections of a devout reader towards that awful passage in the New Testament,—words which fell from the lips of the Saviour of mankind: "For what is a man profited, if he shall gain *the whole world*, and lose his own soul? Or what shall a man give in exchange for his soul? FOR the Son of man shall come in the glory of His Father, with His angels, and then He shall reward every man according to his works."* These two questions (to say nothing of the significance of the expression with reference to the subject now under discussion, "the whole world") and the reason which is proposed to those who would answer the question, as that which should govern the choice between their own soul and the whole world, justify our attaching the highest conceivable value and importance to man, as a rational, a moral, an accountable being.

In the *Dialogue*, an objector suggests, "But in your inclination to make man the centre of creation, and the object of all the rest of the universe, are you not forgetting the admonitions of those who warn us against this tendency to self-glorification? You will recollect how much of this warning there is in the *Essay on Man*:—

> 'Ask for what end the heavenly bodies shine?
> Earth, for whose use? Pride answers, 'Tis for mine.'

* Matt. xvi. 26, 27.

To imagine ourselves of so much consequence in the eyes of the Creator is natural to us, self-occupied as we are, till philosophy rebukes such conceit." To which it is justly answered — "It is quite right to attend to such warnings. But warnings may also be useful on the other side: warnings against self-disparagement; against the belief that man is *not* an important object in the eyes of the Creator. I do not know what philosophy represents man as insignificant in the eyes of the Deity; and still less does religious philosophy favour the belief of man's insignificance in the eyes of God. What great things, according to the views which religion teaches, has He done for mankind, and for each man!"*

But man's intellectual and moral nature being of such dignity and value in the estimation of God, other circumstances connected with him tend in the same direction, says Dr Whewell, and point him out as a special and unique existence, in every way worthy of his transcendent position. He is created by a direct and special act of the Deity, and placed and continued, under circumstances of a most remarkable character, upon the locality prepared for him through a long course of ages. We need hardly say that Dr Whewell repudiates the irreligious, idle, and unphilosophical notion that man is merely the result of material development out of a series of animal existences. This figment Dr Whewell easily demolishes, on philosophical grounds, in common with all the great scientific men of the age; and having vindicated for man the dignity of his origin, and differing not only in his kind, but in his order, from all other orders of creation, proceeds to consider his recently developed relations to his earthly abode. This brings us to the second stage of the argument, to be found in two chapters of the *Essay*, the fifth and sixth, respectively entitled, "Geology;" and "the Argument from Geology;" both written with uncommon ability, and exhibiting proofs of the great importance

* *Dialogue*, pp. 53, 54.

attached to them by the author. Even those who may altogether dissent from his main conclusions, will appreciate the interesting and instructive, the masterly and suggestive outline which he gives of this noble twin sister of Astronomy, Geology. We are disposed to hazard a conjecture, that the governing idea developed in these chapters, was the origin of the whole speculation to which the *Essay* is devoted.*

Before entering, however, on this second stage of the inquiry, and that detailed examination which may enable us to grasp the scope of this curious and interesting discussion, let us briefly recapitulate, and fix our mind on the precise nature of the question, which, since the foregoing pages were written, we have seen more than once the subject of misconception.

The heavenly bodies around us, some or all of them, are, or are not, in point of fact, the abodes of intellectual and moral beings *like ourselves*—that is, be it observed, consisting of body and soul. That there are other and higher orders of intelligent existence, both the Christian and the mere philosopher may, and the former must, admit as an article of his "creed;" but what may be the mode of that existence, and its relations to that physical world of which we are sensible, we know not, and conjecture would be idle. That beings like ourselves exist elsewhere than here, is not revealed in Scripture; and the question, consequently, for us to concern ourselves with is, whether there nevertheless exist rational grounds for believing the fact to be so. The accomplished and eminent person who has so suddenly started this discussion, has, since his *Essay* appeared, † and in strict consistency with it, emphatically declared—"As I conceive the unity of the world to be the result of its being the work of one Divine Mind, exercising creative power according to His

* Since this was written, we have had some reason to believe that this conjecture is well founded.

† *Dialogue*, p. 37.

own Ideas; so it seems to me not unreasonable to suppose that man, the being which can apprehend, in some degree, those Ideas, is a creature unique in the creation." But what says Sir David Brewster, speaking of the greatest known member of our planetary system, Jupiter?

"With so many striking points of resemblance between the Earth and Jupiter, the unprejudiced mind cannot resist the conclusion, that Jupiter has been created, like the Earth, for the express purpose of being the seat of animal and intellectual life. The Atheist and the Infidel, the Christian and the Mohammedan, men of all creeds, nations, and tongues, the philosopher and the unlettered peasant, have all rejoiced in this universal truth; and we do not believe that any individual who confides in the facts of astronomy seriously rejects it. If such a person exists, we would gravely ask him, for what purpose could so gigantic a world have been framed?" *

I am such a person, would say Dr Whewell; and I own that I cannot tell why Jupiter was created. "I do not pretend to know for what purpose the stars were made, any more than the flowers; † or the crystalline gems, or other innumerable beautiful objects. * * * No doubt the Creator might make creatures fitted to live in the stars, or in the small planetoids, or in the clouds, or on meteoric stones; but we cannot believe that he *has* done this, without further evidence." ‡ And as to the "facts of astronomy," let me patiently examine them, and the inferences you seek to deduce from them. Besides which, I will bring forward certain facts in that science, and in another, of which you seem to have taken no account.

As we foresaw, Dr Whewell's *Essay* is attracting increased attention; and, as far as we can ascertain the scope of contemporaneous criticism hitherto pronounced, it is hostile to his views, while uniformly recognising the power and scientific knowledge with which they are enforced. "We scarcely expected," observes one of his

* *More Worlds than One*, p. 59.

† See the Note at the end of this paper.

‡ *Dialogue*, pp. 5, 6.

reviewers, "that in the middle of the nineteenth century, a serious attempt would have been made to restore the exploded ideas of man's supremacy over all other creatures in the universe; and still less that such an attempt would have been made by any one whose mind was stored with scientific truths. Nevertheless a champion has actually appeared, who boldly dares to combat against all the rational inhabitants of other spheres; and though as yet he wears his vizor down, his dominant bearing, and the peculiar dexterity and power with which he wields his arms, indicate that this knight-errant of nursery notions can be no other than the Master of Trinity College, Cambridge." * The reviewer falls, it appears to us, into a serious error as to the sentiments of Dr Whewell, when charging him with requiring us "to assume that, in the creation of intelligent beings, Omnipotence must be limited, in its operations, to the ideas which human faculties can conceive of them: that such beings must be men like ourselves, with similar powers, and have had their faculties developed by like means." In the very passage cited to support this charge, Dr Whewell will be found thus exactly limiting his proposition so as to exclude so impious and absurd a supposition: "In order to conceive, on the Moon, or on Jupiter, a race of beings intelligent *like man*, we must conceive there colonies of men, with histories resembling, more or less, the histories of human colonies: and, indeed, resembling the history of those nations whose knowledge we inherit, far more closely than the history of any other terrestrial nation resembles that part of terrestrial history." † In the passage which we have so recently quoted, Dr Whewell expressly declares, as of course he could not help de-

* Dr Whewell is now almost avowedly the author of this *Essay*; for he not only sanctions by silence the universally received statement that he is such, but since the preceding portions of this paper were written, has allowed his publisher to advertise the work to which we have already referred (*Indications of the Creator*), as by him.

† *Essay*, p. 120.

claring, that the Creator no doubt might make creatures fitted to live on the stars, or anywhere; but the passage misunderstood by the reviewer, appears to us possessed of an extensive significance not perceived by the reviewer; and is closely connected with that portion of the author's speculations with which we have already briefly dealt, especially that which regards Man as a being of progressive development.

"The privileges of man," observes Dr Whewell, in a passage essential to be considered by those who would follow his argument, "which make the difficulty in assigning him his place in the Vast Scheme of the universe, we have described as consisting in his being an Intellectual, Moral, and Religious creature. Perhaps the privileges implied in the last term, and their place in our argument, may justify a word more of explanation.

"Religion teaches us that there is open to man, not only a prospect of a life in the presence of God, after this mortal life, but also the possibility, and the duty, of spending *this* life as in the presence of God. This is, properly, the highest result and manifestation of the effect of religion upon Man. Precisely because it *is* this, it is difficult to speak of this effect without having to use the language of enthusiasm; and yet again, precisely because it is so, our argument would be incomplete without a reference to it. There is, for man, a possibility and a duty of bringing his thoughts, purposes, and affections, more and more into continual unison with the will of God. This even Natural religion taught man was the highest point at which he could aim; and Revealed religion has still more clearly enjoined the duty of aiming at such a condition. The means of a progress towards such a state belong to the religion of the heart, and the mind. They include a constant purification and elevation of the thoughts, affections, and will: wrought by habits of religious reflection and meditation—of prayer and gratitude to God. Without entering into further explanation, all religious persons will agree that such a progress is, under happy influences, possible for man; and is the highest condition to which he can attain in this life. Whatever names may have been applied, at different times, to the steps of such a progress—the cultivation of the Divine Nature in us, resignation, devotion, holiness, union with God, living in God, and with God in us—religious persons will not doubt that there is a reality of internal state corresponding to these expressions; and that to be capable of elevation into the condition which these expressions indicate, is one of the especial privileges of man. Man's soul, considered especially as the gift of God's goodness, is often called his *spirit;* and that man is capable of such conformity to the will of God, and approximation to Him, is sometimes expressed by speaking of him as a Spiritual Creature. And though the privilege of being, or of being capable of becoming, in this sense, a spiritual creature, is a part of man's religious privileges, we may sometimes be allowed to use this additional expression, 'spiritual,' in order to remind the reader how great these religious privileges are, and how close is the relation between man and God which they imply. We have given a view of the peculiar character of man's condition, which seems to claim for him a nature and place unique, and incapable of repetition in the scheme of the universe; and to this view, Astronomy, exhibiting to us the habitation of man as only one of many similar abodes, offers no objection. We are therefore now called upon to proceed to exhibit the Answer which a somewhat different view of modern science suggests to this difficulty or objection."

"The difficulty," he proceeds to observe, with equal force and distinctness, "appears great either way of considering it. Can the earth alone be the theatre of such intelligent, moral, religious, and spiritual action? Or can we conceive *such* action to go on in the other bodies of the universe? In the latter alternative, other planets and systems must be peopled with men such as we are, even to their history; for the intellectual and moral condion of man implies a *history* of the species; and the view of man's condition which religion presents, not only involves a scheme of which the history of the human race is a part, but also asserts a peculiar reference had, in the provisions of God, to the nature of man; and even a peculiar relation and connexion between the human and the Divine nature. To extend such suppositions to other worlds, would be a proceeding so arbitrary and fanciful, that we are led to consider whether the alternative supposition may not be more admissible—that man is, in an especial and eminent manner, the object of God's care; that his place in the creation is, not that he occupies merely one among multitudes of similar domiciles, provided in boundless profusion by the Creator of the universe, but that he is the servant, subject, and child of God, in a way unique and peculiar; that his being a spiritual creature (including his other attibutes in the highest, for the sake of brevity) make him belong to a spiritual world, which is not to be judged of merely by analogies belonging to the material universe. Between these two difficulties the choice is embarrassing, and the decision must be unsatisfactory, except we can find some further ground of judgment. But this, perhaps, is not hopeless. We have hitherto referred to the evidence and analogies supplied by one science, namely, Astronomy. But there are other sciences which give us information concerning the nature and history of the Earth. From some of these we may perhaps obtain some knowledge of the place of the Earth in the scheme of creation; how far it is, in its present condition, a thing unique, or only one thing among many like it. Any science which supplies us with evidence or information on this head, will give us aid in forming a judgment upon the question under our consideration."

Thus the accomplished and venturous essayist steps upon the splendid domain of GEOLOGY. To this great but recently consolidated science Dr Chalmers made no allusion in his celebrated *Discourses on the Christian Revelation, viewed in connexion with the Modern Astronomy*,* which were delivered in the year 1817, nearly thirty-seven years ago: and then he spoke, in his first *Discourse*, of Astronomy as "the most certain and best established of the sciences." Dr Whewell, however, vindicates the claims of Geology, in respect of both the certainty and vastness of her discoveries, in a passage so just and admirable, that we must lay it before our readers.

"As to the vastness of astronomical discoveries, we must observe that those of Geology are no less vast. They extend through time, as those of Astronomy do through space; they carry us through millions of years—that is, of the earth's revolutions—as those of Astronomy through millions of diameters of the earth's orbit. Geology fills the regions of duration with events, as Astronomy the regions of the universe with objects. The former carries us backwards by the relation of cause and effect, as the latter carries us upwards by the relations of geometry. As Astronomy steps on from point to point of the universe by a chain of triangles, so Geology steps from epoch to epoch of the earth's

* One or two of these *Discourses*, all of which were delivered in the Tron Church, Glasgow, at noon on the week day, were heard by the writer of this paper, then a boy. He had to wait nearly four hours before he could gain admission as one of a crowd, in which he was nearly crushed to death. It was with no little effort that the great preacher could find his way to his pulpit. As soon as his fervid eloquence began to stream from it, the intense enthusiasm of the auditory became almost irrestrainable; and in that enthusiasm the writer, young as he was, fully participated. He has never since witnessed anything equal to the scene.

history by a chain of mechanical and organical laws. If the one depends on the axioms of geometry, the other depends on the axioms of causation. So far, then, Geology has no need to regard Astronomy as her superior; and least of all, when they apply themselves, together, to speculations like these. But in truth, in such speculations, Geology has an immeasurable superiority. She has the command of an implement, in addition to all that Astronomy can use; and one, for the purpose of such speculations, adapted far beyond any astronomical element of discovery. She has, for one of her studies—one of her means of dealing with her problems—the knowledge of life, animal and vegetable. Vital organization is a subject of attention which has, in modern times, been forced upon her. It is now one of the main parts of her discipline. The geologist must study the traces of life in every form—must learn to decipher its faintest indications and its fullest development. On the question, then, whether there be, in this or that quarter, evidence of life, he can speak with the confidence derived from familiar knowledge; while the astronomer, to whom such studies are utterly foreign, because he has no facts which bear upon them, can offer, on such questions, only the loosest and most arbitrary conjectures, which, as we have had to remark, have been rebuked by eminent men as being altogether inconsistent with the acknowledged maxims of his science." *

Before we proceed to state the profoundly suggestive argument derived from this splendid science,† we may apprise the reader that Dr Whewell's primary object is to show that even "*supposing* the other bodies of the universe to resemble the earth, so far as to seem, by their materials, forms, and motions, no less fitted than she to be the abodes of life, yet that, knowing what we know of Man, we can believe the earth to be tenanted by a race who are the *special* objects of God's care."‡ The grounds for entertaining, or rather impugning, that supposition he subsequently deals with after his own fashion in

* *Essay*, pp. 193, 194.

† In the *Dialogue*, Dr Whewell states that it was not till after the publication of his *Essay* that he became acquainted with the fact of the coincidence of his views, on the subject of Geology, with those of Mr Hugh Miller, in his *First Impressions of England*, with reference to astronomical objections to Revelation.

‡ *Essay*, chap. vii., sec. 1, p. 206.

Chapters VII., VIII., IX., X.; but the two with which we are at present concerned are the fifth and sixth.

The exact object at which this leading section of the *Essay* is aimed is, in the essayist's words, this:—"A complete reply to the difficulty which astronomical discoveries appear to place in the way of religion:—the difficulty of the opinion that Man, occupying this speck of earth but as an atom in the universe, surrounded by millions of other globes larger, and to all appearance nobler, than that which he inhabits, should be the object of the peculiar care and guardianship of the favour and government of the Creator of All, in the way in which religion teaches us that he is."*

What is that "complete *reply?*" The following passage contains a key to the entire speculation of the essayist, and deserves a thoughtful perusal:—

"The scale of man's insignificance is *of the same order in reference to Time, as to Space.* Man—the Human Race from its origin till now—has occupied but an atom of time as he has occupied but an atom of space. * * * If the earth, as the habitation of Man, be a speck in the midst of an infinity of space, the Earth, as the habitation of Man, is also a speck at the end of an infinity of time. If we be as nothing in the surrounding universe, we are as nothing in the elapsed eternity—or rather in the elapsed organic antiquity during which the Earth has existed, and been the abode of life. If Man be but one small family in the midst of innumerable possible households, he is also but one small family, the successor of innumerable tribes of animals, not possible only, but actual. If the planets may be the seats of life, we know that the seas, which have given birth to our mountains, were so. If the stars *may* have hundreds of systems of tenanted planets rolling round them, we know that the secondary group of rocks *does* contain hundreds of tenanted beds, witnessing of as many systems of organic creation. If the Nebulæ may be planetary systems in the course of formation, we know that the primary and transition rocks either show us the earth in the course of formation, as the future seat of life, or exhibit such life as already begun.

"How far that which Astronomy thus asserts as possible, is probable—what is the value of these possibilities of life in distant

* *Essay*, chap. vi., sec. 27, p. 190.

regions of the universe, we shall hereafter consider: but in what Geology asserts, the case is clear. It is no possibility, but a certainty. No one will now doubt that shells and skeletons, trunks, and leaves, prove animal and vegetable life to have existed. Even, therefore, if Astronomy could demonstrate all that her most fanciful disciples assume, Geology would still have a complete right to claim an equal hearing—to insist on having *her analogies* regarded. She would have a right to answer the questions of Astronomy, when she asks, How can we believe this? And to have her answer accepted." *

The great Fact sought to be established in these two chapters is, that immense numbers of tribes of animals have tenanted the earth, for countless ages, before the present state of things, to which belong the existence and history of man, began to be. That many of our highest hills are formed of materials raised from the depth of ocean, is a proposition which cannot be doubted by any one who fairly examines the evidence of that fact which Nature offers; and the change, or changes, converting the bottom of the ocean into the centre of our greatest continents and highest mountains, were undoubtedly gradual, successive, and long continued. This is one of those prodigious facts developed by Geology, with as much certainty as any human inquiries admit of, and which may be set against some of the grandest facts established by Astronomy: but it is only introductory to another still more worthy of our profound wonder—the successive creation and disappearance of animal life on this globe. We entreat the attention of those of our readers, who have not hitherto devoted attention to such matters, to a brief and plain account of the evidence supporting such immense conclusions.

The masses of our mountain chains were deposited, as sediment, at the bottom of a sea, and there hardened; and consist entirely of *successive layers* of such sediment. How long must have been required for the deposit of a mass of ten thousand feet thick of these sedimentary

* *Essay*, pp. 191, 192.

strata? Surely a long course of ages. But these different strata are not found always lying level on one another, or parallel, but in a totally different position—the lower ones often of steep inclination, while the upper ones are level and wide-spreading, as if the lower had been broken up and thrown into disorder, and then a new series of strata deposited horizontally on their fragments. By whatever mysterious agency these complex rocky layers were formed, however, they contain the shells, and other remains, of creatures *living in the sea*, and in vast profusion, as in those parts of the ocean now most alive with them! And each of these beds of shells, corals, and fishes, must have required, probably, centuries for the growth and development of the successive individuals and generations of which it consists; and it is reasonable to infer that each of the periods is at least as long as, and perhaps far longer than, that during which the dry land has had its present form!

But incomparably the most remarkable fact remains to be stated: that the various series of petrified tenants of these rocky sepulchres, or tiers of sepulchres, are almost all different from those now occupying our existing seas: different in *species*, and different in *genera!* Dead as individuals, extinct as species! Belonging to a terrestrial period, and an animal creation, long passed away, as though it had never existed! The series of wonders, however, does not stop here: these marine relics are intermingled with a vast series of different tribes, *fresh*-water and land animals and plants, successively, and at great intervals of time, occupying the earth, its seas, and rivers; their number, variety, multiplicity, and strangeness, infinitely exceeding anything that could have been previously imagined! Strata beneath strata all swarming with these mute chronicles of past animal and vegetable existence; becoming fewer and fewer in their general types, simpler and simpler in their organization; such as have forced on the minds of geologists and naturalists the general impression that, as we descend in this long staircase of natural steps, we are brought in view of a state of the earth in which life was scantily manifested, so as to be near its earliest stages.* Nor must the reader imagine that these strata are slight layers: on the contrary, several are hundreds, and many thousands, of feet thick! Thus affording an astounding record of the time of their respective accumulation, and during which these successive groups of animals must have been brought into existence, lived, and propagated their species.

"This series of creations, or of successive periods of life, is, no doubt, a very striking and startling fact, very different from anything which the imagination of man, in previous stages of investigation of the earth's condition, had conceived; but still, is established by evidence so complete, drawn from an examination and knowledge of the structures of living things so exact and careful, as to leave no doubt whatever of the reality of the fact, on the minds of those who have attended to the evidence, founded, as it is, upon the analogies, offices, anatomy, and combinations of organic structures. The progress of human knowledge on this subject has been carried on and established by the same alternations of bold conjectures and felicitous confirmations of them, of minute researches and large generalizations, which have given reality and solidity to the other most certain portions of human knowledge. That the strata of the earth, as we descend from the highest to the lowest, are distinguished in general by characteristic or organic fossils, and that these forms of organization are different from those which now live on the earth, are truths as clearly and indisputably established in the minds of those who have the requisite knowledge of geology and natural history, as that the planets revolve round the sun, and the satellites round the planets." †

The question obviously arises, By what agency, and at what intervals, did this amazing series of organic creations succeed each other on the earth? Suffice it here to say, that in the opinion of the most eminent geologists, some of these epochs of organic transition had also been those of mechanical violence, on a vast and wonderful scale—as it were, an indefinite series of successive periods of

* *Plurality,* &c., p. 146.

† Ibid. pp. 149, 150.

alternate violence and repose. The general nature of such change is thus graphically sketched by the essayist:—

> "It appeared that, at some of these epochs at least, the strata previously deposited, as if in comparative tranquillity, had been broken, thrust up from below, or drawn, or cast, downwards; so that strata which must at first have been nearly level, were thrown into positions highly inclined, fractured, set on edge, contorted, even inverted. Over the broken edges of these strata, thus disturbed and fractured, were found vast accumulations of the fragments which such rude treatment might naturally produce; these fragmentary ruins being spread in beds comparatively level, over the bristling edges of the subjacent rocks, as if deposited in the fluid which had overwhelmed the previous structure; and with few or no traces of life appearing in this mass of ruins: while in the strata which lay over them, and which appeared to have been the result of quieter times, new forms of organic life made their appearance in vast abundance." *

The dislocation, disruption, and contraction of the vast masses of previously existing mountains, by which their frame-work was broken up, and its ruins covered with beds of its own rubbish, many thousand feet thick, could hardly have taken place but in hundreds or thousands of years. Then, again, all these processes of deposition, thus arranging loose masses of materials into level beds, must have taken place *at the bottom of deep oceans.* And the beds of these oceans must have been elevated into the position of the mountain ridges which they now occupy, by some stupendous operation of nature, comparatively tranquil, since it has not materially disturbed these more level beds; † and that operation must consequently have been long continued. When, therefore, we find strata bearing evidence of such a mode of deposit, and piled up to the height of thousands and tens of thousands of feet, we are naturally led to regard them as the production of myriads of years; and to add *new* myriads, as often as we are brought to new masses of strata of the like kind; and

* *Plurality,* &c., pp. 151, 152.

† Ibid. p. 153.

again to interpolate new periods of the same order, to allow for the transition from one group to another. *

The best geologists and naturalists are utterly at fault, in attempting to account for the successive introduction of these numerous *new species*, at these immense intervals of time, except by referring them to the exercise of a series of distinct Acts of Creation. The chimerical notion of some natural cause effecting a transmutation of one series of organic forms into another, has been long exploded, as totally destitute of proof: and "the doctrine of the successive CREATION of species," says the essayist, "remains firmly established among geologists." † There is nothing known of the cosmical conditions of our globe, to contradict the terrestrial evidence for its vast antiquity as the seat of organic life, ‡ says Dr Whewell: and then proceeds thus, in a passage which is well worth the reader's attention, and has excited the ire of Sir David Brewster:—

"If, for the sake of giving *definiteness to our notions*, we were to assume that the numbers which express the antiquity of these four periods—the present organic condition of the earth; the tertiary period of geologists which preceded that; the secondary period which was anterior to that; and the primary period which preceded the secondary—were *on the same scale* as the numbers which express these four magnitudes:—The magnitude of the earth; that of the solar system compared with the earth; the distance of the nearest fixed stars compared with the solar system; and the distance of the most remote nebulæ compared with the nearest fixed stars,—there is in the evidence which geological science offers, nothing to contradict such an assumption. And as the infinite extent which we necessarily ascribe to space allows us to find room, without any mental difficulty, for the vast distances which astronomy reveals, and even leaves us rather embarrassed with the infinite extent which lies beyond our furthest explorations; so the infinite duration which we, in like manner, necessarily ascribe to past time, makes it easy for us, so far as our powers of intellect are concerned, to go millions of millions of years backwards in order to trace the beginning of the earth's existence—the

* *Essay*, p. 154. † Ibid. p. 166. ‡ Ibid. p. 155.

first step of terrestrial creation. * * * It is as easy for the mind of man to reason respecting a system which is billions or trillions of miles in extent, and has endured through the like number of years or centuries, as it is to reason about a system—the earth, for instance—which is forty millions of feet in extent, and has endured for a hundred thousand millions of seconds—that is, a few thousand years."

To return, however, to the course of the argument. We hear the oppressed observer asking, as he ascends this "long staircase of natural steps" which had brought time down to the mystic origin of animal existence; his eye dimmed with its efforts to "decipher," in the picturesque language of Sir David Brewster, "downwards, the pale and perishing alphabet* of the Chronology of Life"—WHERE, ALL THIS WHILE, WAS MAN?

Were Europe at this moment to be submerged beneath the ocean, or placed under a vast rocky stratum, what countless proofs would present themselves to the exploring eyes of remote future geologists, of the existence of both Man and his handiwork!—of his own skeleton, of the products of his ingenuity and power, and the various implements and instruments with which he had effected them!

"If," says the essayist, "with the illustrious Cuvier, we liken the fossil remains, by which the geölogist determines the age of his strata, to the medals and coins in which the antiquary finds the record of reigns and dynasties, we must still recollect that a coin really discloses a vast body of characteristics of man, to which there is nothing approaching in the previous condition of the world. *For how much does a coin, or medal, indicate?*—Property; exchange; government; a standard of value; the arts of mining, assaying, coining, drawing, and sculpture; language, writing, reckoning; historical recollections, and the wish to be remembered by future ages. All this is involved in that small human work, a COIN. If the fossil remains of animals may, as has been said, be

* *More Worlds than One*, p. 52.

termed medals struck by nature to record the epochs and their history, medals must be said to be not merely, like fossil remains, records of material things, but are the records of Thought, Purpose, Society, long continued, and improved, supplied with multiplied helps;—and are the permanent results, in a minute compass, of a vast progress, extending through all the ramifications of human life."

Not a coin only, but any, the very rudest conceivable work of human art would carry us to any extent backward, but it is not to be found! Man's existence and history incontestably belong to the existing condition of the earth; and the essayist now addresses himself to the two following propositions:—

*First*, That the existence and history of man are facts of an Entirely Different Order from any which existed in any of the previous states of the earth.

*Secondly*, That his history has occupied a series of years which, compared with geological periods, may be regarded as very brief and limited.

Here opens the "Argument from Geology"—and with it Chapter VI.

That the existence of man upon the earth is an event of an order entirely different from any previous part of the earth's history; and that there is no transition from animals to MAN, in even his most degraded, barbarian, and brutish condition, the essayist demonstrates, with affecting eloquence, and with great argumentative power. No doubt there are kinds of animals very intelligent and sagacious, and exceedingly disposed and adapted to companionship with man; but by elevating the intelligence of the brute, we do not make it become that of the man; nor by making man barbarous, do we make him cease to be man. The brute has its special capacity, which may be carried very far, and can approach to, and exceed human sagacity; yet, however well trained, its progress is very narrowly limited;—and the creature soon reaches an impassable boundary. MAN, however, has a capacity, not for becoming sagacious, but *rational*,—or rather he has a capacity for PROGRESS, in virtue of his being rational.

In LANGUAGE, he possesses a wonderful vehicle, and an awful evidence of his peculiar and exalted condition and endowment.

"His bodily organs can, by a few scarcely perceptible motions, shape the air into sounds which express the kinds, properties, actions, and relation of things, under thousands of aspects, in forms infinitely more general and recondite than those in which they present themselves to his senses; and he can, by means of these forms, aided by the use of his senses, explore the boundless regions of space, the far recesses of past time, the order of nature, the working of the Author of nature. This man does, by the exercise of his reason, and by the use of language, a necessary implement of his reason for such purposes."

That brutes have anything which can be termed LANGUAGE, in the sense here spoken of—as admitting of *general* expressions, abstractions, address to number, eloquence—is utterly at variance with any interpretation we can put upon their proceedings. The broad distinction between instinct and reason, however obscure it may be, yet seems to be described most simply, by saying that the brutes do not apprehend their impressions *under general forms*, and that man does. Brutes are shut up in their sphere of sensation; passing from one impression to another by various associations, established by circumstances, but still having access to no wider intellectual region, through which lie lines of transition purely abstract and mental. Nor need we be disturbed in our conclusions by observing the condition of savage and uncultivated tribes, ancient or modern—the Scythians and Barbarians, the Australians and Negroes. The history of man, in the earliest times, is as truly a history of a wonderful, intellectual, social, political, spiritual creature, as it is at present. The savage and ignorant is not the state of nature out of which civilised life has everywhere emerged: their savage condition is one rather of civilization degraded and lost, than of civilization incipient and prospective. And even were it to be assumed to be otherwise—that man, naturally savage, had a tendency to become civilized—that TENDENCY is an endowment no less wonderful than those endowments which civilization exhibits.

"The capacity is as extraordinary as the developed result, for the capacity involves the result. If savage man be the germ of the most highly civilized man, he differs from all other animal germs, as man differs from brute. And add to this again, that, in the tribes which we call savage, and whose condition most differs in external circumstances from ours, there are, after all, a vast mass of human attributes; thought, purpose, language, family relations; generally property, law, government, contract, arts, and knowledge, to no small extent; and in almost every case, religion. Even uncivilized man is an intellectual, moral, social, religious creature; nor is there, in his condition, any reason why he may not be a spiritual creature, in the highest sense in which the most civilized man can be so."

When, however, we know not only what man is, but what he may become, both intellectually and morally, as we have already seen; when we cast our mind's eye over the history of the civilized section of our race, wherever authentic records of their sayings and doings exist, we find repeated and radiant instances of intellectual and moral greatness, rising into sublimity: such as compel us to admit, that man is incomparably the most perfect and highly endowed creature which appears to have ever existed on the earth.

"How far previous periods of animal existence were a necessary preparation of the earth as the habitation of man, or a gradual progression towards his existence, we need not now inquire. But this, at least, we may say, that man, now that he is here, forms a climax to all that has preceded; a term incomparably exceeding in value all the previous parts of the series; a complex and ornate capital to the subjacent column; a personage of vastly greater dignity and importance than all the preceding line of the procession." *

If we are thus to regard man as the climax of the

* *Essay*, pp. 198, 199.

creation in space, as in time, "can we point out any characters," finally asks the essayist, "which may tend to make it conceivable that the Creator should thus distinguish him, and care for him—should prepare his habitation, if it be so, by ages of chaotic and rudimentary life, and by accompanying orbs of brute and barren matter? If man be thus the head, the crowned head of the creation, is he worthy to be thus elevated? Has he any qualities which make it conceivable that, with such an array of preparation and accompaniment"—the reader will note the sudden and perhaps artful introduction of these elements of the question, the "*accompanying orbs!*" —"he should be placed upon the earth, his throne? Does any answer *now* occur to us, after the views which have been presented to us? That answer," continues the essayist, "is the one which has been already given:" the transcendent intellectual, moral, and religious character of man—such as warrants him in believing that God in very deed is not only mindful of him, but visits him."*

This may be, the objector is conceived to say; but my difficulty haunts and harasses me: that, while man's residence is, with reference to the countless glistening orbs revealed by Astronomy, scarcely in the proportion of a single grain of sand to the entire terraqueous structure of our globe, I am required to believe that the Almighty has dealt with him, and with the speck in which he resides, in the awfully exceptional manner asserted in the Scriptures. Let us here remind the reader of a coarser, and an insolent and blasphemous, expression of this "difficulty" —or as he would have it, impossibility—by Thomas Paine, already quoted:—†

"The system of a plurality of worlds renders the Christian faith at once little and ridiculous, and scatters it in the mind like feathers in the air: the two beliefs cannot be held together in the same mind." With such an opponent Dr Whewell expressly states, as we have seen,

* *Essay*, p. 203. † *Ante*, p. 388.

that he has no concern; he deals with a "difficulty felt by a friend:" wishing "rather to examine how to quiet the troubled and perplexed believer, than how to triumph over the dogmatical and self-satisfied unbeliever."

"Let the difficulty," he says, "be put in any way the objector pleases:" and the following four sections are worthy of a reflecting reader's best attention.

I. Is it that it is unworthy of the greatness and majesty of God, according to our conception of Him, to bestow such peculiar care on so SMALL A PART of His creation?*

But a narrow inspection of the atom of space assigned to man, proves that He *has* done so. He has made the period of mankind, though only a moment in the ages of animal life, the only period of Intelligence, Morality, Religion. If it be contrary to OUR conception of Him, to suppose Him to have done so, it is plain that these conceptions are wrong. God has not judged as to what is worthy of Him, as we have presumed to judge. He has deemed it worthy of Himself to bestow upon man this special care, though he occupy so small a portion of TIME:—why not, then, though he occupy so small a portion of SPACE?

II. Or is the difficulty this: That supposing the earth, alone, to be occupied by inhabitants, all the other globes of the universe are WASTED?—turned to NO PURPOSE?*

Is "waste" of this kind to be considered unsuited to the character of our Creator? But here again we have the like "waste" in the occupation of this earth. All its previous ages, its seas and its continents, have been "wasted" upon mere brute life: often, apparently, on the lowest, the least conscious forms of life:—upon sponges, coral, shell-fish. Why, then, should not the seas and continents of other planets be occupied with life of this order, or with no life at all? Who shall tell how many ages elapsed before this earth was tenanted by life at all?

* *Essay*, p. 194. † Ibid. p. 195.

Will the occupation of a spot of land, or a little water, by the life of a sponge, a coral, or an oyster, save it from being "wasted?" If a spot of rock, or water, be sufficiently employed, by its being the mere seat of organization, of however low and simple a type, why not, by its being the mere seat of attraction? cohesion? crystalline power? All parts of the universe appear pervaded by attraction, by forces of aggregation and atomic relation, by light and heat: why may not these be sufficient, in the eyes of the Creator, to prevent the space from being "wasted," as, during a great part of the earth's past history, and over vast portions of its mass in its present form, they are, as far as we are able to discover, actually held by Him to be sufficient? since these powers, or forces, appear all that occupy such portions! This notion, therefore, of the improbability of there being in the universe so vast an amount of "waste" spaces or "waste" bodies, as is implied in the notion that the earth alone is the seat of life, or of intelligence, is confuted by matter of fact, existing, in respect of vast spaces, waste districts, and especially waste times, upon our own earth. The *avoidance* of such "waste," according to our notions of waste, is no part of the economy of creation, so far as we can discern that economy in its most certain exemplification.

III. Or is the difficulty this: That giving such a peculiar dignity and importance to the earth is CONTRARY TO THE ANALOGY OF CREATION?*

This objection, be it remembered, *assumes* that there are so many globes similar to the earth, and like her revolving,—some accompanied as she is, by satellites,—on their axis, and that therefore it is reasonable to suppose the destination and office of all the same; that there are so many stars, each, like our sun, a source of light, probably also of heat; and that it is consequently reasonable to suppose their light and heat, like his, imparted, as from

* *Essay*, p. 196.

so many centres of systems, to uphold life; and that all this affords strong ground for believing all such planets, as well those of our own as of other systems, inhabited like our planet.

But the essayist again directs the eye of the questioner to the state of our own planet, as demonstrated by Geology, in order to show the precariousness, if not futility, of supposing such an analogy to exist. It would lead us to a palpably false conclusion, viz., that during all the vast successive periods of the Earth's history, that Earth was occupied with life of the same order, nay, even, that since the Earth is NOW the seat of an intelligent population, it must have been so in all its former conditions. For it was then able, and adapted, to support animal life, and that of creatures pretty closely resembling man* in physical structure. Nevertheless, if evidence go for anything, the Earth did not do so! "Even," says Dr Whewell, "those geologists who have dwelt most on the discovery of fossil monkeys, and other animals nearest to man, have not dreamed that there existed, before him, a race of rational, intelligent, and progressive creatures." † Here, however, the acute essayist is mistaken; as we shall presently see Sir David Brewster revelling in such a dream. As, then, the notion that one period of time in the Earth's history must resemble another in the character of its population, because it resembles it in physical conditions, is negatived by the history of the Earth itself; so the notion that one part *of the universe* must resemble another in its population, because it has a resemblance in physical conditions, is negatived, as a law of creation. Analogy really affords no support to such a notion.

IV. Nay, continues Dr Whewell, ‡ we may go further: instead of the analogy of creation pointing to such entire resemblance of similar parts, it points in the opposite direction: it is not entire resemblance, but universal

* Even of monkeys there have been found fossil remains.

† *Essay*, p. 197. ‡ Ibid. p. 198.

difference, that we discover: not the repetition of exactly similar cases, but a series of cases perpetually dissimilar, presents itself: not constancy, but change, perhaps advance: not one permanent and pervading scheme, but preparation, and completion of successive schemes: not uniformity, and a fixed type of existences, but progression and a climax.

Viewing the advent of Man, and what preceded that advent, it seems the analogy of nature that there should be inferior, as well as superior, provinces in the universe, and that the inferior may occupy an immensely larger portion of Time, than the superior. Why not, then, of Space?

"The earth was brute and inert, compared with its present condition; dark and chaotic, so far as the light of reason and intelligence are concerned, for countless centuries before man was created. Why then may not other parts of creation be still in this brute and inert and chaotic state, while the earth is under the influence of a higher exercise of creative power? If the earth was for ages a turbid abyss of lava and of mud, why may not Mars or Saturn be so still? If the germs of life were gradually and at long intervals inserted in the terrestrial slime, why may they not be just inserted, or not yet inserted, in Jupiter? Or why should we assume that the condition of these planets resembles ours, even so far as such suppositions imply? Why may they not, some or all of them, be barren masses of stone and metal, slag and scoriæ, dust and cinders? That some of them are composed of such materials, we have better reason to believe, than we have to believe anything else respecting their physical constitution, as we shall hereafter show. If, then, the earth be the sole inhabitated spot in the work of creation, the oasis in the desert of our system, there is nothing in this contrary to the analogy of creation. But if, in some way which perhaps we cannot discover, the earth obtained, for accompaniments, mere chaotic and barren masses, as conditions of coming into its present state: as it may have required, for accompaniments, the brute and imperfect races of former animals, as conditions of coming into its present state, as the habitation of man; the analogy is against, and not in favour of, the belief that they too (the other masses, the planets, &c.) are habitations. The possibility that the planets are such rude masses, is quite as tenable, on astronomical grounds, as the possibility that the planets resemble the earth, in matters of which astronomy can tell us nothing. We say, therefore, that the example of geology refutes the argument drawn from the supposed analogy of one part of the universe with another; and suggests a strong suspicion that the force of analogy, better known, may tend *in the opposite direction.*" *

We have now gone through a large portion, embracing two of the three sections into which we had divided this startling *Essay;* presenting as full and fair an account of it as is consistent with our limits. Though the author professes that he "does not pretend to disprove the Plurality of Worlds, but to deny the existence of arguments making the doctrine probable," his undisguised object is to assign cogent reasons for holding the opposite to be the true doctrine—the Unity of the World. What has gone before is, moreover, on the assumption that the other bodies of the universe are fitted, equally with the Earth, to be the abodes of life. Before passing on, however, to the remaining section of the *Essay*, which is decidedly hostile to that assumption, let us here introduce on the scene Dr Whewell's only hitherto avowed antagonist, Sir David Brewster.

Though it is impossible to treat otherwise than with much consideration whatever is published by this gentleman, we must express our regret, if on only his own account, that he did not more deliberately approach so formidable an opponent as Dr Whewell, and, as we are compelled to add, in a more calm and courteous spirit. We never read a performance less calculated than this *Essay*,—from its modesty and moderation of tone, and the grave and abstract nature of the topics which it discusses with such powerful logic, and such a profusion of knowledge of every kind,—to provoke an *acrimonious* (!) answer. It is happily rare, in recent times, for one of two philosophic disputants, to speak, as does Sir David Brewster, of the other's "exhibiting an amount of knowledge so massive as occasionally to smother his reason;"† "to

* *Essay*, pp. 199, 200.

† *More Worlds than One*, p. 237 (we quote from the first edition).

ascribe his sentiments only to some morbid condition of the mental powers, which feeds upon paradox, and delights in doing violence to sentiments deeply cherished, and to opinions universally believed;"* to characterise some of his reasonings as "dialectics in which a large dose of banter and ridicule is seasoned with a little condiment of science;"† and an elaborate argument, of great strength and originality, whether sound or not, as "the most ingenious, though shallow piece of sophistry which *we!* (Sir David Brewster) have encountered in modern times;"‡ to refer his "theories and speculations to no better a feeling than a love of notoriety."§ It is not to be supposed that Sir David was not aware who his opponent was;‖ a circumstance which may well occasion extreme surprise at the tone adopted throughout *More Worlds than One.* In his preface he assigns, as a cause of his anger, that he found that "the author" of the *Essay,* "under a title calculated to mislead the public, had made an elaborate attack upon opinions consecrated, as Sir David had thought, by reason and revelation;"—that the author had not only adopted a theory (the Nebular) so universally condemned as a dangerous speculation, "but had taken a view of the condition of the solar system calculated to disparage the science of astronomy, and throw a doubt over the noblest of its truths." We dismiss this topic with a repetition of our regret, that so splendid a subject was not approached in a serener spirit; that greater respect was not shown by a contemporary for one of the most eminent men of the age; and that sufficient time was not taken, in order to avoid divers

* *More Worlds than One,* p. 230. † Ibid. p. 240.
‡ Ibid. p. 202. § Ibid. p. 199.

‖ In fact, in a note to page 247, Sir David thus slily alludes to those "conjectures" of Dr Whewell in his *Bridgewater Treatise,* to which we have referred, *ante,* pp. 390 391 :—"A very different opinion is stated by Dr Whewell, in his *Bridgewater Treatise;*" adding, after citing the passages, "The rest of the chapter, 'On the Vastness of the Universe,' is well worthy of the perusal of the reader, and forms a striking contrast with the opinions of the essayist."—This is perfectly fair, and also amusing.

surprising *maculæ*, occurring in even the composition, and certain rash, unguarded, and highly objectionable expressions and speculations.

If Dr Whewell may be regarded as (*pace tanti viri!*) a sort of Star-Smasher, his opponent is in very truth a Star-Peopler. Though he admits that "there are some difficulties to be removed, and some additional analogies to be adduced, before the mind can admit the startling proposition* that the Sun, Moon, and all the satellites, are inhabited spheres"—yet he believes that they are:† that all the supposed planets of their respective systems are so; as well as all the single stars, double stars, and *nebulæ*, with all planets and satellites circling about them! —though "our *faltering reason utterly fails* us!" he owns,‡ "when called on to believe that even the *Nebulæ* must be surrendered to life and reason! Wherever there is matter *there must* be life!" One can by this time almost pardon the excitement, the alarm rather, and anger with which Sir David ruefully beheld Dr Whewell go forth on his exterminating expedition through Infinitude! It was like a father gazing on the ruthless slaughter of his offspring. Planet after planet, satellite after satellite, star after star, sun after sun, single suns and double suns, system after system, nebula after nebula, all disappeared before this sidereal Quixote! As for Jupiter and Saturn, the pet planets of Sir David, they were dealt with in a way perfectly shocking! The former turned out, to the disordered optics (as Sir David would say) and unsteady brain of the essayist, to be a sphere of water, with perhaps a few cinders at the centre, and peopled "with cartilaginous and glutinous monsters—boneless, watery, pulpy creatures, floating in the fluid;" while poor Saturn may be supposed turning aghast on being told that, for all his grand appearance, he was little else than a sphere of vapour, with a little water, tenanted, if at all, by "aqueous, gelatinous creatures, too sluggish almost to

* *More Worlds than One*, p. 98. † Ibid. p. 108. ‡ Ibid. p. 166.

be deemed alive, floating in their ice-cold waters, shrouded for ever by their humid skies!" But talk hereafter of the pensive Moon? "She is a mere cinder! a collection of sheets of rigid slag, and inactive craters!" This could be borne no longer; so thus Sir David pours forth the grief and indignation of the Soul Astronomic, in a passage fraught with the spirit, and embodying the results, of his whole book, and which we give, as evidently laboured by the author, as far as his perturbation permitted, with peculiar care.

"Those ungenial minds that can be brought to believe that the earth is the only inhabited body in the universe, will have no difficulty in conceiving that it also might have been without inhabitants. Nay, if such minds are imbued with geological truth, they must admit that for millions of years the earth was without inhabitants; and hence we are led to the extraordinary result, that for millions of years there was not an intelligent creature in the vast dominions of the universal King; and that before the formation of the protozoic strata, there was neither a plant nor an animal throughout the infinity of space! During this long period of universal death, when Nature herself was asleep—the sun, with his magnificent attendants—the planets, with their faithful satellites—the stars in the binary systems—the solar system itself, were performing their daily, their annual, and their secular movements unseen, unheeded, and fulfilling no purpose that human reason can conceive; lamps lighting nothing—fires heating nothing—waters quenching nothing—clouds screening nothing—breezes fanning nothing—and everything around, mountain and valley, hill and dale, earth and ocean, all meaning nothing.

'The stars
Did wander darkling in the eternal space.'

To our apprehension, such a condition of the earth, of the solar system, and of the sidereal universe, would be the same as that of our own globe if all its vessels of war and of commerce were traversing its seas with empty cabins and freightless holds; as if all the railways on its surface were in full activity without passengers and goods; and all our machinery beating the air and gnashing their iron teeth without work performed. A house without tenants, a city without citizens, present to our minds the same idea as a planet without life, and a universe without inhabitants. Why the house was built, why the city was founded, why the planet was made, and why the universe was created, it would be difficult even to conjecture. Equally great would be the difficulty were the planets shapeless lumps of matter, poised in ether, and still and motionless as the grave. But when we consider them as chiselled spheres, and teeming with inorganic beauty, and in full mechanical activity, performing their appointed motions with such miraculous precision that their days and their years never err a second of time in hundreds of centuries, the difficulty of believing them to be without life is, if possible, immeasurably increased. To conceive any one material globe, whether a gigantic clod slumbering in space, or a noble planet equipped like our own, and duly performing its appointed task, to have no living occupants, or not in a state of preparation to receive them, seems to us one of those notions which could be harboured only in an ill-educated and ill-regulated mind—a mind without faith and without hope: but to conceive a whole universe of moving and revolving worlds in such a category, indicates, in our apprehension, a mind dead to feeling and shorn of reason." *

"It is doubtless possible," observes Sir David, however, a little further on,† as if with a sudden twinge of misgiving, "that the Almighty Architect of the universe may have had other objects in view, incomprehensible by us, than that of supporting animal and vegetable life in these magnificent spheres." Would that Sir David would allow himself to be entirely influenced by this rational and devout sentiment! His book is, on the contrary, crammed with assertions from beginning to end, and of a peremptory and intolerant character, unknown alike to the spirit of humble piety and genuine philosophy.

The essayist, however, is not incapable of quiet humour: and the following pregnant passage is at least worthy to stand side by side with that which we have just quoted from his indignant and eloquent opponent:—

"Undoubtedly all true astronomers, taught caution and temperance of thought by the discipline of their magnificent science, abstain from founding such assumptions upon their discoveries. They know how necessary it is to be upon their guard against the tricks which fancy plays with the senses; and if they see appearances of which they cannot interpret the meaning, they are content that they should have no meaning for them, till the due explana-

* *More Worlds than One*, pp. 180, 183. † Ibid. p. 185.

tion comes. We have innumerable examples of this wise and cautious temper in all periods of astronomy. One has occurred lately. Several careful astronomers, observing the stars by day, had been surprised to see globes of light glide across the field of view of their telescopes, often in rapid succession, and in great numbers. They did not, as may be supposed, rush to the assumption that these globes were celestial bodies of a new kind, before unseen, and that, from the peculiarity of their appearance and movement, they were probably inhabited by beings of a peculiar kind. They proceeded differently. They altered the focus of their telescopes, looked with other glasses, made various changes and trials; and finally discovered that these globes of light were the winged seeds of certain plants, which were wafted through the air, and which, illuminated by the sun, were made globular by being at distances unsuited to the focus of the telescopes!" *

Before proceeding to give our readers some idea of the mode in which Sir David Brewster encounters Dr Whewell, let us offer a general observation concerning both these eminent gentlemen. While the latter exhibits, throughout his *Essay*, a spirit of candour and modesty, without one harsh expression or uncharitable insinuation with reference to the holder of doctrines which he is bent upon impugning with all his mental power and multifarious resources; the former, as we have seen, uses language at once heated, uncourteous, and unjustifiable: especially where he more than insinuates that his opponent, whose great knowledge and ability he admits, either deliberately countenances doctrines tending really to Atheism, or may be charitably believed "*ignorant of* their tendency, and to have forgotten the truths of Inspiration, and even those of Natural Religion."† To venture, however circuitously, to hint such grievous imputations upon an opponent whom he had the slightest reason for suspecting to be a gentleman of such high and responsible academic position, is an offence equally against personal courtesy and public propriety; as we think Sir David Brewster would, on reflection, acknowledge. Both Dr Whewell and Sir David Brewster must

* *Essay*, ch. vii. sec. 17, p. 221.

† *More Worlds than One*, p. 248.

excuse us, if, scanning both through the cold medium of impartial criticism, their speculations, questions, or assertions appear to us disturbed and deflected by a leading prepossession or foregone conclusion, which we shall indicate in the words of each.

Dr WHEWELL.—"The Earth is really the largest Planetary body in the Solar system; its domestic hearth, and the Only World [*i.e.*, collection of intelligent creatures] in the Universe."*

Sir DAVID BREWSTER.—"Life is almost a property of matter [ ! ] * * * Wherever there is Matter, there must be Life :—Life Physical, to enjoy its beauties: Life Moral, to worship its Maker; and Life Intellectual, to proclaim His wisdom and His power. * * * Universal Life upon Universal Matter, is an idea to which the mind instinctively clings. * * * Every star in the Heavens, and every point in a nebula which the most powerful telescope has not separated from its neighbour, is a sun surrounded by inhabited planets like our own. * * * In peopling such worlds with life and intelligence, we assign the cause of their existence; and when the mind is once alive to this great Truth, it cannot fail to realise the grand combination of infinity of life with infinity of matter."†

The composition of Sir David Brewster, though occasionally too declamatory and rhetorical, and so far lacking the dignified simplicity befitting the subjects with which he deals, has much merit. It is easy, vivid, and vigorous, but will bear retrenchment, and lowering of tone. As to the substantial texture of his work, we think it betrays, in almost every page, haste and impetuosity. Another feature of *More Worlds than One*, is a manifest desire *provocare ad populum*—a greater anxiety, in the first instance, to catch the ear of the million, than to convince the "fit audience, though few."

Now, however, to his work; and, as we have already said, on him lies the labouring oar of proof. All that his opponent professes to do, is to ask for arguments "rendering probable" that "doctrine" which Sir David pledges himself to demonstrate to be not only the "*hope*" of the Christian, but the "*creed*" of the philosopher: as much, that

* *Essay*, chap. x. sec. 10, pp. 308, 309; chap. xii. sec. 1, p. 359.

† *More Worlds than One*, pp. 178, 179.

is, an article of his belief, as the doctrines of attraction and gravitation, or the existence of demonstrable astronomical facts.

He commences with a brief introduction, sketching, but in a perfunctory manner, the growth of the belief in a plurality of worlds—one steadily and firmly increasing in strength, he says, till it encountered the rude shock of the essayist, whose "very remarkable work" is "ably written," and who "defends ingeniously his novel and extraordinary views:" "the direct tendency of which is to ridicule and bring into contempt the grand discoveries in sidereal astronomy by which the last century has been distinguished." In his next chapter, Sir David discusses "the religious aspect of the question," representing man, especially the philosopher, as always having pined after a knowledge of the scene of his future existence. He declares that neither the Old nor the New Testament contains "a single expression incompatible with the great truth, that there are other worlds than our own which are the seats of life and intelligence;" but that, on the contrary, there are "other passages which are inexplicable without admitting it to be true." He regards, as we have seen, the noble exclamation of the Psalmist, "What is man?" as a "positive argument for a plurality of worlds;" and "cannot doubt" that he was gifted with a plenary knowledge of the starry system, inhabited as Sir David would have it to be! Dr Chalmers, let us remark, in passing, expressed himself differently, and with a more becoming reserve: "It is not for us to say whether inspiration revealed to the Psalmist the wonders of the modern astronomy," but "even though the mind be a perfect stranger to the science of these enlightened times, the heavens present a great and an elevating spectacle, the contemplation of which awakened the piety of the Psalmist"—a view in which Dr Whewell concurs. Sir David then comes to consider the doctrine of "Man, in his future state of existence, consisting, as at present, of a spiritual nature residing in a corporeal frame." We must, therefore, he says, find for the race of Adam, "*if not for the races which preceded him!*"* "a material home upon which he may reside, or from which he may travel to other localities in the universe." That house, continues this philosopher, cannot be the earth, for it will not be big enough—there will be such a "population as the habitable parts of our globe could not possibly accommodate;" wherefore, "*we can scarcely doubt* that their future abode must be on some of the primary or secondary planets of the solar system! whose inhabitants have ceased to exist, like those on the earth; or on planets which have long been in a state of preparation, as our earth was, for the advent of intellectual life!"

Here, then, is the "creed of the philosopher," as well as "the hope of the Christian!" Passing, according to the order adopted in this paper, from the first chapter, "Religious Aspect of the Question," we alight on the seventh, entitled, "*Religious Difficulties.*" We entertain too much consideration for Sir David Brewster as a gentleman of great distinction in the scientific world, to speak harshly of anything falling from his pen; but we think ourselves justified in questioning whether this chapter—dealing with speculations of an awful nature, among which the greatest religious and philosophical intellects tremble as they "go sounding on their dim and perilous way"—shows him equal to cope with his experienced and very learned opponent; whom every page devoted to such topics shows to have fixed the DIFFICULTY, with which he proposed to deal, fully and steadily before his eyes, in all its moral, metaphysical, and philosophical bearings, and to have discussed it at once luminously, cautiously, and reverently. We shall content ourselves with briefly indicating Sir David's course of observation on that "difficulty;" leaving it to the discreet reader to form his own

* *More Worlds than One*, p. 18.

judgment whether Sir David has left the difficulty where he found it, or removed, lessened, or enhanced it.

Dr Whewell, in his *Dialogue*, thus temperately and effectively deals with this section of his opponent's lucubrations :—

"If he cannot see the difficulties which the question involves, he is not one of those for whom I wrote ! I am sorry that he has allowed me to obliterate, metaphysically, the brightness of his perceptions.

"*A.* He does, however, speak of the religious difficulty ; and says that Dr Chalmers 'has rather cut than untied the knot.'

"His own solution of the question concerning the redemption of other worlds appears to be this, that the provision made for the redemption of man, by what took place upon earth eighteen hundred years ago, may have extended its influence to other worlds.

"*Z.** In reply to which astronomico-theological hypothesis three remarks offer themselves: In the first place, the hypothesis is entirely without warrant or countenance in the revelation from which all our knowledge of the scheme of redemption is derived; in the second place, the events which took place upon earth eighteen hundred years ago, were connected with *a train of events in the history of man*, which had begun at the creation of man, and extended through all the intervening ages ; and the bearing of this whole series of events upon the condition of the inhabitants of other worlds must be so different from its bearing on the condition of man, that the hypothesis needs a dozen other auxiliary hypotheses to make it intelligible ; and, in the third place, this hypothesis, making the earth, insignificant as it seems to be in the astronomical scheme, the centre of the theological scheme, ascribes to the earth a peculiar distinction, quite as much at variance with the analogies of the planets to one another, as the supposition that the earth alone is inhabited ; to say nothing of the bearing of the critic's hypothesis on the other systems that encircle other suns." †

"*A.* Your critic does not allow, as I have already told you, that man and his history are an especial care of God. He says, 'The lily that neither toils nor spins ; the ravens that neither sow nor reap ; the sparrows, though of less value than man ; the crushed insect ; the broken planet ; the twinkling star ; are all as special objects of God's care as the wise elephant, the illiterate biped, the presumptuous philosopher, and the great globe itself, and all that it inherits.'

* "*A.*" indicates the objector ; "*Z.*" the author. † *Dialogue*, pp. 62–64.

"*Z.* But surely a scheme for the redemption of man, bound up with the whole history of man, and establishing a special relation between man and God, shows a care more special than the Divine operation which clothes the lily and feeds the sparrow; and this was implied, when it was said, 'Fear not, ye are of more value than many sparrows.'"

"In freely discussing the subject of a Plurality of Worlds," confidently observes Sir David, "there can be no collision between Reason and Revelation." He regrets the extravagant conclusion of some, that the inhabitants of all planets but our own "are sinless and immortal beings that never broke the Divine Law, and enjoying that perfect felicity reserved for only a few of the less favoured occupants of earth. Thus chained to a planet," he mournfully remarks, "the lowest and most unfortunate in the universe, the philosopher, with all his analogies broken down, may justly renounce his faith in a Plurality of Worlds, and rejoice in the more limited but safer creed of the anti-Pluralist author, who makes the earth the only world in the universe, and the special object of God's paternal care." * He proceeds, in comfortable accordance with "men *of lofty minds*, and undoubted piety," to regard the existence of Moral Evil as a necessary part of the general scheme of the universe, and consequently affecting all its Rational Inhabitants. † With Huygens, he concludes that the inhabitants of the other planets must be endowed with the same vices and virtues as man, otherwise they would be far more degraded than the occupants of the earth. He "rejects the idea that the inhabitants of the planets do not require a Saviour; and maintains the more rational opinion, that they stand in the same moral relation to their Maker as the inhabitants of the earth; and seeks for a solution of the difficulty—how can there be inhabitants in the planets, when God had but One Son, whom He could send to save them? If we can give a satisfactory answer to this question, it may

* *More Worlds than One*, p. 131.

† Ibid.

destroy the objections of the Infidel, while it relieves the Christian from his difficulties." † * * * "When our Saviour died, the influence of His death extended backward, in the Past, to millions who never heard His name; in the Future, to millions who never will hear it, * * * a Force which did not vary with any function of the distance. ‡ * * * Emanating from the *middle* planet of the system"

—— The *earth* the *middle* planet of the system! How is this? In an earlier portion of his book (p. 56), Sir David had demonstrated that "our earth is neither the *middle* [his own italics] planet, nor the planet *nearest* the sun, nor the planet furthest from that luminary: that therefore the earth, as a planet, has no pre-eminence in the solar system, to induce us to believe that it is the only inhabited world. * * * *Jupiter* is the *middle* planet (p. 55), and is otherwise highly distinguished!" How is this? Can the two passages containing such direct contradictions have emanated from the same scientific controversialist?

— "Emanating from the middle planet of the system, why may it not have *extended to them all*, * * * to the Planetary Races in the Past, and to the Planetary Races in the Future? * * * But to bring our argument more within the reach of an ordinary understanding"—he supposes our earth split into two parts! the old world and the new, as Biela's comet is supposed to have been divided in 1846, at the beginning of the Christian era! § —"would not *both fragments* have shared in the beneficence of the Cross—the penitent on the shores of the Mississippi, as richly as the pilgrim on the banks of the Jordan? * * * Should this view prove unsatisfactory to the anxious inquirer, we may suggest another sentiment, even though we ourselves may not admit it into our creed. * * * May not the Divine Nature, which can

† *More Worlds than One*, p. 138.
‡ Ibid. p. 139. § Ibid. p. 140.

neither suffer, nor die, and which, in our planet, once only clothed itself in humanity, *resume elsewhere a physical form, and expiate the guilt of unnumbered worlds?*" *

We repeat, that we abstain from offering any of the stern strictures which these passages almost extort from us.

He denies that either "a Theist or Christian of the smallest mental capacity could imagine the Almighty prevented, by the many worlds under His management, from taking care of the earth and its inhabitants; and denies that if they do, the discoveries of the microscope have the slightest tendency to remove them;" differing here from both Dr Chalmers and Dr Whewell: and we ourselves are not disposed to pronounce an opinion upon the matter.

Sir David proceeds to declare himself incompetent to comprehend the Difficulty "put in a form so unintelligible" by the essayist—that of a kind of existence, similar to that of men, in respect of their intellectual, moral, and spiritual character, and its *progressive* development, existing in any region occupied by beings other than men. He denies that Progression has been the character of the history of man,† but rather frequent and vast retrogressions, ever since the Fall; and asks "which of these ever-changing conditions of humanity is the *unique* condition of the essayist—incapable of repetition in the scheme of the Universe?"‡ Why may there not be an intermediate race between that of man and the angelic beings of Scripture, where human reason shall pass into the highest form of created mind, and human affections into their noblest development?—

"Why may not the intelligence of the spheres be ordained for the study of regions and objects unstudied and unknown on earth? Why may not labour have a better commission than to earn its bread by the sweat of its brow? Why may it not pluck its loaf from the bread-fruit tree, or gather its manna from the ground, or

* *More Worlds than One*, pp. 141–2. † Ibid. p. 151.
‡ Ibid. p. 152.

draw its wine from the bleeding vessels of the vine, or *inhale its anodyne breath from the paradise gas of its atmosphere?*" *

And Sir David thus concludes the chapter:—

"The difficulties we have been considering, in so far as they are of a religious character, have been very unwisely introduced into the question of a Plurality of Worlds. We are not entitled to remonstrate with the sceptic; but we venture to doubt the soundness of that philosopher's judgment, who thinks that the truths of natural religion are affected by a belief in planetary races, and the reality of that Christian's faith who considers it to be endangered by a belief that there are other Worlds than his own."

This last paragraph induces us to go so far as to doubt whether Sir David Brewster has really or deliberately addressed his understanding to the subject to which so large a portion of the most elaborate reasonings of Dr Whewell have been directed; and if there lurk in the paragraph which we have last quoted, an insinuation against the sincerity of his opponent's belief in the Christian religion, it is utterly unpardonable.

Sir David does not quarrel with the essayist's account of the constitution of man; and we must now see how he deals with his arguments drawn from Geology.

Sir David "is not disposed to grudge the geologist even periods so marvellous" as "millions of years required for the formation of strata, provided they be considered as merely hypothetical;" and admits that "our seas and continents have nearly the same locality, and cover nearly the same area, as they did at the creation of Adam;" but demurs to the conclusion that the earth was prepared for man by causes operating so gradually as the diurnal changes going on around us. "Why may not the Almighty have deposited the earth's strata, during the whole period of its formation, by a *rapid* precipitation of their atoms from the waters which suspended them, so as to reduce the period of the earth's formation to little more than the united generations of the different orders of plants and animals constituting its organic remains? Why not still further shorten

* *More Worlds than One*, p. 47.

the period, by supposing that plants and animals, requiring, in our day, a century for their development, may in primitive times have shot up in rank luxuriance, and been ready, in a few *days!* or months! or years, for the great *purpose of exhibiting*, by their geological distribution, the progressive formation of the earth?"*

These questions, of which a myriad similar ones might be asked by any one, we leave to our geological readers; and hasten to inform them, that, as it appears to us, in involuntary homage to the powerful reasonings of his opponent, Sir David Brewster is fain to question the "inference that man did not exist during the period of the earth's formation;"† and to suggest that there may have existed intellectual races in at present unexplored continental localities, or the immense regions of the earth now under water!—"The future of geology may be pregnant with startling discoveries of the remains of intellectual races, even *beneath* the primitive Azoic‡ formations of the earth! . . . Who can tell what sleeps beyond? Another creation may lie beneath! more glorious creatures may be entombed there! the mortal coils of beings more lovely, more pure, more divine than man, may yet read to us the unexpected lesson, that we have not been the first, and may not be the last, of the intellectual race!"§ Is he who can entertain and publish conjectures like these, entitled to stigmatise so severely those of other speculators, as "inconceivable absurdities, which no sane mind can cherish—suppositions too ridiculous even for a writer of romance?" This wild licence given to the fancy, may not be amiss in a poet, whose privilege it is that his "eye, in a fine phrensy rolling, may"

> "Give to airy nothing,
> A local habitation and a name;"

* *More Worlds than One*, pp. 44–47. † Ibid. p. 47.

‡ It may be proper to intimate to persons not familiar with such expressions, that the word "Azoic" signifies those primary rocks which contain no traces of organic life, no remains of plants or animals.

§ *More Worlds than One*, p. 52.

but when set in the scale, by a man of science, against the solemnly magnificent array of facts in the earth's history established by Geology, may be somewhat summarily discarded.

The essayist suggests a most striking and original analogy between man's relation to Time and to Space; but it appears to us not understood, in either its scope or nature, by Sir David Brewster. At this we are as much surprised, as at the roughness with which he characterises the argument, as "the most ingenious though shallow piece of sophistry he has ever encountered in modern dialectics." The essayist suggests a comparison between the numbers expressing the four magnitudes and distances, of the earth, the solar system, the fixed stars, and the nebulæ, and the numbers expressing the antiquity of the four geological periods, but only "*for the sake of giving definiteness to our notions.*" Sir David abstains from quoting these last expressions, and alleges that the essayist, "quitting the ground of analogy," founds an elaborate argument on the mutual relation of an atom of time and an atom of space. The "argument" Sir David thus presents to his readers, the capital and italic letters being his own: "That is, *the earth, the* ATOM OF SPACE, *is the only one of the planetary and sidereal worlds that is inhabited, because it was so long without inhabitants, and has been occupied only an* ATOM OF TIME."* "If any of our readers," he heatedly adds, "see the force of this argument, they must possess an acuteness of perception to which we lay no claim. To us, it is not only illogical; it is a mere sound in the ear, without any sense in the brain." This is the language possibly befitting an irritated professor towards an ignorant and conceited student, but hardly suitable when Sir David Brewster is speaking of such an antagonist as he cannot but know that he has to deal with.

It does not appear to us the essayist's attempt, or pur-

* *More Worlds than One,* p. 206.

pose, to establish any arbitrary, absolute *relation* between time and space, or definite proportions of either, as concurring or alternative elements for determining the probability of a plurality of worlds. But he says to the dogmatic astronomical objector to Christianity, Such arguments as you have hitherto derived from *your* consideration of SPACE, MULTITUDE, and MAGNITUDE, for the purpose of depressing man into a being beneath his Maker's special notice, I encounter by arguments derived from recent disclosures concerning another condition of existence—DURATION, or TIME. Protesting that neither Time nor Space has any true connexion with the subject, nevertheless I will turn your own weapons against yourself. My argument from Time shall at least neutralise yours from Space: mine shall involve the conditions of yours, fraught with their supposed irresistible force, and falsify them in fact, as forming premises whence may be deduced derogatory inferences concerning man. The essayist's ingenious and suggestive argument is intended, not to prove an opinion, but *to remove an objection;* which, according to the profound thinker, Bishop Butler, is the proper office of analogy. It is asked, for instance, *how* can you suppose that man, such as he is represented to be, occupies only an immeasurably minute fraction of existing matter? And it is answered, I find that man occupies only an immeasurably minute fraction of elapsed time: and this is, to me, an answer to the "*How*," as concluding improbability. *How* is balanced against *How:* difficulty against difficulty: they neutralise each other, and leave the great question, the great reality, standing as it did, before either was suggested, to be dealt with according to such evidence as God has vouchsafed us. We, therefore, do not see that the essayist is driven to say, as Sir David Brewster alleges he is, either that because man has occupied only an atom of space, he must live only an atom of time on the earth;*

* *More Worlds than One*, pp. 206, 207.

or that because he has lived only an atom of time, he must occupy but an atom of space. In dismissing this leading portion of the essayist's reasonings, we shall say only that we consider it worthy of the attention of all persons occupied in speculations of this nature, as calculated to suggest trains of novel, profitable, and deeply interesting reflection.

Thus far the essayist, as followed by his opponent, on the assumption that the other bodies of the universe are fitted, equally with the earth, to be the abodes of life. *But are they?* Here we are brought to the last stage of the essayist's speculations: he asking, What physical EVIDENCE have we that the other bodies of the solar system,—besides the earth,—the fixed stars, and the nebulæ, are structures capable of supporting human life, of being inhabited by rational and moral beings?

The great question, in its physical aspect, is now fully before us: Is there that analogy on which the pluralist relies?

For the existence of life, several conditions must concur; and any of these failing, life, so far as we know anything about it, is impossible. Not air only, and moisture, are necessary, but a certain temperature, neither too hot nor too cold, and a certain consistence, on which the living frame can rest. Without the other conditions, an atmosphere alone does not make life possible; still less, prove its existence. A globe of red-hot metal, or of solid ice, however well provided with an atmosphere, could not be inhabited, so far as we can conceive. The old maxim of the logicians is true: that it requires all the conditions to establish the affirmative, but that the negative of any one proves the negative.

First, as to the smallest tenants of our system, the thirty* planetoids, some of which are certainly no larger

* A thirtieth planetoid was discovered by Mr Hind since the publication of the second edition of the *Essay*, and a thirty-first while the third edition was being printed. It is believed that even since then, two more have been discovered! [December 1854.]

than Mont Blanc, moving in the great space between Mars and Jupiter, in orbits so complex and anomalous as to have suggested to most astronomers (Sir David Brewster boldly states it as almost placed beyond doubt) that they may be portions of a shattered planet, once circling between Mars and Jupiter; and fragments are being discovered latterly almost monthly! "It may yet, however," discreetly observes Mr Hind, who has discovered so many of these strange occupants of our system, "be found that these small bodies, so far from being portions of the wreck of a great planet, were created in their present state, for some wise purpose, which the progress of astronomy in future ages may eventually unfold."

Sir David Brewster dare not venture to suggest that these planetoids are inhabited, or in a condition to become so, any more than meteoric stones, which modern science regards as masses of matter, moving, like the planets, in the celestial spaces, subject to the gravitating attraction of the sun; the earth encountering them occasionally, either striking directly upon them, or approaching to them so closely that they are drawn by the terrestrial attraction, first within the atmosphere, and afterwards to the earth's surface.* Here our essayist gives a thrust at our pluralist not to be parried: asking him why he shrunk from asserting the planetoids and meteoric stones to be inhabited? If it be because of their being found to be uninhabited, or of their smallness, then "the argument that they *are* inhabited *because* they are planets fails him."†

"There is, then," says elsewhere the wary essayist,‡ "a degree of smallness which makes you reject the supposition of inhabitants. But where does that degree of smallness begin? The surface of *Mars* is only one-fourth that of the Earth. Moreover, if you allow all the planetoids to be uninhabited, those planets which you acknowledge to be probably uninhabited, far outnumber those with regard to which even the most resolute pluralist holds to be inhabited. The majority swells every year; the planetoids are now [upwards of] thirty.

* Lardner, *Museum of Science and Art,* vol. i. p. 156.
† *Dial.*, p. 60. ‡ Ibid., p. 28.

The fact of a planet being inhabited, then, is, at any rate, rather the exception than the rule; and therefore must be proved, in each case, by special evidence. Of such evidence I know not a trace!"

We may add, also, that Dr Lardner, vouched by Sir David Brewster, as we shall soon see, to be a thoroughly competent witness, gives up the planetoids as seats of habitation for animal life.*

Let us now, would say our essayist, proceed on our negative tour, so to speak, and hasten to pay our respects to the Moon, our nearest neighbour, and whose distance from the Sun is admitted to adapt her, so far, for habitation.† If it appear, by strong evidence, that the Moon is not inhabited, then there is an end of the general principle, that *all* the bodies of the solar system are inhabited, and that we must begin our speculation about each with this assumption. If the Moon appear not to be inhabited, then, it would seem, the belief that each special body in the system *is* inhabited, must depend upon reasons specially belonging to that body, and cannot be taken for granted without these reasons.‡ Now, as to the Moon, we have latterly acquired the means of making such exact and minute inquiries, that at the meeting of the British Association at Hull last year [1853], Mr Phillips, an eminent geologist, stated that astronomers can discern the shape of a spot on the Moon's surface, only a few hundred feet in breadth. At the recent [Sept. 1854] meeting of the same association at Liverpool, moreover, the most assiduous and able observants of the Moon re-asserted,

* *Museum*, &c., vol. i. p. 64.

† P. 271. Her distance from us is 24,000 miles; and our essayist, by the way, tells us (chap. ix. sec. 7) that "a railroad carriage, at its ordinary rate of travelling, would reach her in *a month*." We should not like, however, to travel by the Lunar Express, but would prefer the Parliamentary train, and hope, starting from the Hanwell station, to get to the terminus in a couple of years or so. Good Bishop Wilkins intended to be taken up by birds of flight trained for the purpose! When the Duke of Newcastle asked him where he intended to bait by the way, he answered, "Your Grace is the last person to ask me the question, having built so many *castles in the air!*" In the third edition, the month is expanded into *six*.

‡ *Essay*, p. 272.

with increased confidence, their conviction that there is not upon her surface either water, vapour, air, or active volcanoes.* Passing by, however, the essayist's brief but able account of the physical condition of this satellite of ours, we will cite the recent testimony of one accredited by Sir David Brewster† as "a mathematician and a natural philosopher, who has studied more than any preceding writer the analogies between the Earth and the other planets"—Dr Lardner; who, in the third volume of the work placed at the head of this article, thus concludes his elaborate account of the Moon, as now regarded by the most enlightened astronomers—after proving it to be "as exempt from an atmosphere as is the utterly exhausted receiver of a good air-pump!"

> "In fine, the entire geographical character of the moon, thus ascertained by long-continued and exact telescopic surveys, leads to the conclusion, that no analogy exists between it and the earth which could confer any probability on the conjecture that it fulfils the same purposes in the economy of the universe; and we must infer, that whatever be its uses in the solar system, or in the general purposes of creation, it is not a world inhabited by organised races such as those to which the earth is appropriated."‡

We must leave Sir David and Dr Lardner to settle their small amount of differences on this score together; for Sir David will have it that "the moon exhibits such proofs of an atmosphere that we have a new ground from analogy for believing that she either has, or is in a state of preparation for receiving, inhabitants;"§ who, "with monuments of their hands," he "hopes may be discovered with some magnificent telescope which may be constructed!" ‖ And he is compelled to believe that "all the other unseen satellites of the solar system, are homes to animal and intellectual life!"¶

The essayist would seem not to have deemed it necessary to deprive the SUN of inhabitants; but our confi-

* *Essay*, Pref. to Third Ed. p. viii. † Pp. 80, 81.
‡ *Museum*, &c., vol. iii. p. 48. § P. 108. ‖ P. 24. ¶ P. 109.

dent pluralist will not surrender the stupendous body so easily. His friend Dr Lardner properly regards it "as a vast globular furnace, the heat emitted from each square foot of which is seven times greater than the heat issuing from a square foot of the fiercest blast-furnace: to what agency the light and heat are due, no one being able to do more than conjecture. According to our hypothesis, it is a great ELECTRIC LIGHT in the centre of the system;"* and "entirely removed from all analogy with the earth"—"utterly unsuited for the habitation of organised tribes."† Nevertheless Sir David stoutly believes that this great electric light, "the sun, is richly stored with inhabitants," the probability "being doubtless greatly increased by the simple consideration of its enormous size," a "domain so extensive, so blessed with perpetual light;" and, beyond all this, it would seem that "if it be inhabited," it is probably "occupied by the highest orders of intelligence!"‡ who, however, are allowed to enjoy their picturesque, and, it must be owned, somewhat peculiar, but doubtless blessed position, only by peeping every now and then through the sun's spots, and so "seeing distinctly the planets and stars"—in fact, "large portions of the heavens!"§ Perhaps it may be thought that this is not a very handsome way of dealing with such exalted beings!

The essayist has now our seven principal sister-planets to deal with, the two *infra*-terrestrial, Mercury and Venus; and the five *extra*-terrestrial, Mars, Jupiter, Saturn, Uranus, and Neptune: and as to all these the question continues, do they so *resemble* the earth in physical conditions, as to lead us safely to the conclusion that they resemble it in that other capital particular, of being the habitations of intellectual and moral beings? Here, be it observed, that every symptom of unlikeness which the essayist can detect, greatly augments the burthen of proof incumbent upon his opponents.

* *Museum,* &c. vol. iii. p. 112.
† Ibid. vol. i. p. 63.
‡ *More Worlds than One,* pp. 97, 101.
§ Pp. 99, 100.

When it was discovered that the old planets in certain important particulars resembled the earth, being opaque and solid bodies, having similar motions round the sun and on their own axes, some accompanied by satellites, and all having arrangements producing day and night, summer and winter, who could help wondering whether they must not also have inhabitants, reckoning and regulating their lives and employments by days, months, and years? This was, at most, however, a mere guess or conjecture; and whether it is now more probable than then, depends on the intervening progress of astronomy and science in general. Have subsequent discoveries strengthened or impugned the validity of the conjecture? The limits of our system have been since vastly extended by the discovery of Uranus and Neptune; and the planetary sisterhood has also increased in number by upwards of thirty little and very eccentric ones.

Now, as to NEPTUNE, says the essayist, in substance, what reason has a sensible person for believing it peopled, as the earth is, by human beings, *i. e.*, consisting of body and soul? He is thirty times further than we are from the sun, which will appear to it a mere star—about the size of Jupiter to us; and Neptune's light and heat will be nine hundred times less than ours! * If it, nevertheless, contain animal and intellectual life, we must try to conceive how they get on with such a *modicum* of those useful elements!

If any planet have sufficient light, heat, clouds, winds, and a due adjustment of gravity, and the strength of the materials of which organisation consist, there *may* be found in it life of some sort or other. Now we can measure and weigh the planets, exactly, by the law of gravitation, which embraces every particle of matter in our system; and the mass of our earth we have found to be only five times heavier than water. Comparing it with JUPITER, the bulk of which is thirteen hundred and thirty-one times greater

* *Essay*, p. 278.

than that of the earth, his density is, as a whole, only a quarter of that of the earth, not greater than it would be as a sphere of water. Such he is conjectured to be; and his belts lines of clouds, fed with vapours raised by the sun's action on such a watery sphere—the lines of such clouds being of so steady and determined a character, in consequence of his great rotatory velocity. Equal bulk for equal bulk, he is lighter than the earth, but of course much heavier altogether; and as he is five times the earth's distance from the sun, he must get a proportionally smaller amount of light and heat, and even that diminished by the clouds enveloping him to so great an extent. What a low degree of vitality, and what kind of organisation must animal existence possess, says Dr Whewell, to suit such physical conditions, especially with reference to gravity, which at his surface is nearly two and a half times that on the earth! Boneless, watery, pulpy, must be the inhabitants of the cold waters; or they may be frozen so far as to exclude the idea of animal existence; or it may be restricted to shallow parts in a planet of ice.* But if this be so, to what end his gorgeous array of satellites?—his four moons? "Precisely the same," answers our pertinacious essayist, "as the use of our moon during the countless ages before man was placed on the earth, while it was tenanted by corals, madrepores, shell-fish, belemnites, the cartilaginous fishes of the old red sandstone, or the Saurian monsters of the lias. With these *differences*, asks the essayist, complacently, what becomes of analogy—of resemblances justifying our belief that Jupiter is inhabited like ourselves?

To this answers Sir David Brewster, substantially, thus. Jupiter's great size "is alone a proof that it must have been made for some grand and useful purpose:" it is flattened at its poles; revolves on its axis in nearly ten hours; has different climates and seasons; and is abundantly illuminated, in the short absence of the sun, by its four moons,

* *Essay*, pp. 281, 289.

giving him, in fact, "perpetual moonlight." *Why* does the sun give it days, nights, and years? Why do its moons irradiate its continents and seas? Its equatorial breezes blow perpetually over its plains? To what purpose could such a gigantic world have been framed, unless to supply the wants, and minister to the happiness, of living beings? Still, it is admitted, with a sort of qualm, "that certain objections or difficulties naturally present themselves."* The distance of Jupiter from the sun precludes the possibility of sufficient light and heat from that quarter, to support either such vegetable or animal life as exists on the earth; the cold must be very intense—its rivers and seas must be tracks and fields of ice.† But it may be answered, that the temperature of a planet depends on other causes: the condition of its atmosphere, and the internal heat of its mass—as is the case with our earth; and such "may" be the case in Jupiter; and,

* Brewster, p. 60.

† To descend, for a moment, to details. Sir David Brewster will not allow himself to be driven to elect between the icy or watery constituency of Jupiter. He declares direct experiment to have proved that it is neither: that if Jupiter were a sphere of water, the light reflected from his surface, when in his quadratures, must contain, as it does *not*, a large portion of polarised light; and if his crust consist of mountains, precipices, and rocks of ice, some of whose faces must occasionally reflect the incident light at nearly the polarising angle, the polarization of their light would be distinctly indicated. The essayist, in his *Dialogue*, "doubts whether the remark is applicable; for Jupiter's watery or icy mass must be clothed in a thick stratum of air, and aqueous vapour, and clouds. But even were the planet free from clouds, the parts of the planet's surface from which polarised light would be reflected, would be only as points compared with the whole surface; and the common light reflected from the whole surface would quite overwhelm and obliterate the polarised light."—*Dial.* p. 64. We cite this as a sample of the ingenuity of both disputants in a point of scientific contest. Whether Sir David's conjectural polarised light be or be not thus obliterated, in our view the item in dispute is quite lost in the general question, and the great principles on which its solution depends. If driven to elect between ice and water, asks Sir David, playfully, "may we not, upon good grounds, prefer the probable ice to the possible water, and accommodate the inhabitants of Jupiter with very comfortable quarters, in huts of snow and houses of crystal, warmed by subterranean heat, and lighted with the hydrogen of its waters, and its cinders not wholly deprived of their bitumen?"—Pp. 236, 237. The answer of his opponent would be obvious.

"if" so, may secure a temperature sufficiently genial to sustain such animal and vegetable life as ours; yet, it is owned, it cannot "increase the feeble light which Jupiter derives from the sun;" but "an enlargement of the pupil of the eye, and increased sensibility of the retina, would make the sun's light as brilliant to Jovians as to us."* Besides, a brilliant phosphorescent light "may" be excited in the satellites by the sun's rays. Again, the day of ten hours may be thought insufficient for physical repose; but, it is answered, five hours' repose are sufficient for five of labour. "A difficulty of a more serious kind, however, is presented by the great force of gravity on so gigantic a planet as Jupiter;"† but Sir David gives us curious calculations to show that a Jovian's weight would be only double that of a man on the earth.

Staggered by such a formidable array of differences, when he was in quest of *resemblances* only,

"Alike, but, oh! how different!"

Sir David rebukes the sceptic for forming so low an opinion of Omnipotent Wisdom, as to assume that "the inhabitants of the planets must be either men, or anything resembling them;—is it," he asks, "necessary that an immortal soul should be hung upon a skeleton of bone, or imprisoned in a cage of cartilage and skin? Must it see with two eyes, and hear with two ears, and touch with ten fingers, and rest on a duality of limbs? May it not rest in a Polyphemus with one eyeball, or in an Argus with a hundred? May it not reign in the giant forms of the Titans, and direct the hundred hands of Briareus?"‡ "The being of another world may have his home in subterranean cities, warmed by central fires; or in crystal caves, cooled by ocean tides; or he may float with the Nereids upon the deep; or mount upon wings as eagles; or rise upon the pinions of the dove, that he may flee away, and be at rest!"§

* Brewster, p. 61. † Ibid. p. 62. ‡ Ibid. pp. 65, 66. § Ibid. pp. 68, 69.

Let us pause at this point, and see how the question stands on the showing of the respectively imaginative, and matter-of-fact, disputants themselves. Sir David Brewster, being bound to show that analogy forces us to believe Jupiter inhabited, is compelled to admit a series of signal discrepancies in physical condition; expecting his opponent, in turn, to admit such a series of essential alterations, both of inert matter and organization, as will admit of what?—*totally different* modes of animal and intellectual existence—so different, as to drive a philosopher into the fantastic dreams in which we have just seen him indulging. Not so the essayist,—a master of the Inductive Philosophy. He does not presume impiously to limit Omnipotence; but reverently owns His power to create whatever forms and conditions of existence He pleases. When, however, it is asserted that He has, in fact, made beings wholly different from any that we see, "he cannot believe this without further *evidence*."* And on this very subject of the imaginary inhabitants of Jupiter, after reading what his heated and fanciful opponent has advanced, "You are hard," he makes an objector say, "on our neighbours in Jupiter, when you will not allow them to be anything better than 'boneless, watery, pulpy creatures.'" To which he answers, "I had no disposition to be hard on them when I entered upon these speculations. I drew, what appeared to me, probable conclusions from all the facts of the case. *If the laws of attraction, of light, of heat, and the like, be the same there as they are here, which we believe to be certain, the laws of life must also be the same; and, if so, I can draw no other conclusions than those which I have stated.*"†

Says the essayist, in effect, I know that my Maker can invest with the intellect of a Newton, each of

"The gay motes that people the sunbeams;"

but before I believe that He *has* done so, give me reason-

* *Dialogue*, p. 6. † Ibid. p. 23.

able and adequate evidence of so wonderful and sublime a fact; or I must believe in any kind of nonsense that any one would palm upon me.

The planet Jupiter affords a fair sample of the procedure of the essayist and his opponent, with reference to all the other primary planets of the solar system. From Mercury, in red-hot contiguity to the Sun, to Neptune, which is at thirty times the Earth's distance from it, and from which, as we have seen, it derives only *one nine-hundredth* part of the light and heat imparted to ourselves by the Sun, Sir David Brewster will have all inhabited, and the physical condition of each correspondingly altered to admit of it!—Central heat, and eyes the pupils of which are sufficiently enlarged, and the retina's sensibility sufficiently increased, to admit of seeing with nine hundred times less light than is requisite for our own organs of sight. "Uranus and Neptune," concludes the triumphant pluralist,* — nothing daunted by the overwhelming evidences of physical difference of condition,—"are *doubtless*," with the Sun, "the abodes of Life and Intelligence: the colossal temples where their Creator is recognised and worshipped; the remotest watch-towers of our system, from which His works may be *better* studied, and His glories *more easily* descried!"

Why, with such elastic principles of analogy as his, should he stop short of peopling the Meteoric Stones with rational inhabitants, whom, and whose doings, as in the case of the Moon, "some magnificent" instrument, yet to be constructed, may discover to us?

This much for the planets: before quitting which, however, we may state that, according to Dr Lardner,—about as staunch a pluralist as his admirer Sir David Brewster, —a greater rapidity of rotation, and smaller intervals of light and darkness, are among the characteristics distinguishing the group of major planets from the terrestrial group. He also adds that another "striking distinction"

* *Dialogue*, p. 76.

is the comparative lightness of the matter constituting the former. The density of Venus, Mars, and our Earth, is nearly equal—about the same as that of ironstone; while the density of the thoroughly-baked planet Mercury is equal to that of gold. "Now it appears, on the contrary," he continues, "that the density of Jupiter very little exceeds that of water; that of Uranus and Neptune is exactly that of water; while Saturn is so light, that it would float in water like a globe of pine wood. The seas and oceans of these planets must consist of a liquid far lighter than water. It is computed that a liquid on Jupiter, which would be analogous to the terrestrial oceans, would be three times lighter than sulphuric ether, the lightest known liquid; and would be such that cork would scarcely float in it!"* Rather queer comrades of ours, must be the Jovian or Saturnian sailors!

Commending these trifling discrepancies to Sir David's attention, while manufacturing his planetary inhabitants in conformity with them, shall we now follow his flight beyond the solar system, and get among the Fixed Stars? Here we are gazing at the Dog-Star! "I allow," says a pensive objector to the essayist,† "that if you disprove the existence of inhabitants in the planets of our system, I shall not feel much real interest in the possible inhabitants of the Sirian system. Neighbourhood has its influence upon our feelings of regard,—even neighbourhood on a scale of millions of miles!"

Among the FIXED STARS our pluralist is quite at home, and evidently in great favour. They twinkle and glitter with delight at his gleeful approach, to invest them with moral and intellectual dignity, and at the same time, perhaps, select "some bright particular" one, to be hereafter favoured and distinguished as the seat of his own personal existence; whence he is to spend eternity in radiating astronomical emanations throughout infinitude.

> "Then, unembodied, doth he trace,
> By steps each planet's heavenly way?

* *Museum,* &c., vol. i. p. 35.

† *Dialogue,* p. 23.

A Thing of Eyes, that all survey,
A Thought Unseen, yet seeing all!"*

He stands in the starry solitude, waving his wand, and lo! he peoples each glistening speck with intellectual existence, with the highest order of intelligence, as in the case of that little star, the Sun, which he has quitted.

Now, as to these same FIXED STARS, we can easily guess the steps of Sir David's brief and, to himself, satisfactory argument, which we may call a sublime celestial hop, step, and jump. *If* the stars be suns, they are inhabited like ours; and if they be suns, each has its planets, like our sun; and if they have planets, they are inhabited like our planets; and if they have satellites like some of ours, they are also inhabited. But the stars *are* suns; and they *have* planets, and at least some of these planets, satellites; therefore, all the fixed stars, with their respective planetary systems, are inhabited—Q. E. D. Here are the very words of the Star-Peopler:—"We are compelled to draw the conclusion that wherever there is a sun, there must be a planetary system, and wherever there is a planetary system, there must be Life and Intelligence."† This is the way in which, it seems, we worms of the earth feel ourselves at liberty to deal with our Almighty Creator: dogmatically insisting that every scene of existence in which He may have displayed His omnipotence, is but a repetition of that particular one in which we have our allotted place! As if He had but one pattern for universal creation! Only one scheme for peopling and dealing with infinitude! Oh, that *the clay* should think thus of *Him that fashioneth it!*‡ Forgetting, in an exulting moment of insect blindness and presumption, His own awful words, *My thoughts are not your thoughts, neither are your ways my ways. For as the heavens are higher than the earth, so are my ways higher than your ways, and my thoughts than your thoughts!* §

* Lord Byron—*Hebrew Melodies.* "The philosopher will scan," says Sir David, at the close of his eloquent treatise, "with a new sense, the lofty spheres in which he is to study."—P. 259.

† *More Worlds than One,* pp. 164, 165. ‡ Isaiah xlv. 9. § Isaiah lv. 8, 9.

We are now, however, about to people the fixed stars. The only proof that they are the centres of planetary systems, resides in the assumption that these stars are like the sun; and as resembling him in their nature and qualities, so having the same offices and appendages; being independent sources of light, and thence probably of heat; therefore having attendant planets, to which they may impart such light and heat; and these planets, inhabitants living under and enjoying those benign influences. Everything here depends on this proposition, that the stars are like the sun; and it becomes essential to examine what evidence we have of the exactness of this likeness.* In the Preface to his Second Edition, the essayist, whose scientific knowledge few will venture to impugn, boldly asserts that " man's knowledge of the physical properties of the luminaries which he discerns in the skies, is, even now, *almost nothing;*" and " such being the state of our knowledge, as bearing on the doctrine of the plurality of worlds, the time appeared to be not inopportune for a calm discussion of the question,—upon which, accordingly," he adds, " I have ventured in the following pages." In the same Preface he has ably condensed into a single paragraph his views on the nature and extent of our present knowledge on the subject of the fixed stars:—†

" In more recent times, many of the astronomical discoveries which have been made, tend to render the conjecture of the plurality of inhabited worlds improbable on physical grounds. * * * Again: It was found that many of the Fixed Stars are physically double, and therefore cannot be the centres of simple systems of planets, as the Sun is. And that such double stars have planets revolving or moving near them at all, is a supposition arbitrary, quite unsupported by any analogy, and never yet shown to be physically possible. Again, there are variable stars, which are evidently in very important respects unlike our Sun. Moreover, these cases of double stars, which were at first supposed to be rare exceptions to a general rule, are now, by recent examination, found to be very numerous,—not less numerous than one-third of the

* *Essay*, p. 244. † Pp. vii. viii.

whole number of stars. And the variable stars also are very numerous. So that it appears to be not improbable that a single permanent star like the Sun, even leaving its planets out of consideration, is a rare exception, instead of being the rule. And with all these negative indications, there is found in the heavens no vestige of anything like a planet revolving round a fixed star!"

In the opening of the chapter devoted to this subject (ch. viii.), he admits "the special evidence," as to the probability of these stars containing, in themselves, or in accompanying planets, inhabitants of any kind, "is, indeed, slight, *either way*."

As to clustered and double stars, they appear to give us, he says, but little promise of inhabitants. In what degree of condensation the matter of these binary systems is, compared with that of our solar system, we have no means whatever of knowing: but even granting that each individual of the pair were a sun like ours, in the nature of its material, and its state of condensation, is it probable that it resembles our sun also in having planets revolving about it? A system of planets revolving about, or among, a pair of suns, which are at the same time revolving about one another, is so complex a scheme (apparently), so impossible to arrange in a stable manner, that the assumption of the existence of such schemes, without a vestige of evidence, can hardly require refutation. No doubt, if we were really required to provide such a binary system of suns, with attendant planets, this would be best done by putting the planets so near to one sun that they should not be sensibly affected by the other; and this is accordingly what has been proposed. For, as has been well said by Sir John Herschell, of the supposed planets, in making this proposal, "unless closely nestled under the protecting wing of their immediate superior, the sweep of the other sun in his perihelion passage round their own, might carry them off, or whirl them into orbits utterly inconsistent with the existence of their inhabitants." "To assume the existence of the inhabitants," says our essayist, "in spite of such dangers, and to provide against those dangers by placing the planets so close to one sun as to be out of the reach of the other, though the whole distance of the two may not, and as we know in some cases does not, exceed the dimensions of our solar system, is showing them all the favour which is possible. But in making this provision, it is overlooked that it may not be possible to keep them in permanent orbits so near to the selected centre. Their Sun may be a vast sphere of luminous vapour; and the planets plunged into this atmosphere may, instead of describing regular orbits, plough their way in spiral paths through the nebulous abyss of its central nucleus." *

In dealing with the single stars, which are, like the sun, self-luminous, can they be proved, like him, to be definite dense masses? *his* density being about that of water. Or are they, or many of them, luminous masses in a far more diffused state, visually contracted to points through their immense distance? Some of those which we have the best means of examining are one-third, or even less in mass, than he: and if Sirius, for instance, be in this diffused condition, though that would not of itself prevent his having planets, it would make him so unlike our sun, as much to break the force of the presumption that he must have planets as the sun has. Again: As far back as our knowledge of our sun extends, his has been a permanent condition of brightness: yet many of the fixed stars not only undergo changes, but periodical, and possibly progressive changes:—whence it may be inferred, perhaps, that they are not, generally, in the same permanent condition as our sun. As to the evidence of their revolution on their axis, this has been inferred from their having periodical recurrences of fainter and brighter lustre; as if revolving orbs with one side darkened by spots. Of these, five only can be at present spoken of by astronomers † with precision.‡ Nothing is more probable

* *Essay*, pp. 243, 244.

† See them specified, p. 251.

‡ (1.) *Omicron*, in the constellation *Cetus*, revolves in 331 days. (2.) *Algol*, in the constellation *Perseus*, revolves in 2 days, 21 hours. (3.) *Delta*,

than that these periodical changes indicate the revolution of these stellar masses on their axes—a universal law, apparently, of all the large compact masses of the universe, but by no means inferring their being, or having accompanying planets, inhabited. The sun's rotation is not shown intelligibly connected with its having near it the inhabited earth.

In the mean time, in so far as these stars are periodical, they are proved to be, not like, but *unlike* our sun. The only real point of resemblance, then, is that of being self-luminous; in the highest degree ambiguous and inconclusive, and furnishing no argument entitled to be deemed one from analogy. Humboldt deems the force of analogy to tend even in the *opposite* direction. "After all," he asks,* "is the assumption of satellites [attendant planets] to the fixed stars so absolutely necessary? If we were to begin from the outer planets, Jupiter, &c., analogy might seem to require that all planets have satellites:—yet this is not so with Mars, Venus, Mercury;" to which may now be added the thirty [one] Planetoids—making a much greater number of bodies that have not, than that have, satellites. The assumption, then, that the fixed stars are of exactly the same nature as the sun, was originally a bold guess; but there has not since been a vestige of any confirmatory fact:—no planet, nor anything fairly indicating the existence of one revolving round a fixed star, has ever hitherto been discerned;—and the subsequent discovery of nebulæ; binary systems; clusters of stars; periodical stars; of varied and accelerating periods of such stars,—all seem to point the other way: leaving, though possibly facts small in amount, the original assumption a mere guess, un-

in the constellation *Cepheus*, revolves in 5 days, 9 hours. (4.) *Beta*, in the *Lyre*, revolves in 6 days, 10 hours -possibly, from one revolution having been taken for two, in 12 days, 21 hours. (5.) *Eta, Aquilær*, 7 days, 4 hours. There are about thirty more stars supposed to be subject to such changes.

* *Cosmos*, iii. 373.

supported by all that three centuries of most diligent, and in other respects, successful research, have been able to bring to light. All the knowledge of times succeeding Copernicus, Galileo, and Kepler,—who might well believe the stars to be in every sense suns;—among other things, the disclosure of the history of our own planet, as one in which such grand changes have been constantly going on; the certainty that in by far the greatest part of the duration of its existence, it has been tenanted by creatures entirely different from those which give an interest, and thence a persuasiveness, to the belief of inhabitants in worlds appended to each star; the impossibility which appears, on the gravest consideration, of transferring to other worlds such interests as belong to our race in this world;—all these considerations, it would seem, should have prevented that old and arbitrary conjecture from growing up, among a generation *professing philosophical caution and scientific discipline*, into a settled belief. Finally, it will be time enough to speculate about the inhabitants of the planets which belong to such systems, as soon as we shall have ascertained that there are such planets,—or that there is one such.*

In the *Dialogue*, written after the first edition of the "Essay" had appeared, the essayist greatly strengthens the position for which he had contended in it, by an important passage containing the results of the eminent astronomer *M. Struve's* recent examination of double stars, and the result of his elaborate and comprehensive comparison of the whole body of facts in stellar astronomy. Among the brighter stars, M. Struve arrives at the conclusion, that every FOURTH such star is physically double; and that a completed knowledge of double stars may prove every THIRD bright star to be physically double! And in the case of stars of inferior magnitude, that the number of *insulated* stars, though indeed greater than that of such compound systems, is nevertheless only three times, perhaps only twice as great. Thus the loose evidence of

* Ch. viii., *passim.*

resemblance between our sun and the fixed stars becomes feebler the more it is examined; and the assumption of stellar *planetary* systems appears, when closely scrutinised, to dwindle away to nothing.*

Now, to so much of the foregoing grave and formidably arrayed facts and speculations concerning the fixed stars, as are contained in the Essay, from which we have faithfully and carefully extracted the substance, in order that our readers may be able, in some degree, to judge for themselves, Sir David Brewster answers, in effect, and generally in words, thus.

The greatest and grandest truth in astronomy, is the motion of the solar system; advancing with all the planets and satellites in the heavens, at the rate of fifty-seven miles a second, round some distant invisible body, in an orbit of such inconceivable dimensions, that millions of years may be required for a single orbit. When we consider that this centre must [?] be a sun with attendant planets like our own, revolving in like manner round our sun, [?] or round their common centre of gravity, the mind rejects, almost with indignation, the ignoble sentiment that Man is the only being performing this immeasurable journey; and that Jupiter, Saturn, Uranus, and Neptune, with their bright array of regal train-bearers, are but as colossal blocks of lifeless clay, encumbering the Earth as a drag, and mocking the creative majesty of Heaven. From the birth of man *to the extinction of his race* [!] the system to which he belongs will have described but an infinitesimal arc in that grand cosmical orbit in which it is destined to move. This affords a new argument for the plurality of worlds. Since every fixed star must have planets, the fact of our system revolving round a similar system of planets, furnishes a new argument from analogy; for as there is at least one inhabited planet in the one system, there must for the same reason be one in the other, and consequently as many as there are systems in the Uni-

* *Dial.*, pp. 20–23.

verse.* Thus our system is not absolutely fixed in space, but is connected with the other systems in the Universe.

The fixed stars, continues Sir David, are suns of other systems, "whose planets are invisible from their distance, as are ours from the nearest fixed star. Every *single* star shining by its own native light is the centre of a planetary system like our own—the lamp that lights, the stove that heats, and the power that guides in their orbits, inhabited worlds like our own. Many are *double*, with a system of planets round each, or the centre of gravity of both. No one can believe that two suns would be placed in the heavens, for no other purpose than to revolve round their common centre of gravity. It is "highly probable," that *our Sun is one of a binary System*, and has at present an unseen partner; and we are "entitled to conclude" that all the other binary systems have at least an inhabited planet: wherever there is a self-luminous fixed or movable sun there must be a planetary system; and wherever there is a planetary system, there must be life and intelligence.†

Apart from the assertion of his cardinal principle, with which we are familiar from his peremptory assertions, namely, that since our sun has an inhabited planet, all others must, and also that all planets must, be inhabited; —the argumentative value of these two chapters seems to lie in this, that they annihilate one of the essayist's leading points of *unlikeness* between our Sun and other Fixed Stars, inasmuch as it, together with so many of them, is one of a binary system: wherefore what is true of it, is true of them, *et vice versâ.* He bases this proposition, viz., that our sun is one of a binary system, on "high probability," from "the motion of our own system round a distant centre." ‡ The great truth of this motion, he accuses the essayist of having "completely misrepresented, foreseeing its influence on the mind as an argument for more worlds

* *More Worlds than One,* Ch. vi., *passim.* † Ibid. Ch. viii. *passim.*
‡ Ibid. p. 164.

than one." * What the essayist had said on the subject, was this: † he spoke of "the *attempt* to show that the sun, carrying with it the whole solar system, is in motion; and the further *attempt* to show the direction of that motion;—and again, the *hypothesis* that the sun itself revolves round some distant object in space." These "minute inquiries and bold conjectures," he says, "cannot throw any light on the question, whether any part besides the earth *be inhabited:* any more than the investigation of the movements of the ocean and their laws can prove or disprove the existence of *marine plants and animals.* They do not, on that account, cease to be important and interesting objects of speculation, but they do not belong to our subject." As to the sun's motion, however, we are bound to say, that the Astronomer Royal has recently declared, "that every astronomer who has examined the matter carefully, has come to a conclusion very nearly the same as that come to by Sir William Herschell,—that the whole solar system is moving bodily towards a point in the constellation Hercules; but it is a thing in which the computation is not very accurate, and it will probably remain inaccurate for many years to come." ‡ Before quitting this part of the subject, we may state that the essayist, in his second Preface,§ points out the insecure character of astronomical calculations as to the amount of absolute light ascribed to some of the fixed stars. It has been estimated that the illuminating power of *Alpha* Centauri, the nearest to our system, is nearly double that of the sun, placed at that distance, which is two hundred thousand times as far off as is the sun; but Sir John Herschell will not concur in more of the calculation than attributes to the star the emission of *more* light than our sun. Surely the critical and precarious character of such calculations, should not be lost sight of by candid and compe-

* *More Worlds than One,* Ch. viii. p. 119. † *Essay,* p. 257.

‡ *Lect. on Astron.,* 2d edit. (1849), sec. v. p. 174.

§ Pp. ix. x.

tent inquirers; but incline them to scan somewhat closely any pretensions tinctured by astronomic dogmatism.

One immense step more, however, but our last, brings us to the "outskirts of creation," as the essayist calls it,—the *Nebulæ;* and here we find him once more confronted by his indefatigable and implacable opponent. We must therefore take our biggest and best mental telescope to behold these two Specks intellectual, so far off in infinitude, wrangling about a faint cloud vastly further off than themselves.—Do you see how angry one of them looks, and how provokingly stolid the other? One of them is vehemently gesticulating and protesting that the other *will* not see, what that other, gazing intently, declares he really cannot. 'Tis all about the nature of that same cloud, or nebula; and perhaps we are catching, in their dispute, a chord or two of the music of the spheres! The essayist is required, by his brother speck, to believe that the faintly-luminous patch at which they are gazing—a thousandth part of the visible breadth of our own sun—contains in it more life than exists in as many such systems as the unassisted eye can see stars in the heavens on the clearest winter night! A view of the greatness of creation so stupendous, this, that the astounded speck, the essayist, asks for a moment's breathing time to consider the matter. "We are entitled to draw the conclusion," says the other, with lively emotion, "that these *nebulæ* are clusters of stars, at such an immense distance from our own system, that each star of which they are composed is the sun or centre of a system of planets; and that these planets are inhabited: are, like our earth, the seat of vegetable, animal, and intellectual life:"* that all the nebulæ are resolvable into stars; and appear as nebulæ only because they are more distant than the region in which they can appear as stars.†

"Each Nebula," says Sir David, "corresponds with our hill of

* *More Worlds than One*, p. 176. † *Essay*, p. 211.

microscopic infusorial animals: each System, with a cubic inch of its materials; and each planet with a cubic line. If we have seen with our own eyes, in the microscope, the individual animal only the two-thousandth part of an inch in size, and if we have seen the hill which is an accumulation of them, need we wonder at nebulæ being stars, stars being suns, and at *planets being inhabited!*"*

The conclusion, however, at which the essayist arrives, after an elaborate examination of evidence, and especially of the latest discoveries in this dim and distant region, by Sir John Herschell and the Earl of Rosse, is—that nebulæ are vast masses of incoherent or gaseous matter, of immense tenuity, diffused in forms more or less irregular, but all of them destitute of any regular system of solid moving bodies. "So far, then," he concludes, "as these nebulæ are concerned, the improbability of *their* being inhabited appears to amount to the highest point that can be conceived. We may, by the indulgence of fancy, people the summer clouds, or the beams of the aurora borealis, with living beings of the same kind of substance as those bright appearances themselves; and in doing so, we are not making any bolder assertion than when we stock the nebulæ with inhabitants, and call them, in that sense, distant worlds."† The essayist contends that the argument for the vastness of the scheme of the Universe, suggested by the resolution of the nebulæ, is found to be untenable:—inasmuch as the greatest astronomers now agree in believing nebulæ to have *distances of the same order* as Fixed Stars. Their filmy appearance is a true indication of a highly attenuated substance: so attenuated as to destroy all probability of their being inhabited worlds. With this opinion as to the tenuity of nebulæ, agrees the absence of all *observed* motion among their parts; while the extraordinary spiral arrangement of many of them, proves that nevertheless many of them really *have* motion, and suggests modes of calculating their tenuity, and showing how extreme it is. "It is probable," said Lord Rosse,

* P. 169. † *Essay*, pp. 235, 236.

in a paper which we ourselves heard him read not long ago, from the chair of the Royal Society, of which he is one of the brightest ornaments, "that in the nebular systems, motion exists. If we see a system with a distinct spiral arrangement, all analogy leads us to conclude that there has been motion; and that if there has been motion, that motion still continues." "Among the nebulæ," he says, "there are vast numbers, much too faint to be sketched or measured with any prospect of advantage: the most powerful instruments we possess showing in them nothing of an organised structure, but merely a confused mass of nebulosity, of varying brightness."* The essayist makes powerful use, moreover, of Sir John Herschell's celebrated observation of the Magellanic Clouds,† lying near the South Pole; exhibiting the co-existence, in a limited compass, and in indiscriminate position, of stars, clusters of stars, nebulæ regular and irregular, and nebular streaks and patches, things different not merely to us, but in themselves; nebulæ, side by side with stars and clusters of stars; nebulous matter resolvable, close to nebulous matter irresolvable;—the last and widest step by which the dimensions of the universe have been expanded, in the notions of eager speculators, being checked by a completer knowledge, and a sager spirit of speculation.‡ In discussing such matters as these, he finely observes, "It is difficult to make men feel that so much ignorance can lie close to so much knowledge; to make them believe that they have been allowed to discover so much, and yet are not allowed to discover more." §

In alluding to the nebulæ, as subjects of our most powerful telescopic observation, the essayist had presumed to

* *Dialogue*, p. 18.

† By the *Magellanic Clouds* is meant, a certain pair of remarkably bright spaces of the skies, filled with a cloudy light, which lie near the Southern Pole; and which, having been unavoidably noticed by the first Antarctic voyagers, are called after the name of "*Magellan.*"

‡ *Essay*, p. 214. § Ibid. p. 216.

speak in a tone of slightly sarcastic raillery concerning the "*shining dots*"—"the *lumps of light*" which are rendered apparent amidst them: asking, what are these lumps? (1.) How large? (2.) At what distances? (3.) Of what structure? (4.) Of what use?—adding, he must be a bold man who undertakes to answer the question, that each is a sun, with attendant systems of planets. Sir David, exceedingly irate, answers: "We accept the challenge, and appeal to our readers—(1.) The size of the dot, or lump, is large enough to be a sun. (2.) This cannot be answered, for want of 'knowing the apparent distance between the centres of the dots.' (3.) Like our sun, 'it will consist of a luminous envelope, enclosing a dark nucleus.' (4.) Of no conceivable use, but to give light to planets, or to the solid *nuclei* of which they consist!" In his turn, he asks the essayist—what is the size, distance, structure, and use of the dots, upon his hypothesis? The essayist, he observes, is silent;* but in his *Essay* he had said, distinctly enough, "Let us not wrangle about words. By all means let these dots be stars, if we know about what we are speaking: if a star mean merely a luminous dot in the sky. But that these stars shall resemble, in their nature, stars of the first magnitude, and that such stars shall resemble our sun, are surely very bold structures of assumption to build on such a basis. Some nebulæ are resolvable into distinct points; but what would it amount to? That the substance of all nebulæ is not continuous; separate, and separable into distinct luminous elements:—nebulæ are, it would then seem, as it were of a curdled or granulated texture; they have run into *lumps* of light, or been formed originally of such lumps." And then follow some ingenious and refined speculations, into which we have not space to enter. We may, indeed, be well content with what we have done; having already travelled from a tolerable depth in the crust of our own little planet, past planet after planet, star after

* *More Worlds than One*, p. 215.

star, till we reached the nebulous "outskirts of creation;" accompanied by two Mentors of Infinitude, whispering into our ear—one, that life, animal, intellectual, moral, was swarming around us at every step; the other, that intellectual and moral life ceased with our own earth, as far as we were able to detect its existence; and giving us solemn and mysterious reasons why it should be so.

Our essayist, however, is not exhausted by the efforts he has made in his destructive career. If he be a proud "setter down" of cosmological systems, he determines, in turn, to be a "putter up:" and so presents us with his own *Theory of the Solar System;* and an explanation of the mode in which he conceives it possible that all appearances in the universe beyond, may be reconciled with it. "It may serve," he says, "to confirm his argument, if he give a description of the system, which shall continue and connect his views of the constitution and peculiarities as to physical circumstances, of each of the planets. It will help us in our speculation, if we can regard them as not only a collection, but a scheme;—if we can give not an Enunciation only, but a Theory. Now such a SCHEME, such a THEORY, appears to offer itself to us."* The scope of this scheme, or theory, is, as we some time ago saw, to make our earth, in point of astronomical fact and reality, the largest planetary body in the solar system; its domestic hearth; the only part of the frame, revolving round the sun, which has become a "WORLD." We must, however, be very brief, earnestly commending this part of his work to the attention of the philosophical reader.

The planets exterior to Mars, especially Jupiter and Saturn, appear spheres of water, or aqueous vapour. The Earth has a considerable atmosphere of air and of vapour; while on Venus or Mercury, so close to the Sun, we see nothing of a gaseous or aqueous atmosphere; they and Mars differing little, in density, from the Earth.

* *Essay*, p. 298.

"Now," he asks, "does not this look as if the water and the vapour belonging to the solar system were driven off into the outer regions of its vast circuit; while the solid masses, nearest to the focus of heat, are all, approximately, of the same nature? So that the Earth is situated nearly in that region of the system where the existence of matter, in both a solid, a fluid, and a gaseous condition, is possible. Outside her orbit—or at least that of the planetoids—there is apparently no solid matter, or, if any, a vast preponderance of watery and vaporous matter. Inside of that orbit, we see no traces of water, vapour, or gas, but solid matter. The Earth alone is placed at the border where the conditions of life are combined: ground to stand upon; air to breathe; water to nourish vegetables, and thus animals; solid matter to supply the materials for their more solid parts: and with this, a due supply of light and heat,—a due energy of the force of weight. All these are conditions requisite for life; and that they meet elsewhere than in the neighbourhood of the Earth's orbit, we see strong reason to disbelieve. The Earth, then, seems to be the abode of life: not because *all* the globes, revolving round the Sun, may be assumed to be the abodes of life, but because the Earth is *fitted* to be so, by a complex combination of properties and relations, not at all applying to the others. That the *Earth* is inhabited, is not a reason for believing that the other planets are so, but for believing that they are not. * * * Can we see any physical reason for the probable fact, that all the water and vapour of this system is gathered in its outward parts?"

Now THE EARTH'S ORBIT, according to the essayist's theory, IS THE TEMPERATE ZONE OF THE SOLAR SYSTEM; where only the play of hot and cold, moist and dry, is possible. Water and gases, clouds and vapours, form, mainly, the planets in the outer part of the solar system; while masses, such as result from the fusion of the most solid materials, lie nearer the Sun, and are found principally within the orbit of Jupiter. After a further exposition of his "theory," the essayist observes that it agrees with the nebular hypothesis, so FAR as it applies to the *solar system;* exactly, and very sternly, repudiating that hypothesis as it applies to the universe in general.* "If we allow ourselves," says he, "to speculate *at all*, on physical grounds, respecting the origin of the Earth, the hypo-

* *More Worlds than One*, p. 315, and note.

thesis, that it has passed through a fluid and a gaseous condition, does not appear more extravagant than any other cosmogonical hypothesis: not even if we suppose that the other bodies of the solar system have shared in the like changes. *But*, that all the stars and the nebulæ have gone, or are going through, a series of changes such as those by which the solar system has been formed,—the nebular hypothesis, as it applies to the *universe* in general, is precisely the doctrine which I here reject, giving my reasons."*

The whole of the chapter devoted to "the Theory of the Solar System," is distinguished by remarkable ingenuity and originality. It is, however, that entitled "the Argument from Design" which, independently of all connexion with the speculations of the author, as already laid before our readers, is worthiest of consideration by all interested in natural theology. It touches many topics which must have occupied the profoundest thoughts of mankind, and touches them with the utmost caution and delicacy. In the 34th section of that chapter (xi.), will be found a passage of singular boldness and imaginative eloquence; but liable, in our opinion, to serious misconception, and susceptible of misrepresentation—by those, at least, who are either unable or indisposed to weigh the entire chapter, and ascertain its real value and tendency. Certain expressions have startled ourselves, we own, not a little, when reflecting that they relate to the possible mode of action of Omniscient Omnipotence; and we shall be gratified by seeing them vindicated, or explained, in the next edition of his *Essay*.†

* In his Third Edition, written since these papers appeared, Dr Whewell alludes to the attempt of his assailant to fasten on him "what is intended to be an odious imputation"—that of holding "the nebular hypothesis:" "forgetting," he continues, "that the nebular hypothesis is a hypothesis *about the nebulæ*. That the nebulæ are *not* in a state of progress towards becoming systems of worlds, is a doctrine prominently asserted and argued for in the Essay;—that they *are*, is commonly held in conjunction with the assertion of the "plurality of worlds."

† See Note at the end of the paper.

Each of our speculators closes his book with a chapter devoted to "The Future." The ideas of Sir David concerning the duration of the human race upon the earth, which Inspiration warns us is so awfully uncertain, and will be cut short suddenly—in a moment—*in the twinkling of an eye*, seem to be curiously definite; since we have seen him stating, in his sixth chapter, that "from the birth of man to the extinction of his race, the solar system to which he belongs will have described but an infinitesimal arc in that grand cosmical orbit in which it is destined to move." Without pausing to ask who told him this, let us give our readers "THE FUTURE OF THE UNIVERSE," according to Sir David Brewster. He says that the scientific truths on which depends the plurality of worlds, are intimately associated with the future destiny of man: who turns to the future of the sidereal systems, as the hallowed spots in which is to be spent his immortal existence. Scripture has not spoken articulately of the future locality of the blest; but Reason has combined the scattered utterances of Inspiration, and with an almost oracular voice declared that the Maker of the worlds will place, *in these*, the beings of His choice! In what region, Reason does not determine; but it is *impossible* for man, with the light of Revelation as his guide, to doubt for a moment that on the celestial spheres his future is to be spent, in lofty inquiries; social intercourse; the renewal of domestic ties; and in the service of his Almighty Benefactor. The Christian's future, not defined in his creed, enwrapt in apocalyptic mysteries, evades his grasp: it is only Astronomy that opens the mysterious expanse of the universe to his eye, and creates an intelligible paradise in the world to come. Wherefore, says Sir David, we must impregnate the popular mind with the truths of natural science; teaching them in every school, and recommending, if not illustrating, them from every pulpit: fixing in the minds and associating in the affections, alike of age and youth, the great truths, in the planetary and sidereal universe, on which the doctrine of More Worlds than One must respectively rest—the philosopher scanning with a new sense the spheres in which he is to study; and the Christian, the temples in which he is to worship.—Such, in his own words, is Sir David Brewster's final and authoritative exposition of the CREED of the Philosopher, and the HOPE of the Christian! Of such a nature, it appears, are to be the *new heavens and the new earth wherein dwelleth righteousness;* and such, henceforth, as he has vouchsafed to indicate, becomes the duty of the Christian teacher in the Family, in the School, in the Pulpit! So absolutely and irrefragably, it seems, are demonstrated the stupendous facts of astronomical science, on which this Creed and this Faith depend; so unerring are our telescopes and other instruments; that he who does not receive this "Creed" is no philosopher, nor he who rejects the "Hope," a Christian! But, in the mean time, surely it occurs to any one to reflect how inconceivably embarrassing to *such* a philosopher, and to *such* a Christian, is the possibility that many, or a few years hence, such immense improvements may be made in telescopes, or such other modes devised of acquiring a knowledge of the celestial structures, as to demonstrate to the sense, as well as reason, of us impatient and presumptuous tenants of the earth, that the planets are *not* inhabited! that the fixed stars are not suns, and have not a planet a-piece—no, not even a solitary planet among them! Thus rendering our astounded and dismayed philosopher homeless and "*creedless*," and the Christian helpless and "*hopeless:*"—the former one of those who, *professing themselves to be wise, become fools;** the latter, *likened unto a foolish man which built his house upon the sand.*†

The *Future* of the essayist is of a different kind, and adumbrated with becoming humility and diffidence. "I did not," he says, "venture farther than to intimate, that when we are taught, that *as we have borne the image*

* Romans i. 22. † Matthew vii. 26.

*of the earthy, we shall also bear the image of the heavenly,* we may find, in even natural science, reasons for opening our minds to the reception of the cheering and elevating announcement."*

Whatever may be the future of our earth, and whatever be the scenes destined to be enacted upon it, with reference to its present human occupants, and independently of the revelations of Scripture, the possibilities reverently put forward by the essayist he declares so vague and doubtful, as far as any scientific analogies lead, that it would be most unwise to attempt to claim for them any value, as points in which Science supplies support to Religion. Those persons who most deeply feel the value of religion, and are most strongly convinced of its truths, will be the most willing to declare that religious belief is, and ought to be, independent of any such support, and must be, and may be, firmly established on its own proper basis. We find no encouragement, then, he says, for any attempt to obtain from science, by the light of the analogy of the past, any definite view of a future condition of the creation. But he concludes his labours by saying, that they will not have been without profit, if they have left upon our minds these convictions:—

"That if the analogy of science prove anything, it proves that the Creator of man can make a creature as far superior to man, as man, when most intellectual, moral, religious, and spiritual," is superior to the brutes.

And again, "That man's intellect is of a divine, and therefore of an immortal nature.

"Those persons who can, on any basis of belief, combine these two convictions, so as to feel that they have a personal interest in both of them—those who have such grounds as religion, happily appealed to, can furnish, for hoping that their imperishable element may, hereafter, be clothed with a new and more glorious apparel by the hand of its Almighty Maker,—may be well content to acknowledge that science and philosophy could not give them this combined conviction in any manner in which it could minister that consolation, and that trust in the Divine power and goodness, which human nature in its present condition requires."

* *Dialogue*, p. 74.

In this impressive and dignified tone, and these deeply-considered expressions, the essayist concludes his Inquiries and Speculations, in the true spirit of a Christian Philosopher.

We have now placed before our readers the substance of the arguments for and against a plurality of worlds, so far as developed in the reasonings of Dr Whewell, and the assertions of Sir David Brewster. The essay of the former is a work so replete with subtle thought, bold speculation, and knowledge of almost every kind, used with extraordinary force and dexterity, as to challenge the patient and watchful attention of the most thoughtful reader; and that, whether he be or be not versed in astronomical speculations. Great as are the powers and resources of the author, however, we detect no trace of dogmatism or arrogance, but, on the contrary, a true spirit of fearless, but patient and candid, inquiry. It is a mighty problem of which he proposes a solution, and he does no more than propose it: in his Preface declaring that, to himself at least, his arguments "appear to be of no small philosophical force, though he is quite ready to weigh carefully and candidly any answer which may be offered to them."

We feel grateful to him for the storehouse of authentic facts, and the novel combination of unsuspected inferences from them, with which he has presented us; and are not aware that he has supplied, in a single instance, just reason to regret confiding in his correctness or candour. In travelling with him through his vast and chequered course, we feel that we have accompanied not only the philosopher and the divine, but the gentleman: one who, while manifestly knowing what is due to himself, as manifestly respects his intelligent reader. In several of his astronomical assumptions and inferences we may be unable to concur, particularly in respect of the nebulous stars. Nor do we desire to be considered as any more committing ourselves to his bold and ingenious Theory of the

Solar System, than we should think of denying his right to propose his Theory, or have it deliberately considered. Where all is speculation, why should not *he* speculate, if he do so consistently with established facts?

We may, however, well falter at expressing a decisive *Ay* or *No* to the great question proposed by him for discussion. Yet we acknowledge that he has sensibly shaken our opinion as to the validity of the reasons usually assigned for believing in a plurality of worlds. He remorselessly ties us down to EVIDENCE, as he ought to do; and all the more rigorously, because the affirmative conclusion, at which many heedless persons are disposed to jump, is one which, if well founded, occasions religious difficulties of a grave character among the profoundest and perhaps even devoutest thinkers. To suppose that Omnipotence may not have peopled already, or contemplate a future peopling of the starry spheres with intelligent beings, of as different a kind and order as it is possible for our limited faculties to conceive, yet in some way involved in physical conditions, altogether inexplicable to us, would be the acme of impious presumption. When we look at Sirius, in his solitary splendour in the midnight sky, pouring forth *possibly* fifty times the light and heat of our sun, upon *possibly* a prodigiously greater planetary system than our own, it is natural to conjecture whether, among many other *possibilities*, it may be the seat of intelligence, perhaps of a transcendant character. Here the imagination may disport itself as it pleases: yet we shall feel ourselves compelled—those who can *think* about the matter—to own that our imaginations are, as it were, "cabined, cribbed, confined," by the objects and associations to which we are at present restricted; and as the late eminent Prussian astronomer, Bessel, observed, those who imagine inhabitants in the moon and planets, "supposed them, in spite of all their protestations, as like to *men*, as one egg to another." But when we proceed further, and insist on likening these supposed inhabitants to ourselves, intellectually and morally, then it is that both philosophy and religion concur in rebuking us, and enjoining a reverent diffidence. What do you really, what do you suppose, that you mean, would say the essayist, when you say it is probable that the heavenly bodies are peopled by beings *like ourselves?* Have you weighed the expression? Have you ascertained the conditions which it involves and presupposes?

We have probably read as much on these subjects as many of our readers, and that with deep interest and due attention; but we never met with so cogent a demonstration as is contained in this Essay, of the theological difficulties besetting the popular doctrine of a plurality of worlds. Had God vouchsafed to tell us that it was so, there would have been an end of the matter, and with it all difficulty would have disappeared, to one whose whole life, as the Christian's ought to be, is one continued act of faith; but God has thought fit to preserve an awful silence concerning his dealings with other scenes of physical existence: while he has as distinctly revealed that of spiritual beings whose functions are vitally connected with man, as he exists upon the earth, the subject of a sublime economy, which, we are assured by Inspiration, that *the angels desire to look into.* The Christian implicitly and joyfully believes that there IS a HEAVEN, where the presence of the adorable Deity constitutes happiness, to the most exalted of His ministers and servants, perfect and ineffable: happiness in which He has solemnly assured us that we may hereafter participate: *for since the beginning of the world, men have not heard, nor perceived by the ear, neither hath the eye seen, O God, beside Thee, what He hath prepared for him that waiteth for Him.** This, our Maker has told us; he has not told us the other, nor anything about it: no, not when He visited the earth, unless we can dimly see such a significance in the words, "In my Father's house—*οἰκίᾳ*—are many *mansions—μοναί*—: if

* Isaiah, xliv. 4. This verse is quoted by St Paul in 1 Cor. ii. 9.

it were not so, I would have told you. I go to prepare a place—τόπον—for you." The word μονή is used twice in the New Testament, and in the same chapter:* in the verse already quoted, and in the 23d—"If a man love me, he will keep my words: and my Father will love him, and we will come unto him, and make our abode, μονὴν, with him." Here are the three words in the same verse, οἰκία, μονή, τόπος. In my Father's house there are μοναὶ πολλαὶ, many places of *abode*. Heaven is the οἰκία, our common place, and it has many subdivisions, room enough for angels, as well as for the spirits of just men made perfect. It is possibly an allusion to the temple, God's earthly house, which had many chambers in it. But who shall require us to believe that this μονὴ was a star, or planet? It may be so, it may not; there can be no sin in a devout mind conjecturing on the subject; but the essayist does not meddle with these solemn topics: confining himself to the physical reasons for conjecturing, with more or less probability, that the stars are habitations for human beings. To him who reverently receives the cardinal doctrine of Christianity, the Divinity of our Saviour, his silence on the subject before us, speaks with awful eloquence to the soul. But we forbear to prosecute a subject so grand, so solemnizing, so sublimely suggestive. Giving our full meed of applause to the author of the *Essay* before us, for the sincere and pious discretion which he uniformly exhibits in dealing with such subjects, we take our leave of him with an admirable passage from his *Dialogue*:—

"*U.* But your arguments are merely negative. You prove only that we do not know the planets to be inhabited.

"*Z.* If, when I have proved that point, men were to cease to talk as if they knew that the planets *are* inhabited, I should have produced a great effect.

"*U.* Your basis is too narrow for so vast a superstructure, as that all the rest of the universe, besides the earth, is uninhabited.

* John xiv. 2, 23.

"*Z.* Perhaps; for my philosophical basis is only the earth—the only known habitation. But on this same narrow basis, the earth, you build up a superstructure that other bodies ARE inhabited. What I do is, to show that each part of your structure is void of tenacity, and cannot stand.

"It is probable that when we have reduced to their real value all the presumptions drawn from physical reasoning, for the opinion of planets and stars being either inhabited, or uninhabited, the force of these will be perceived to be so small, that *the belief of all thoughtful persons on this subject will be determined by moral, metaphysical, and theological consideration.*" *

In these few words may be found the essence of the entire Essay.

"More Worlds than One," will not, we are constrained to say, in our opinion, add to the well-earned reputation of Sir David Brewster. It is a hasty and slight performance, entirely of a popular character, and disfigured throughout, not only by an overweening confidence and peremptoriness of assertion, but by tinges of personality, and outbursts of heat, which are indeed strange disturbing forces in a philosophical discussion. Dr Whewell's Essay is a work requiring, in a worthy answer, great consideration; and we do not think that "More Worlds than One," evidences a tithe of such consideration. Its author does not show a proper respect for his opponent; nor has he taken a proper measure of his formidable proportions, as a logical and scientific disputant!—one who should be answered in a cold and exact spirit, or it were much better to leave him alone. Sir David must forgive us if we quote a sentence or two from devout old John Wesley, a man who had several points of greatness in him:—

"Be not so *positive*, especially with regard to things which are neither easy, nor necessary to be determined. When I was young, I was *sure* of everything. In a few years, having been mistaken a thousand times, I was not half so sure of most things as before. At present I am hardly sure of anything, but what God has revealed to me! Upon the whole, an ingenious man may easily

* *Dialogue*, p. 42.

flourish on this head. How much more glorious is it for the great God to have created innumerable worlds than this little globe only! But, after all, I would ask one plain question: Suppose there are more worlds than sands on the sea-shore, is not the universe finite still? It must be, unless it be God. And if it be finite, it can still bear no proportion to Him that is INFINITE, any more than this ball of earth does. How large soever it be, still, compared TO HIM, it is as nothing, or the small dust of the balance. Do you ask, then, what is this Spot to the great God? Why, as much as millions of systems. GREAT and LITTLE have place with regard to us; but before Him, they vanish away! Enlarge the bounds of Creation as much as you please, still it is but a drop to the Creator." *

We said, in an early portion of this paper, that after the two questions, Why should there be more worlds than one? and, Why should there not? we should ask a third, on our own account, and of a practical character: *What if there be?* With this we must, however, deal briefly, since our own views have been sufficiently indicated in what has gone before.

We have always doubted whether any one, disquieted by qualms and misgivings concerning the truths of revelation, derived from such astronomical speculations as we have been considering, has really reflected with sufficient depth and reverence upon the character and attributes of God, with reference to his creatures, and the nature of a professed revelation from him! especially of such a revelation as the Scriptures purport to contain. What do we, too frequently, see in such discussions, but Omnipotence attempted to be measured and limited by impotence—Omniscience by ignorance?—The forbearing Creator, *remembering that we are but dust*, by his presumptuous creature? Because man cannot himself attend completely to many things at once, and considers that numbers infer equality of claims to notice and importance; So, forsooth, he thinks it must be with the Almighty; and presumes to suggest to the High and Holy One, inhabiting eternity, what it is likely or unlikely, that he should do with the work of his own hands!

* *Wisdom of God in the Worlds of Creation,* vol. iii. p. 265.

We, ourselves, see no difference between the case of only two bodies, throughout infinitude, like the earth, and one of them selected to be the scene of such an event as the incarnation of the Son of God, as well as those other special dealings revealed in Scripture, and one out of two hundred, two millions, or any conceivable number of other bodies—and that, too, reasoning on the assumption that we know as much about every other body as about that one which we inhabit. But how is the impious absurdity heightened, when, to raise the objection, we jump at the conclusion that there *is* such a likeness, and snatch at every vestige of possible coincidence, in order to lay the basis of unbelief! Unbelief—of what? Of a professed message from God himself to his creatures, which, if believed, instantly and for ever concludes the whole matter. *Let God be true, though every man a liar:* and we may well stand aghast at the idea of raising such an issue as the truth or falsehood of God. He may, very fearfully, have given us a revelation which he has also left us at liberty to accept, or reject: but he has supplied us with evidence, and the power of judging of it: and is it not barely rational to address our faculties to *that evidence*—its absolute intrinsic claims to our assent? But beyond this, we are to remember that he professes to tell us, that it is not a matter of the head alone, but also of the heart; that *with the heart man believeth unto righteousness*—it is a matter of the will as well as the understanding; and if a man, instead of fastening his startled attention upon the one great subject and question of this life, will choose to set forth on a butterfly tour through infinitude, fluttering round about this and then about the other shining speck in the heavens, in order to impugn the profound truth of God—why, he must settle the matter with his Maker.

It has been well observed by Dr Chalmers, that the object of God's mysterious and merciful message to the earth " is not to convey information to us about the state of the planetary regions. This is not the matter with which it is fraught. It is a message from the throne of God to this rebellious province of His dominions; and the purpose of it is, to reveal the fearful extent of our guilt and of our danger, and to lay before us the overtures of reconciliation. Were a similar message sent from the metropolis of a mighty empire to one of its remote and revolutionary districts, we should not look to it for much information about the state or concerns of the intermediate provinces." Whether or not such a Proclamation may contain any casual reference to other quarters of the Empire, surely the concern of those to whom the document is sent, is with its direct bearing *on themselves*, to whom it professes to be directed: and a temper of insolent distrust, and presumptuous scrutiny, concerning these collateral matters, is the last that befits a reverent and rational being.

The Christian revelation is of a nature to satisfy, by its vastness and profundity, the utmost capacity of which man is conscious, as a moral and intellectual being. The more frequent and deep are his meditations upon it, the more he becomes invested with strength and grandeur of mind and character; the more frequent, solemnising, and elevating will be the internal evidences graciously afforded him, of the adaptation of revelation to his moral nature. Among the countless stars, his eye will be fixed on Him who made them, and who desires to become personally more and more intimately related to him; for religion is verily a personal matter between God and man.

An astronomical unbeliever is really a very poor yet pretentious thing. His little armoury is soon exhausted. His only weapon is—Is it *likely?* If answered, "How can that signify, if the fact be so?" he has no reply to make, but to deny the fact, because—it is not *likely!* *Likely*, in the estimation of an insect like himself!

"Newton," says Dr Chalmers, in his Discourse on the Modesty of True Science, "knew the boundary which hemmed him. He knew that he had not thrown one particle of light on the moral or religious history of these planetary regions. He had not ascertained what visits of communication *they* receive, from the God who upholds them; but he knew that the Fact of a Real Visit to This Planet had such evidence to rest upon, that it was not to be disputed by any aërial imagination." This is the true, the culminating point of all these inquiries; and if we negligently or wilfully lose sight of it, we may fearfully, hereafter as well as here, find that *the wisdom of this world was foolishness with God.*

Horace Walpole, that flippant, brilliant trifler, thought differently from Sir Isaac Newton. He said that Fontenelle's book had made him a sceptic: that on the assumption of a plurality of worlds, any revelation was impossible: that the reception of this opinion was sufficient with him to destroy the credibility of all Revelation! He and Thomas Paine were thus, it seems, of one mind on this matter—Sir Isaac Newton of another. Let the noble and devout spirit of Newton, however, be in us; both Faith and Reason assuring us that we stand, in scriptural truth, not *like a foolish man which built his house upon the sand,* but safe and immovable, *like a wise man which built his house upon a rock.*

Surely, sublime is such an attitude, and magnificent the spirit capable of reposing upon the assurance of its Maker, regardless of everything else whatever. It is thus that, as we have already said, the life of the Christian is one long-sustained Act of FAITH. He knows that full light is reserved for hereafter, because he has been expressly told, that here we know but in part. *He* may then wake up out of his self-abasement, amidst scenes of wonder and blessedness, shut out for ever from the dismayed and confuted unbeliever.

Finally, we repeat the question, What if there *be* a Plurality of Worlds? Suppose every luminary, great and small, whether Sun, Planet, or Satellite, and in as great numbers as the imagination can conceive, to be the seat of anything that we can deem rational and moral existence: what then? *What is it to us?* Why must we meddle with other worlds, instead of attending to that allotted to ourselves? We could at best but satisfy our curiosity, by discovering inhabitants of other worlds: and could such knowledge be otherwise than a mere disturbing force in the discharge of our duties? Let us be very sure, that had our Maker deemed it conducive to our welfare, or His glory, or consistent with the purpose of His infinite wisdom, to disclose to us that which we are so impotently panting and straining for, He would have done so—but He has not. Why, therefore, should "More Worlds than One," be either the "hope of the Christian," or the "creed of the philosopher?" To the former, it is, undoubtedly, open to form innocent conjectures on the subject, even as affecting, possibly, in some way at present inconceivable, his own personal interests hereafter. If he choose, he may "hope" to tenant a star; but it is not "THE hope" of the Christian, because he has no such sufficient ground or warrant as alone he would found a hope upon. And why the "creed" of the philosopher? Had not such language fallen from a veteran in science like Sir David Brewster, we should have been disposed to call such language ridiculous: and echoing his own inapplicable and uncourteous expressions to his opponent, declare that they are "mere sound in the ear, without any sense in the brain."

Need we remind any one of what is required to constitute an item in a *creed*, and moreover, the creed of a philosopher?

The Christian can dispense with such "hope;" and the philosopher discards the "creed" sought to be foisted upon him.

And finally, we would close this paper by deprecating the indulgence, by speculators of this class, in unseemly suggestions and suppositions—unseemly up to the point of irreverence and profanity—concerning the nature and extent of that awful item of the Christian's creed, the Atonement with reference to a plurality of worlds :—as to whether or not, for instance, all imaginary inhabitants of other worlds have, or have not, need of a Saviour; and whether the efficiency of His incarnation extends to such other extra-terrestrial beings, or is expended upon ourselves. It was with reluctance that we transcribed a passage on this subject from Sir David Brewster; to which we must refer our readers as affording the best evidence of the necessity for these remarks.

## Note.

At page 477, we remarked "that certain expressions" of the essayist, "had startled ourselves, not a little, when reflecting that they related to the possible mode of action of Omniscient Omnipotence; and we should be gratified by seeing them vindicated, or explained, in the next edition of the *Essay*."

The distinguished author has responded to this appeal, in the following paragraph in the Preface to the newly-published [October 1854] Third Edition of the *Essay*. We commend that paragraph to the careful consideration of the reader :—

"Those persons who may have thought that there was too much boldness in some of the author's expressions ;—as when he speaks of '*wasted means*' in the work of creation, of '*failure*' in some parts of its plan, of 'several sketches of which only one has been completed,' and the like ;—will see, I hope, on a further consideration of what is said in the Essay and in the Dialogue, that nothing is involved, in the thought thus expressed, but what is in full harmony with the spirit of reverence which prompts their own sentiment. Such expressions imply the ignorance and blindness of man ; to whom such thoughts as *waste*, and *failure*, and *incompleteness*, are suggested by his first views of many parts of the world, both moral and physical; they do not imply any imperfection in the work which God, with a full comprehension of all relations, and foresight of all consequences, is performing, from the beginning to the end of time, space, and causation. Can it surprise us that we do not fully understand this work? And can our defect of comprehension take any other form than this,—of a *seeming* failure in some parts? Can the pious man see plainly how *everything* has its use? Those who require a palpable use in every part of creation, have been asked, What is the use of the flowers of the field? and no answer has been given. We *know*, but we do not yet *see*, that all things work together for good."

# A FEW PERSONAL RECOLLECTIONS OF CHRISTOPHER NORTH.

On a bright frosty day in December 1827, as I was quitting the mathematical class in the University of Edinburgh, of which I had been a member about two months, one of my class-fellows said suddenly, "If you want to see Christopher North, he 's yonder!" This my companion knew to have been long my desire, for I was in those early days one of Christopher North's most enthusiastic admirers. My curiosity was gratified in a moment. Walking rapidly across the quadrangle towards his class-room (that of Moral Philosophy) with a sort of hasty, impetuous step, as though he were behind his time, was Professor Wilson, then in the very prime of life.* A faded, tattered gown, put on carelessly, fluttered in the keen wind, and seemed a ludicrous appendage to as fine, tall, manly a figure, and free, fearless bearing, as I have ever looked upon. As he came nearer, his limbs and their motions gave the idea of combined strength, agility, and grace; and there was a certain sort of frank, buoyant unaffectedness about his demeanour that seemed to indicate lighthearted consciousness of great mental and physical endowments. When he came near enough for his face to be seen with distinctness, in it I forgot everything else about him; and I shall never forget the impression it produced. What a magnificent head! How finely chiselled his

* He was in his forty-third year.

features! What compression of the thin but beautifully formed lips! What a bright blue flashing

"Eye, like Mars, to threaten or command!"

Add to all this the fair transparent complexion, flowing auburn hair, and the erect commanding *set* of his head upon his shoulders, and surely no Grecian sculptor could have desired anything beyond it. As for his eye, it lightened on me as he passed, and suddenly disappeared.

I had seen power and genius visibly embodied; and, in a word, I think that never before or since can any celebrated man's personal appearance have so far surpassed an admirer's expectation as Professor Wilson's air, face, and figure went beyond what I had imagined. I say this calmly, after the lapse of twenty-seven years, during which I have a thousand times recalled the scene which I have now faintly sketched for the reader; assuring him that no one then knowing this gifted and far-famed man, will think my sketch too highly coloured.

As I heard that many more were crowding into his class-room than were entitled to do so, I followed their example, discarding from my thoughts for the nonce all poor Professor Wallace's sines, co-sines, triangles, and parallelopipeds; and when I entered the Moral Philosophy class, I found that Professor Wilson had just begun his lecture. He read it with considerable rapidity, as it were vehemently urging his words out of lips compressed with the natural energy of his character. Professor Sedgwick, of Cambridge, when speaking in public, has sometimes reminded me of Professor Wilson's manner.

The lecture was eloquent, and greatly relished by the auditory. A small incident showed how he was absorbed with his subject, though the lecture was probably one that he had often read to his class. He had taken out his pocket-handkerchief, and after drawing it across his forehead, crushed it up, and placed it on the left hand side of his paper, partly under a book. By and by, he required his handkerchief, and felt first in one pocket, then in the other; then in his breast, then glanced hastily round, evidently in quest of his handkerchief, but without pausing for a moment in the flow of his impassioned rhetoric. These efforts he renewed several times; but it was not till he had finished his lecture that he suddenly saw what he had been looking for, and which we had seen all the while. He uttered a loud "Oh!" as he thrust it into his pocket, and withdrew. I have several times reminded him of this little circumstance, and he always laughed heartily, saying, "Very likely—very probably. I'm very thoughtless about such things." All I recollect of his lecture was, that it dealt much with Plato; but I was completely occupied with Wilson, feeling that I could pay my respects to Plato at any time. I am bound to say, that this distinguished man did not favourably impress me as a Lecturer on Moral Philosophy; inasmuch as he seemed to lack that calm, didactic manner, alone befitting the treatment of difficult, profound, abstract subjects. I think those who frequented his class must have found it difficult to realise what they had heard from him. I do not indeed recollect seeing any one taking notes; but I do recollect thinking one or two passages in his lecture very fine.

I did not see Professor Wilson again, except perhaps casually, and at a distance, till a few days before I quitted Edinburgh, in the autumn of 1828. I had had no opportunity of meeting him in society; and resolved not to leave Scotland without being able to say that I had spoken to Professor Wilson. But how was this to be done? Having been informed that he had concurred with Professor Pillans in awarding to me the prize for English poetry,* I thought, after many qualms and misgivings, that an allusion to that circumstance might, to a generous man of genius, serve to take off the edge of the liberty I proposed to myself, of calling, as a student quitting the

* *The Martyr Patriots,* note, vol. ii. p. 377.

university, to pay my parting respects to one of the Professors. So, one afternoon, after walking hesitatingly up and down the street in which he lived, and other adjoining ones, I summoned up spirit enough to call at his house, and inquire if he were at home. The answer was, yes; and on being asked my name, I mentioned it, adding, "a student in the university." In a moment or two's time the servant returned, saying, "The Professor would see me." Somewhat nervously I followed, and in a moment found myself, if I am not mistaken, in his library. The room had a disordered appearance, as if its occupant were careless. He had a loose wrapper round him, his shirt collar was thrown open, and he seemed writing. "Pray take a seat," said he, addressing me by name, and then his piercing eyes were fixed on me with what I thought a slightly impatient curiosity. "I feel, sir, that I have taken a great liberty," I began; "but I am an English student, with very few friends in Scotland, and before leaving the university and Scotland, I felt anxious to have the honour of paying my parting respects to you." "Oh, well, I am much obliged to you. So you are leaving the university? Are you the Mr Warren that gained the prize for English verse?" I told him I was; on which his whole manner altered, and became exceedingly cordial and gracious, and his smile was fascinating. "Well," said he, "as you are an Englishman at a Scotch university, I was a Scotchman at an English university—at Oxford;" and he talked with animation on the topic. I explained that the reason why I could not attend his, among other classes, was that I wished to enter at an inn of court immediately. "Oh, pho!" said he, laughing good-humouredly, "you have not lost much by missing *my* lectures! You must read for yourself on these subjects." After some other conversation, I happened to say—"There is only one other person besides yourself, sir, whom I should have liked to see before returning to England." "Who's that?" he asked. "Mr

De Quincy, the 'Opium Eater.'" "Mr De Quincy! Why, he's staying with me now! Well, I dare say I can manage that for you. Come in to-morrow evening about nine o'clock, and I'll introduce you to him. I shall be most happy to see you!" He said this with so much kindness, that I accepted the invitation; and after he had shaken my hand with much friendship of manner, I withdrew, he instantly resuming his pen.

On making my appearance next evening at the appointed hour, I was at once shown into the drawing-room, where were Mrs Wilson, evidently a very amiable and kindly woman, and some of her children. In about ten minutes' time Professor Wilson made his appearance, with one or two other gentlemen, to whom he was talking very energetically. He presently saw me, and shook hands with me cordially. "Oh, you want to see Mr De Quincy!—Come here!" and leading me into the back room, towards a door which stood open, in the angle formed by it with the wall stood a little slight man, dressed in black, pale, care-worn, and with a very high forehead. "Mr De Quincy, this is a young friend of mine—a student in the university, returning to England." After a few words of course, he left us; but Mr De Quincy seemed exceedingly languid. He spoke courteously, though evidently disinclined to talk. Shortly before we went down to supper, Professor Wilson said, "You shall sit opposite to Mr De Quincy"—and I think he added in a whisper and with a smile, "it will be a queer kind of *wine* that you will see him drinking!" Presently we went down to supper. Nothing could exceed the gentle unaffected kindness to me of Mrs Wilson, whom I never saw again after that evening. I saw her watching me once or twice with a good-natured amused smile, as she saw me intent upon Mr De Quincy, and his doings! I cannot at this distance of time pretend to say that his small decanter contained coffee: assuredly it was not wine, but exactly resembled laudanum. He was taciturn for some time, but gradually fell into conversation, in which Professor Wilson joined with vivacity. It was on some metaphysical subject; and at length I well recollect that the discussion turned on the nature of *Forgetfulness*. "Is such a thing as *forgetting* possible to the human mind?" asked Mr De Quincy—"Does the mind ever actually lose anything for ever? Is not every impression it has once received, reproducible? How often a thing is suddenly recollected that had happened many, many years before, but never been thought of since till that moment!—Possibly a suddenly-developed power of recollecting every act of a man's life may constitute the Great Book to be opened before him in the judgment day." I think this is the substance of what was said on the subject, Professor Wilson making several curious remarks as to the nature of mind, memory, and suggestion. I ventured to say—and it was the only thing I did venture to say—that I knew an instance of a gentleman who in hastily jumping from on board the *Excellent*, to catch a boat that was starting for shore, missed it, and fell into the water of Portsmouth harbour, sinking to a great depth. For a while he was supposed drowned. He afterwards said, that all he remembered after plunging into the water was a sense of freedom from pain, and a sudden recollection of all his past life, especially of guilty actions that he had long forgotten. Professor Wilson said that if this were so, it was indeed very startling: and I think Mr De Quincy said that he also had heard of one, if not two or three such cases.

I was so absorbed with watching and listening to the conversation of Professor Wilson and Mr De Quincy, that I left almost supperless, in spite of the kindly pressure of Mrs Wilson. I often saw her look, as I fancied, with fond interest at her famous husband, whose demeanour had a noble simplicity. His eyes sometimes seemed to glitter and flash with the irrepressible fire of genius. I watched him with lynx-like vigilance; but all was spontaneous and genuine: not a vestige of artifice, affectation, or display: no silly "inflicting his eye on you:" but all, whether grave or frolicksome, the exuberance of a gloriously-gifted man of genius. And see how hospitable and kind he was to a young English stranger, whom he had never seen till the preceding day! Before I left, he asked me much about my intentions and prospects; wished me heartily well: and when, about eleven o'clock, I had shaken hands with him and got into the street, the sun of GENIUS no longer shone on me, and I felt dull, and indeed in the dark. As I walked home, I thought myself a poor pigmy, that had just been entertained by a good-humoured giant!

---

I never saw any man who *looked* the man of genius he was, but Professor Wilson. Next to him was Sir Walter Scott. Him I first saw, in his fifty-seventh year, when I was at college in Edinburgh, and had wandered one day, in, I think, the month of June, into one of the law courts to hear Mr Jeffrey plead. The latter's face, let me say in passing, appeared to me that of an acute, refined, sensitive, and somewhat irritable man, but not indicative of power. I had been standing for some time in the Court of Session, in which Sir Walter Scott was one of the principal clerks, who sate at a table below the judges, when my eye fell upon an elderly man, one of those sitting at the table, wearing a rusty-looking old stuff gown. His chin rested on his left hand, and his right hung by his side with a pen in it. Without having an idea who he was, my attention was soon arrested by his lofty forehead, and a pair of eyes that seemed gazing dreamily into a distant world unseen by any but himself. The more I looked at those eyes, the more remarkable appeared their character and expression: not bright, or penetrating, but invested with a grand, rapt, profound air. He sate motionless as a statue, apparently lost to all that was passing around him. A sudden suspicion arose within me that I was looking on the mighty Northern novelist, who had publicly avowed himself the author of Waverley in the preceding February. To make assurance doubly sure, I asked a person standing beside me, who that was, indicating him. "Whaur d'ye come frae?" said he, looking at me rather contemptuously; "d'ye no ken that's *Sir Walter?*" Almost while this was being said, Sir Walter Scott seemed to rouse himself from a reverie, and soon afterwards wrote rapidly on several sheets of paper, and then quitted the court, leaning on his stick, and walking very lame.

Professor Wilson's noble countenance indicated, to even an ordinary observer, the impulsive energy of his character, daring and generous,—also acuteness, refinement, and power; one, in short, to fear, to admire, and to love. Everything petty and mean, he spurned with a scorn that was magnificent; to obscure and timid genius, he extended, with tender kindliness, the hand of, as it were, the King of Letters. To pretenders, however, of all sorts, he was utterly merciless: to them, the crutch of Christopher was annihilation. It was fine to hear him *talk* on such a subject: his eye, his lip, his voice, his gesture, all in fierce and vivid accord.

As an instance of his watchfulness of literary merit, when newly manifested, I recollect his once saying to me, "By the way, do you know any one in the Temple—a special pleader, or something of that kind, called Moile—Nicholas Thirning Moile?"* I told him that I had never heard of the name: on which he pressed me much, and said, "Try to find out, then, for he is a very clever fellow. He has just published a sort of poetical

* It turned out that the name of "Nicholas Thirning Moile" was assumed by a friend of my own, now an eminent Queen's Counsel: who had sent to me the very volume in question in his assumed name; and, after glancing at it for a moment, I acknowledged the receipt of the book to the publisher, but soon afterwards lost sight of it. It was only a few months ago that I discovered the author.

version of two or three of the State Trials, which I have read, and formed a high opinion of them. Some parts are beautiful—he's a man of genius. I shall review the book in the *Magazine;*" and his opinion of the performance may be seen in No. 288.

Professor Wilson read with prodigious rapidity, and it was an *exhaustive* reading: he gathered the purpose, scope, and character of a work, on even a difficult subject, at almost a glance. Instances of this have come under my personal knowledge: and I know the pages in *Blackwood's Magazine* which attest Christopher North's marvellous rapidity and accuracy of critical judgment. As a critic, his perceptions were exquisite, and his resources boundless. He could put a new or an old idea into a sort of kaleidoscopic variety of striking and novel aspects, and with a charming facility. He could bring out a meaning often more distinctly and happily than his author himself. His rich, comprehensive, and penetrating criticism shed new splendour over Homer, Shakspeare, Spenser, Milton, Dryden, and whomsoever else he willed to set before his own and his reader's eye.

One of his most distinguished contemporaries, not apt to bestow eulogy lavishly or unworthily,—I mean Mr Hallam,—in his *Introduction to the Literature of Europe*, while sketching the character of Spenser, thus alludes to a fine series of papers by Professor Wilson on the *Fairy Queen*:—"It has been justly observed by a living writer, of the most ardent and enthusiastic genius, whose eloquence is as the rush of mighty waters, and has left it for others, almost as invidious, to praise in terms of less rapture, as to censure what he has borne along in the stream of unhesitating eulogy, 'that no poet has ever had a more exquisite sense of the beautiful than Spenser:'" adding, in a note, "I allude here to a very brilliant series of papers on the *Fairy Queen*, published in *Blackwood's Magazine*, during the years 1834 and 1835." I think the observation which the Professor makes concerning Spenser, may be well applied to the gifted critic himself. I fear, however, that I am wandering too far from the object of this humble tribute to the memory of Professor Wilson.

I never heard him speak in disparaging terms of any of his contemporaries; but how tremendous, in his earlier years, were his flagellations of those whom he considered deserving of them as literary offenders, is known to all well-informed literary readers. I have conversed with him much about literary men, and often admired his forbearing and generous spirit.

Shortly after Mr Dickens had so suddenly eclipsed in popularity all his contemporaries, Professor Wilson spoke to me of him in terms of high admiration, as a man of undoubted and great genius; and he spoke of "*Nelly*" as a beautiful creation.

Professor Wilson told me that there were two things he specially hated—letter-writing, and being "made a lion of," or, as I recollect him saying contemptuously, "a lion*et*." As for letter-writing, I never received from him but one in my life; and that was written on half a sheet of paper, evidently the blank sheet of some old letter. Mentioning a late accomplished dignitary of the Church, he said, laughingly, "—— —— will continue writing to me, though I never answer his letters, nor will!" One of those letters happened to contain a friendly allusion to myself, and he sent it to me through a common friend, thinking it would please me.

He never called on me in the Temple but once; and then sate a long time, asking a multitude of questions about the Temple,—its history, the nature of chamber life, &c. &c., with lively interest; almost suggesting that he might be thinking of writing something on the subject.

He used to be a daily visitor at Messrs Blackwood's saloon,* in George Street, to chat with them and one or

* This is a spacious room dedicated by Messrs Blackwood to the use of their friends, where are lying numerous newspapers and magazines; and ornamented with busts and pictures of their distinguished literary men.

two other friends, read the newspapers, and skim over the magazines, reviews, and new publications. He was much attached to all the Blackwoods, giving them many proofs of his zealous and affectionate good-will. How pleasantly have I chatted with him in that saloon! How fresh and genial he always was! How sly his humour! How playfully his eye glittered while he was good-humouredly making fun of you! How racy his comments on literary and political topics! How ready and correct his knowledge in all kinds of subjects, even while he professed "to know very little about them!"

I saw him last in that saloon, towards the close of September 1851. I had been for ten days in Edinburgh, superintending—as that was the long vacation—a work which was on the eve of publication, and had lived quite secluded all the time. In passing hastily through the saloon with some proofs in my hand, I came upon Professor Wilson, sitting there as usual; but I had not seen him for several years. He had become a great deal stouter than I had ever seen him before; he was also aged much; but his face was as fine, his eye as bright, and his manner as delightful as ever. He did not, however, speak with his former energy. "They tell me," said he, laughing good-humouredly, "that you've quite buried yourself since you have been here! What have you been about?" I told him. "Ay—it's a capital title, and promises well. You have set us all gaping to know what we're to have! Tell me what it's about—I'm anxious to hear. What's your *idea?*" I told him, as briefly as I could. "Let me hear some of it," said he, after I had given him my notions of the scope of the work; and I read him, at his desire, a considerable portion. How I recollect his full, keen eyes, watchfully fixed upon me as I read!

The next, and last time I saw him, was also the last time that he left his own house. During the intervening years, he had had a paralytic seizure, which affected his powers of motion and speech, and to some extent his mental faculties. He had driven up to Mr Blackwood's door, accompanied by a fond daughter, for the purpose of congratulating one in whom he had always felt deep interest, on his approaching marriage. I was in the saloon at the time; but on being told that he would be pleased to see me, though he was feeble and could not converse, I went to the carriage door. Shall I ever forget father and daughter,* as they sate opposite to each other, she eyeing her gifted but afflicted father with such tender anxiety! Never! His hat was off, and his countenance, on which fell the rays of setting sunlight, was fine as ever; his *eye was not dim*, nor did his *natural force* seem *abated*, as he sate, and looked at me, and stretched forth his hand; but when he attempted to speak, alas! it was in words few, indistinct, and unintelligible. To me it was an affecting moment—but a moment; for he was not allowed to become excited. Again he shook my hand; and I had looked my last on Professor Wilson. The next I heard of him, was his peaceful death; and then a burial befitting one of the great men of Scotland.

I am almost ashamed to commit to the press this sudden and spontaneous, but poor tribute to the memory of such a man of genius and goodness. I am altogether unequal to the task of his intellectual portraiture; but what I have written is true, and comes from my heart; wherefore I hope it will be accepted in the spirit in which it is offered.

Adieu, Christopher North! Adieu, John Wilson!

SAMUEL WARREN.

* Mrs Gordon.

END OF VOLUME SECOND.

BALLANTYNE AND COMPANY, PRINTERS, EDINBURGH.